BLADE
OF THE IMMORTAL

On Silent Wings

P9-DEP-738

publisher
Mike Richardson

series editor
Rachel Penn

collection editor
Chris Warner

collection designers
Amy Arendts
& Harald Graham

**English version produced by Studio Proteus
for Dark Horse Comics, Inc.**

BLADE OF THE IMMORTAL Vol. 4: ON SILENT WINGS
Blade of the Immortal copyright © 1998, 1999 by Hiroaki Samura. All
rights reserved. First published in Japan in 1994 by Kodansha Ltd.,
Tokyo. English translation rights arranged through Kodansha Ltd. New
and adapted artwork and text © 1998, 1999 Studio Proteus and Dark
Horse Comics, Inc. All other material © 1999 Dark Horse Comics,
Inc. All rights reserved. No portion of this publication may be reproduced
by any means without written permission from the copyright holders.
The stories, characters, and incidents in this publication are entirely
fictional. Dark Horse Comics® and the Dark Horse logo are registered
trademarks of Dark Horse Comics, Inc., registered in various categories
and countries. All rights reserved.

This book collects issues nineteen through
twenty-three of the Dark Horse comic-book series,
Blade of the Immortal.

Published by
Dark Horse Comics, Inc.
10956 SE Main Street
Milwaukie, OR 97222

First edition: August 1999
ISBN: 1-56971-412-6

1 3 5 7 9 10 8 6 4 2

Printed in Canada

BLADE
OF THE IMMORTAL

art and story
HIROAKI SAMURA

translation
Dana Lewis & Toren Smith

lettering and retouch
Tomoko Saito

On Silent Wings

DARK HORSE COMICS®

ABOUT THE TRANSLATION

The Swastika

The main character in *Blade of the Immortal*, Manji, has taken the "crux gammata" as both his name and his personal symbol. This symbol is also known as the *swastika*, a name derived from the Sanskrit *svastika* (meaning "welfare," from su — "well" + asti "he is"). As a symbol of prosperity and good fortune, the swastika was widely used throughout the ancient world (for example, appearing often on Mesopotamian coinage), including North and South America and has been used in Japan as a symbol of Buddhism since ancient times. To be precise, the symbol generally used by Japanese Buddhists is the *sauvastika*, which moves in a counterclockwise direction, and is called the *manji* in Japanese. The arms of the swastika, which point in a clockwise direction, are generally considered a solar symbol. It was this version (the *hakenkreuz*) that was perverted by the Nazis. The *sauvastika* generally stands for night and often for magical practices. It is important that readers understand that the *swastika* has ancient and honorable origins, and it is those that apply to this story, which takes place in the 18th century [ca. 1782-3]. *There is no anti-Semitic or pro-Nazi meaning behind the use of the symbol in this story. Those meanings did not exist until after 1910.*

The Artwork

The creator of *Blade of the Immortal* requested that we make an effort to avoi mirror-imaging his artwork. Normally, al of our manga are first copied in a mirror image in order to facilitate the left-to-righ reading of the pages. However, Mr. Samur decided that he would rather see his page reversed via the technique of cutting up the panels and re-pasting them in revers order. While we feel that this often leads to problems in panel-to-panel continuity, we place primary importance on the wishe of the creator. Therefore, most of *Blade c the Immortal* has been produced using th "cut and paste" technique. There are, of course, some sequences where it was impossible to do this, and mirror-imaged panels or pages were used.

The Sound Effects & Dialogue

Since some of Mr. Samura's sound effects are integral parts of the artwork, we decided to leave those in their origina Japanese. When it was crucial to the understanding of the panel that the soun effect be in English, however, Mr. Samur chose to redraw the panel. We hope reader will view the un-retouched sound effects as essential portions of Mr. Samura's extraordinary artwork. In addition, Mr. Samura's treatment of dialogue is quite different from that featured in average samurai manga and is considered to be on of the things that has made *Blade* such a hit in Japan. Mr. Samura has mixed a variet of linguistic styles in this fantasy story where some characters speak in the mannered style of old Japan while others speak as if they were street-corne punks from a bad area of modern-day Tokyo. The anachronistic slang used by some of the characters in the English translation reflects the unusual mix of speech patterns from the original Japanese text.

RIN'S BANE
Part 1

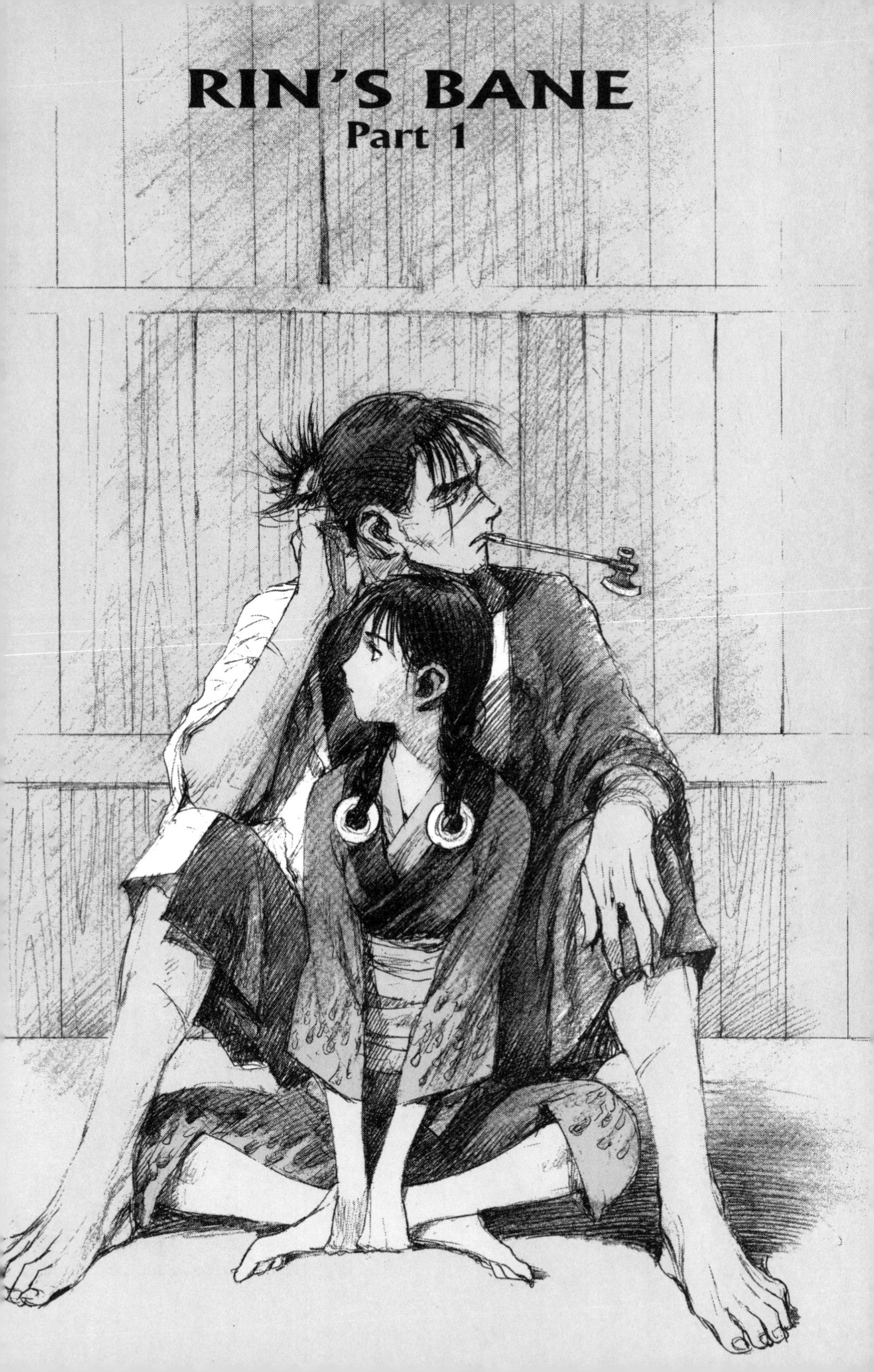

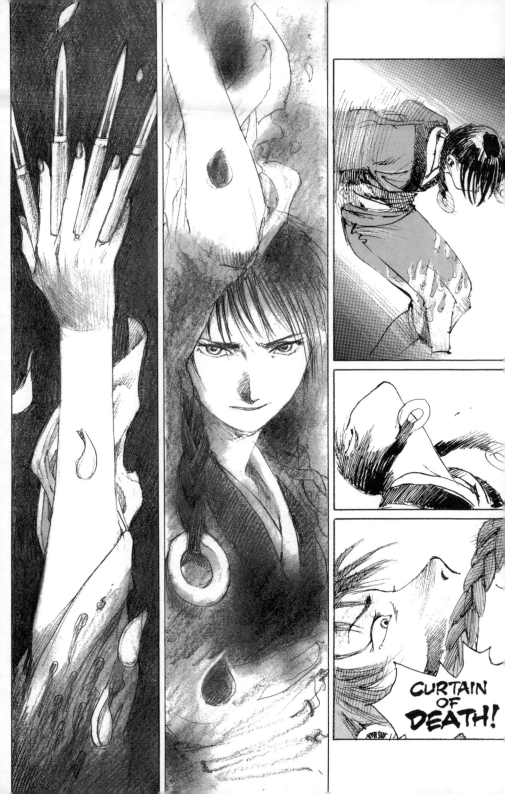

CURTAIN
OF
DEATH!

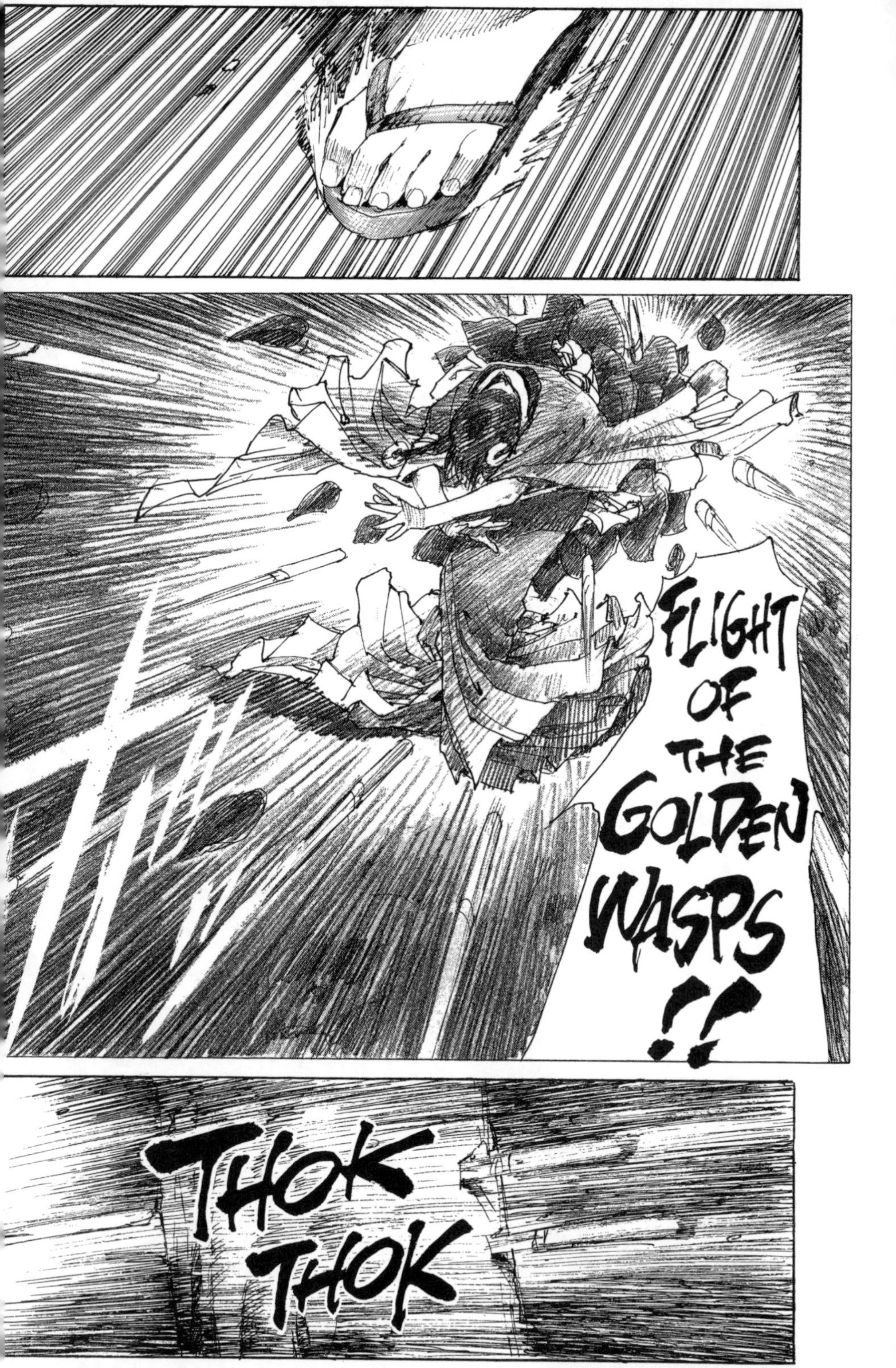
FLIGHT OF THE GOLDEN WASPS !!
THOK THOK

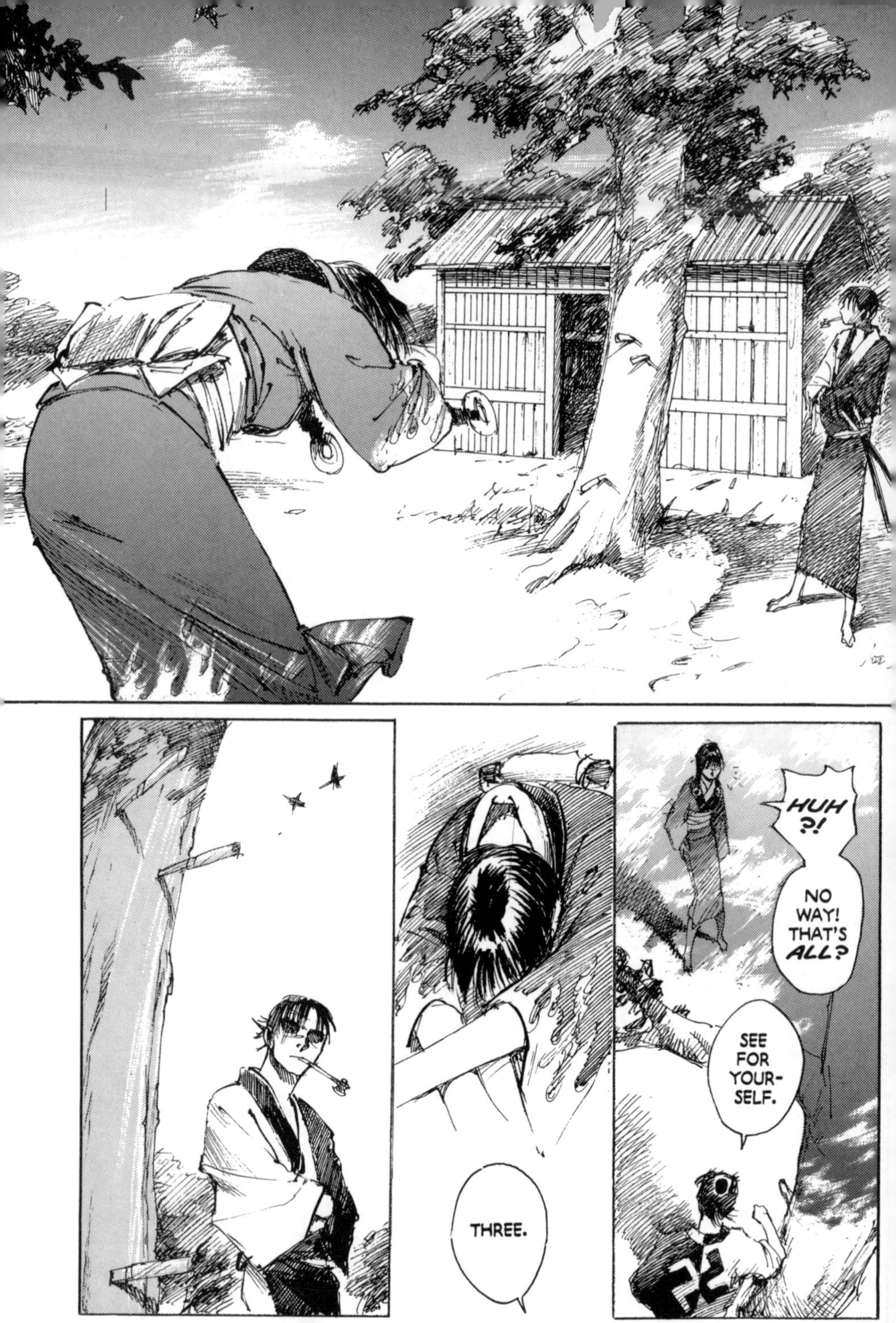
THREE.
HUH?!
NO WAY! THAT'S ALL?
SEE FOR YOURSELF.

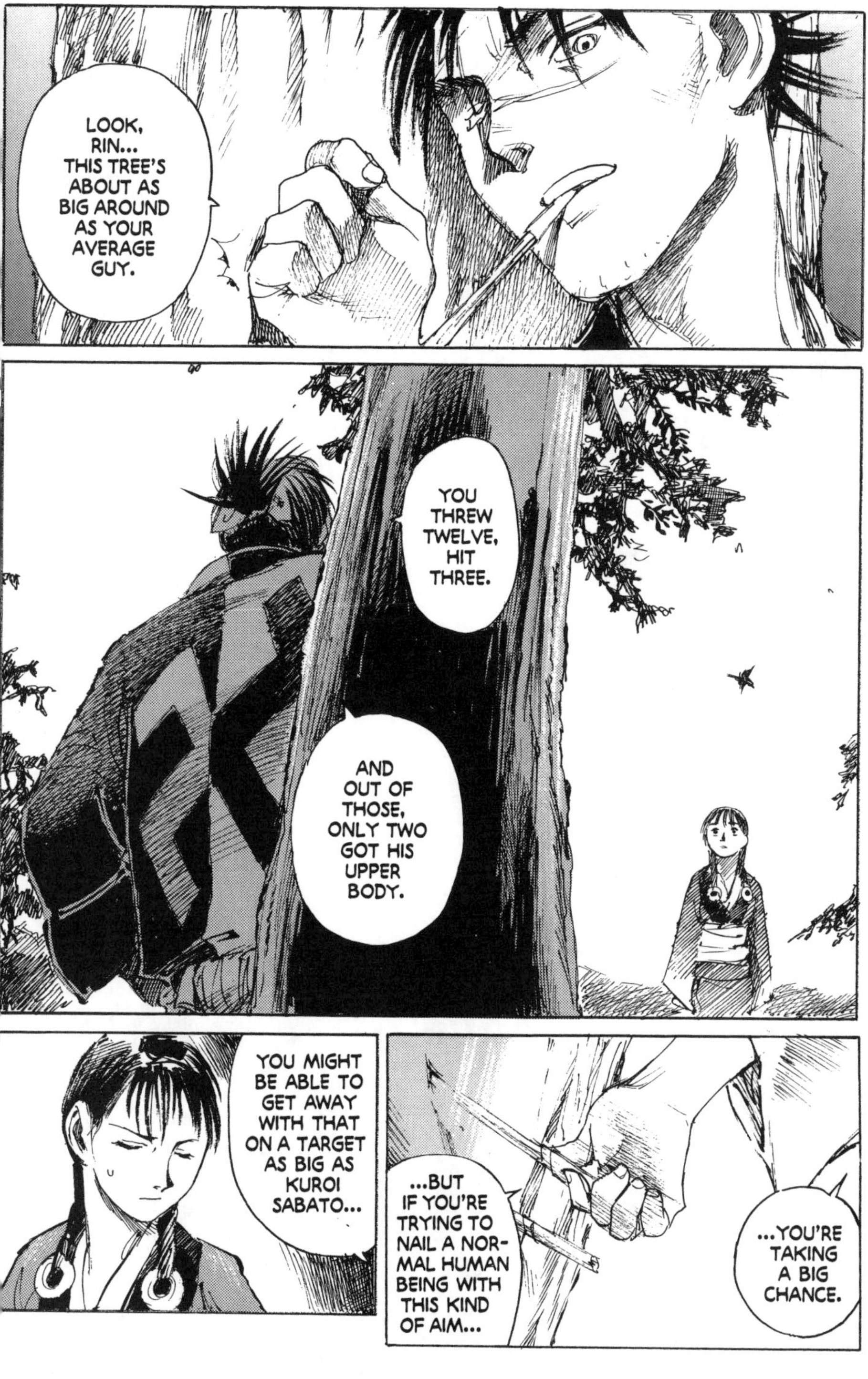
LOOK, RIN... THIS TREE'S ABOUT AS BIG AROUND AS YOUR AVERAGE GUY.
YOU THREW TWELVE, HIT THREE.
AND OUT OF THOSE, ONLY TWO GOT HIS UPPER BODY.
YOU MIGHT BE ABLE TO GET AWAY WITH THAT ON A TARGET AS BIG AS KUROI SABATO...
...BUT IF YOU'RE TRYING TO NAIL A NOR-MAL HUMAN BEING WITH THIS KIND OF AIM...
...YOU'RE TAKING A BIG CHANCE.

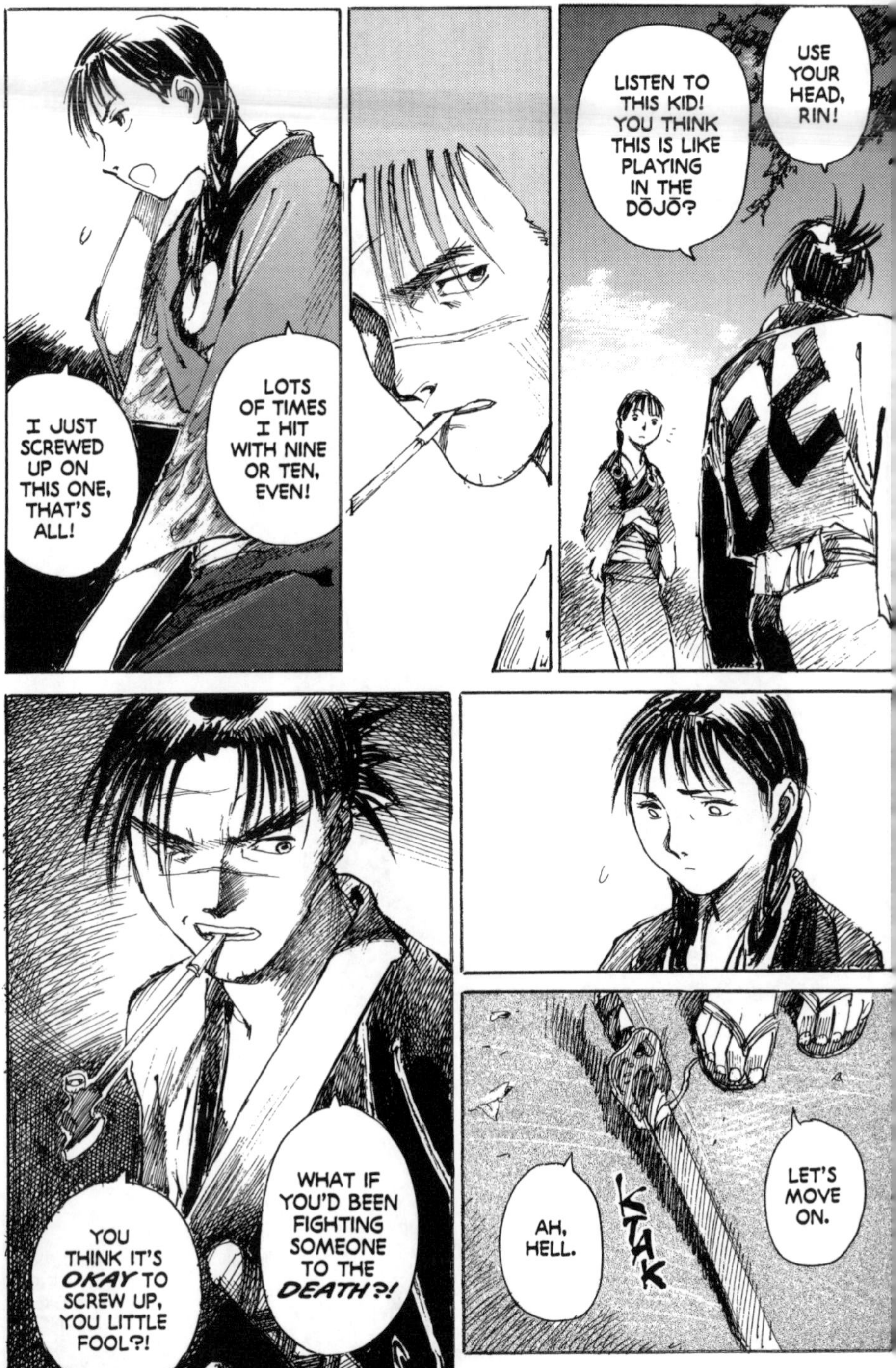
I JUST SCREWED UP ON THIS ONE, THAT'S ALL!
LOTS OF TIMES I HIT WITH NINE OR TEN, EVEN!
LISTEN TO THIS KID! YOU THINK THIS IS LIKE PLAYING IN THE DŌJŌ?
USE YOUR HEAD, RIN!
YOU THINK IT'S *OKAY* TO SCREW UP, YOU LITTLE FOOL?!
WHAT IF YOU'D BEEN FIGHTING SOMEONE TO THE *DEATH*?!
AH, HELL.
KTAK
LET'S MOVE ON.

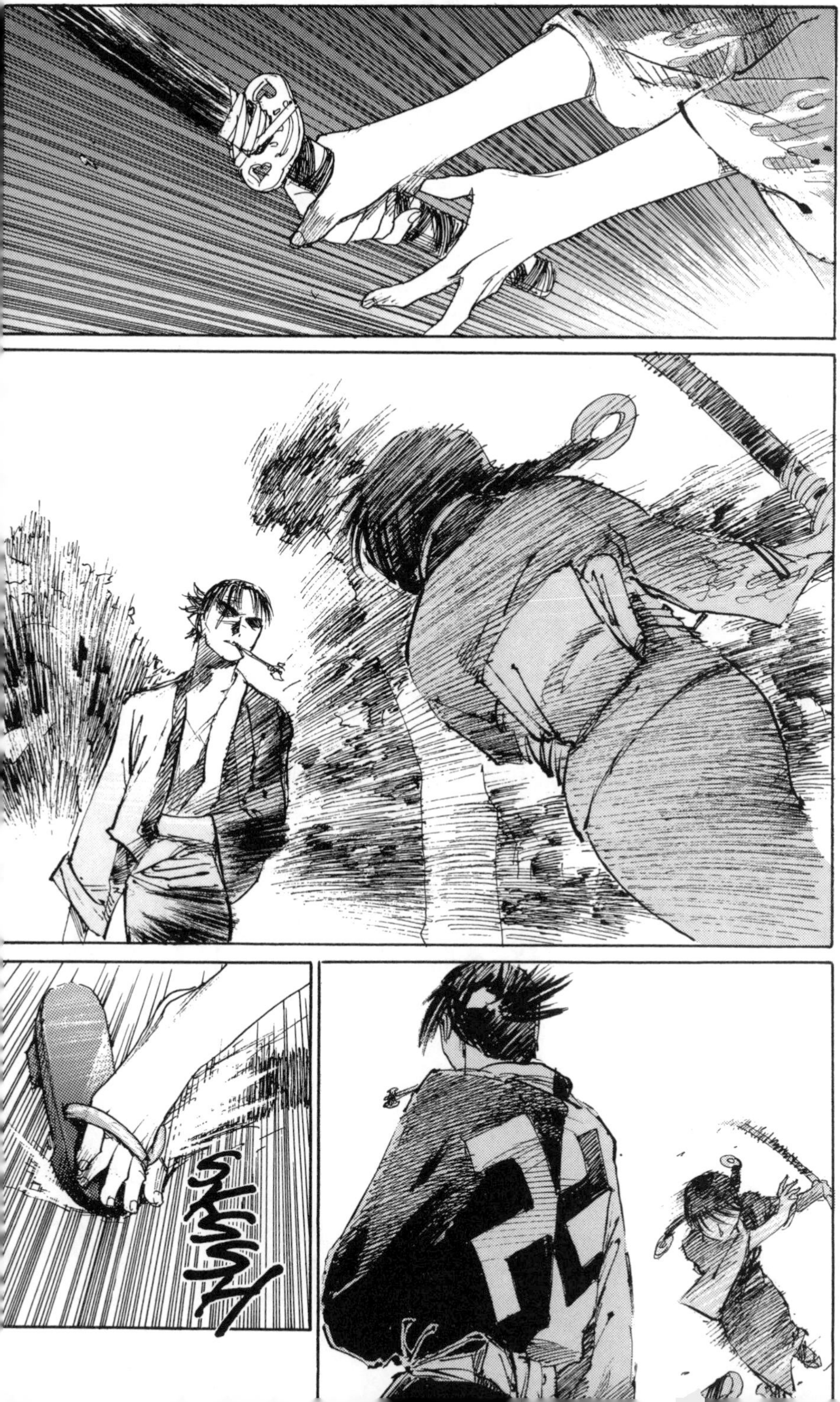
HSSSS

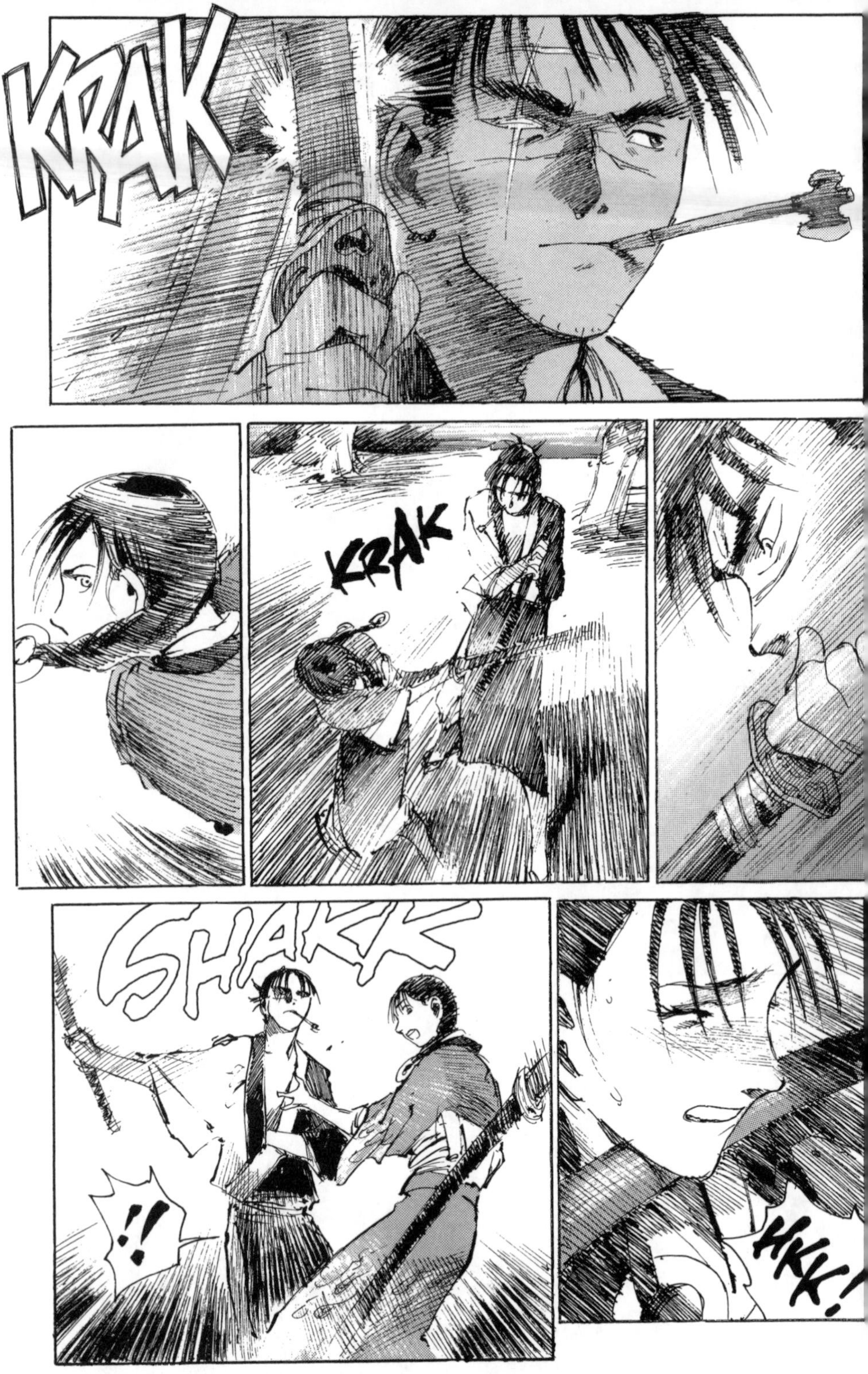
KRAK
KRAK
SHAKK
!!
HKKK!

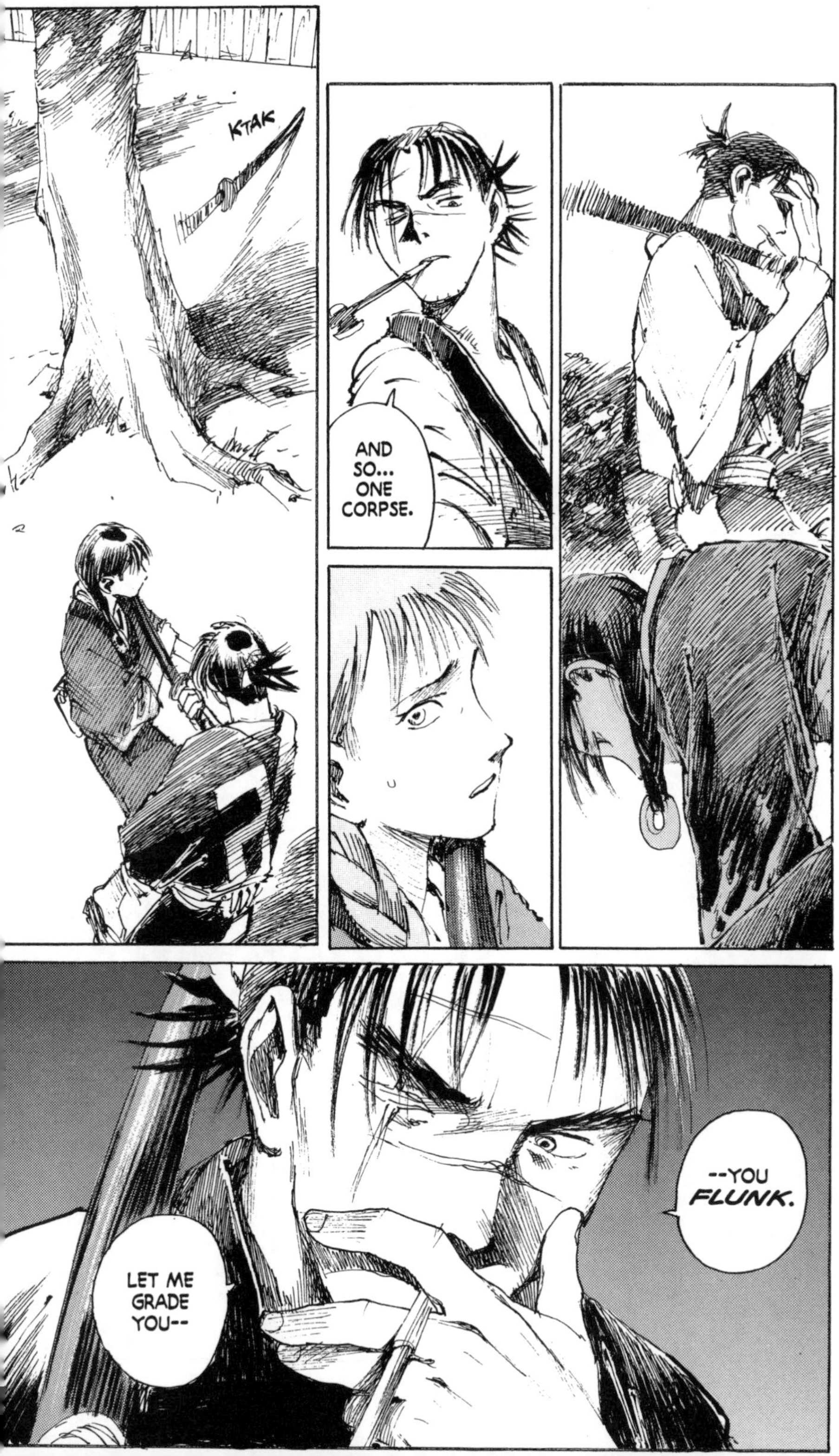
KTAK
AND SO... ONE CORPSE.
LET ME GRADE YOU--
--YOU FLUNK.

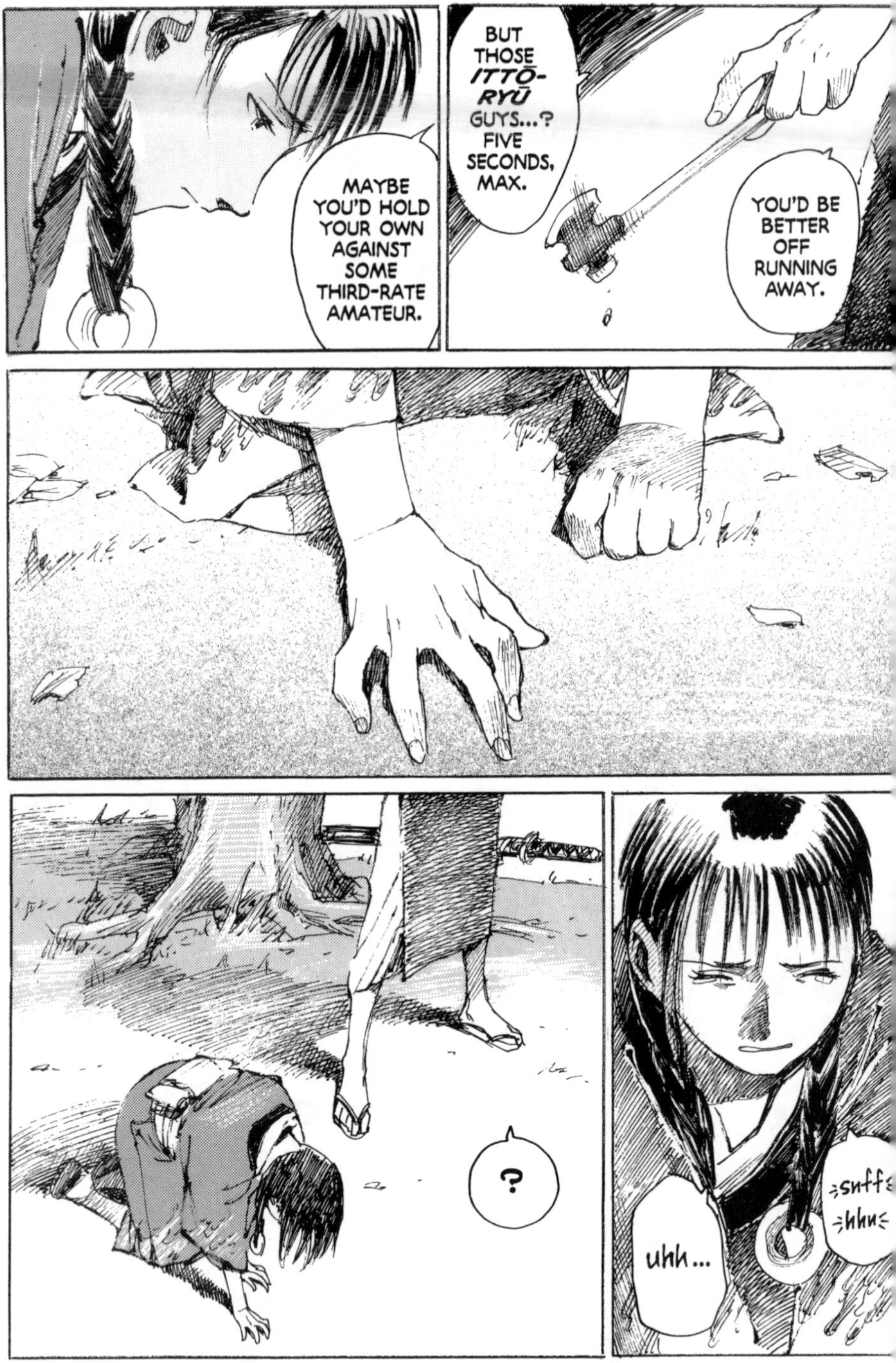
MAYBE YOU'D HOLD YOUR OWN AGAINST SOME THIRD-RATE AMATEUR.
BUT THOSE ITTŌ-RYŪ GUYS...? FIVE SECONDS, MAX.
YOU'D BE BETTER OFF RUNNING AWAY.
?
uhh...
snff
hhn

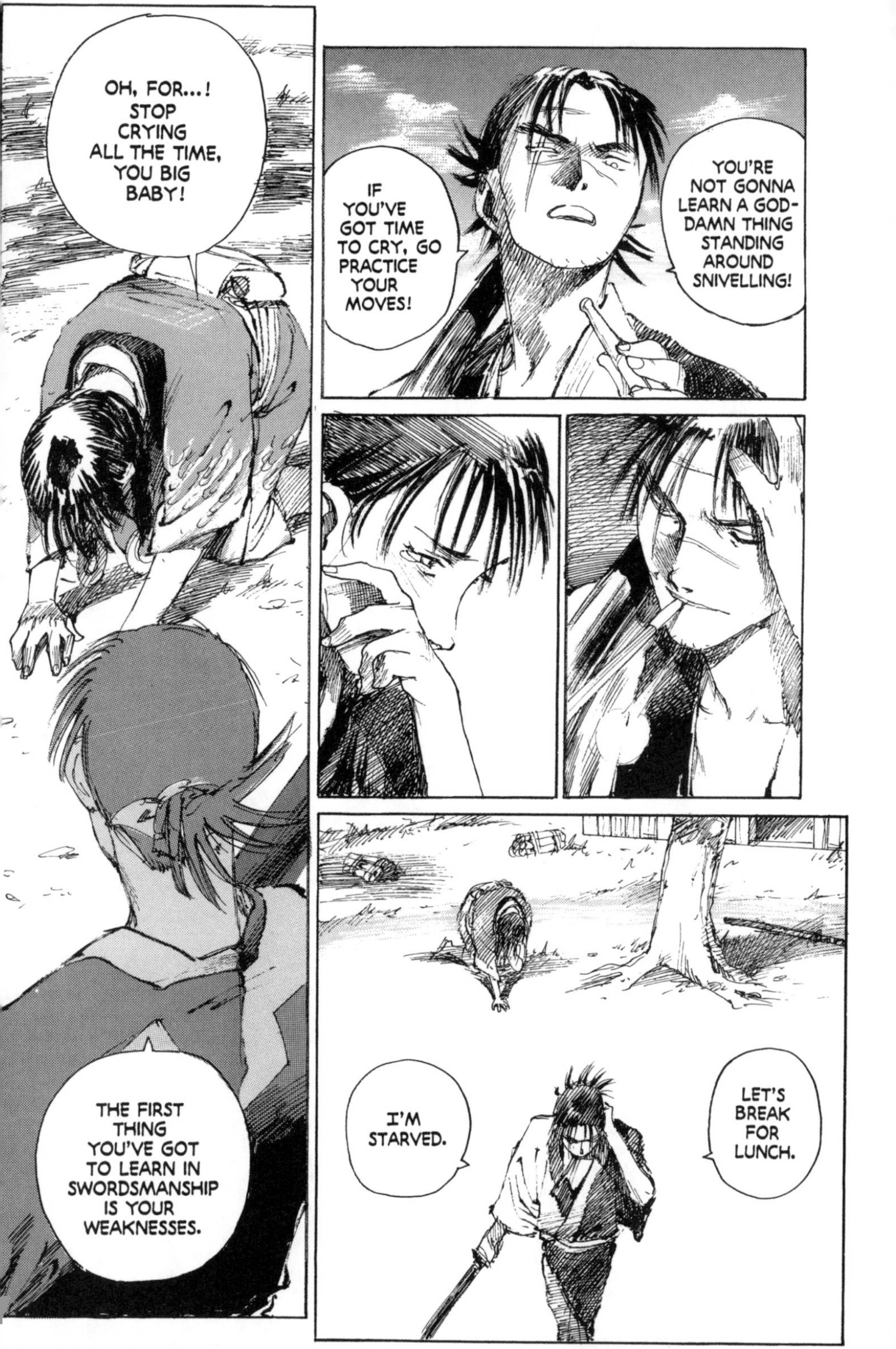
OH, FOR...! STOP CRYING ALL THE TIME, YOU BIG BABY!
THE FIRST THING YOU'VE GOT TO LEARN IN SWORDSMANSHIP IS YOUR WEAKNESSES.
IF YOU'VE GOT TIME TO CRY, GO PRACTICE YOUR MOVES!
YOU'RE NOT GONNA LEARN A GOD-DAMN THING STANDING AROUND SNIVELLING!
I'M STARVED.
LET'S BREAK FOR LUNCH.

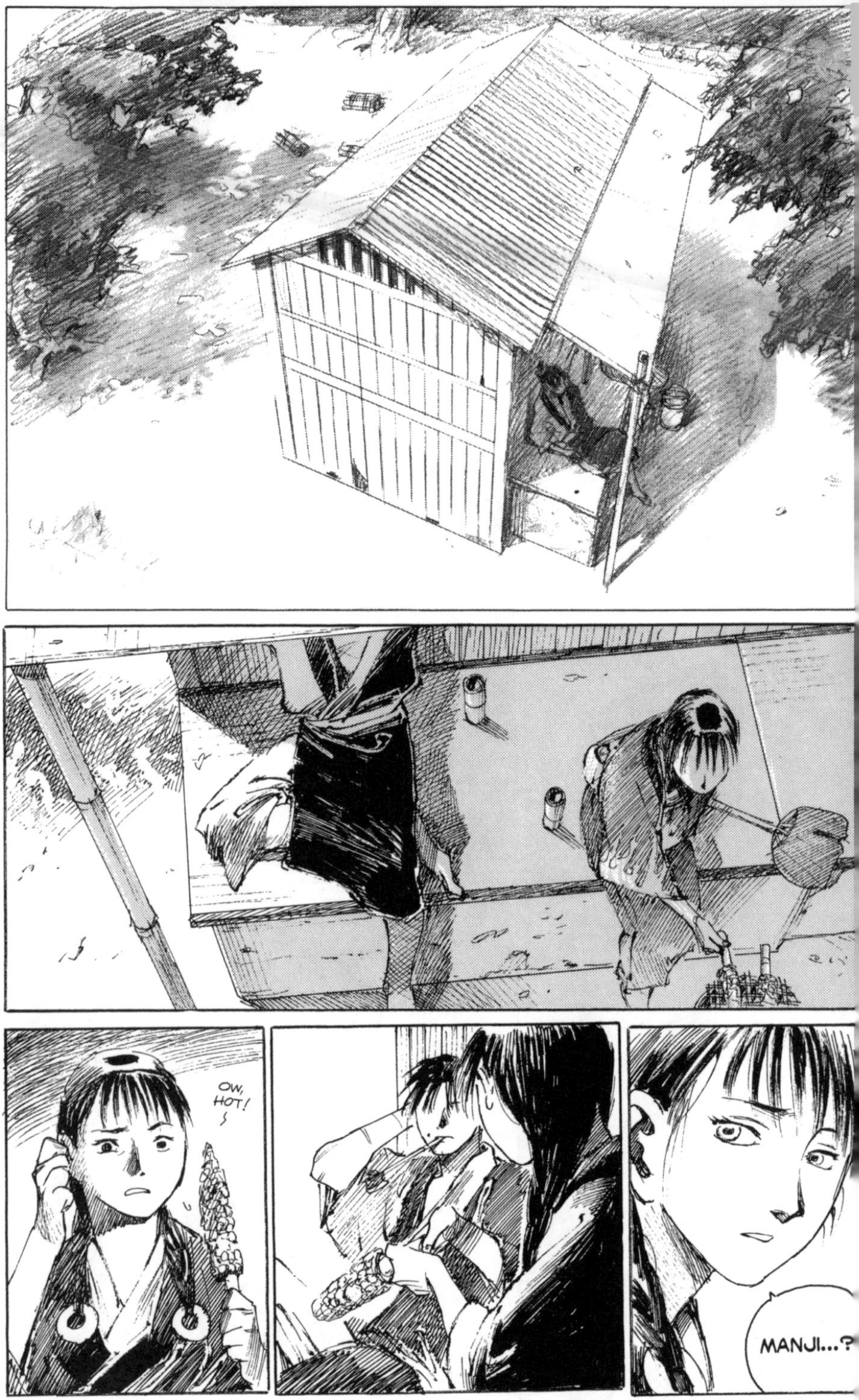
OW, HOT!
MANJI...?

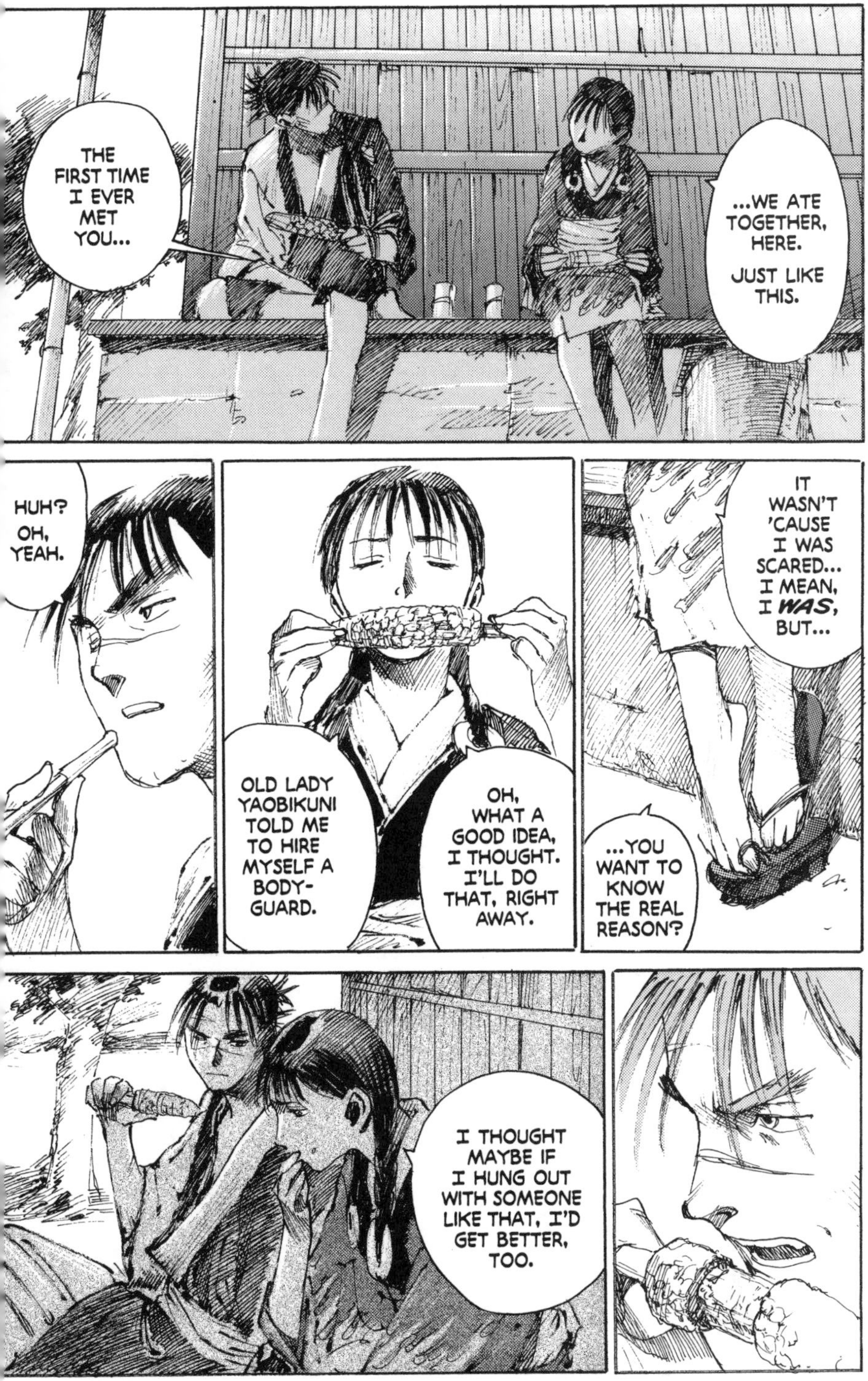
THE FIRST TIME I EVER MET YOU...
...WE ATE TOGETHER, HERE.
JUST LIKE THIS.
HUH? OH, YEAH.
OLD LADY YAOBIKUNI TOLD ME TO HIRE MYSELF A BODY-GUARD.
OH, WHAT A GOOD IDEA, I THOUGHT. I'LL DO THAT, RIGHT AWAY.
IT WASN'T 'CAUSE I WAS SCARED... I MEAN, I *WAS*, BUT...
...YOU WANT TO KNOW THE REAL REASON?
I THOUGHT MAYBE IF I HUNG OUT WITH SOMEONE LIKE THAT, I'D GET BETTER, TOO.

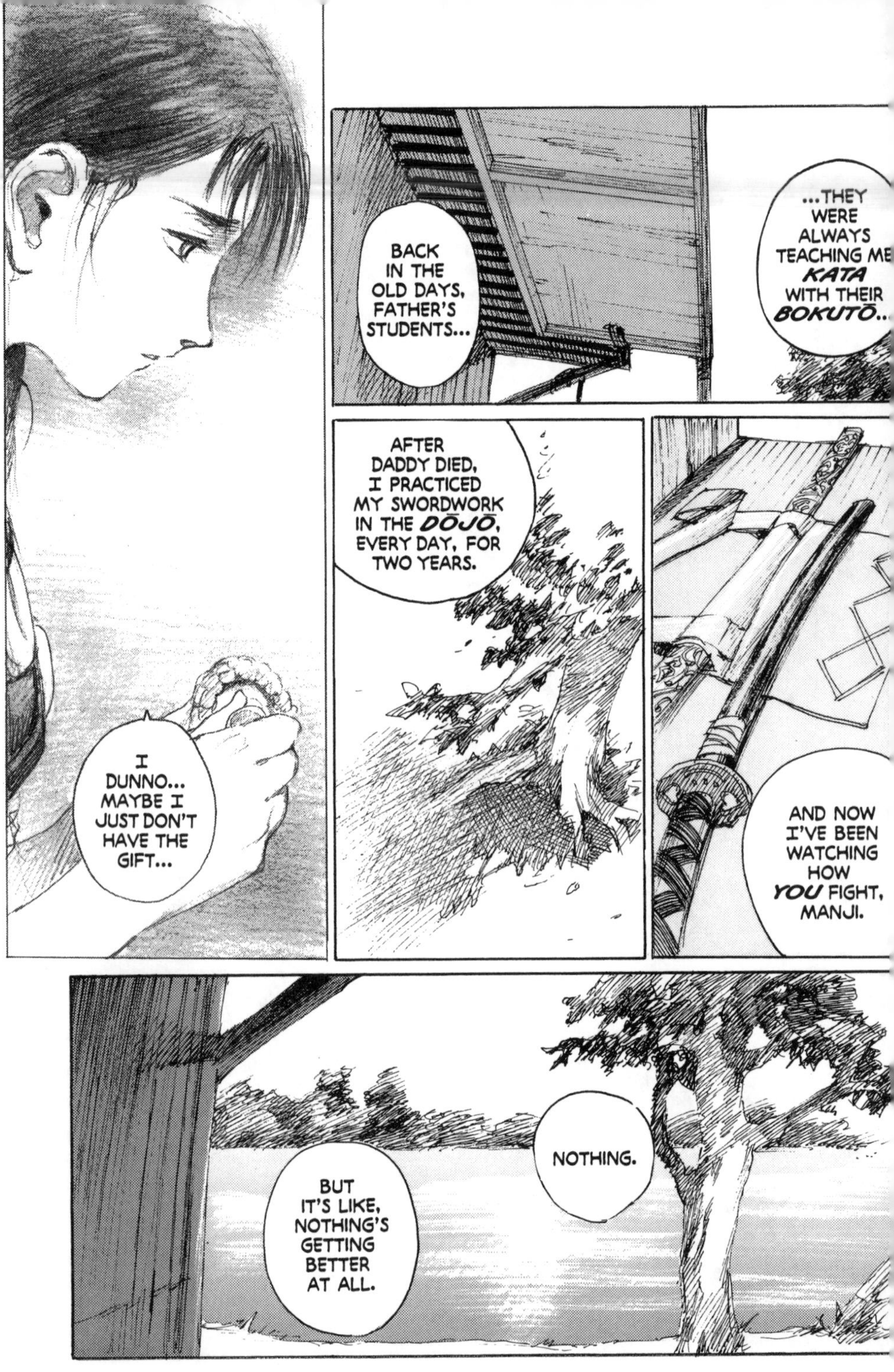
I DUNNO... MAYBE I JUST DON'T HAVE THE GIFT...
BACK IN THE OLD DAYS, FATHER'S STUDENTS...
...THEY WERE ALWAYS TEACHING ME *KATA* WITH THEIR *BOKUTŌ*...
AFTER DADDY DIED, I PRACTICED MY SWORDWORK IN THE *DŌJŌ*, EVERY DAY, FOR TWO YEARS.
AND NOW I'VE BEEN WATCHING HOW *YOU* FIGHT, MANJI.
BUT IT'S LIKE, NOTHING'S GETTING BETTER AT ALL.
NOTHING.

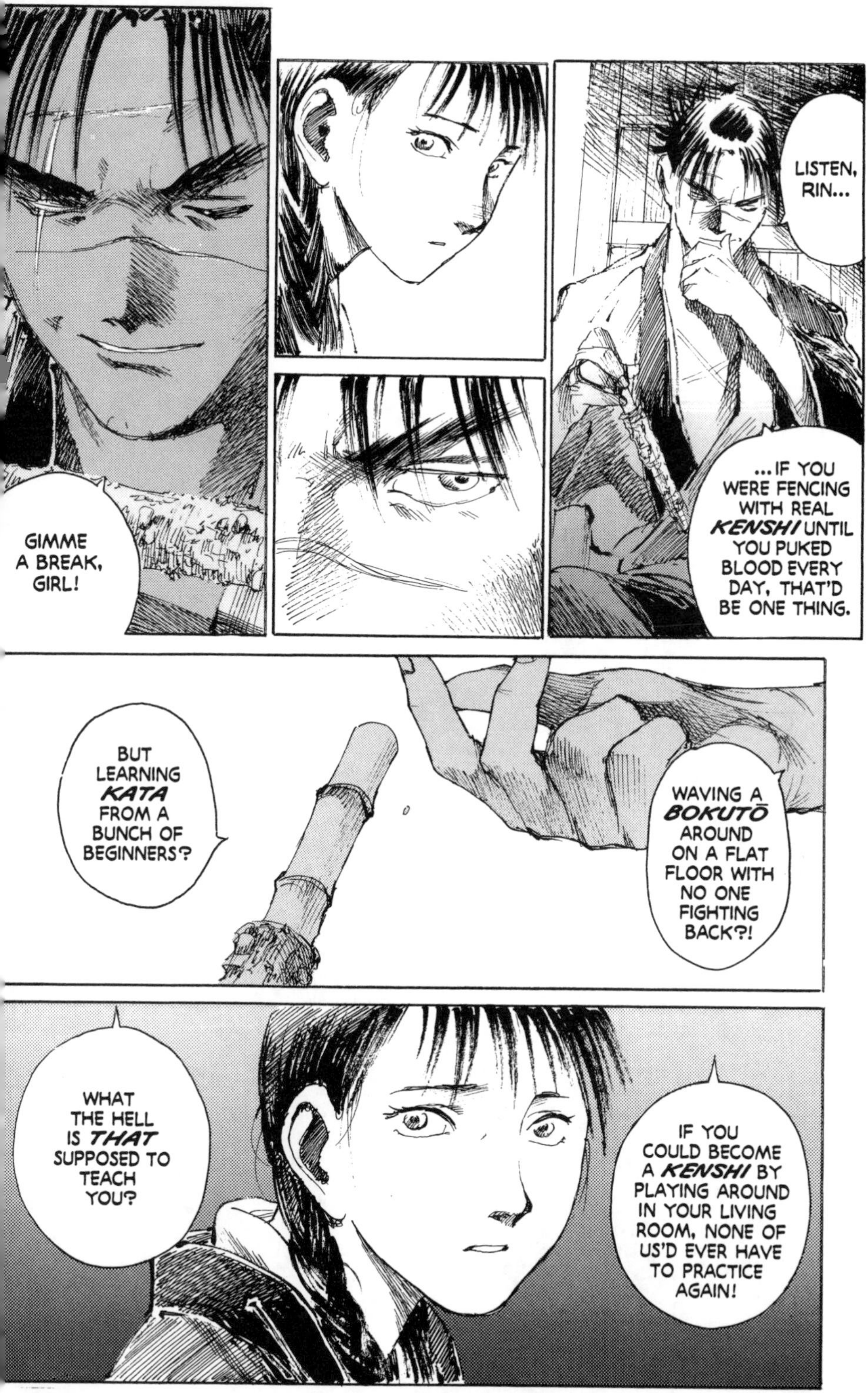
GIMME A BREAK, GIRL!
LISTEN, RIN...
...IF YOU WERE FENCING WITH REAL *KENSHI* UNTIL YOU PUKED BLOOD EVERY DAY, THAT'D BE ONE THING.
BUT LEARNING *KATA* FROM A BUNCH OF BEGINNERS?
WAVING A *BOKUTŌ* AROUND ON A FLAT FLOOR WITH NO ONE FIGHTING BACK?!
WHAT THE HELL IS *THAT* SUPPOSED TO TEACH YOU?
IF YOU COULD BECOME A *KENSHI* BY PLAYING AROUND IN YOUR LIVING ROOM, NONE OF US'D EVER HAVE TO PRACTICE AGAIN!

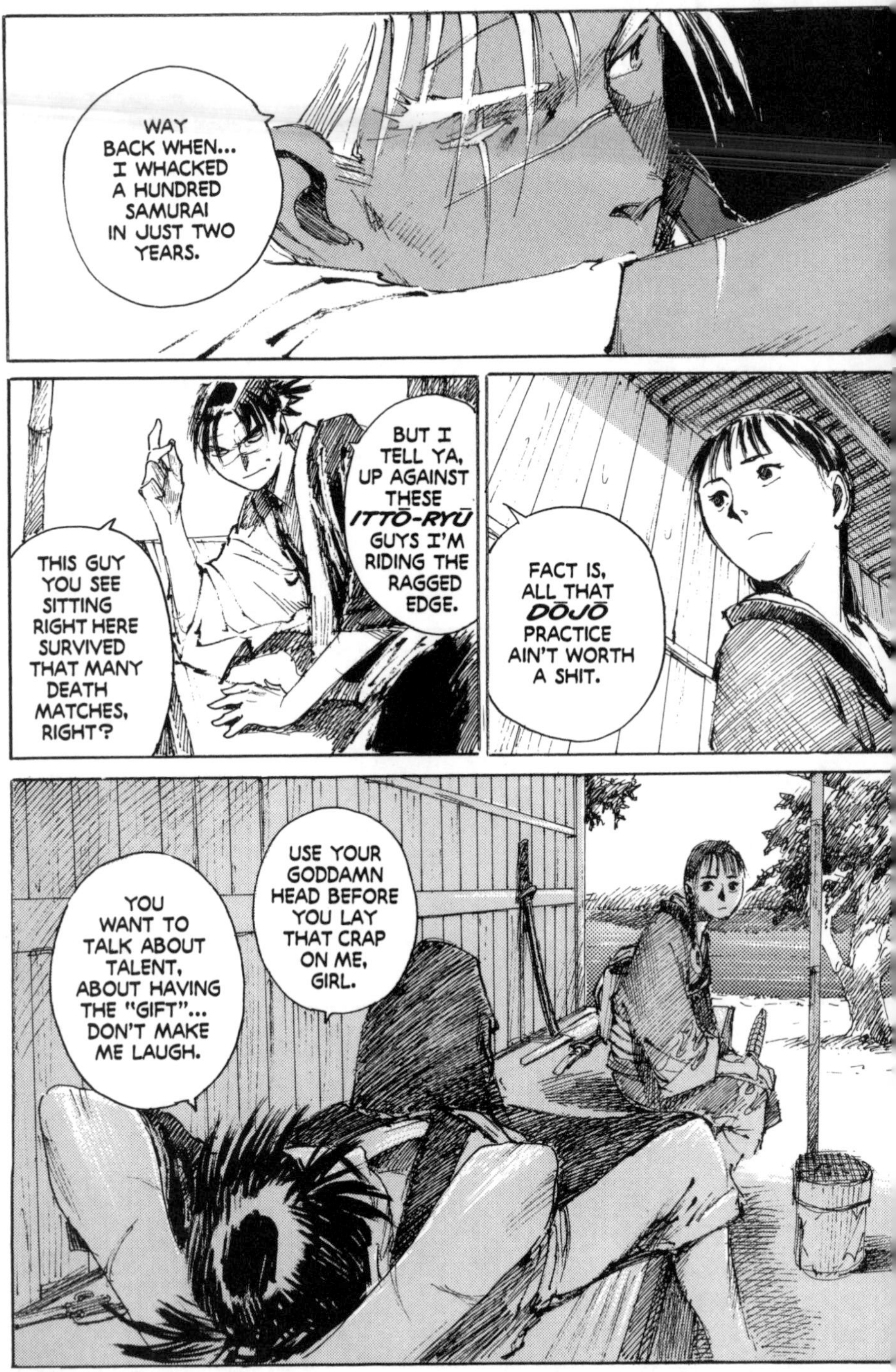
WAY BACK WHEN... I WHACKED A HUNDRED SAMURAI IN JUST TWO YEARS.
THIS GUY YOU SEE SITTING RIGHT HERE SURVIVED THAT MANY DEATH MATCHES, RIGHT?
BUT I TELL YA, UP AGAINST THESE *ITTŌ-RYŪ* GUYS I'M RIDING THE RAGGED EDGE.
FACT IS, ALL THAT *DŌJŌ* PRACTICE AIN'T WORTH A SHIT.
YOU WANT TO TALK ABOUT TALENT, ABOUT HAVING THE "GIFT"... DON'T MAKE ME LAUGH.
USE YOUR GODDAMN HEAD BEFORE YOU LAY THAT CRAP ON ME, GIRL.

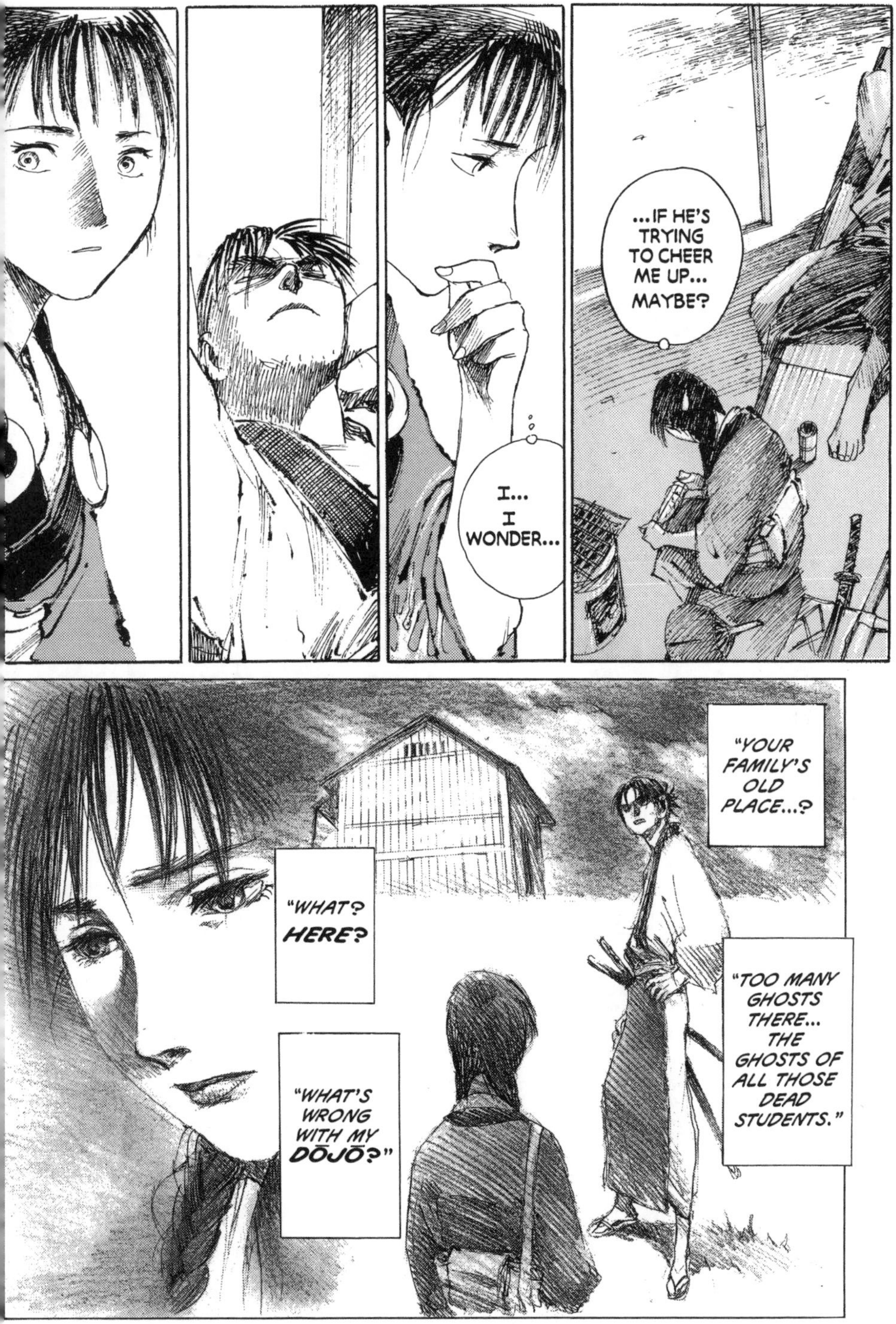
I...
I WONDER...
...IF HE'S TRYING TO CHEER ME UP... MAYBE?
"YOUR FAMILY'S OLD PLACE...?
"WHAT? HERE?
"WHAT'S WRONG WITH MY DŌJŌ?"
"TOO MANY GHOSTS THERE... THE GHOSTS OF ALL THOSE DEAD STUDENTS."

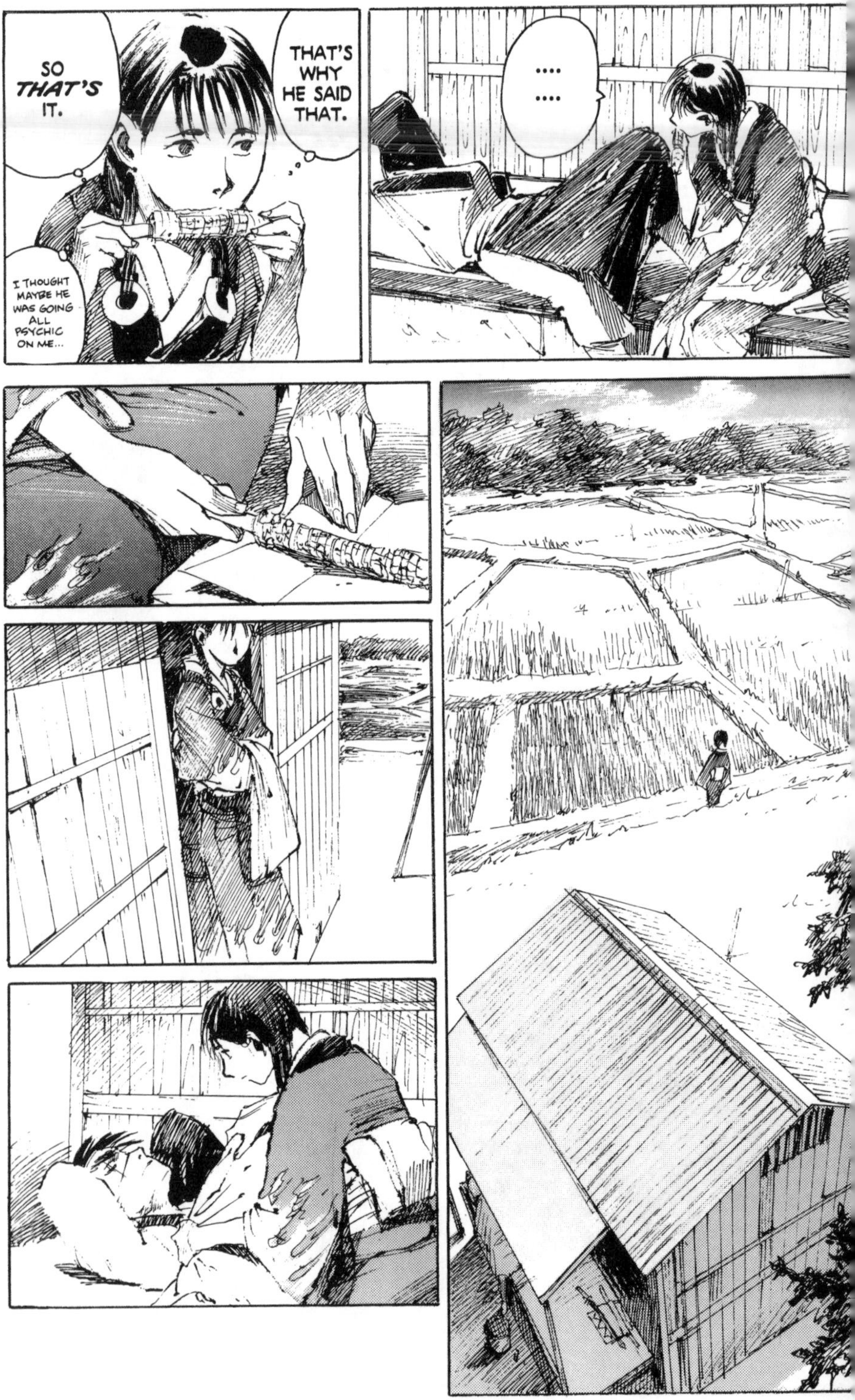
SO THAT'S IT.
THAT'S WHY HE SAID THAT.
I THOUGHT MAYBE HE WAS GOING ALL PSYCHIC ON ME...
....
....

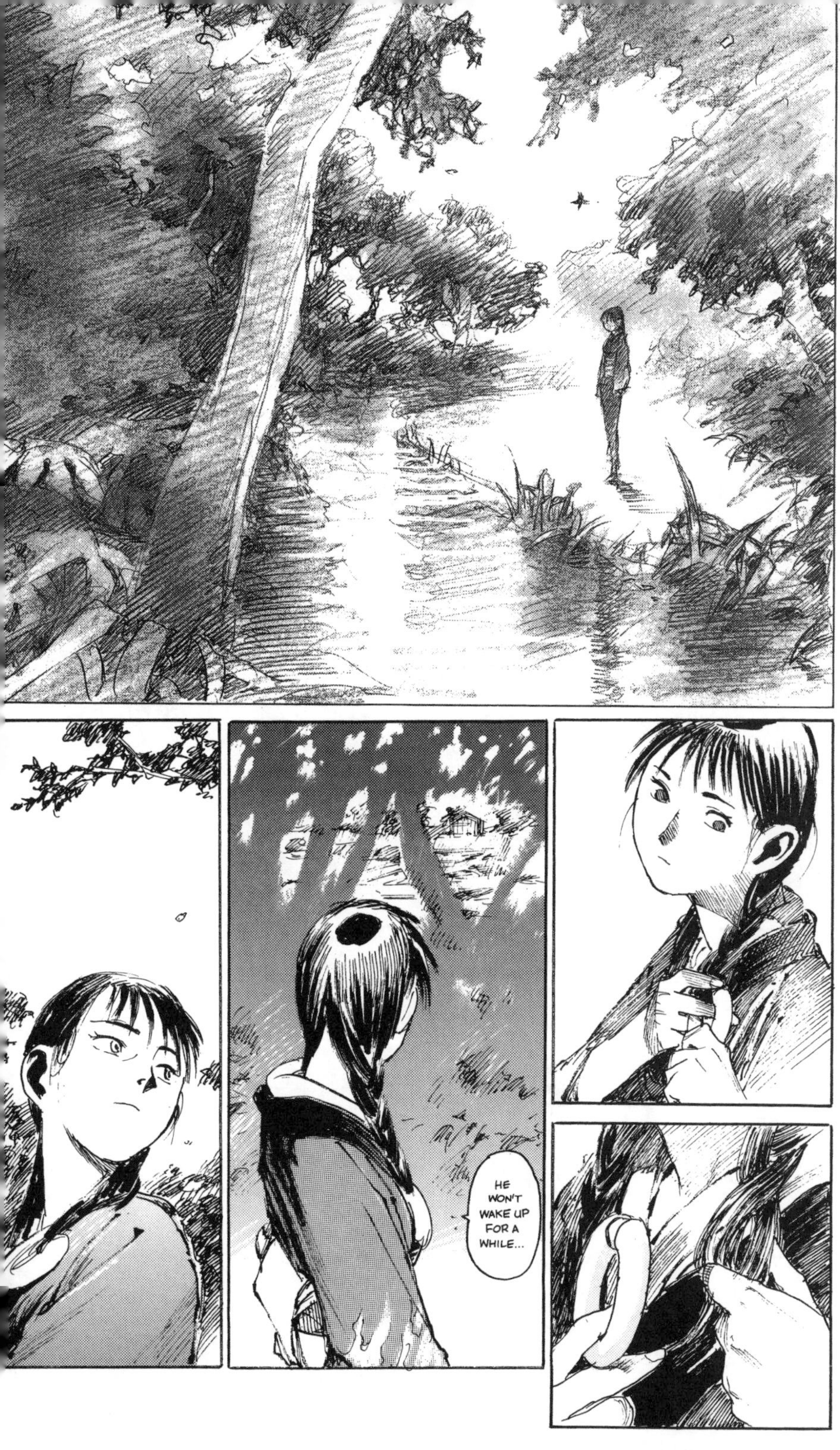
HE WON'T WAKE UP FOR A WHILE...

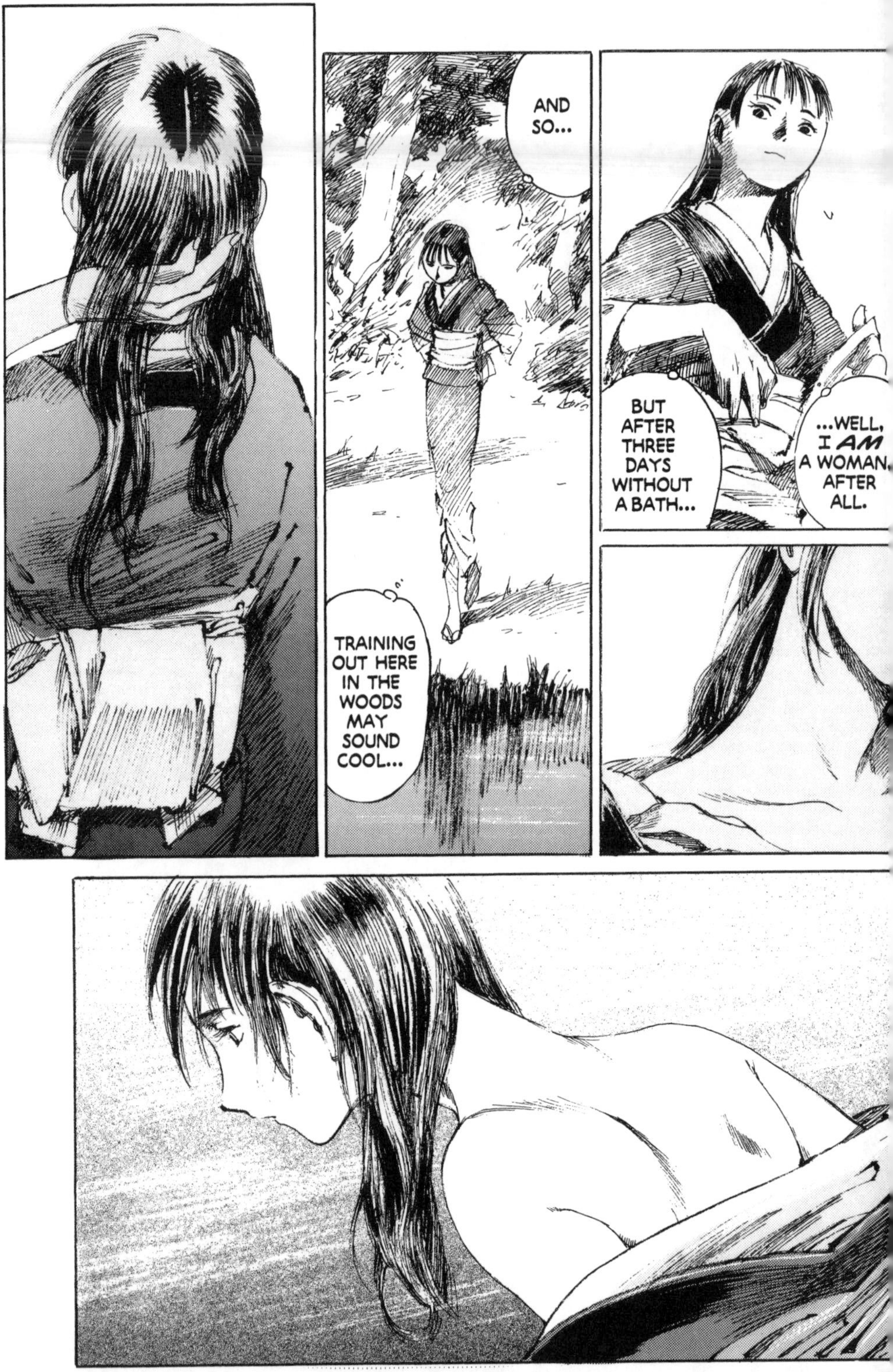
AND SO...
TRAINING OUT HERE IN THE WOODS MAY SOUND COOL...
BUT AFTER THREE DAYS WITHOUT A BATH...
...WELL, I *AM* A WOMAN, AFTER ALL.

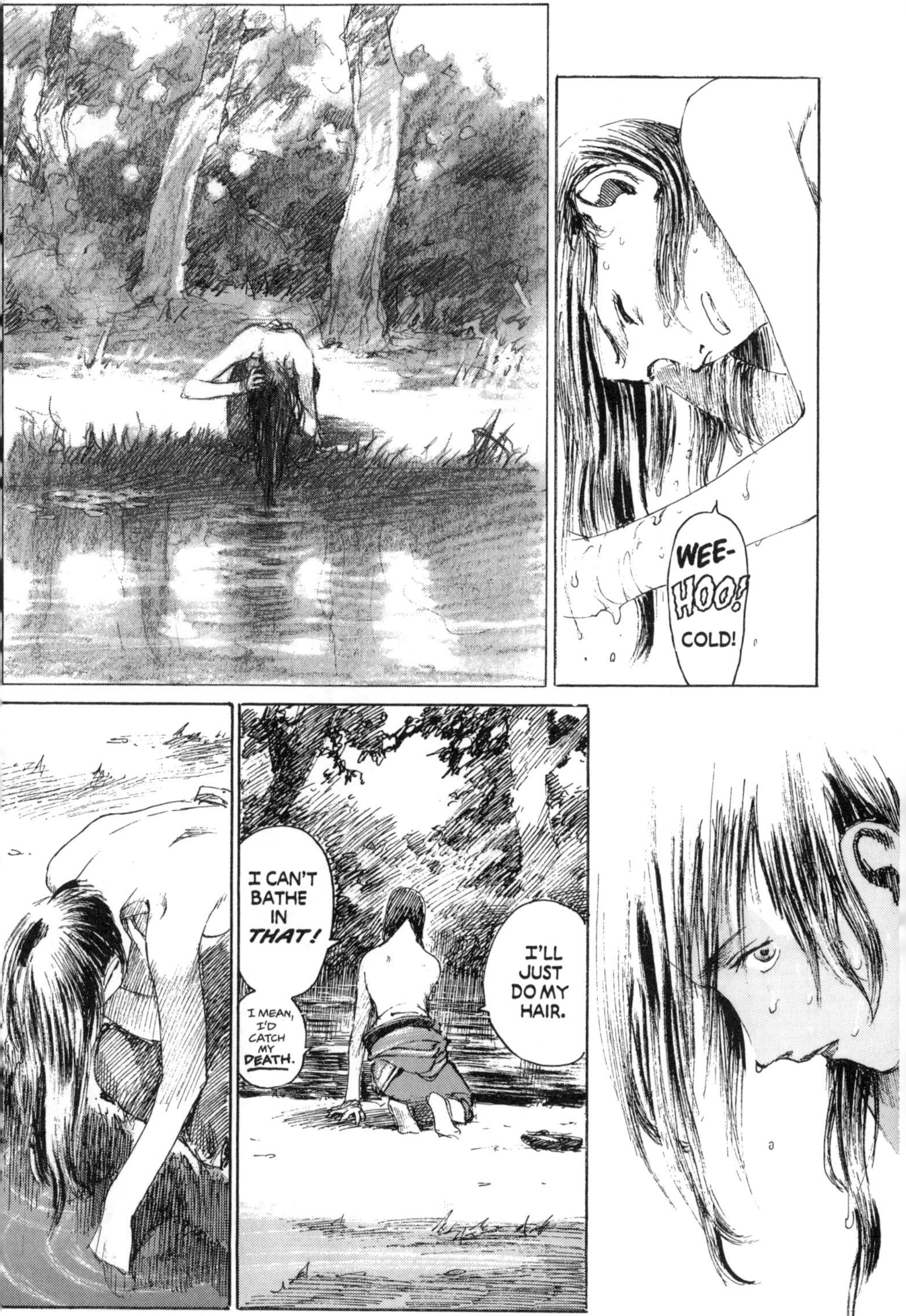
WEE-HOO! COLD!
I CAN'T BATHE IN THAT!
I MEAN, I'D CATCH MY DEATH.
I'LL JUST DO MY HAIR.

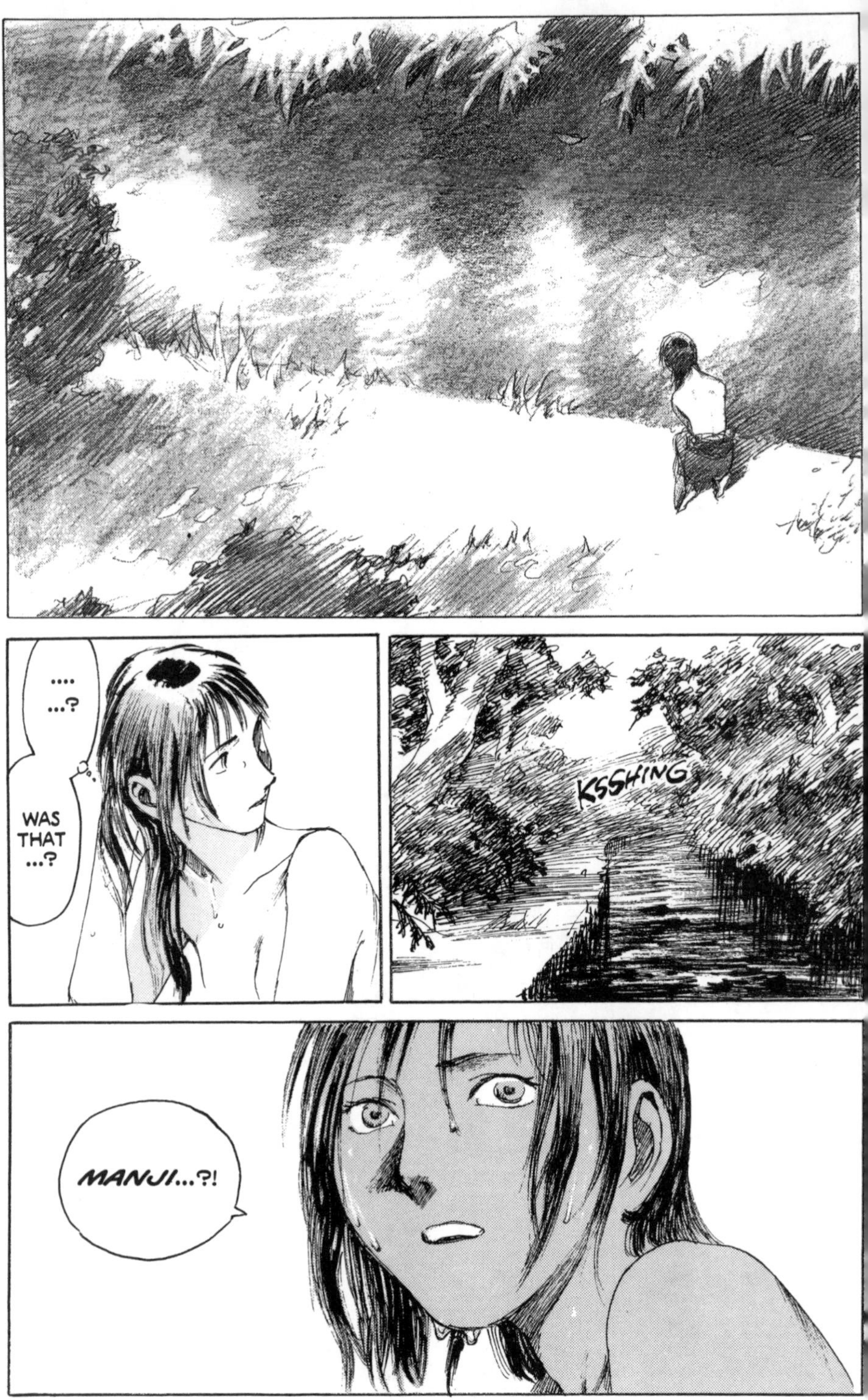
....
...?
WAS THAT ...?
KSSHING
MANJI...?!

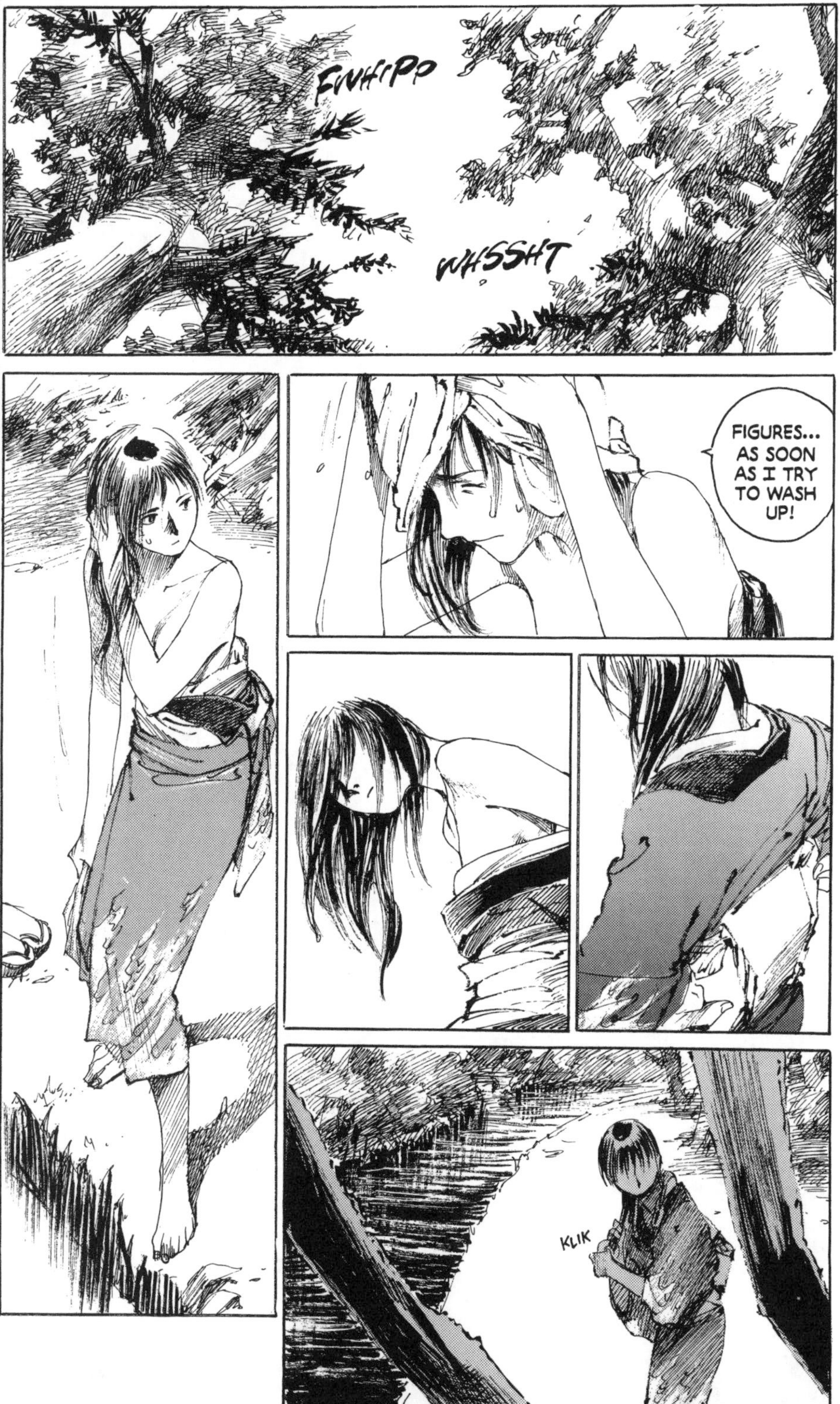
FWHIPP
WHSSHT
FIGURES... AS SOON AS I TRY TO WASH UP!
KLIK

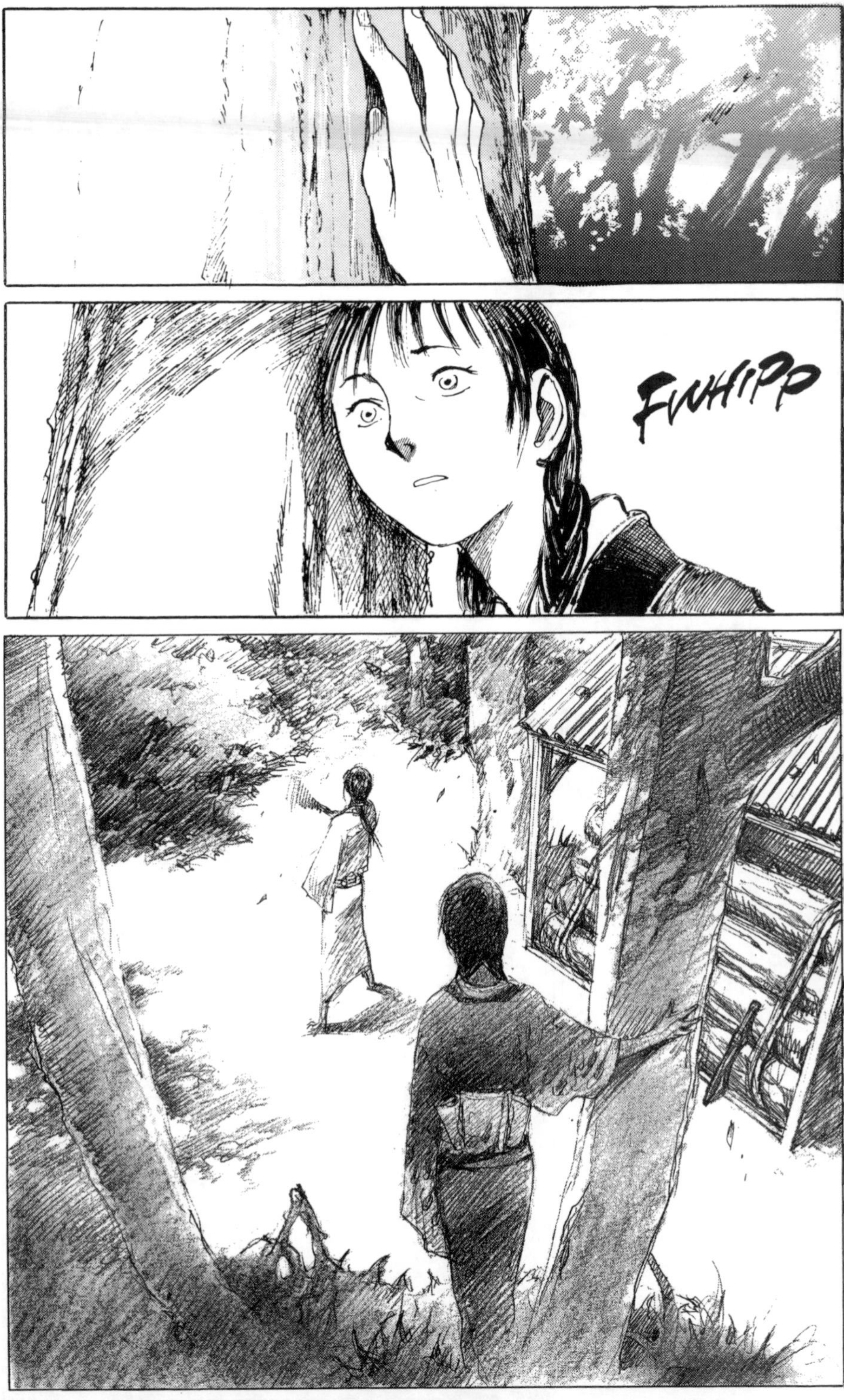
FWHIPP

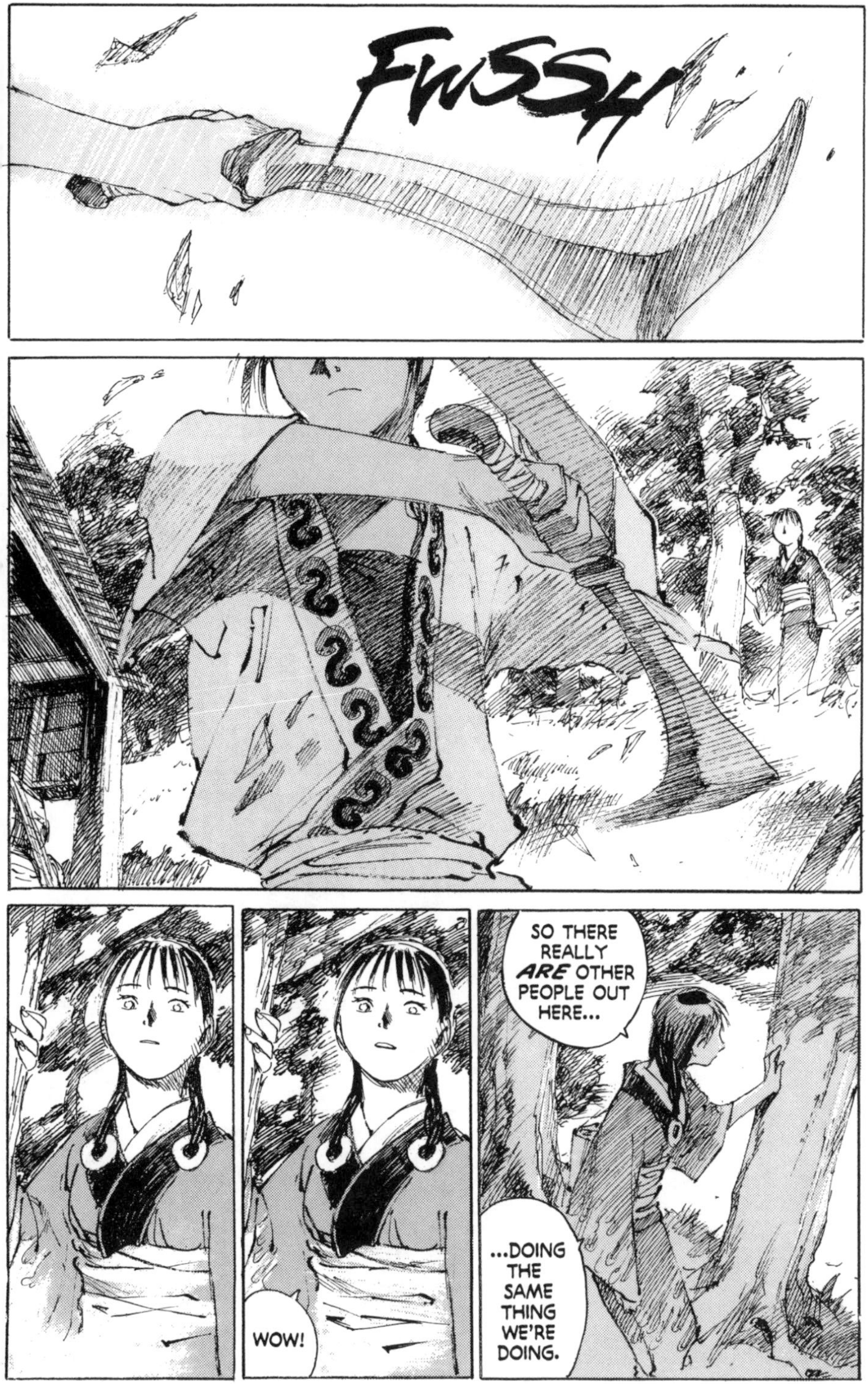
FWSSH
WOW!
SO THERE REALLY *ARE* OTHER PEOPLE OUT HERE...
...DOING THE SAME THING WE'RE DOING.

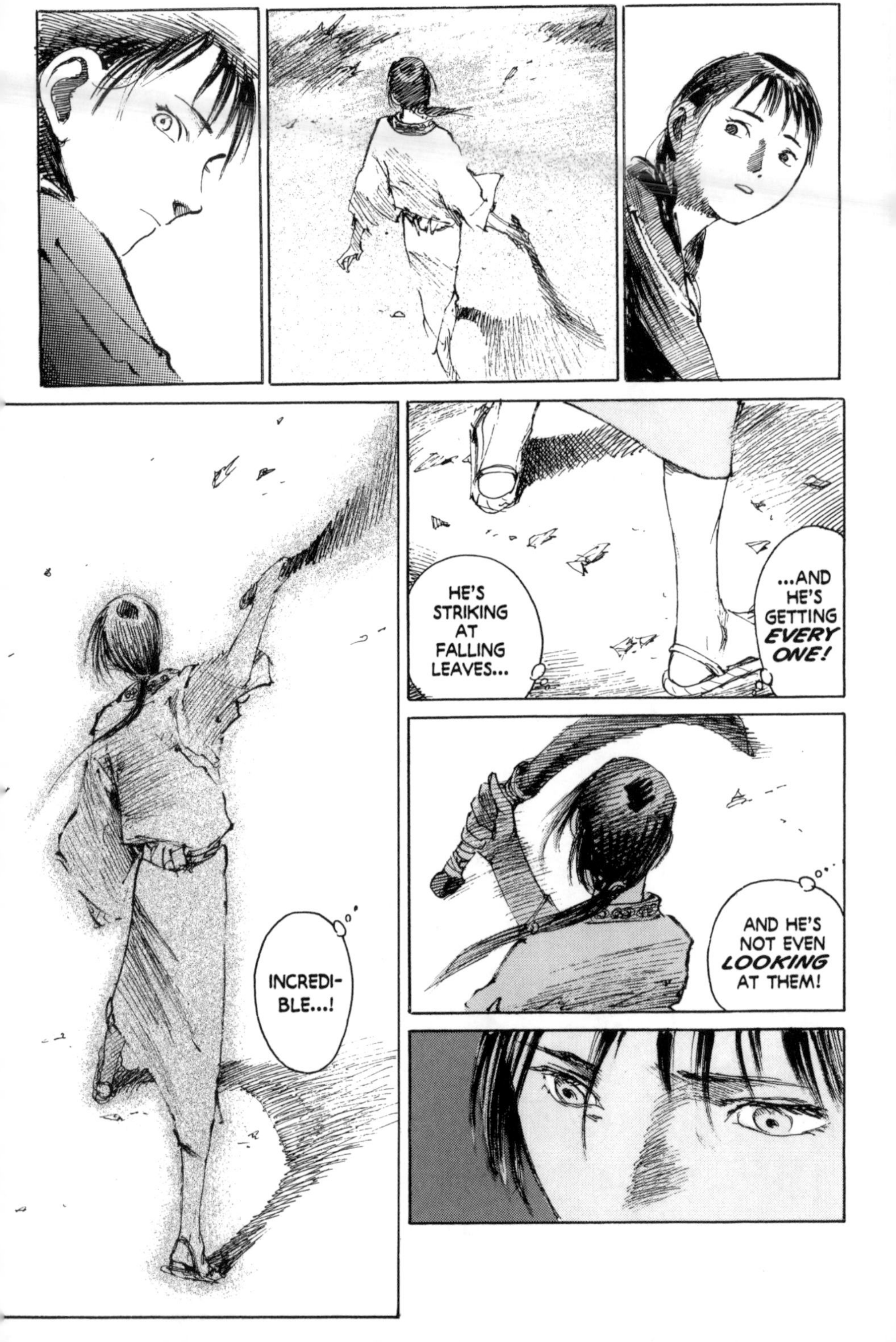
INCREDI-
BLE...!
HE'S STRIKING AT FALLING LEAVES...
...AND HE'S GETTING *EVERY ONE!*
AND HE'S NOT EVEN *LOOKING* AT THEM!

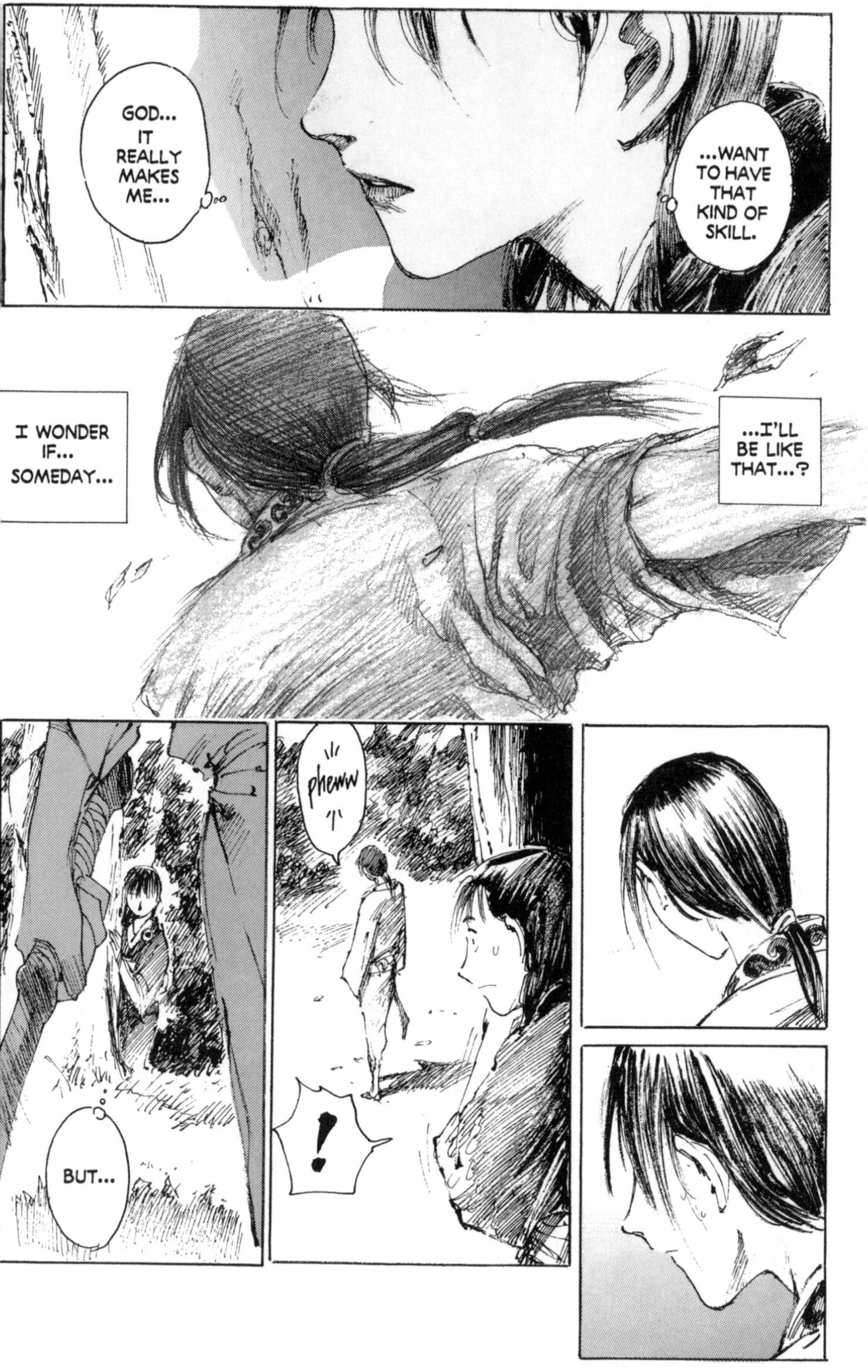
GOD... IT REALLY MAKES ME...
...WANT TO HAVE THAT KIND OF SKILL.
I WONDER IF... SOMEDAY...
...I'LL BE LIKE THAT...?
BUT...
phew
!

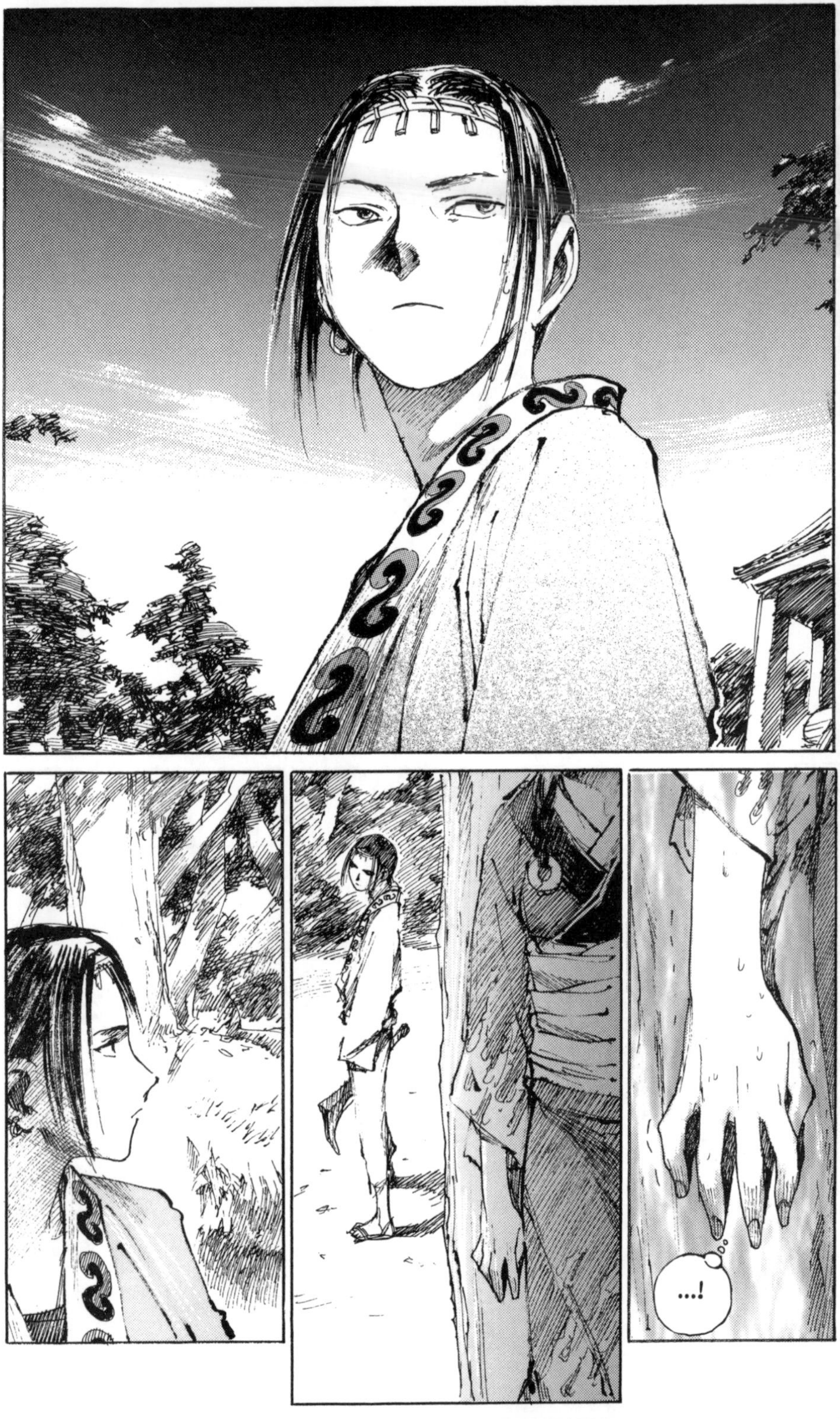
...!

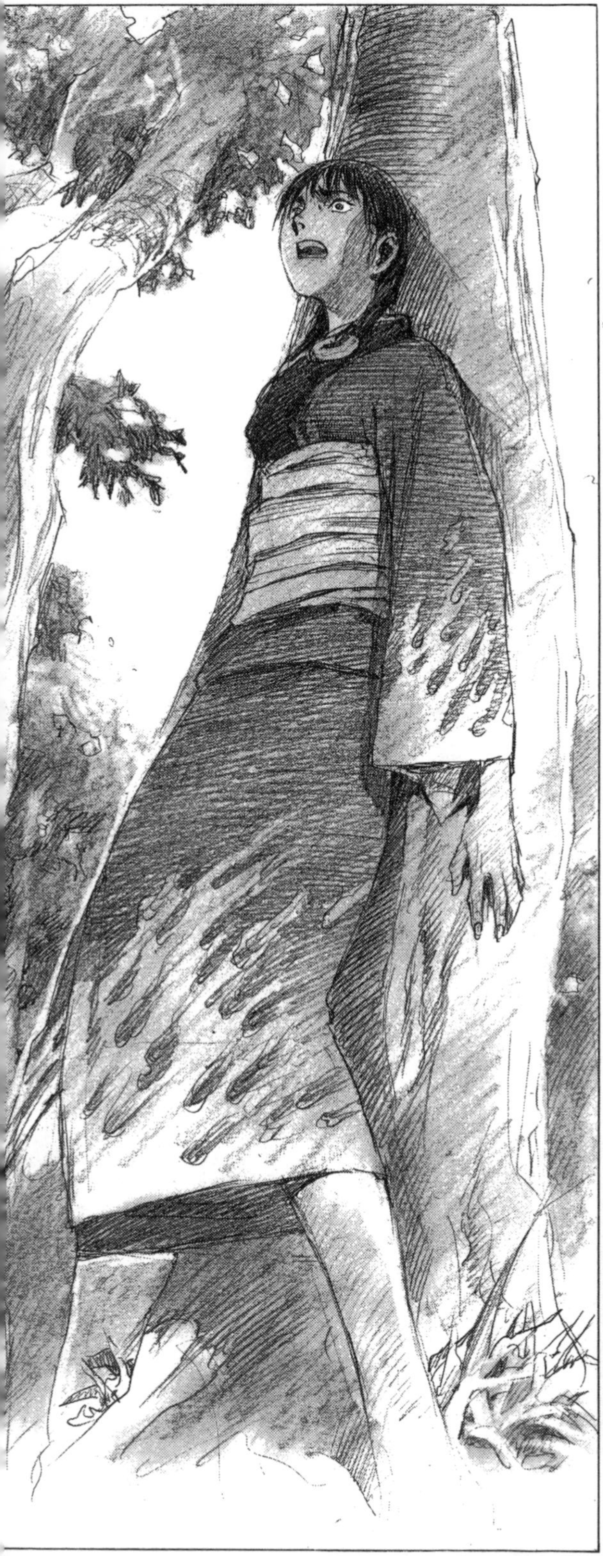
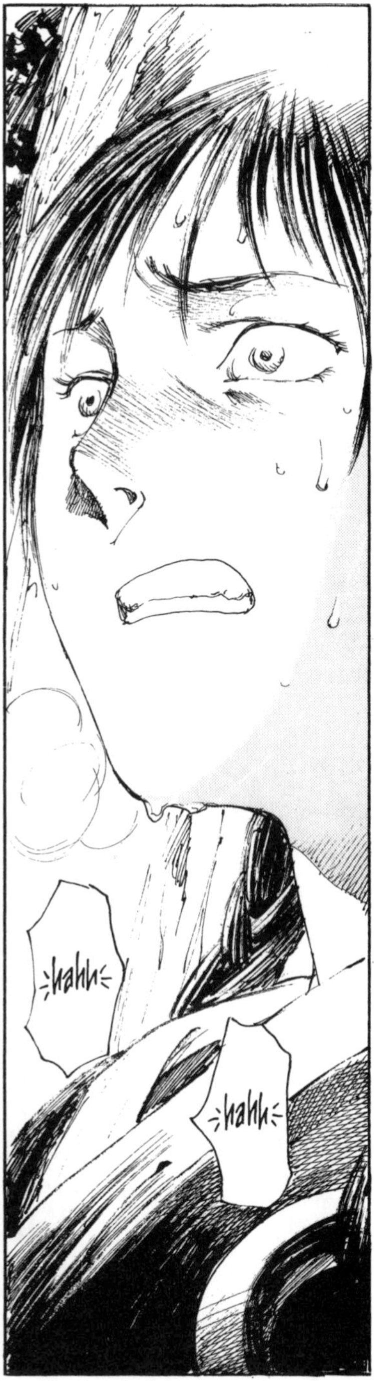
hahh
hahh

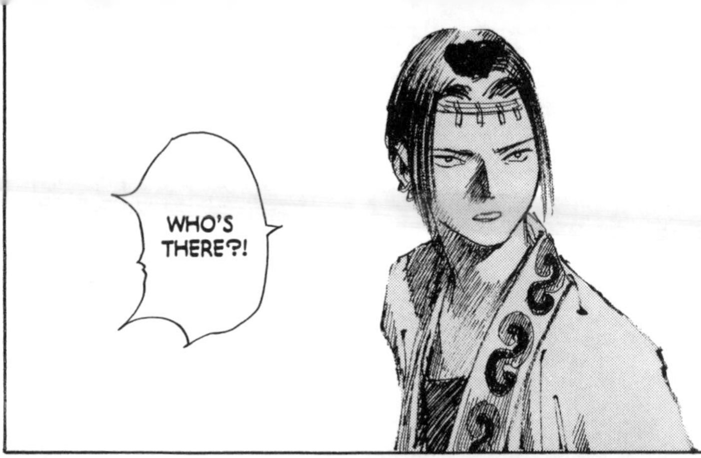
WHO'S THERE?!
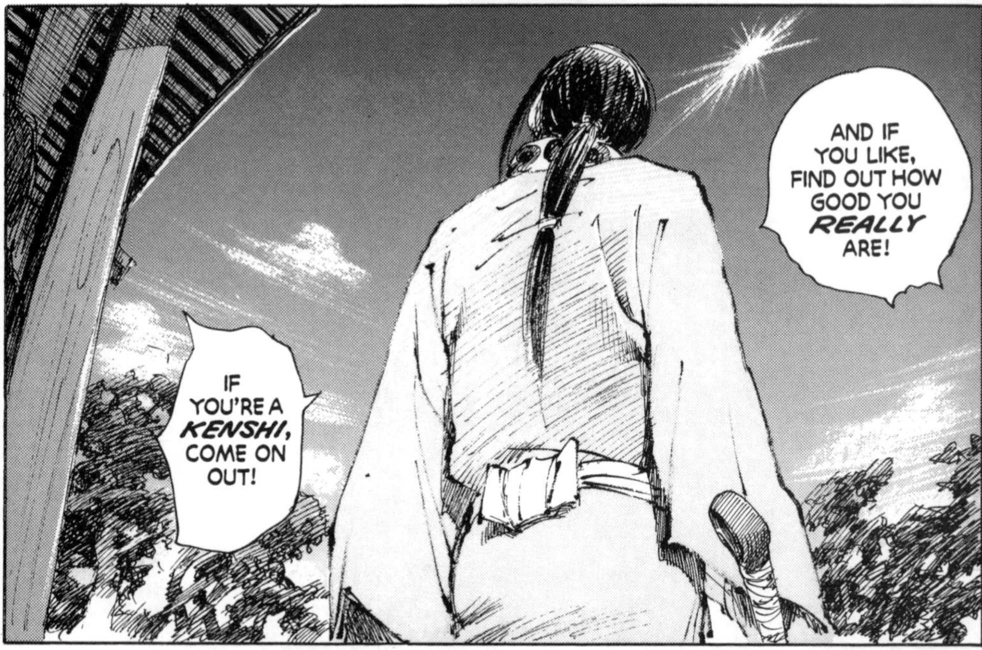
IF YOU'RE A *KENSHI*, COME ON OUT!
AND IF YOU LIKE, FIND OUT HOW GOOD YOU *REALLY* ARE!
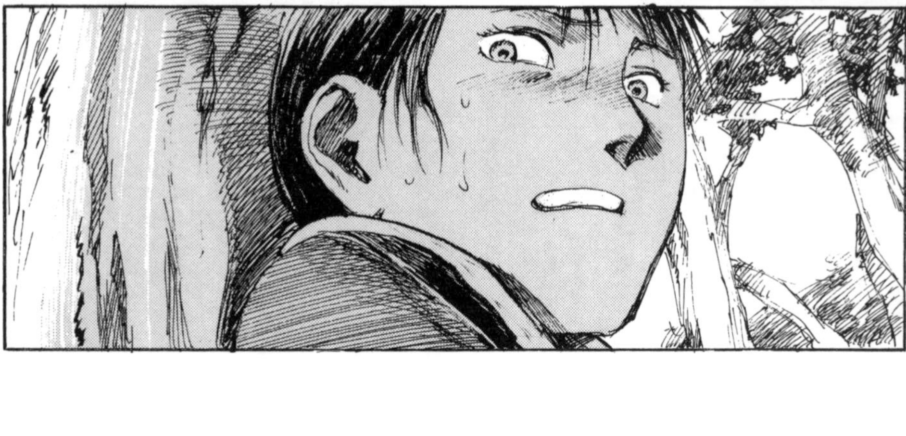

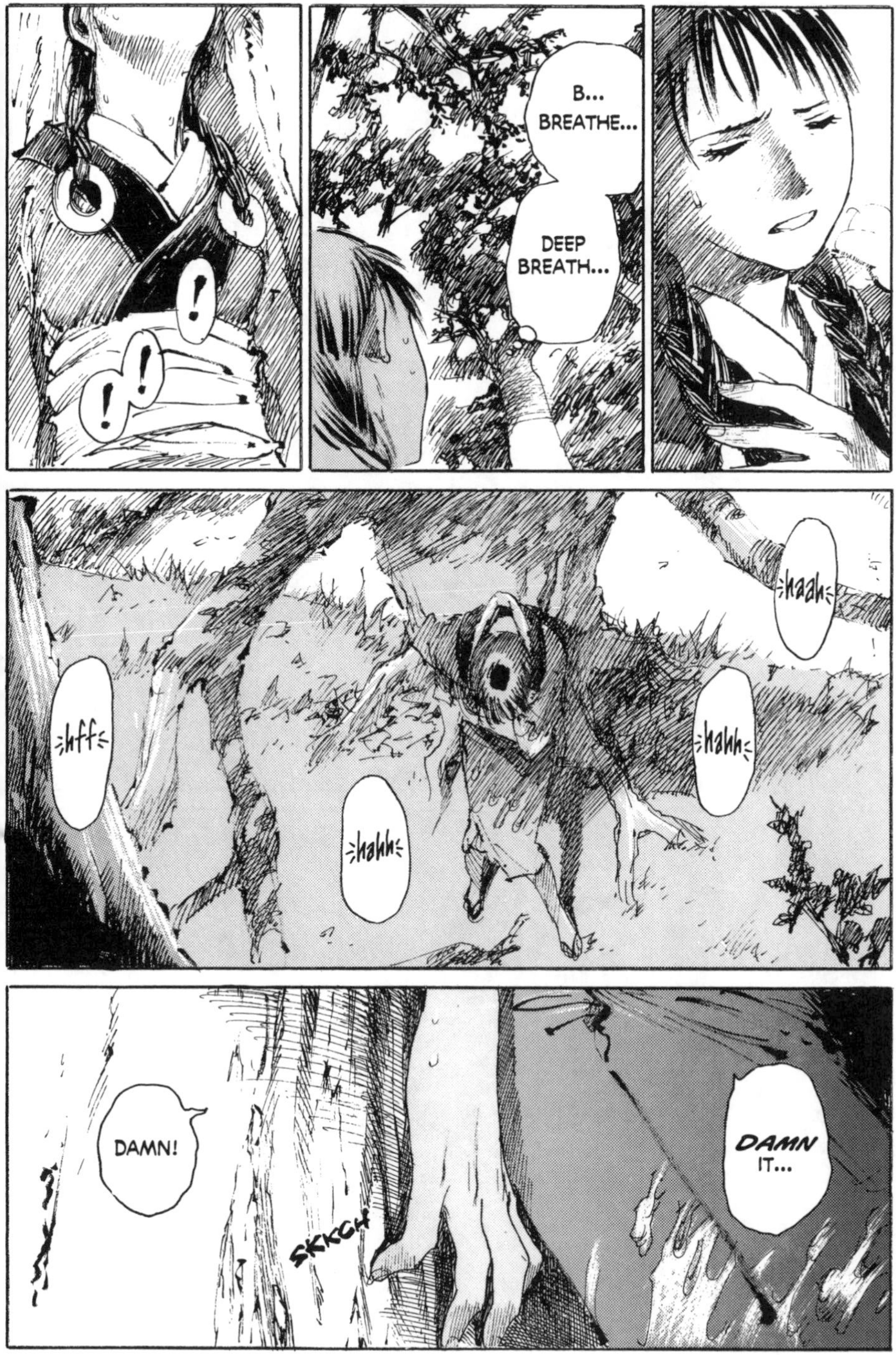
!!!
B... BREATHE...
DEEP BREATH...
hff
hahh
haah
hahh
DAMN!
SKKCH
DAMN IT...

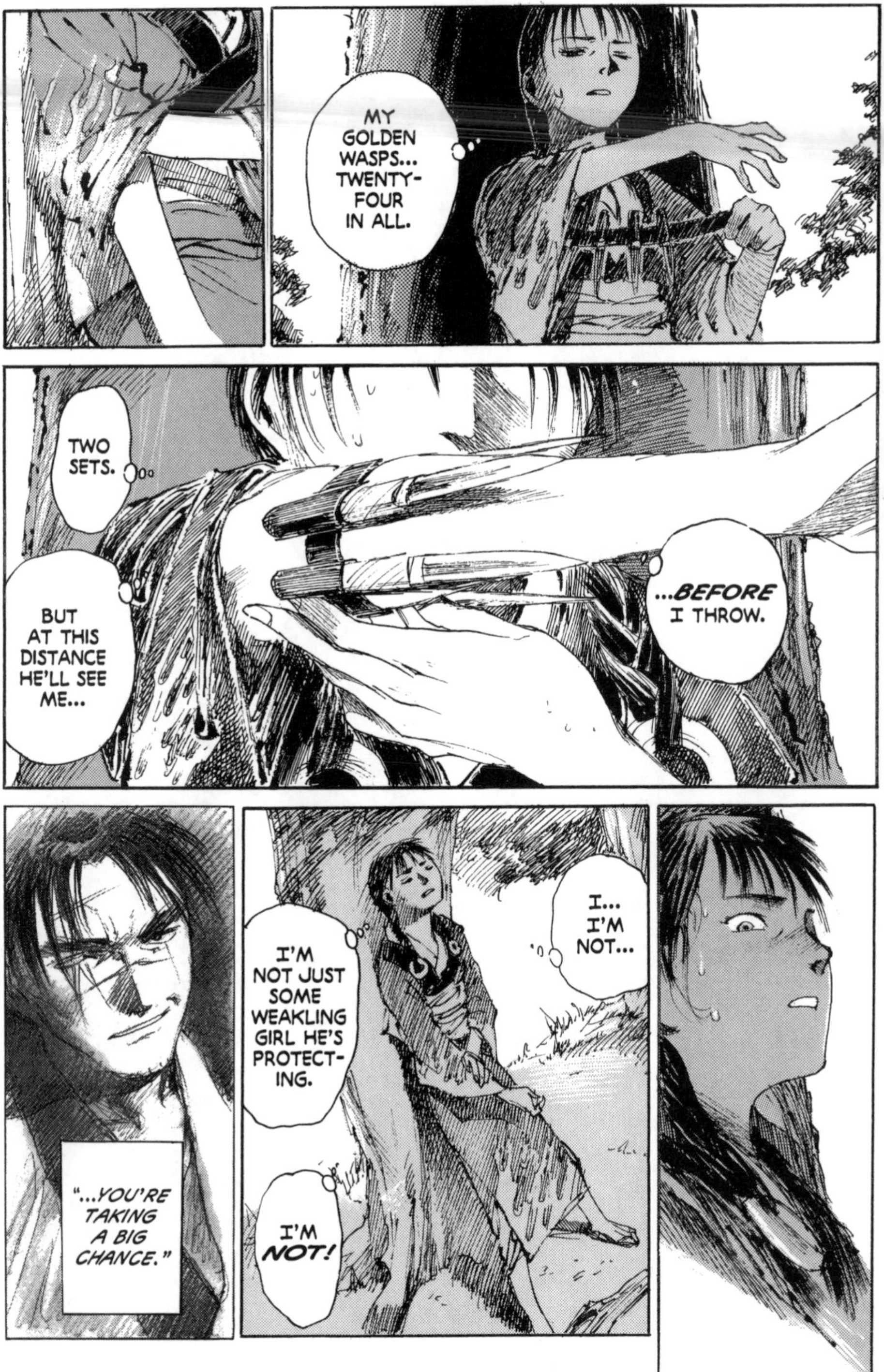
MY GOLDEN WASPS... TWENTY-FOUR IN ALL.
TWO SETS.
BUT AT THIS DISTANCE HE'LL SEE ME...
...*BEFORE* I THROW.
"...*YOU'RE TAKING A BIG CHANCE.*"
I'M NOT JUST SOME WEAKLING GIRL HE'S PROTECT-ING.
I'M *NOT!*
I... I'M NOT...

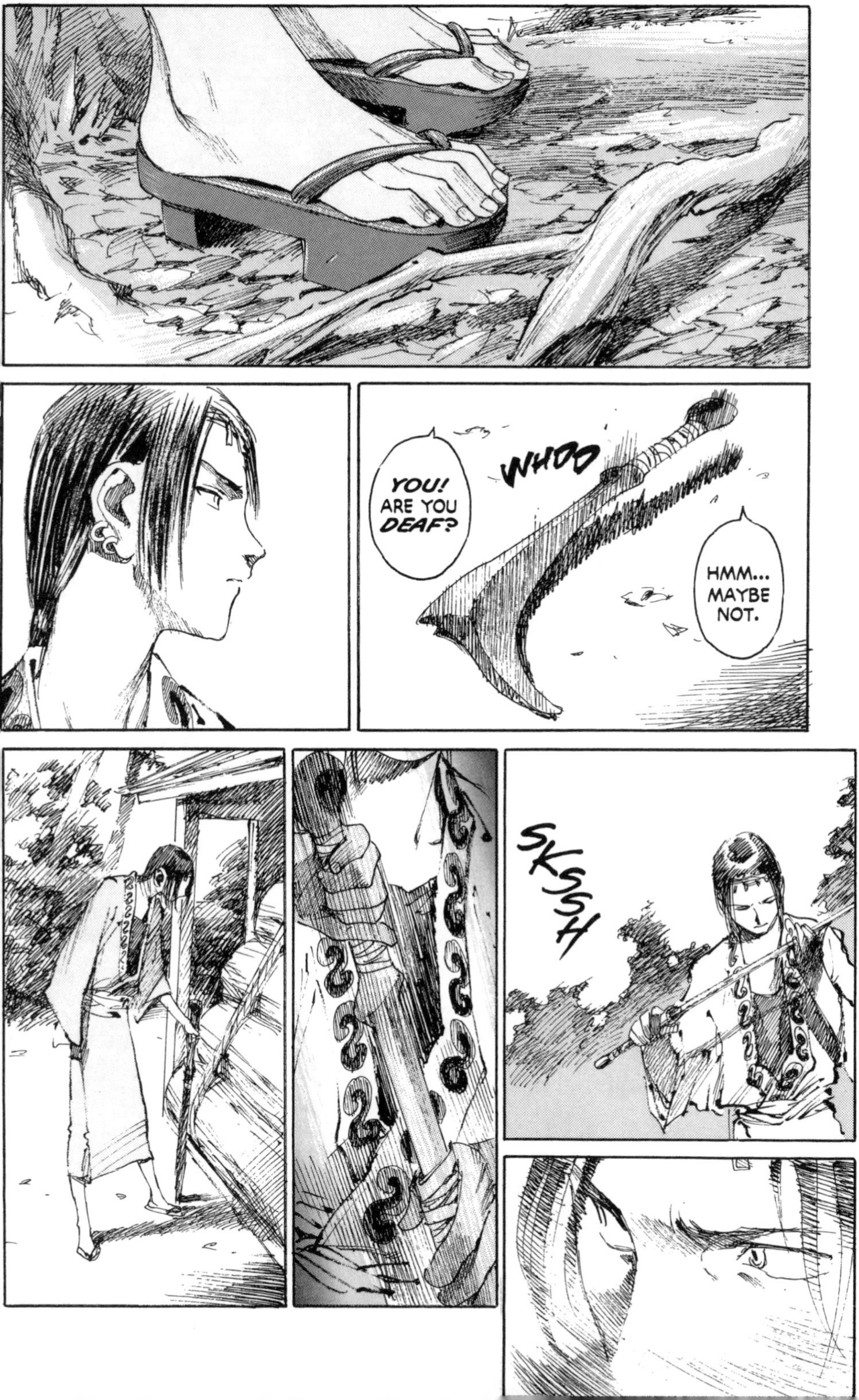
YOU! ARE YOU DEAF?
WHOO
HMM... MAYBE NOT.
SKSSH

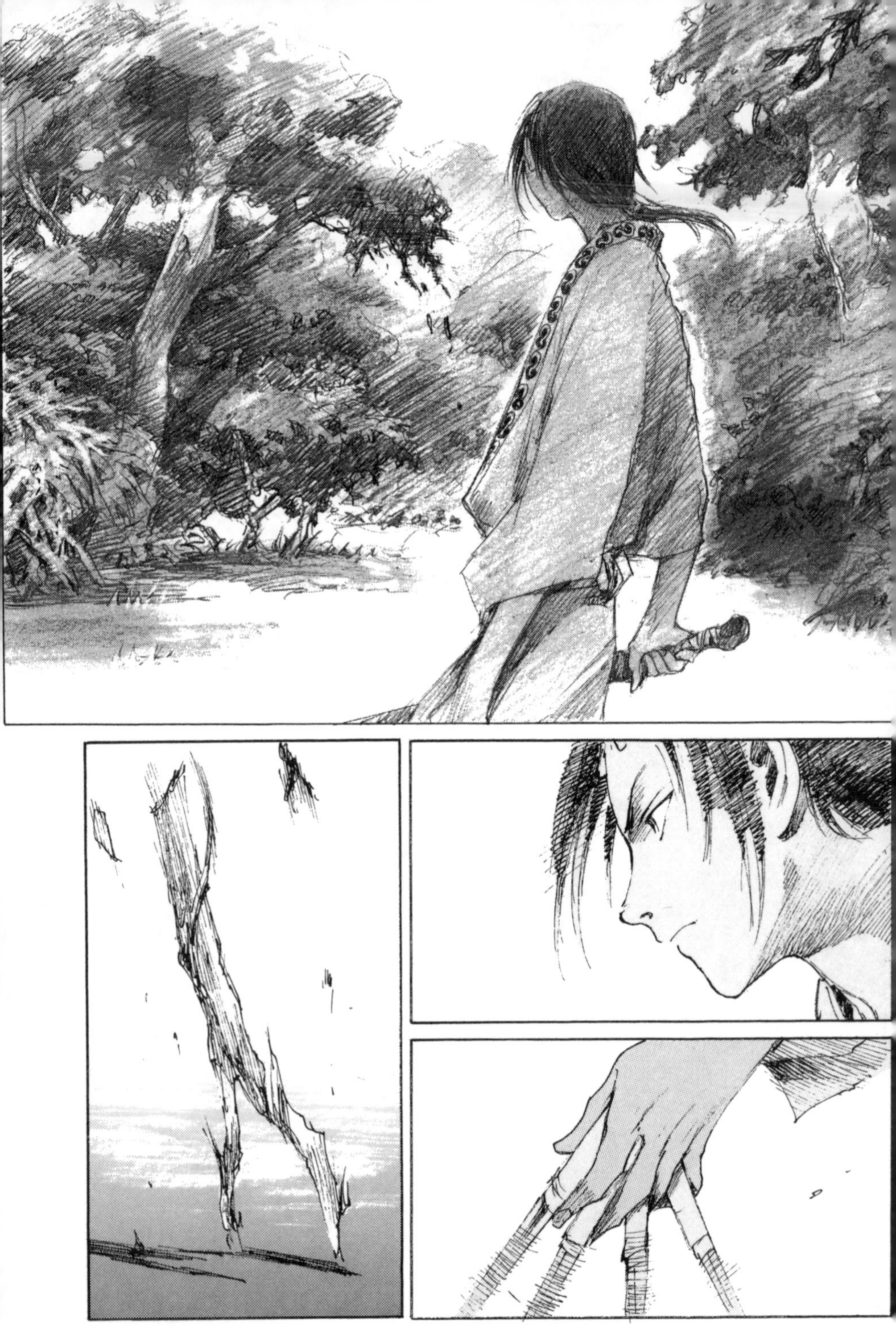

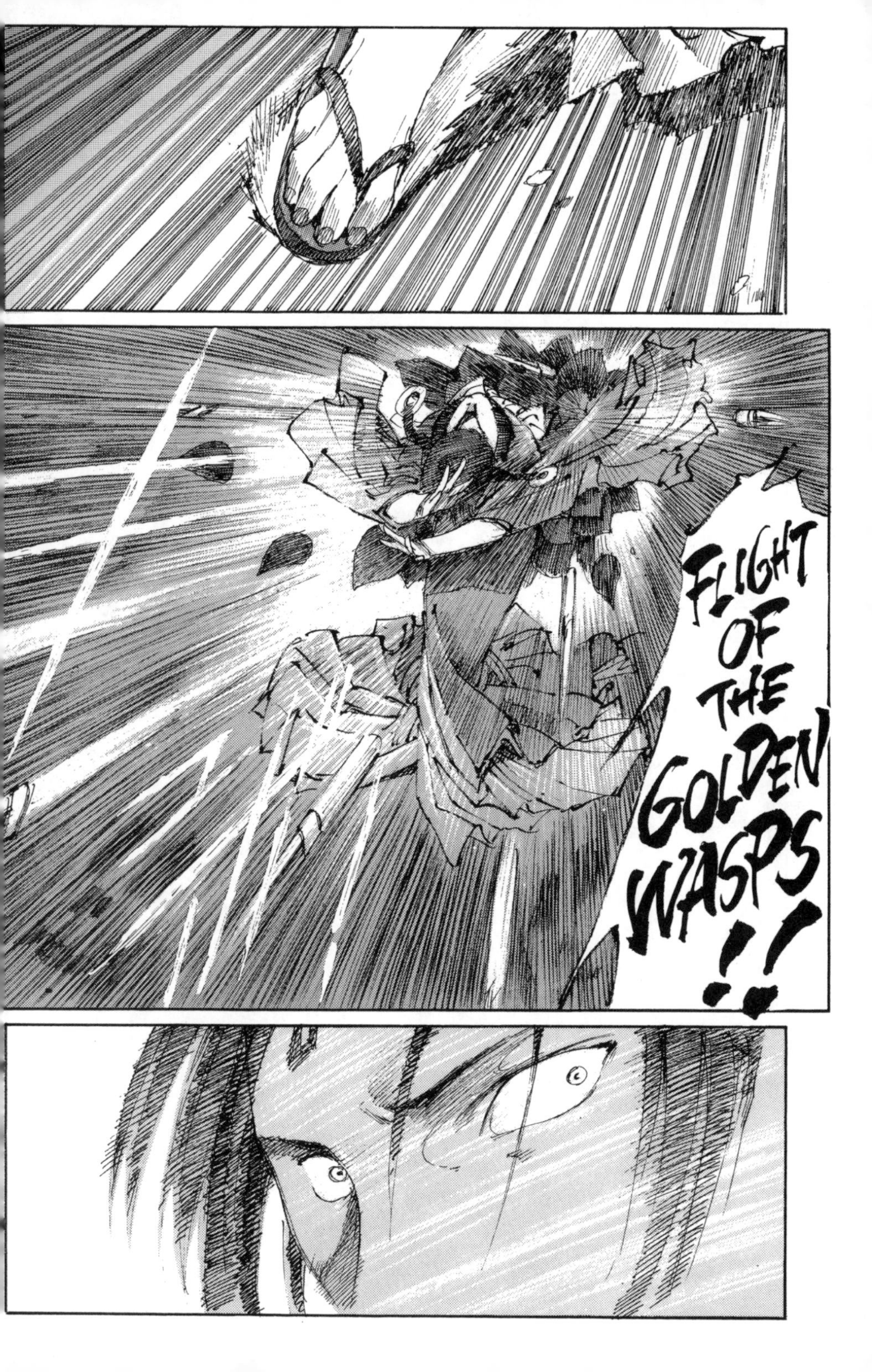
FLIGHT OF THE GOLDEN WASPS!!

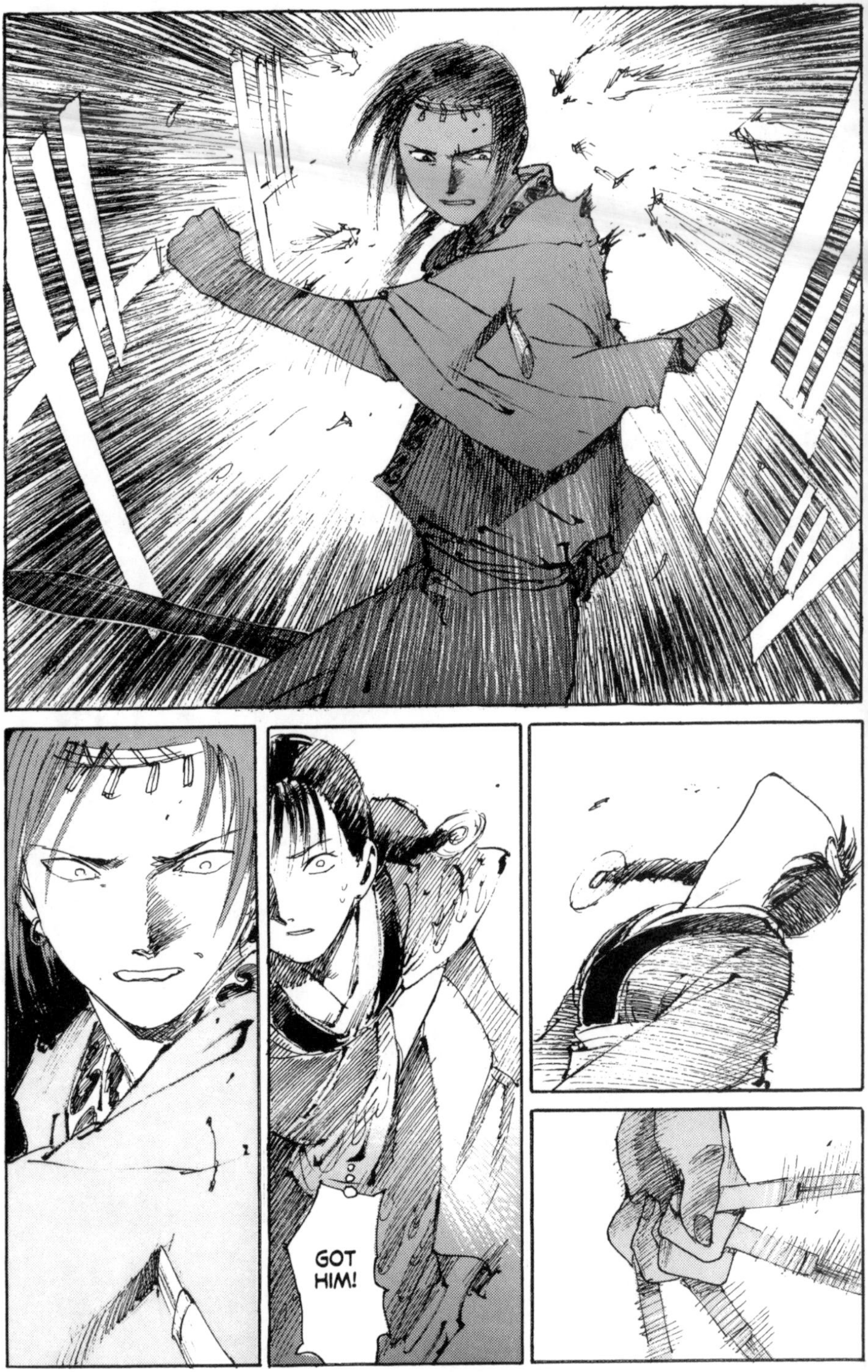
GOT
HIM!

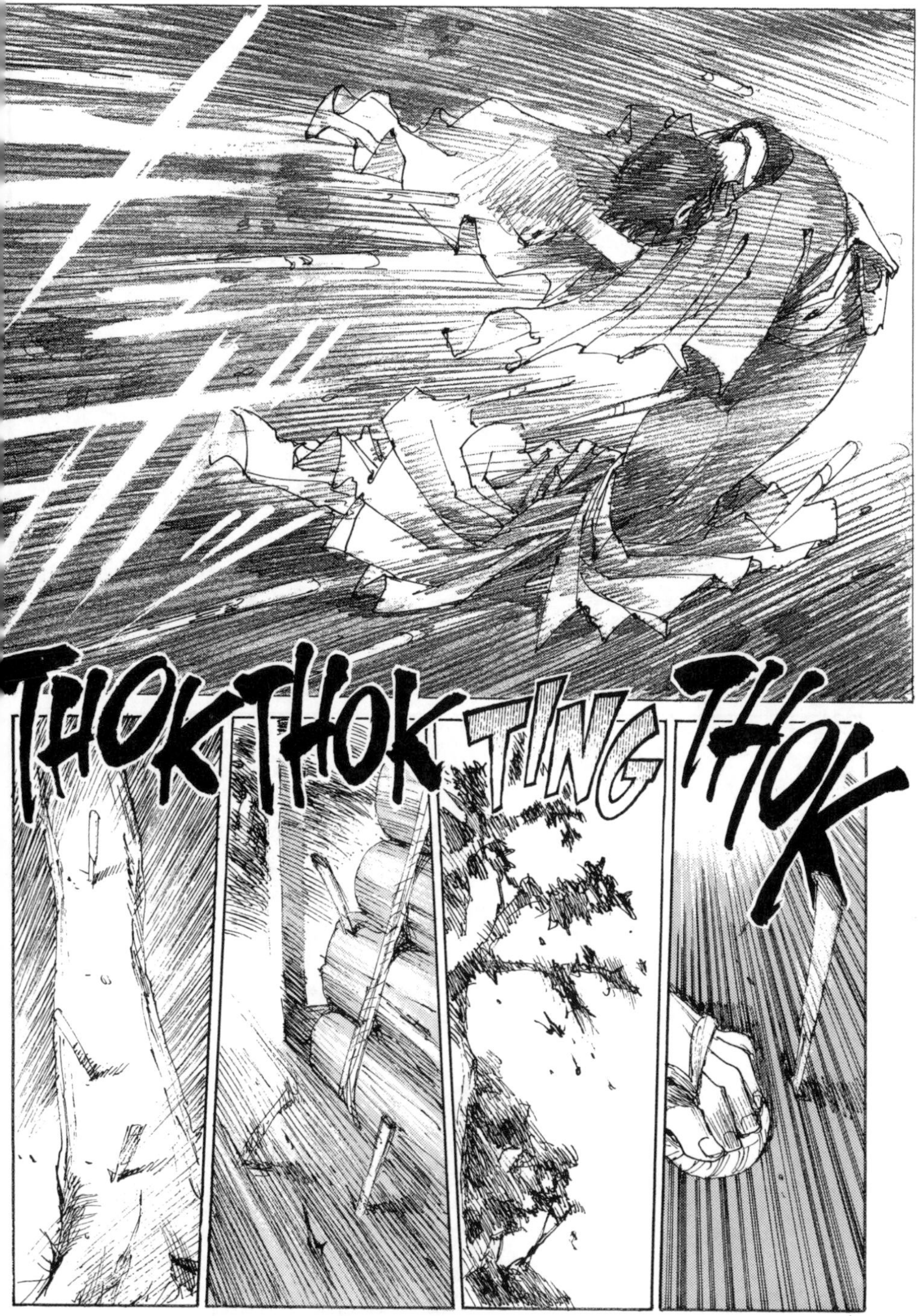
THOK
TING
THOK
THOK

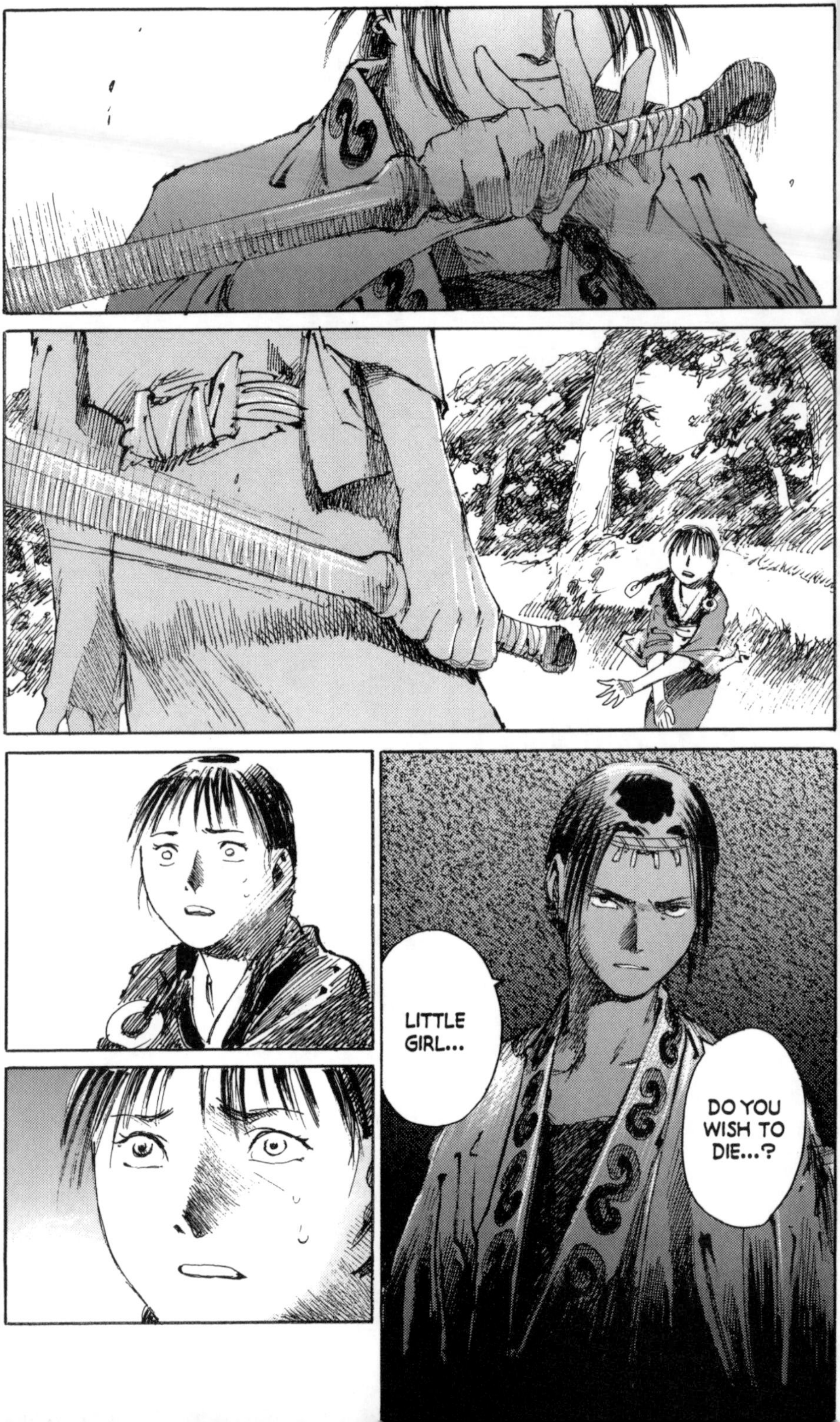
LITTLE GIRL...
DO YOU WISH TO DIE...?

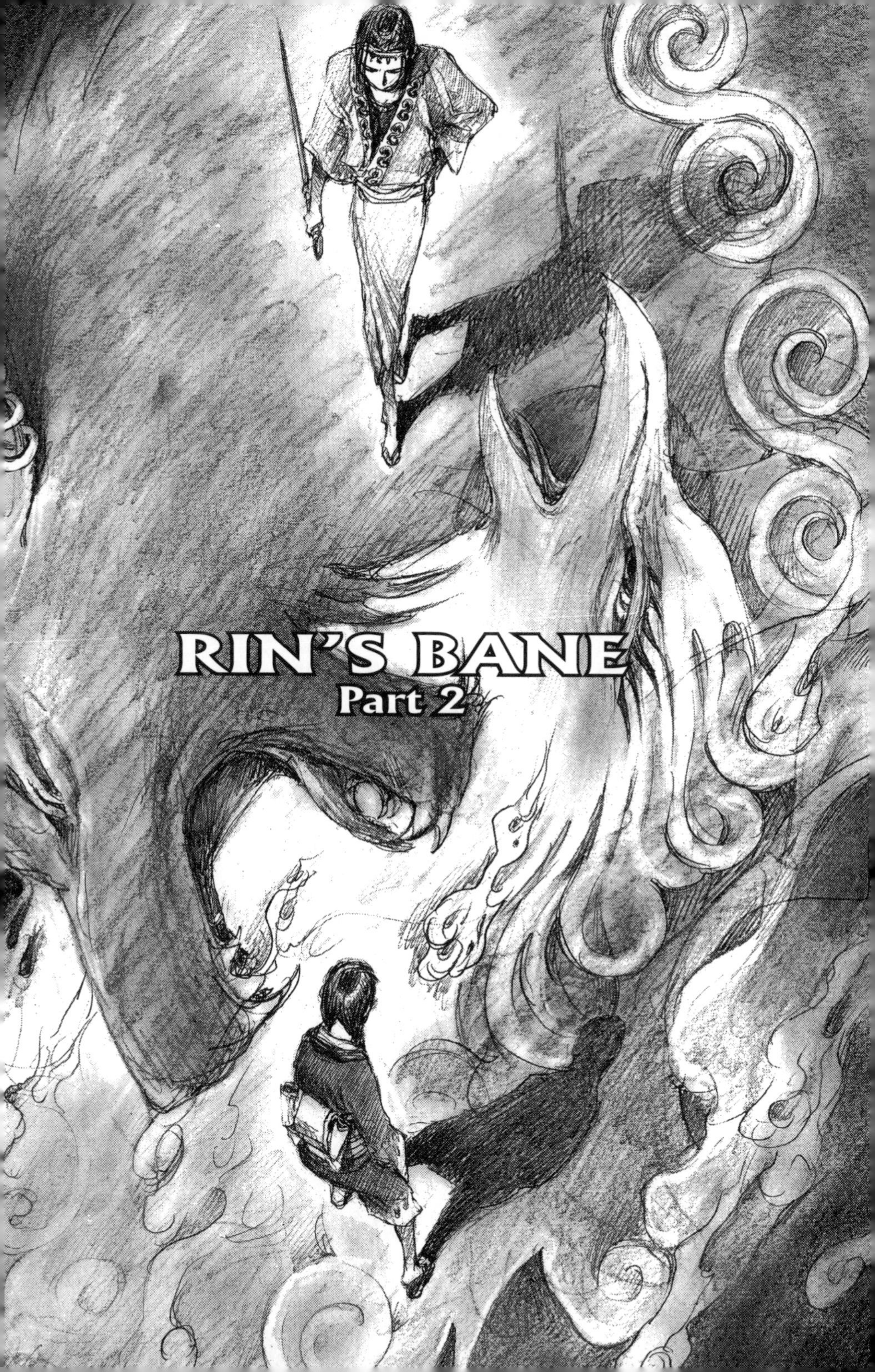
RIN'S BANE
Part 2

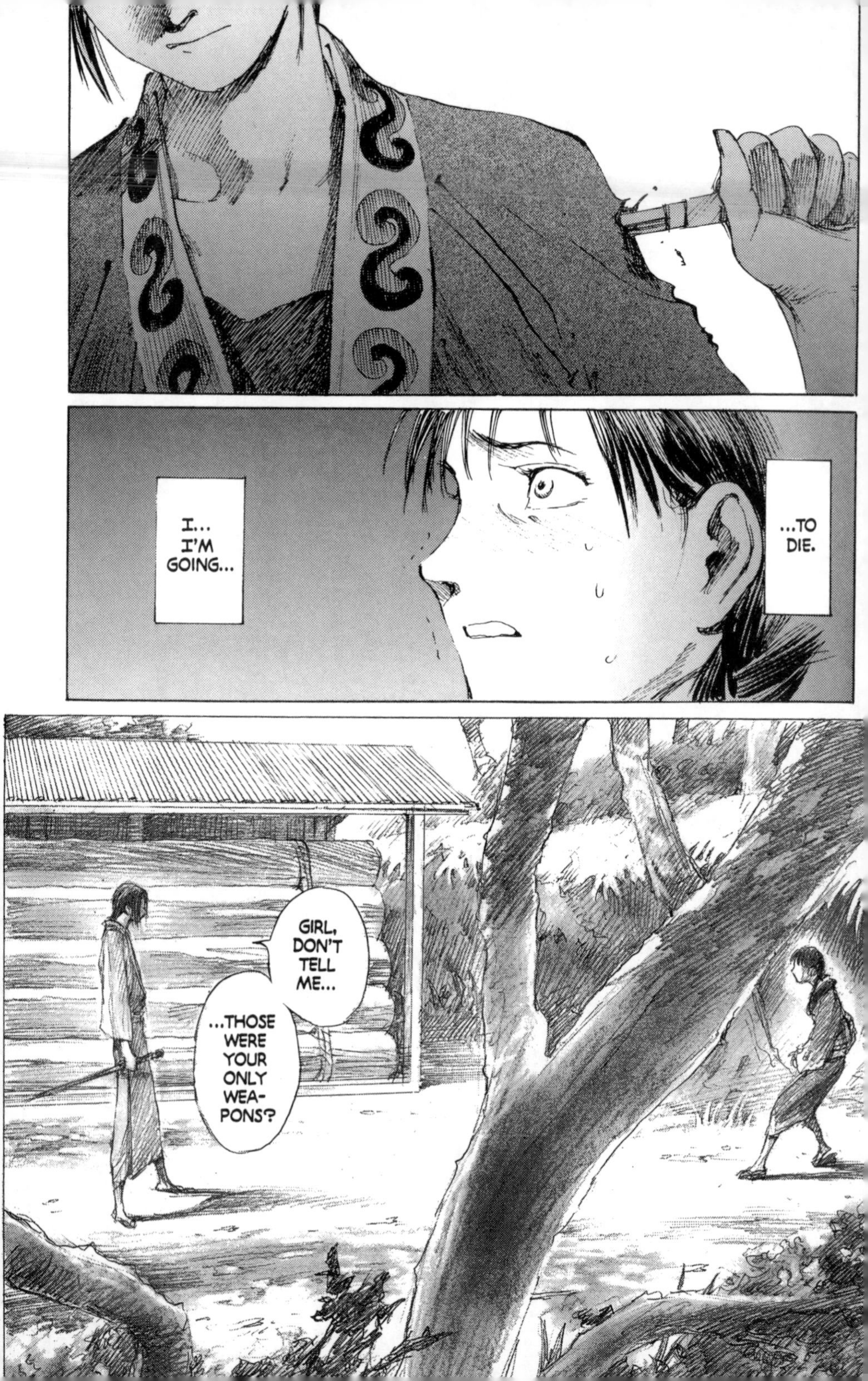
I... I'M GOING...
...TO DIE.
GIRL, DON'T TELL ME...
...THOSE WERE YOUR ONLY WEA-PONS?

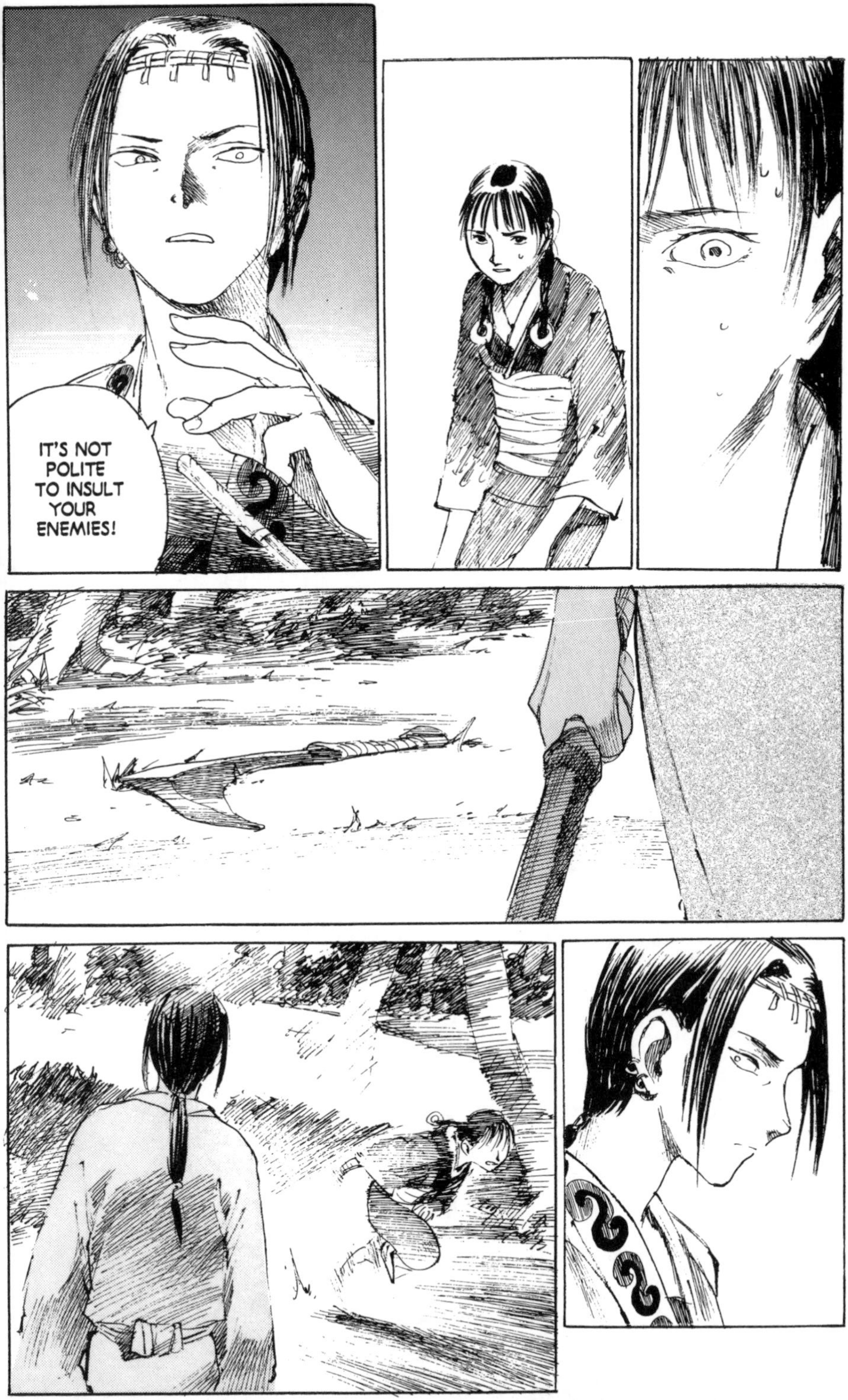
IT'S NOT POLITE TO INSULT YOUR ENEMIES!

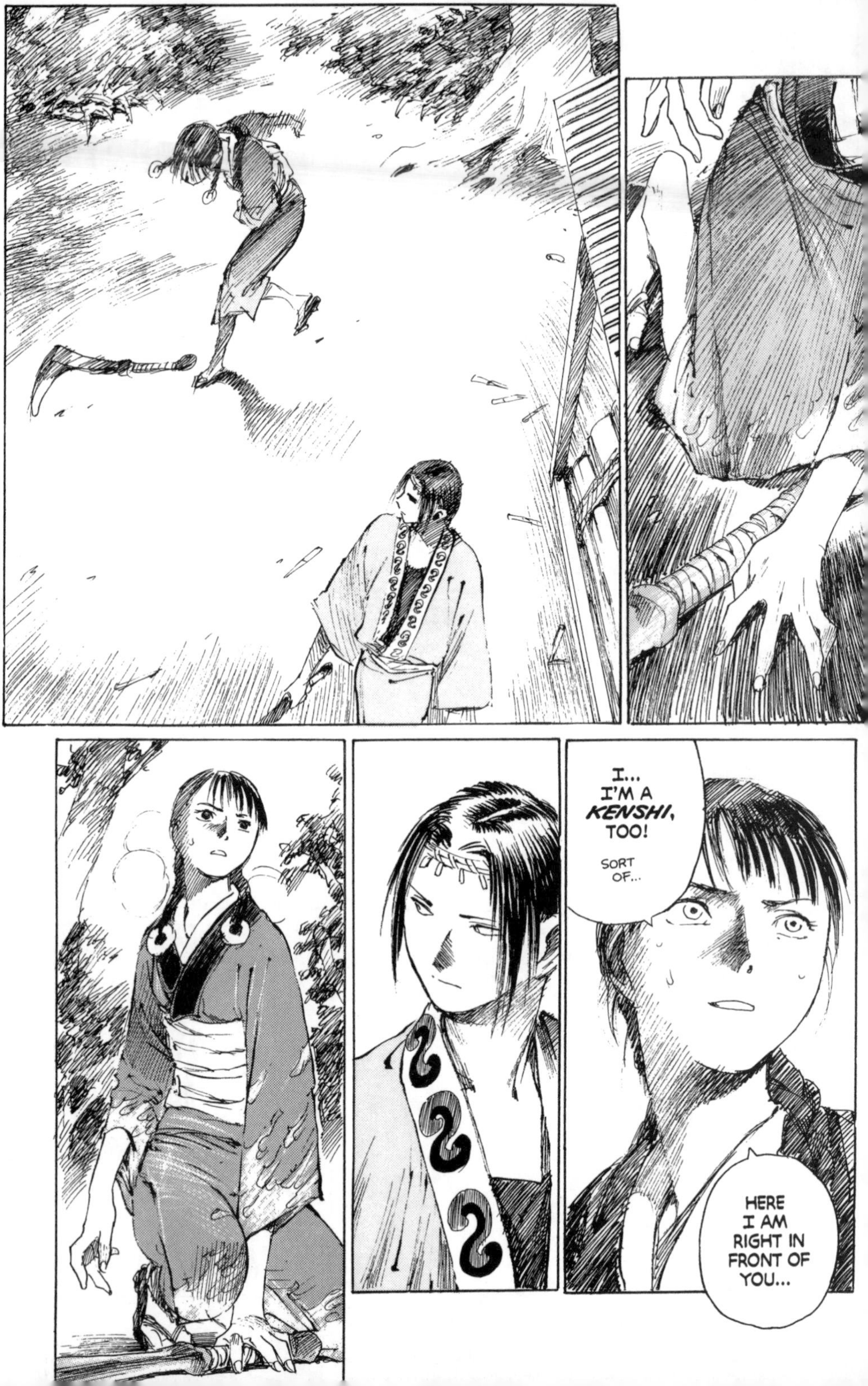

I... I'M A *KENSHI*, TOO!
SORT OF...
HERE I AM RIGHT IN FRONT OF YOU...

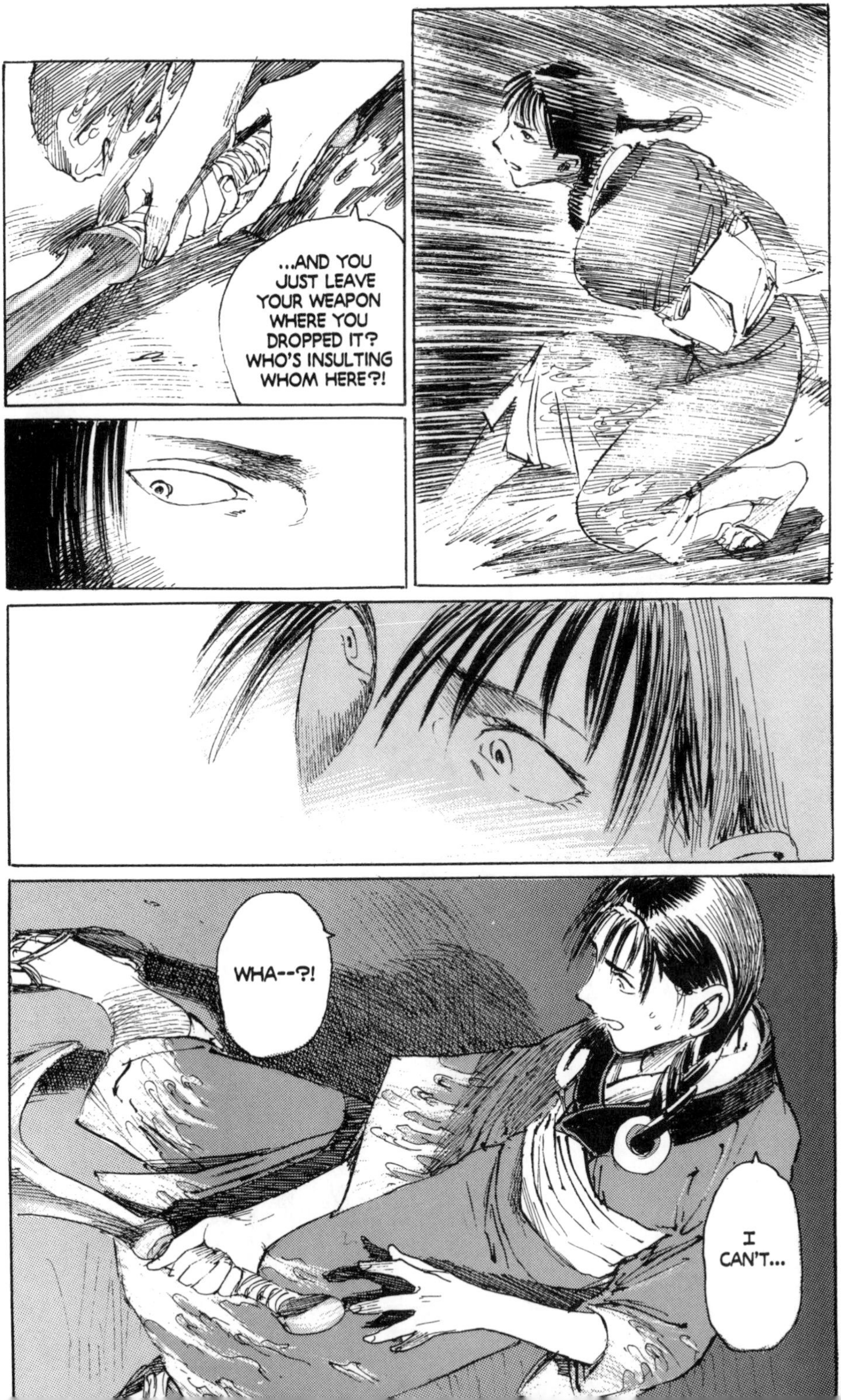
...AND YOU JUST LEAVE YOUR WEAPON WHERE YOU DROPPED IT? WHO'S INSULTING WHOM HERE?!
WHA--?!
I CAN'T...

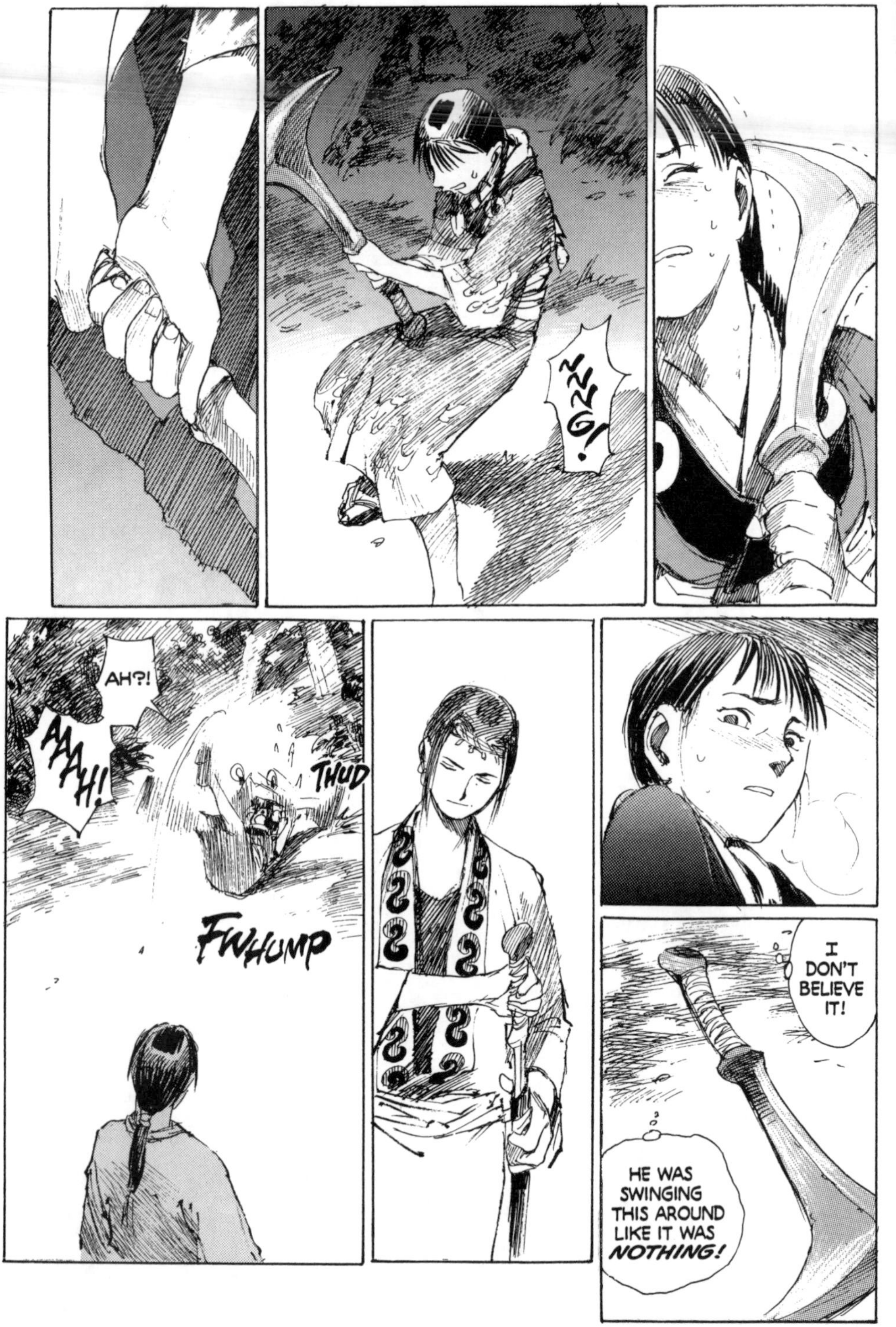
NNNG!
AH?!
AAAAH!
THUD
FWHUMP
I DON'T BELIEVE IT!
HE WAS SWINGING THIS AROUND LIKE IT WAS NOTHING!

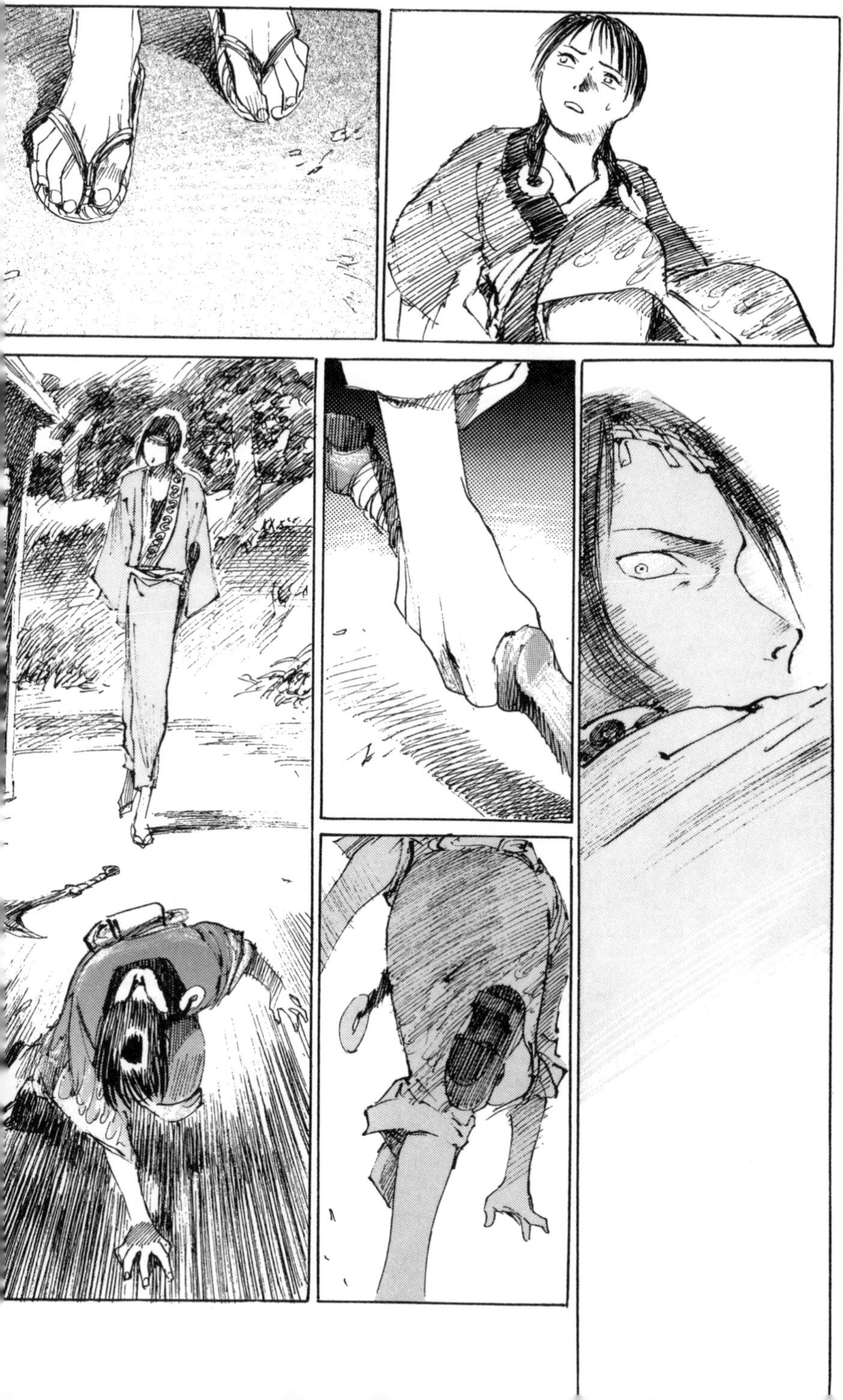

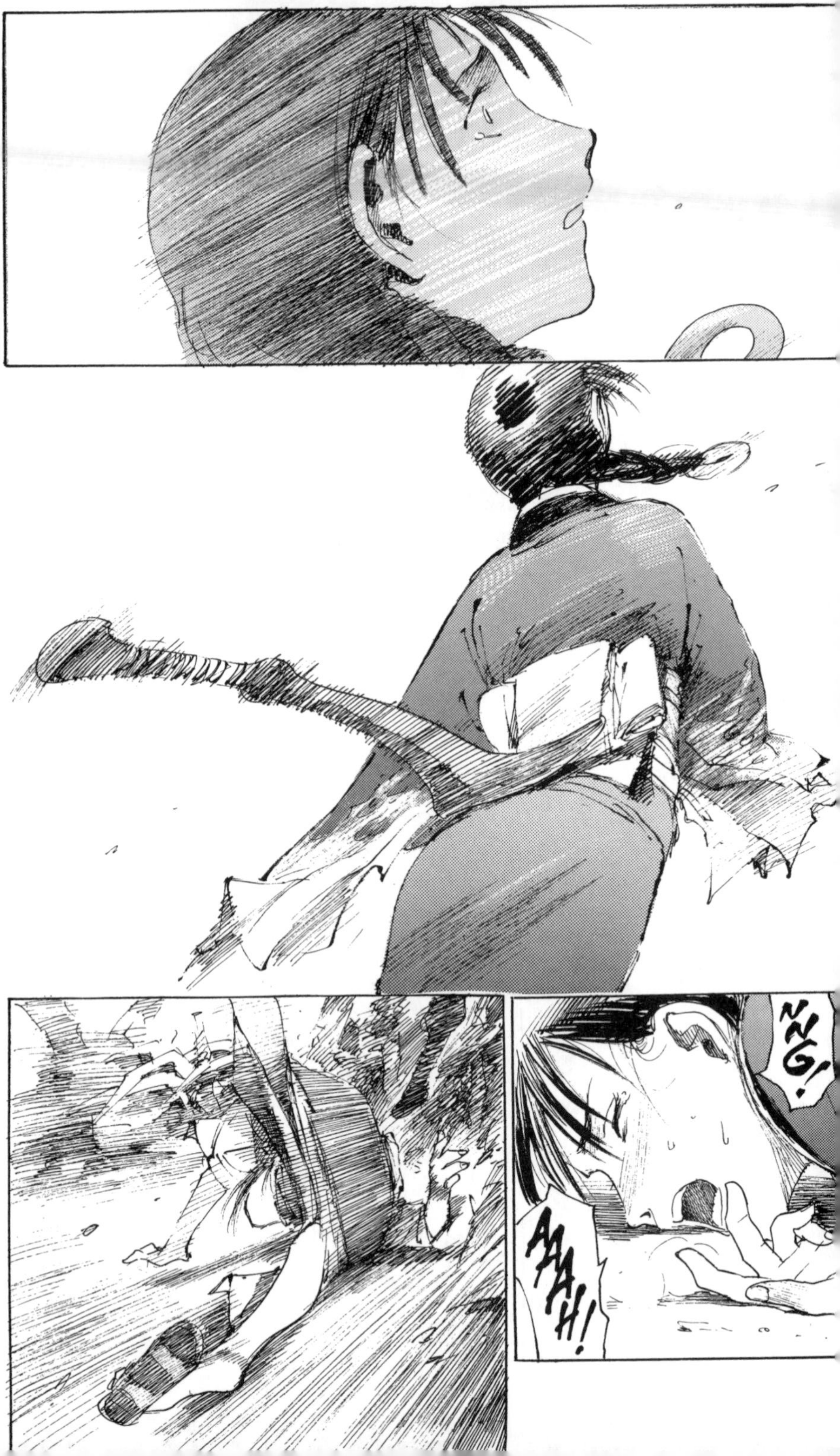
NNG!
AAAAH!

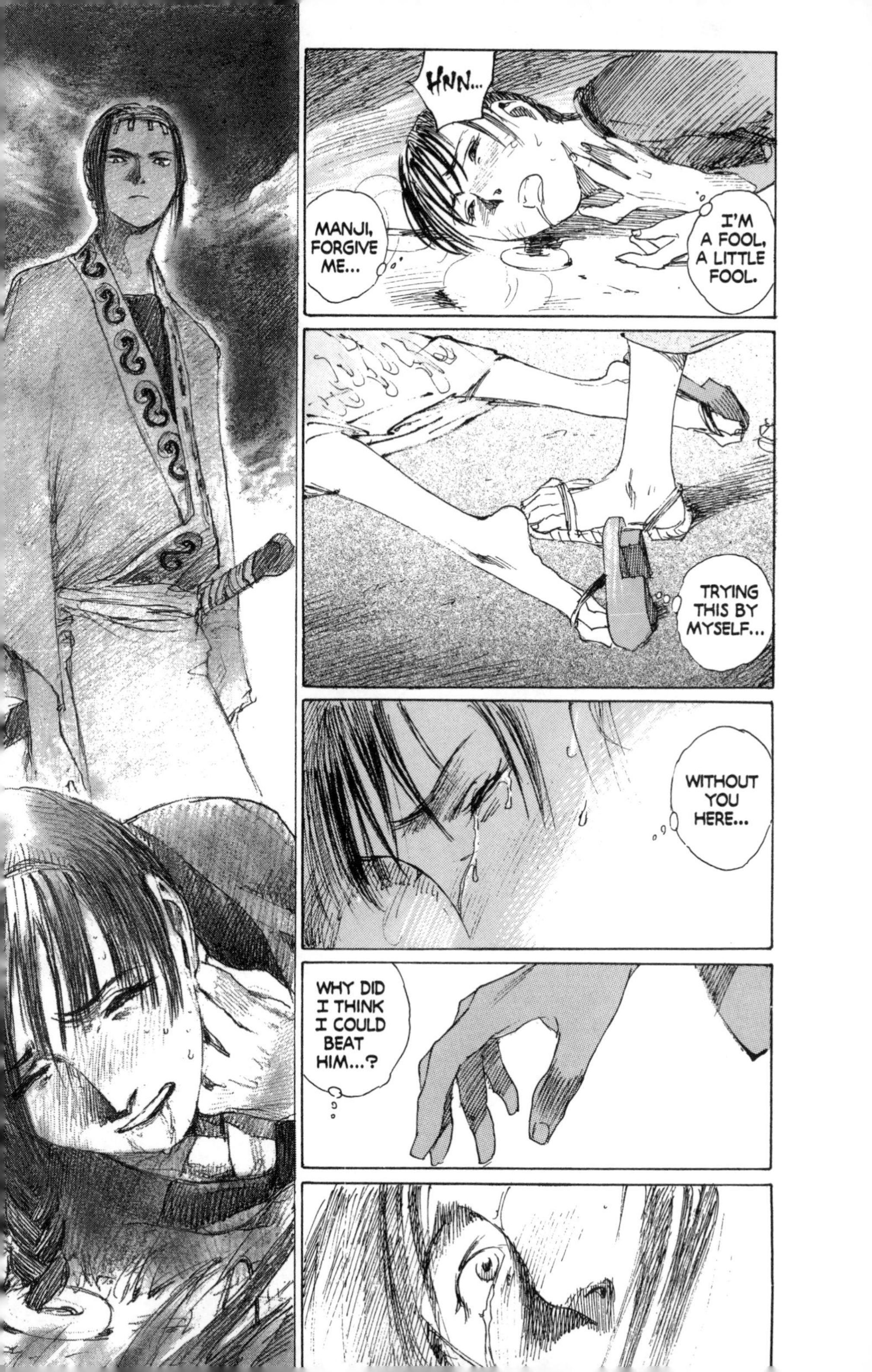
HNN...
MANJI, FORGIVE ME...
I'M A FOOL, A LITTLE FOOL.
TRYING THIS BY MYSELF...
WITHOUT YOU HERE...
WHY DID I THINK I COULD BEAT HIM...?

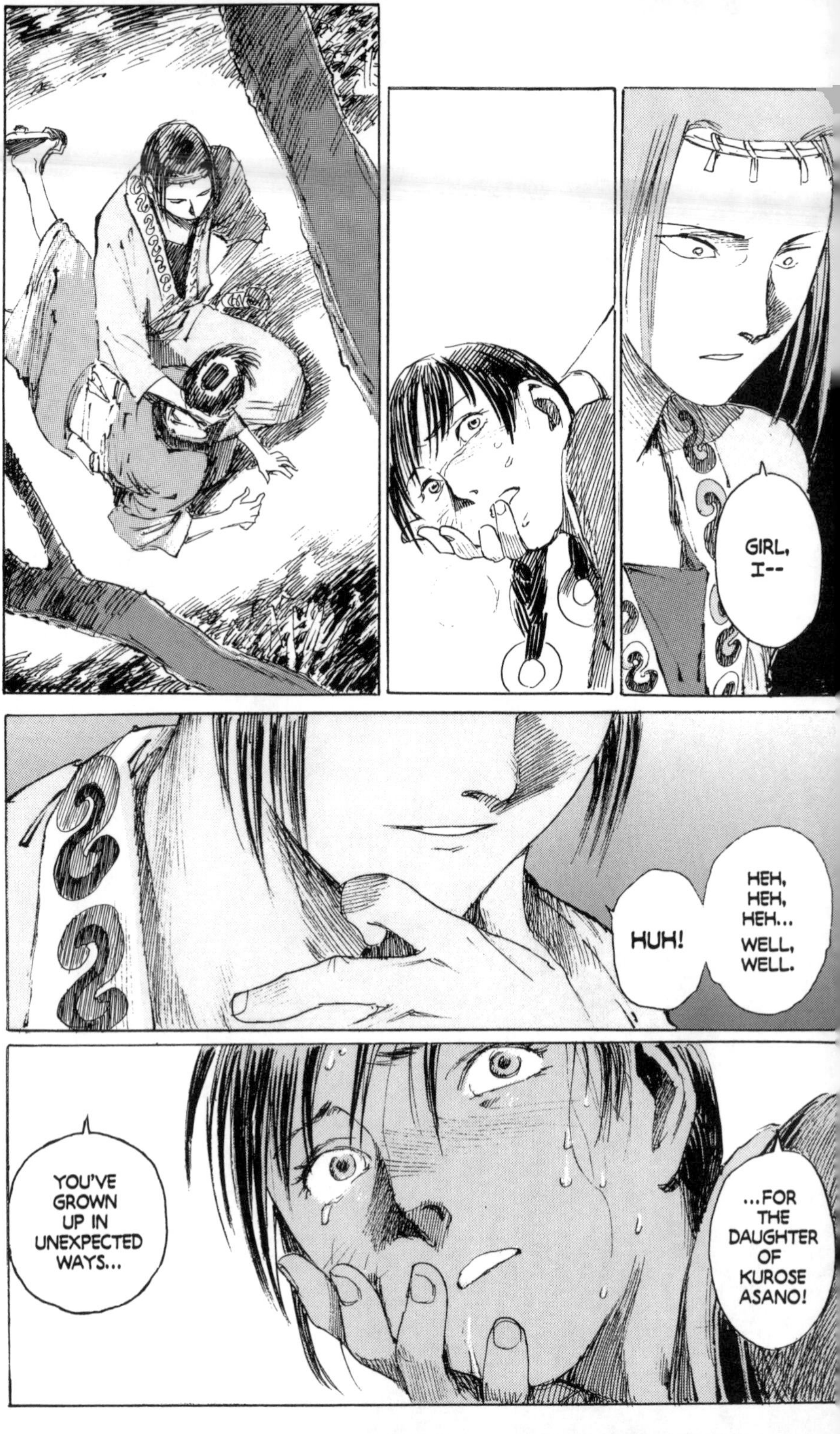
GIRL, I--
HUH!
HEH, HEH, HEH... WELL, WELL.
YOU'VE GROWN UP IN UNEXPECTED WAYS...
...FOR THE DAUGHTER OF KUROSE ASANO!

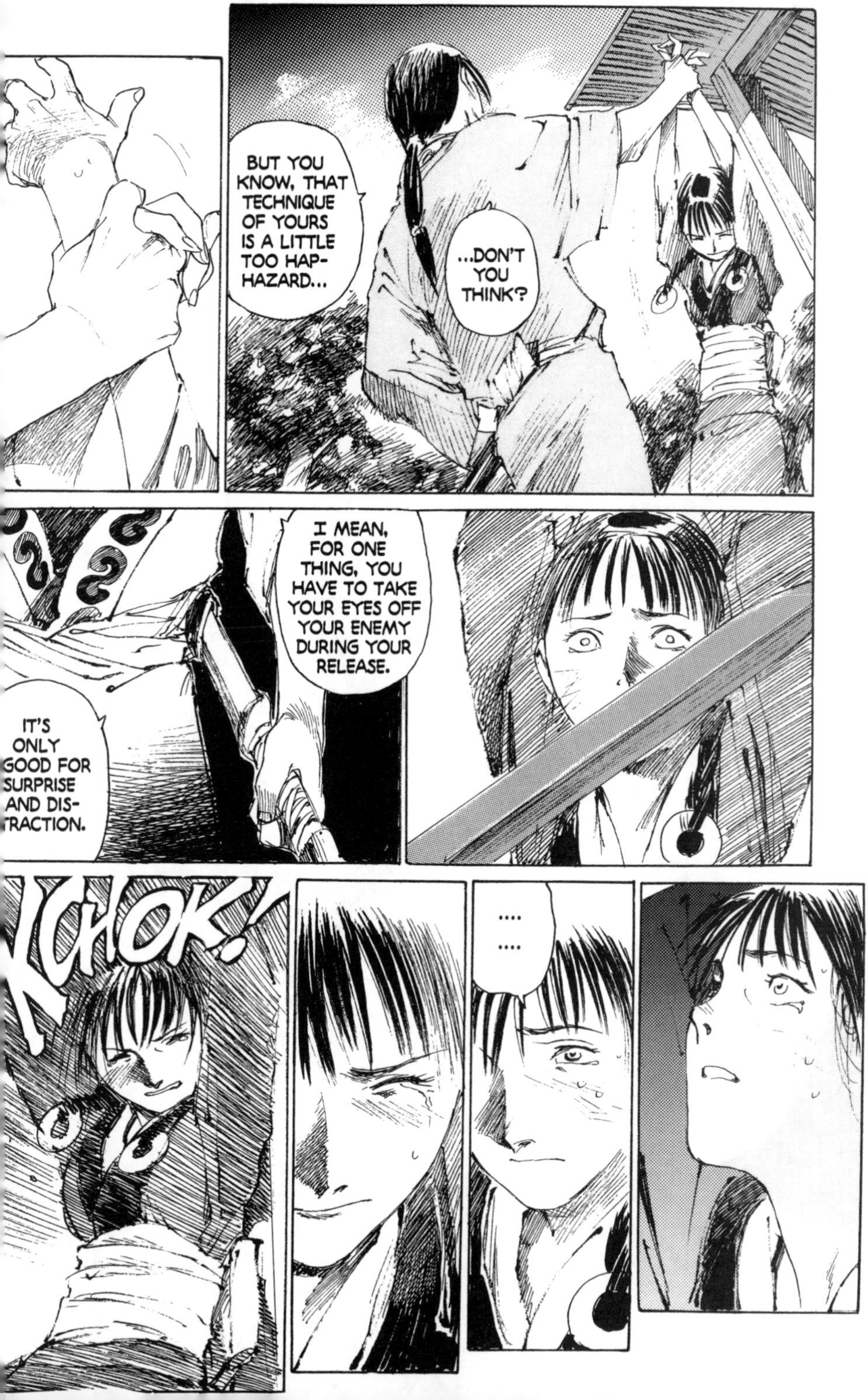
BUT YOU KNOW, THAT TECHNIQUE OF YOURS IS A LITTLE TOO HAP-HAZARD...
...DON'T YOU THINK?
I MEAN, FOR ONE THING, YOU HAVE TO TAKE YOUR EYES OFF YOUR ENEMY DURING YOUR RELEASE.
IT'S ONLY GOOD FOR SURPRISE AND DIS-TRACTION.
CHOK!
....
....

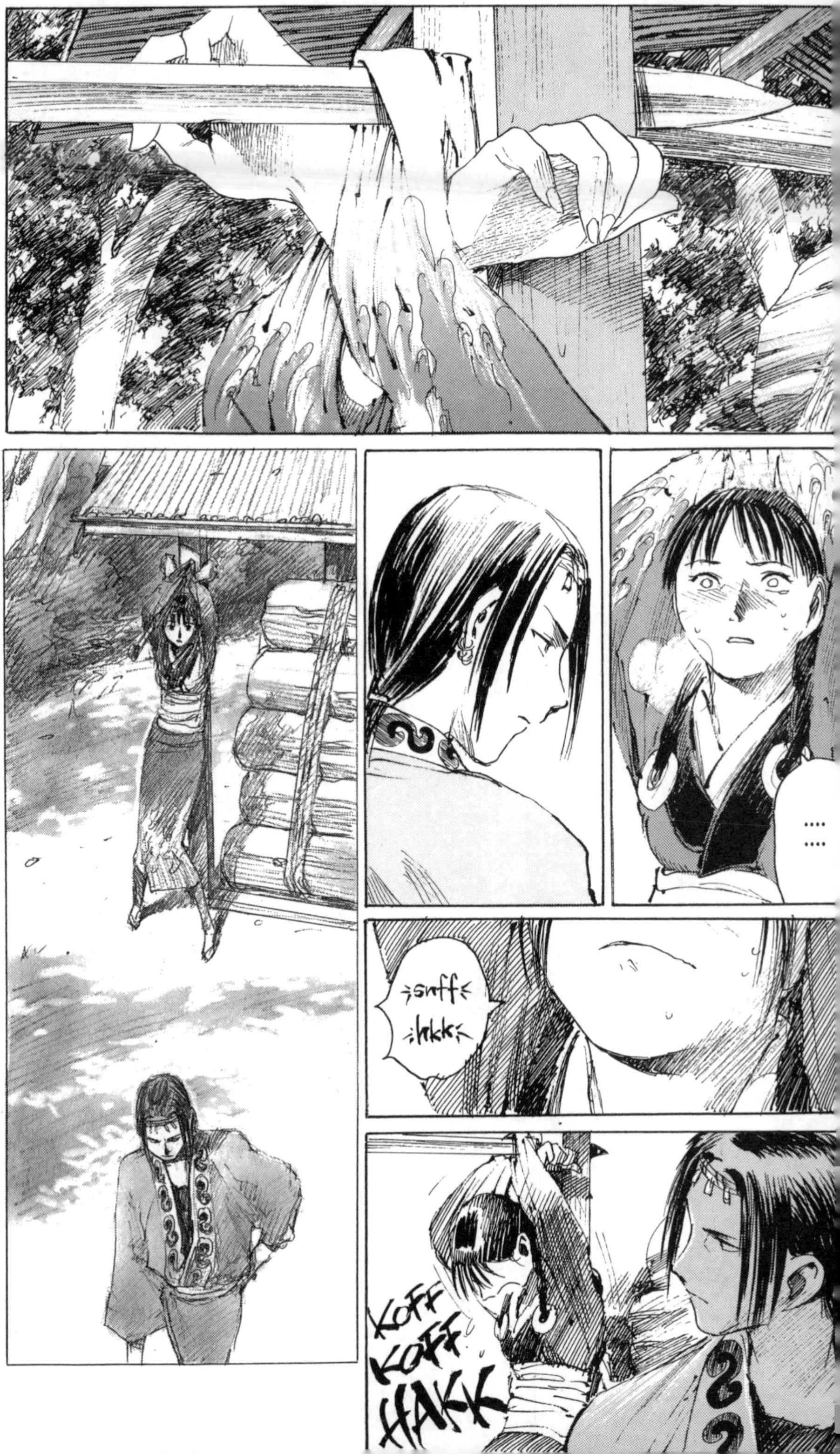
....
....
snff hkk
KOFF KOFF HAKK

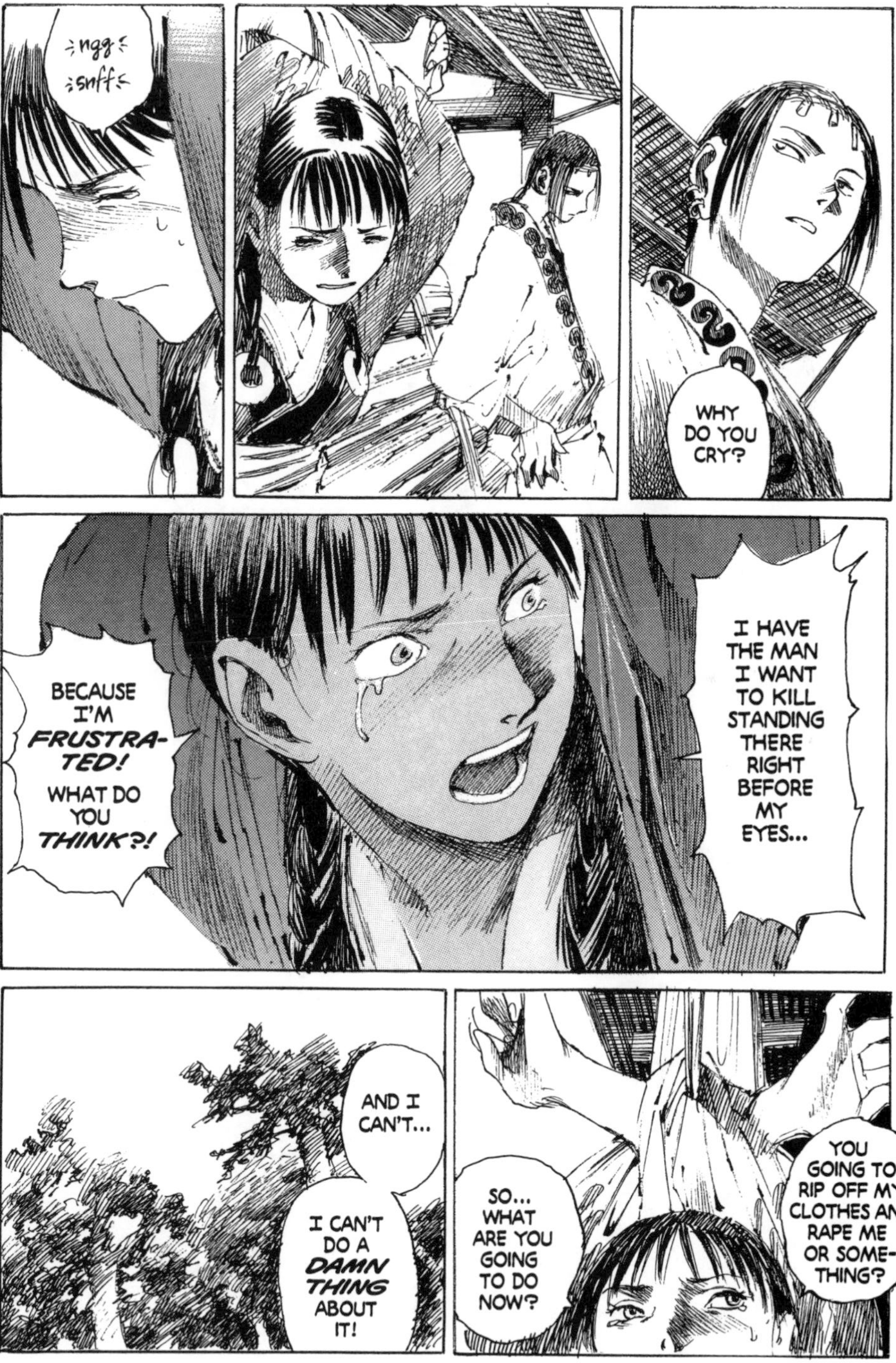
ngg
snff
WHY DO YOU CRY?
BECAUSE I'M *FRUSTRATED!* WHAT DO YOU *THINK?!*
I HAVE THE MAN I WANT TO KILL STANDING THERE RIGHT BEFORE MY EYES...
AND I CAN'T...
I CAN'T DO A *DAMN THING* ABOUT IT!
SO... WHAT ARE YOU GOING TO DO NOW?
YOU GOING TO RIP OFF MY CLOTHES AND RAPE ME OR SOMETHING?

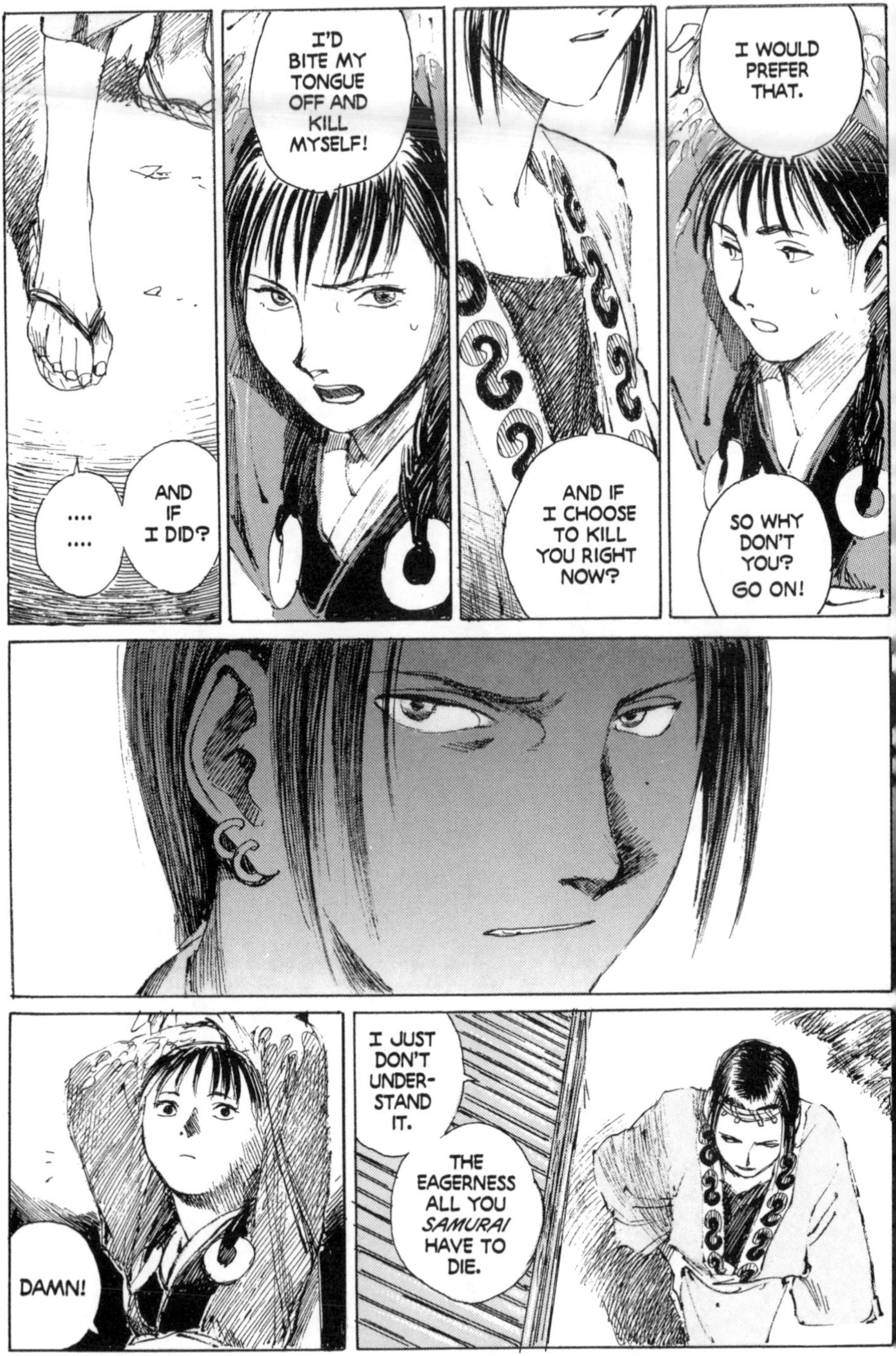

....
....
AND IF I DID?
I'D BITE MY TONGUE OFF AND KILL MYSELF!
AND IF I CHOOSE TO KILL YOU RIGHT NOW?
I WOULD PREFER THAT.
SO WHY DON'T YOU? GO ON!
DAMN!
I JUST DON'T UNDER-STAND IT.
THE EAGERNESS ALL YOU *SAMURAI* HAVE TO DIE.

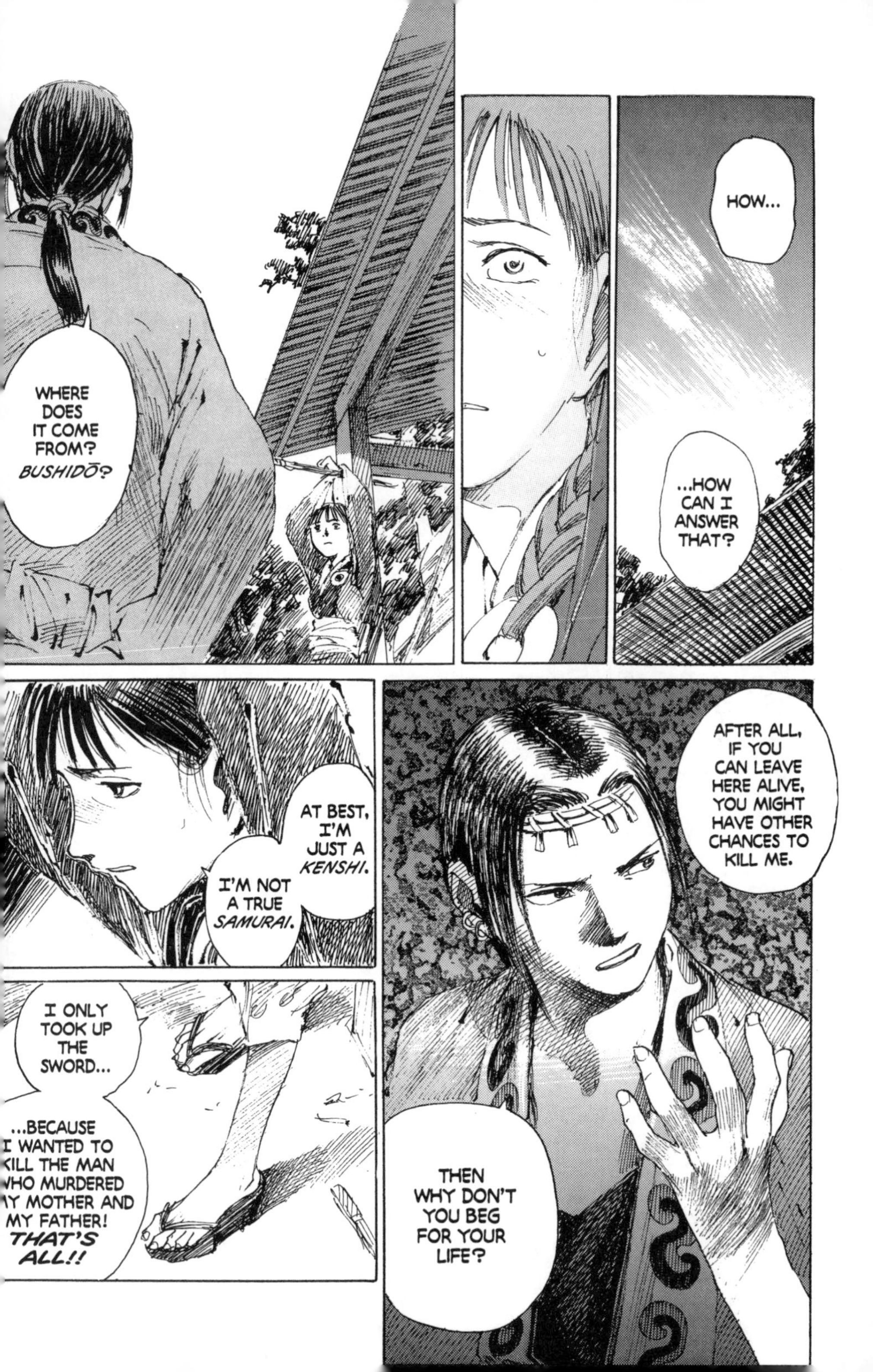
WHERE DOES IT COME FROM? *BUSHIDŌ?*
HOW...
...HOW CAN I ANSWER THAT?
I'M NOT A TRUE *SAMURAI*.
AT BEST, I'M JUST A *KENSHI*.
I ONLY TOOK UP THE SWORD...
...BECAUSE I WANTED TO KILL THE MAN WHO MURDERED MY MOTHER AND MY FATHER! ***THAT'S ALL!!***
THEN WHY DON'T YOU BEG FOR YOUR LIFE?
AFTER ALL, IF YOU CAN LEAVE HERE ALIVE, YOU MIGHT HAVE OTHER CHANCES TO KILL ME.

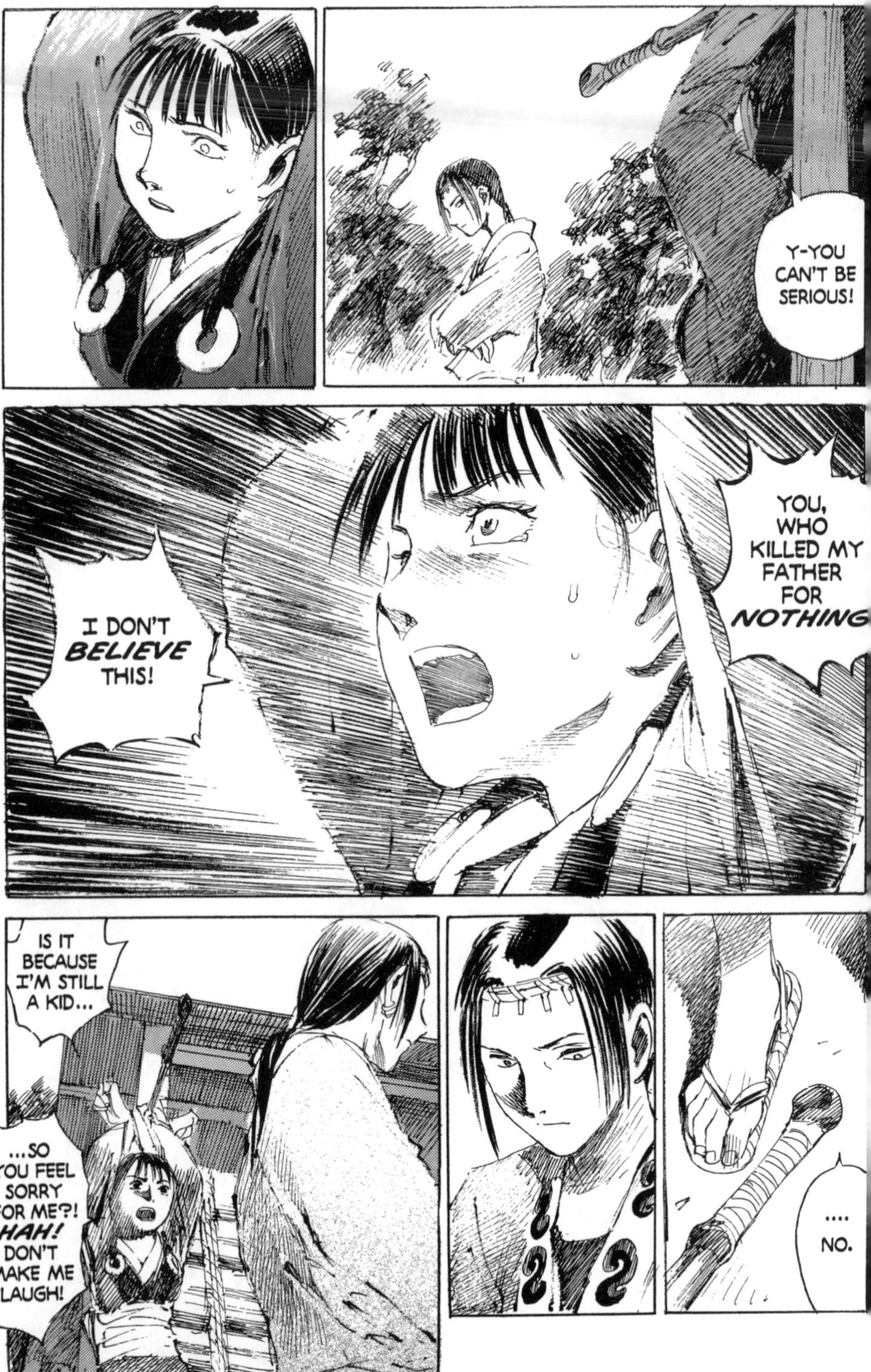
Y-YOU CAN'T BE SERIOUS!
I DON'T *BELIEVE* THIS!
YOU, WHO KILLED MY FATHER FOR *NOTHING*
IS IT BECAUSE I'M STILL A KID...
...SO YOU FEEL SORRY FOR ME?! *HAH!* DON'T MAKE ME LAUGH!
.... NO.

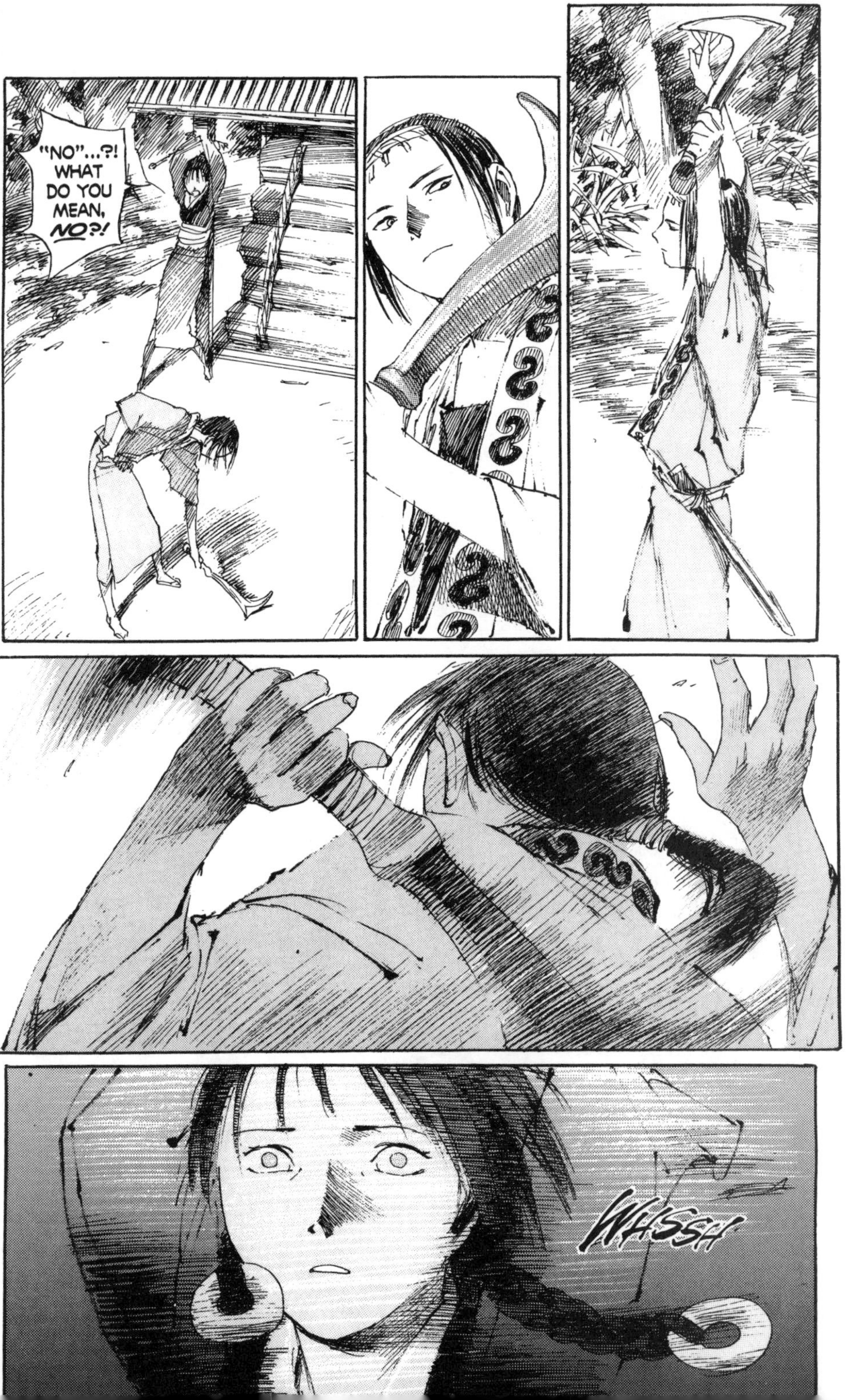
"NO"...?! WHAT DO YOU MEAN, NO?!
WHSSH

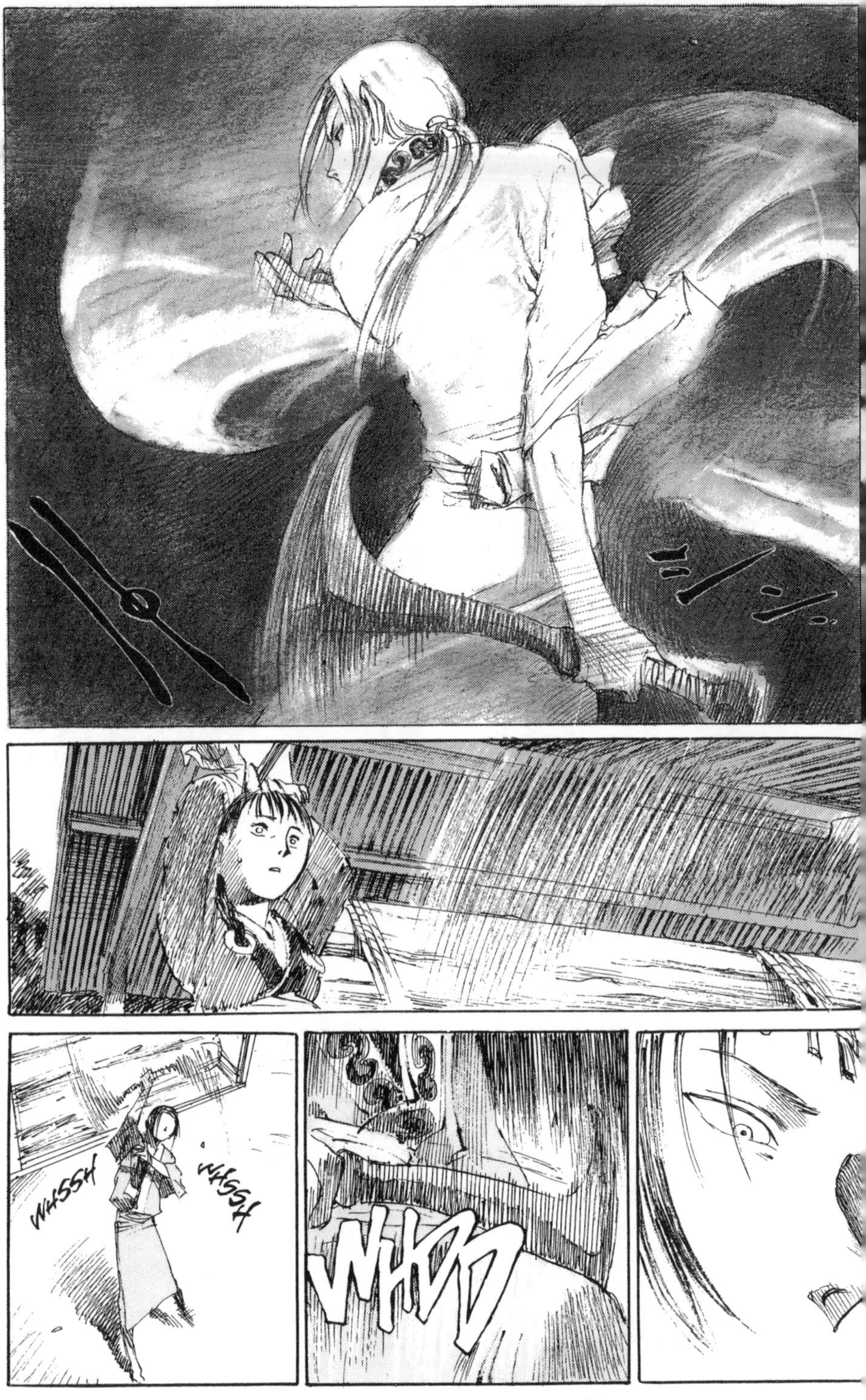
WHSSH
WHSSH
WHOO

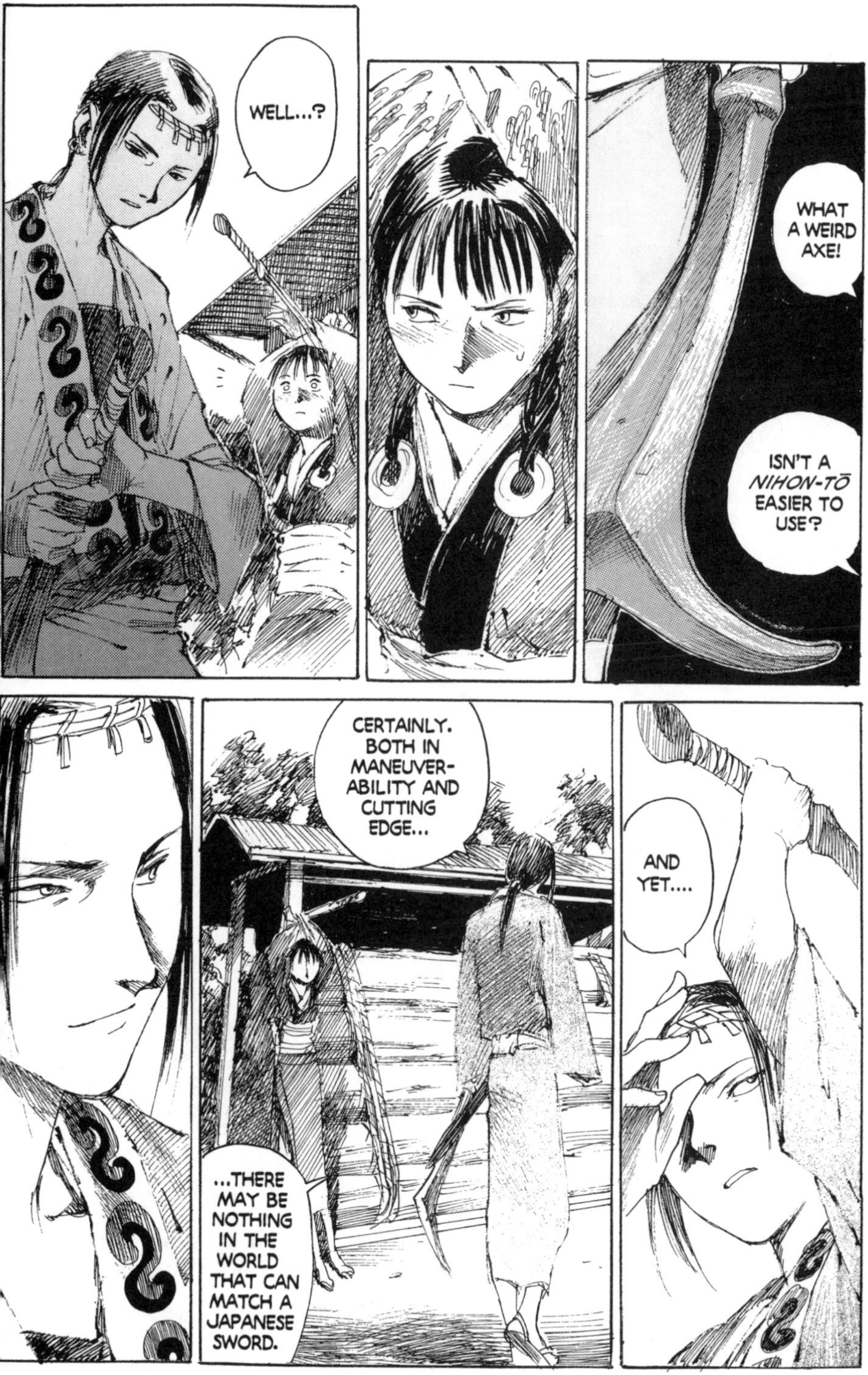
WELL...?
WHAT A WEIRD AXE!
ISN'T A *NIHON-TŌ* EASIER TO USE?
CERTAINLY. BOTH IN MANEUVER-ABILITY AND CUTTING EDGE...
...THERE MAY BE NOTHING IN THE WORLD THAT CAN MATCH A JAPANESE SWORD.
AND YET....

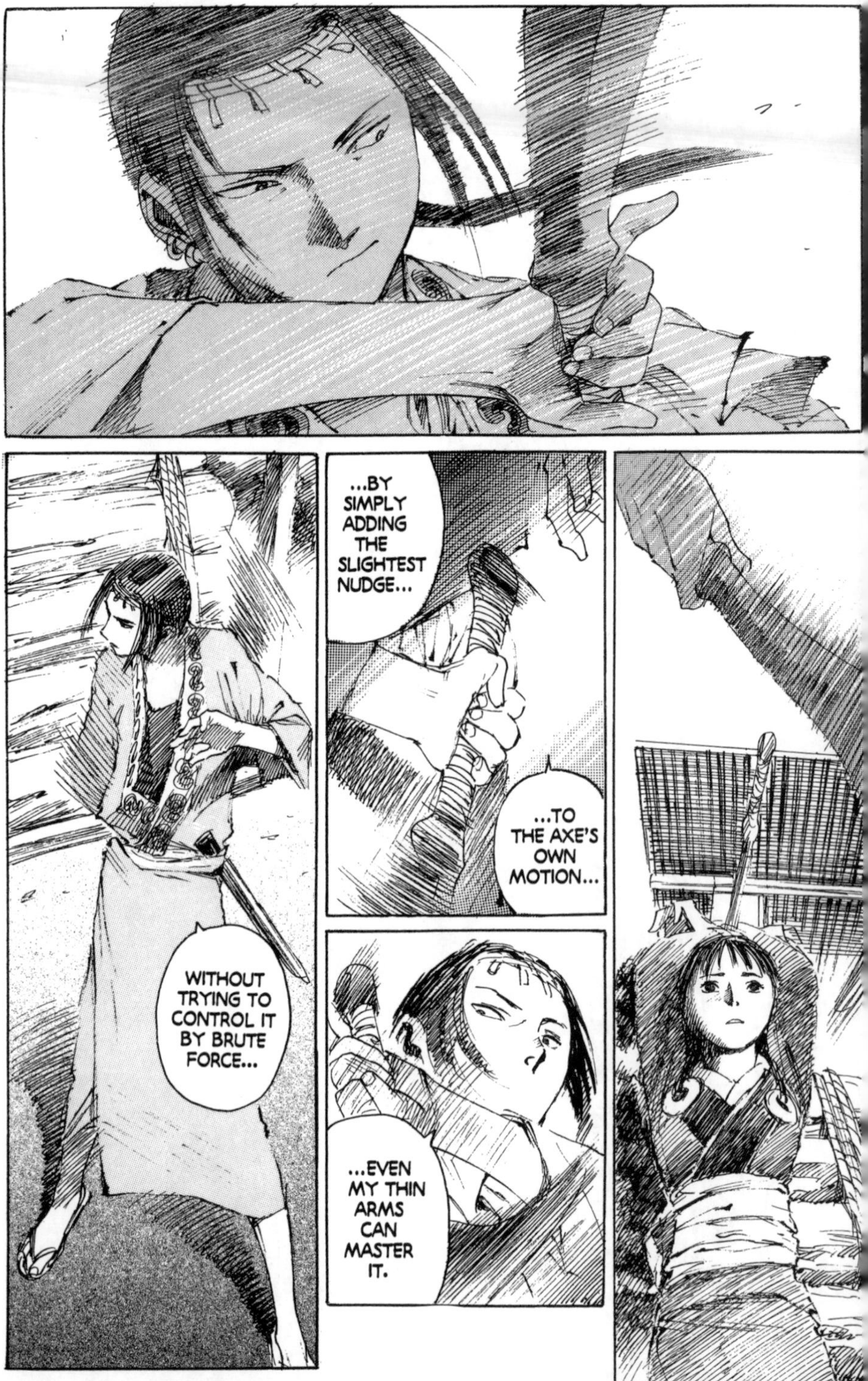
WITHOUT TRYING TO CONTROL IT BY BRUTE FORCE...
...BY SIMPLY ADDING THE SLIGHTEST NUDGE...
...TO THE AXE'S OWN MOTION...
...EVEN MY THIN ARMS CAN MASTER IT.

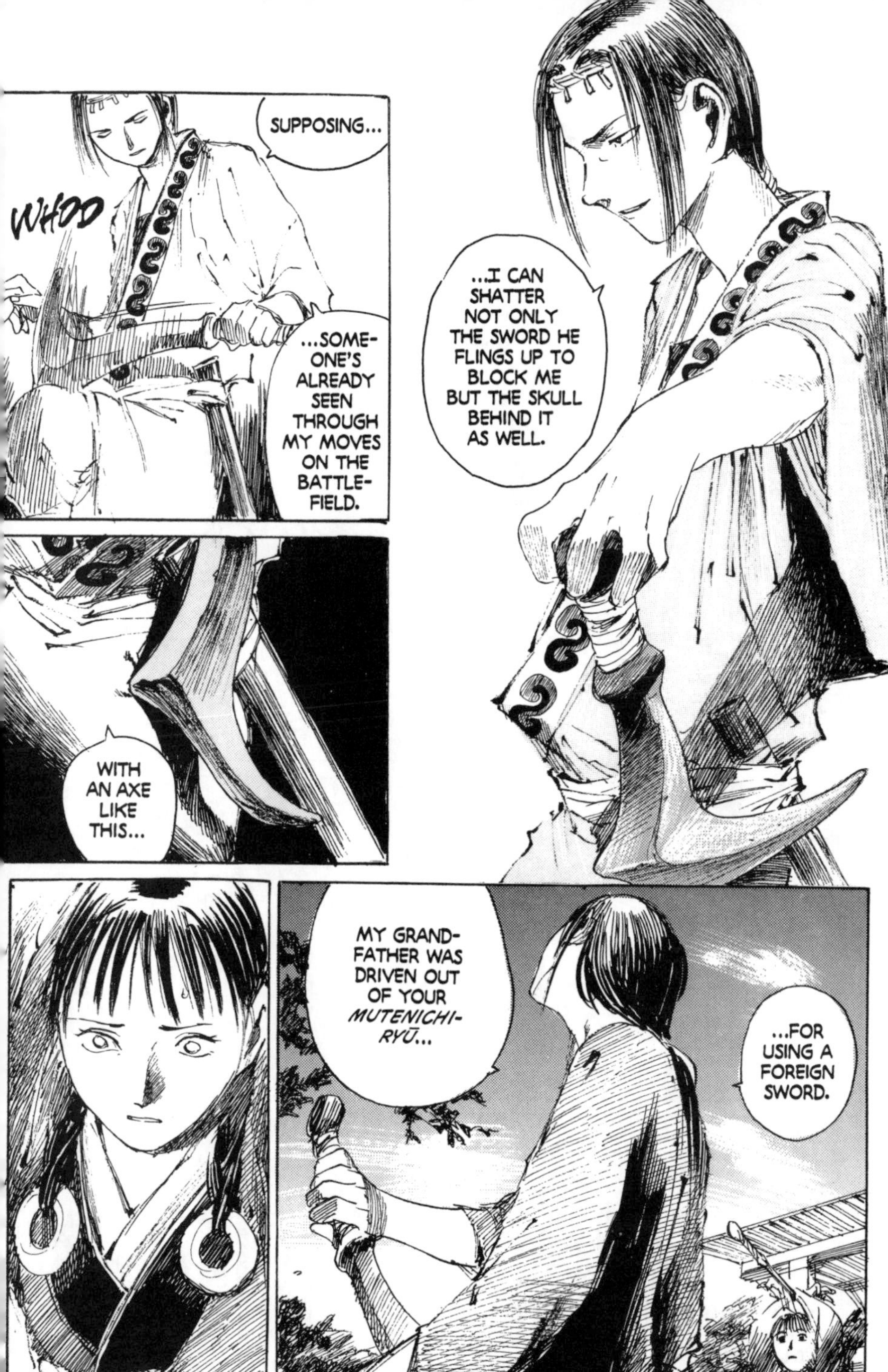
SUPPOSING...
WHOO
...SOMEONE'S ALREADY SEEN THROUGH MY MOVES ON THE BATTLEFIELD.
WITH AN AXE LIKE THIS...
...I CAN SHATTER NOT ONLY THE SWORD HE FLINGS UP TO BLOCK ME BUT THE SKULL BEHIND IT AS WELL.
MY GRANDFATHER WAS DRIVEN OUT OF YOUR *MUTENICHI-RYŪ*...
...FOR USING A FOREIGN SWORD.

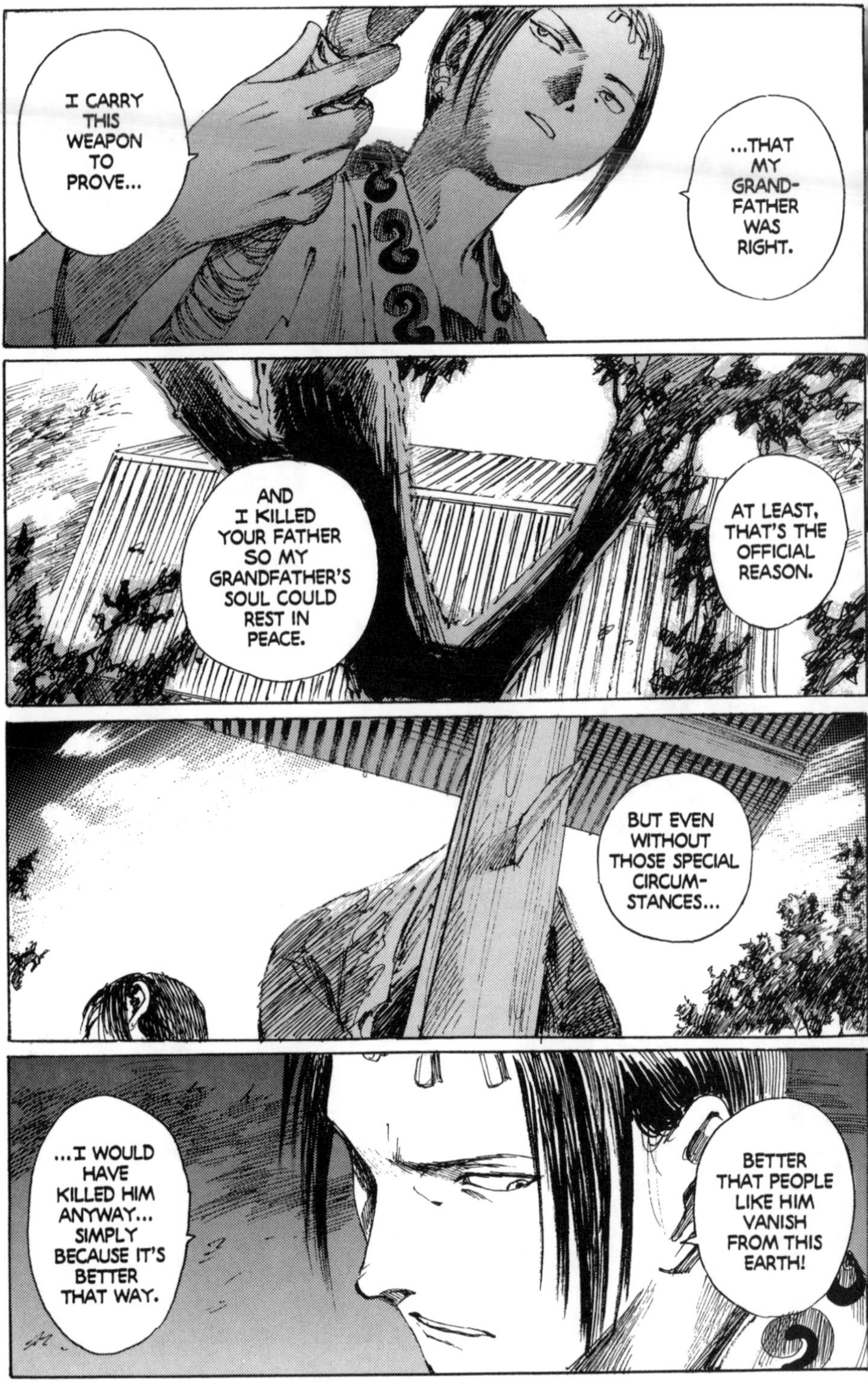
I CARRY THIS WEAPON TO PROVE...
...THAT MY GRAND-FATHER WAS RIGHT.
AND I KILLED YOUR FATHER SO MY GRANDFATHER'S SOUL COULD REST IN PEACE.
AT LEAST, THAT'S THE OFFICIAL REASON.
BUT EVEN WITHOUT THOSE SPECIAL CIRCUM-STANCES...
...I WOULD HAVE KILLED HIM ANYWAY... SIMPLY BECAUSE IT'S BETTER THAT WAY.
BETTER THAT PEOPLE LIKE HIM VANISH FROM THIS EARTH!

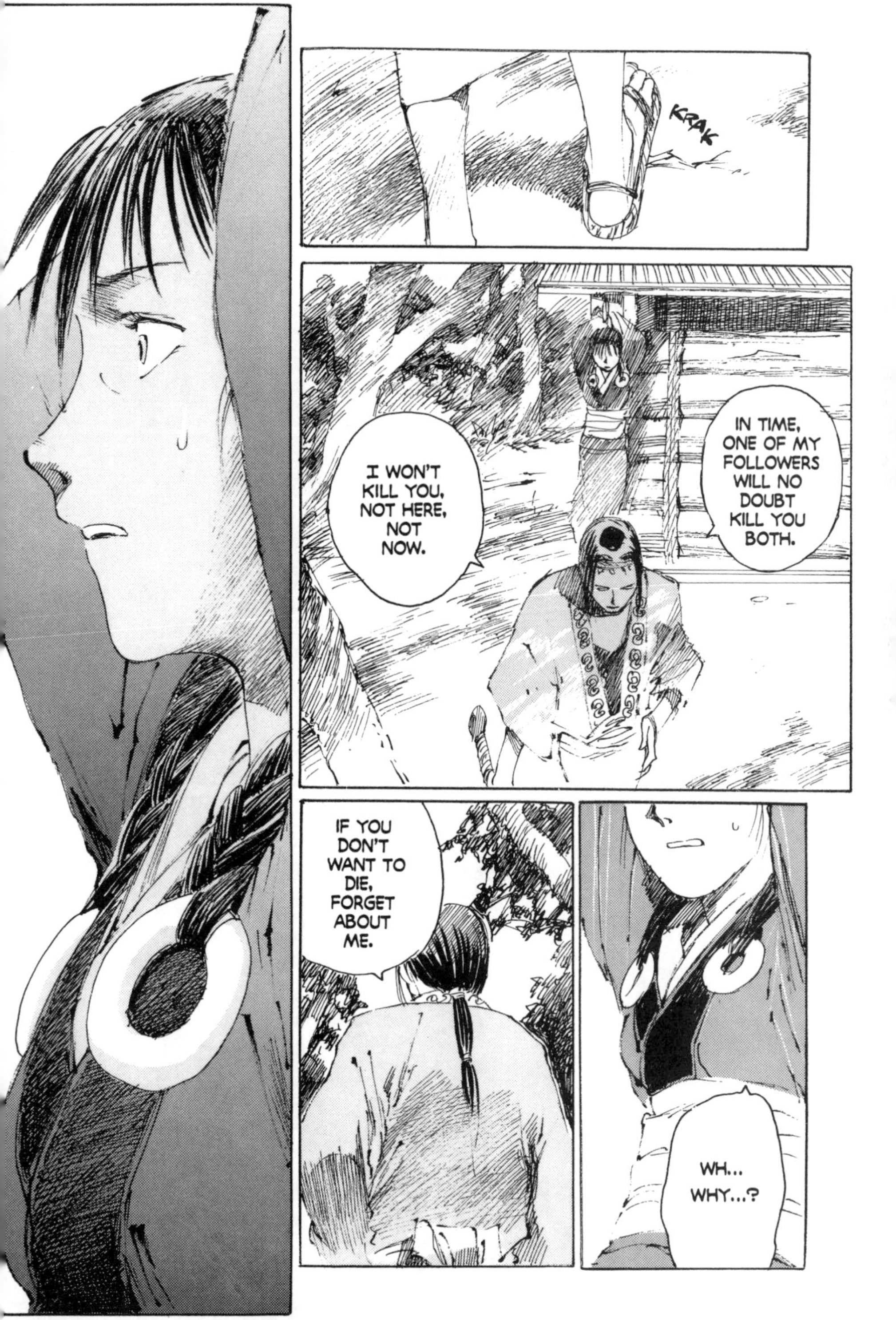
KRAK
I WON'T KILL YOU, NOT HERE, NOT NOW.
IN TIME, ONE OF MY FOLLOWERS WILL NO DOUBT KILL YOU BOTH.
IF YOU DON'T WANT TO DIE, FORGET ABOUT ME.
WH... WHY...?

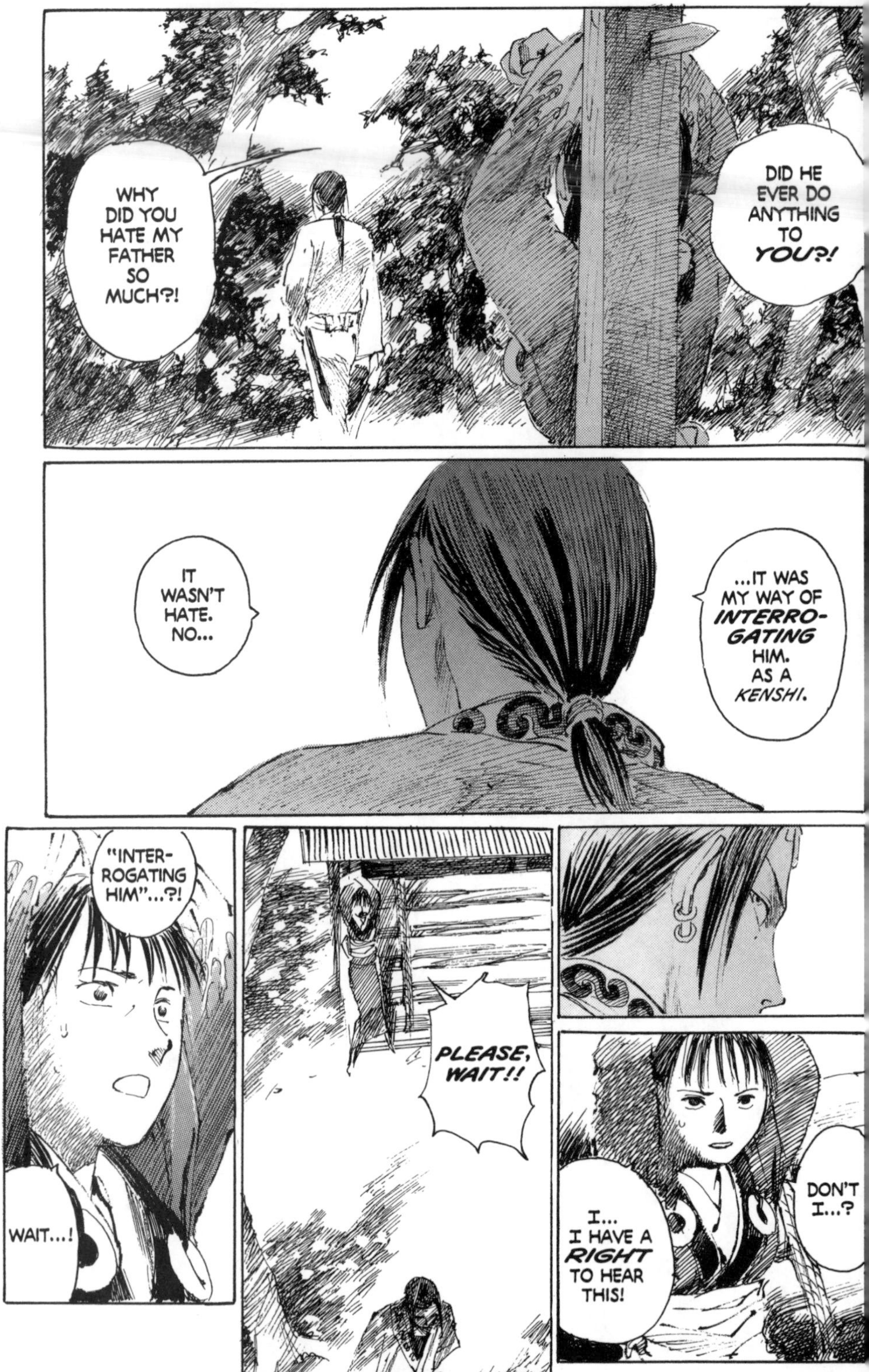
WHY DID YOU HATE MY FATHER SO MUCH?!
DID HE EVER DO ANYTHING TO *YOU?!*
IT WASN'T HATE. NO...
...IT WAS MY WAY OF *INTERROGATING* HIM. AS A *KENSHI*.
"INTERROGATING HIM"...?!
WAIT...!
PLEASE, WAIT!!
I... I HAVE A *RIGHT* TO HEAR THIS!
DON'T I...?

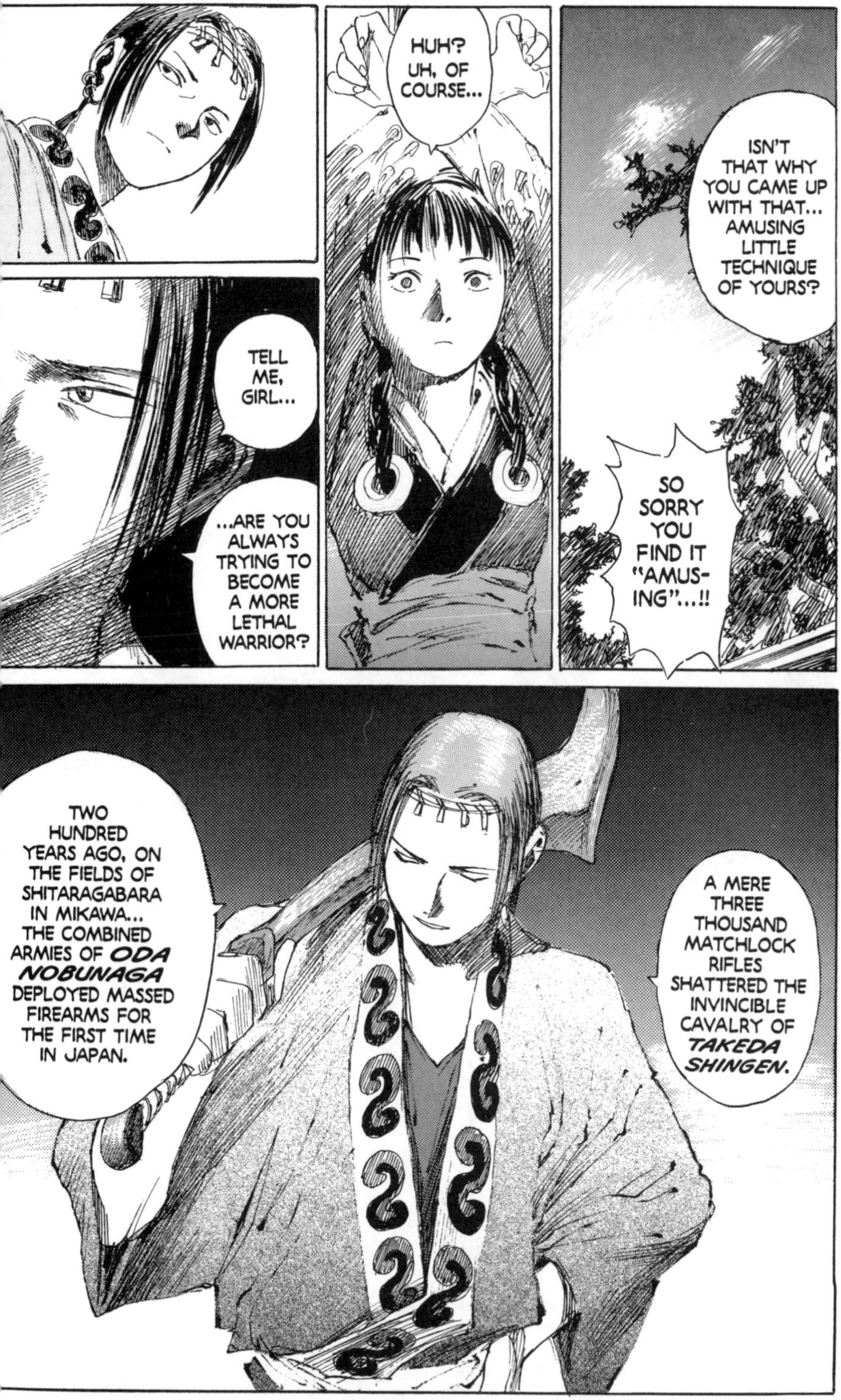
TELL ME, GIRL...
...ARE YOU ALWAYS TRYING TO BECOME A MORE LETHAL WARRIOR?
HUH? UH, OF COURSE...
ISN'T THAT WHY YOU CAME UP WITH THAT... AMUSING LITTLE TECHNIQUE OF YOURS?
SO SORRY YOU FIND IT "AMUS-ING"...!!
TWO HUNDRED YEARS AGO, ON THE FIELDS OF SHITARAGABARA IN MIKAWA... THE COMBINED ARMIES OF *ODA NOBUNAGA* DEPLOYED MASSED FIREARMS FOR THE FIRST TIME IN JAPAN.
A MERE THREE THOUSAND MATCHLOCK RIFLES SHATTERED THE INVINCIBLE CAVALRY OF *TAKEDA SHINGEN*.

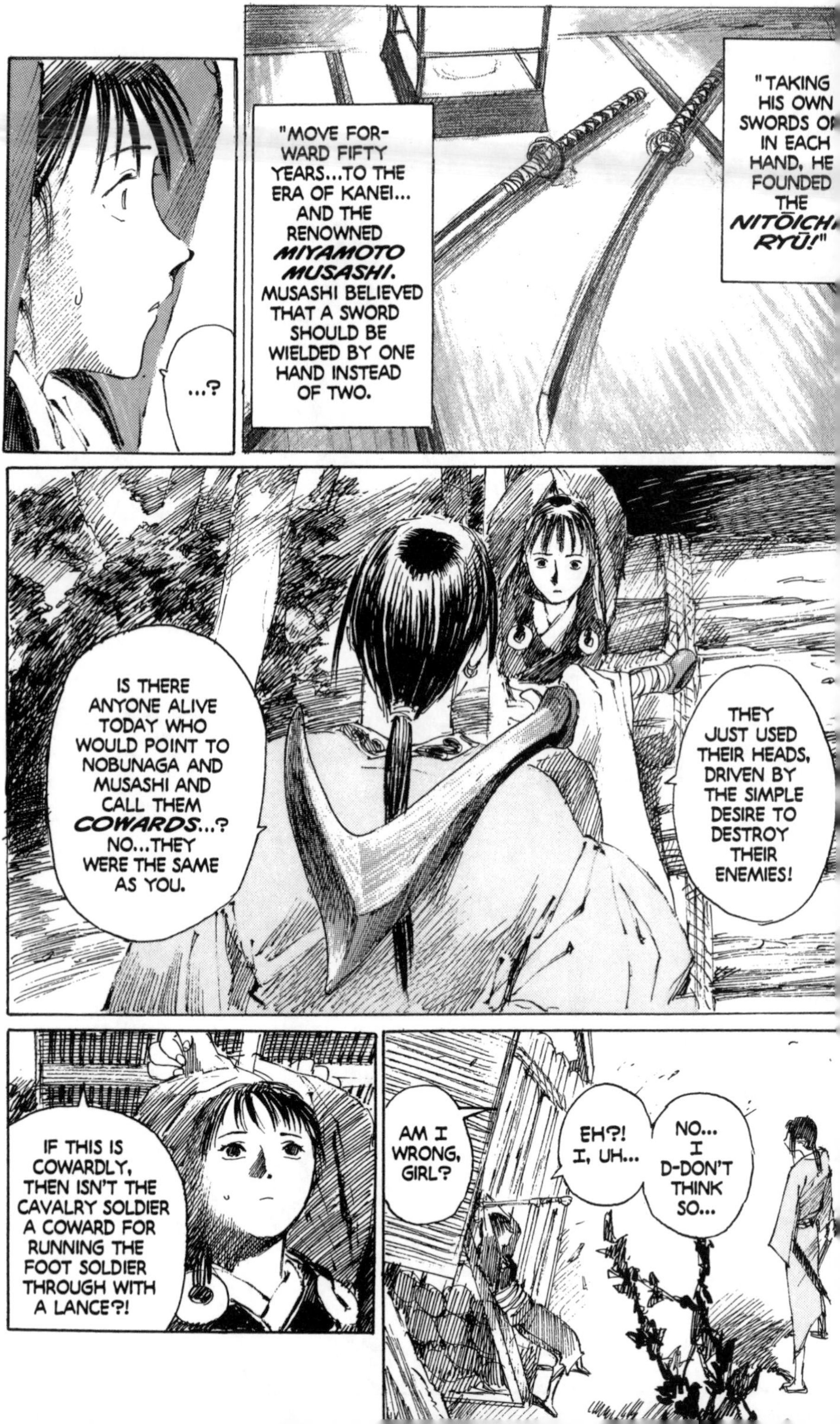
...?
"MOVE FORWARD FIFTY YEARS...TO THE ERA OF KANEI... AND THE RENOWNED *MIYAMOTO MUSASHI*. MUSASHI BELIEVED THAT A SWORD SHOULD BE WIELDED BY ONE HAND INSTEAD OF TWO.
"TAKING HIS OWN SWORDS O IN EACH HAND, HE FOUNDED THE *NITŌICH RYŪ!*"
IS THERE ANYONE ALIVE TODAY WHO WOULD POINT TO NOBUNAGA AND MUSASHI AND CALL THEM *COWARDS*...? NO...THEY WERE THE SAME AS YOU.
THEY JUST USED THEIR HEADS, DRIVEN BY THE SIMPLE DESIRE TO DESTROY THEIR ENEMIES!
IF THIS IS COWARDLY, THEN ISN'T THE CAVALRY SOLDIER A COWARD FOR RUNNING THE FOOT SOLDIER THROUGH WITH A LANCE?!
AM I WRONG, GIRL?
EH?! I, UH...
NO... I D-DON'T THINK SO...

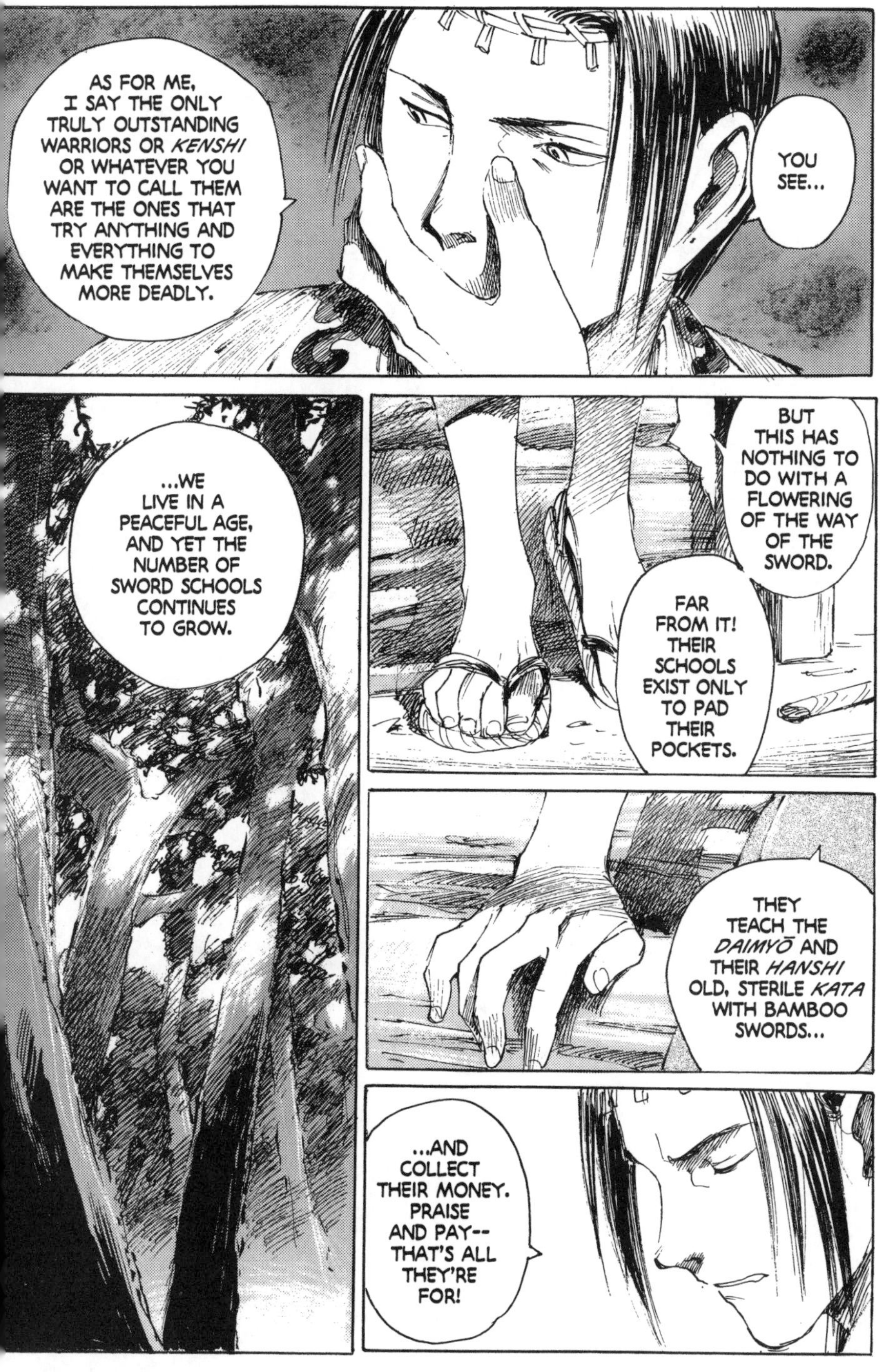
AS FOR ME, I SAY THE ONLY TRULY OUTSTANDING WARRIORS OR *KENSHI* OR WHATEVER YOU WANT TO CALL THEM ARE THE ONES THAT TRY ANYTHING AND EVERYTHING TO MAKE THEMSELVES MORE DEADLY.
YOU SEE...
...WE LIVE IN A PEACEFUL AGE, AND YET THE NUMBER OF SWORD SCHOOLS CONTINUES TO GROW.
BUT THIS HAS NOTHING TO DO WITH A FLOWERING OF THE WAY OF THE SWORD.
FAR FROM IT! THEIR SCHOOLS EXIST ONLY TO PAD THEIR POCKETS.
THEY TEACH THE *DAIMYŌ* AND THEIR *HANSHI* OLD, STERILE *KATA* WITH BAMBOO SWORDS...
...AND COLLECT THEIR MONEY. PRAISE AND PAY--THAT'S ALL THEY'RE FOR!

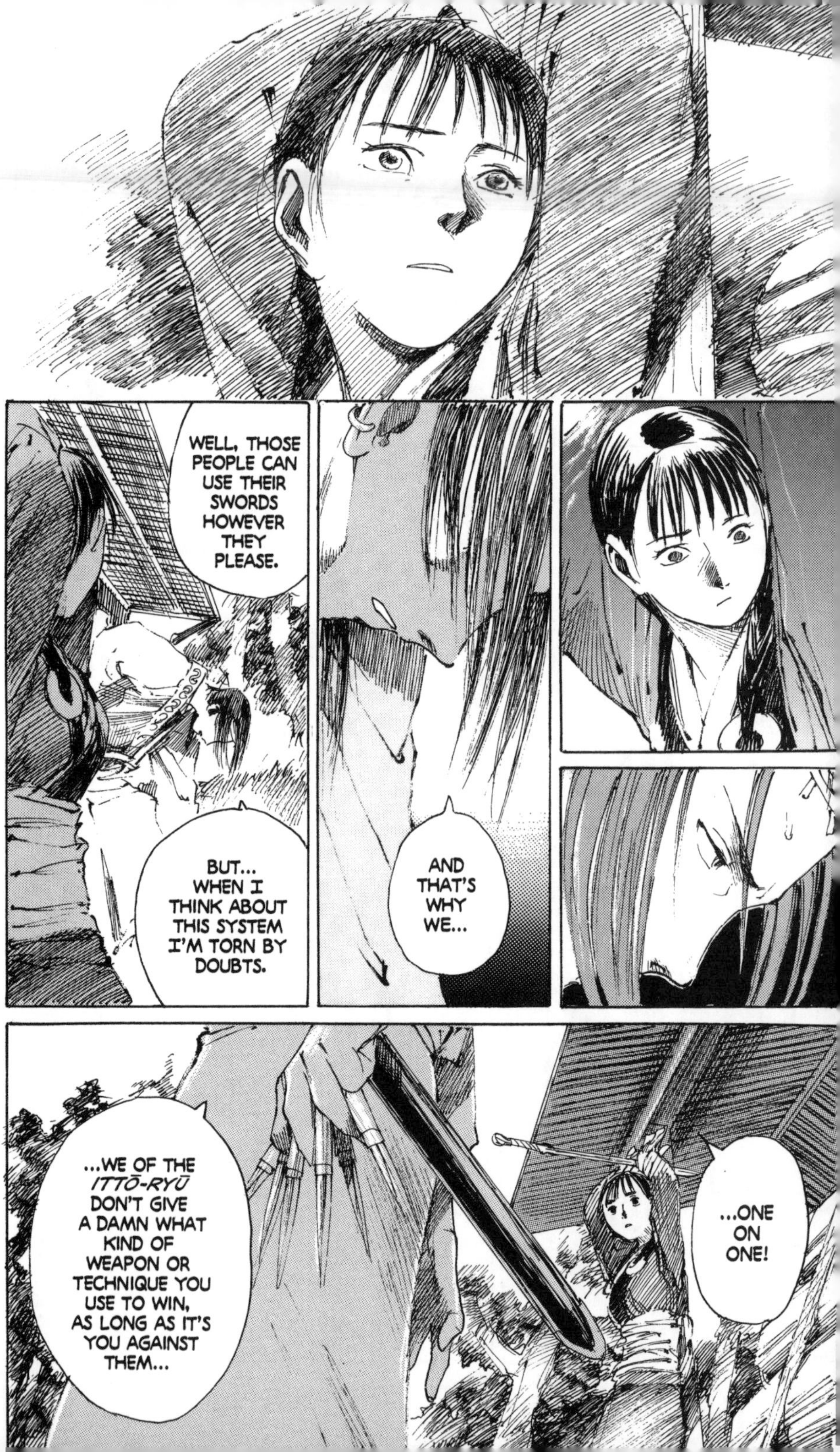
WELL, THOSE PEOPLE CAN USE THEIR SWORDS HOWEVER THEY PLEASE.
BUT... WHEN I THINK ABOUT THIS SYSTEM I'M TORN BY DOUBTS.
AND THAT'S WHY WE...
...WE OF THE *ITTŌ-RYŪ* DON'T GIVE A DAMN WHAT KIND OF WEAPON OR TECHNIQUE YOU USE TO WIN, AS LONG AS IT'S YOU AGAINST THEM...
...ONE ON ONE!

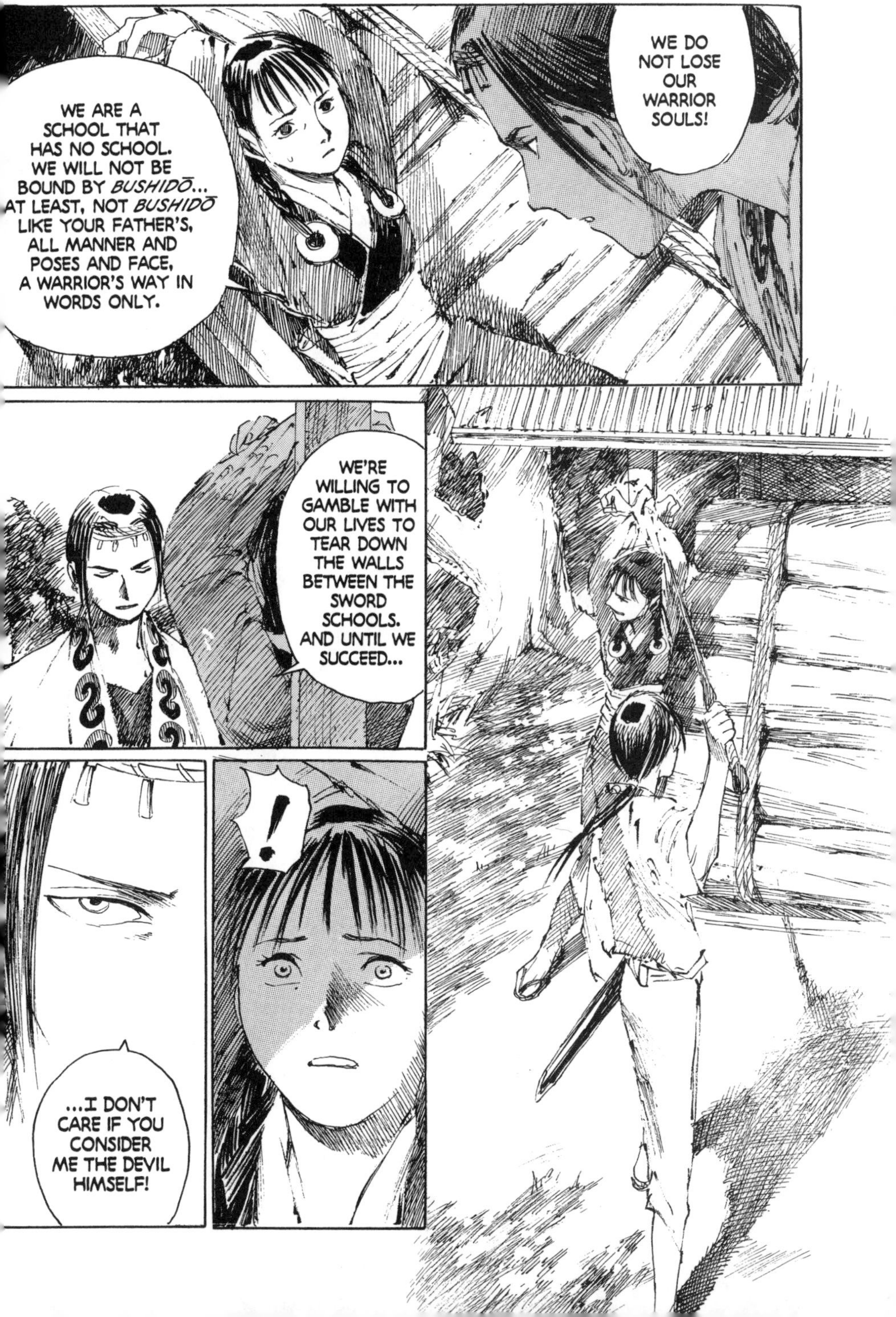
WE ARE A SCHOOL THAT HAS NO SCHOOL. WE WILL NOT BE BOUND BY *BUSHIDŌ*... AT LEAST, NOT *BUSHIDŌ* LIKE YOUR FATHER'S, ALL MANNER AND POSES AND FACE, A WARRIOR'S WAY IN WORDS ONLY.
WE DO NOT LOSE OUR WARRIOR SOULS!
WE'RE WILLING TO GAMBLE WITH OUR LIVES TO TEAR DOWN THE WALLS BETWEEN THE SWORD SCHOOLS. AND UNTIL WE SUCCEED...
...I DON'T CARE IF YOU CONSIDER ME THE DEVIL HIMSELF!
!

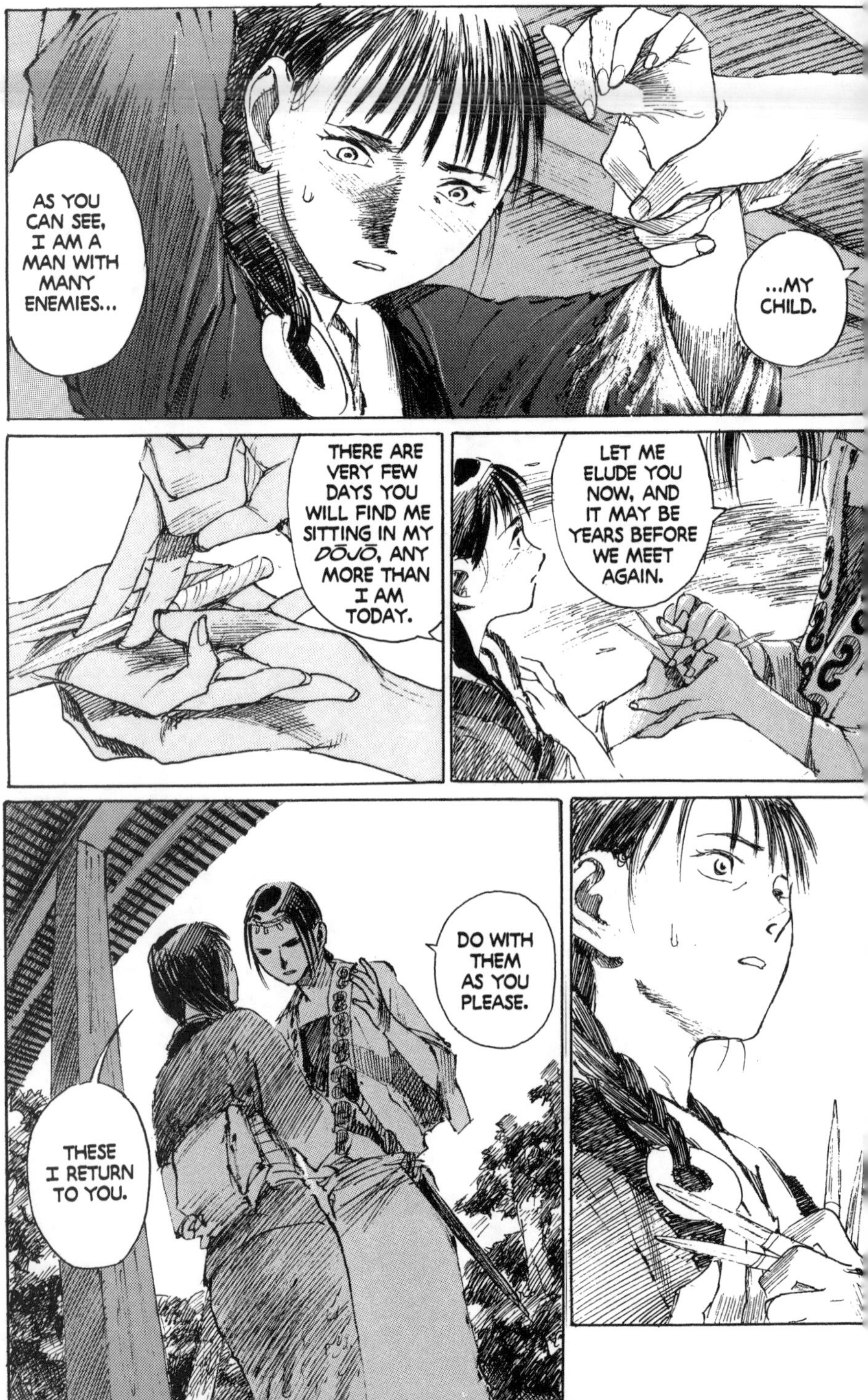
AS YOU CAN SEE, I AM A MAN WITH MANY ENEMIES...
...MY CHILD.
THERE ARE VERY FEW DAYS YOU WILL FIND ME SITTING IN MY *DŌJŌ*, ANY MORE THAN I AM TODAY.
LET ME ELUDE YOU NOW, AND IT MAY BE YEARS BEFORE WE MEET AGAIN.
THESE I RETURN TO YOU.
DO WITH THEM AS YOU PLEASE.

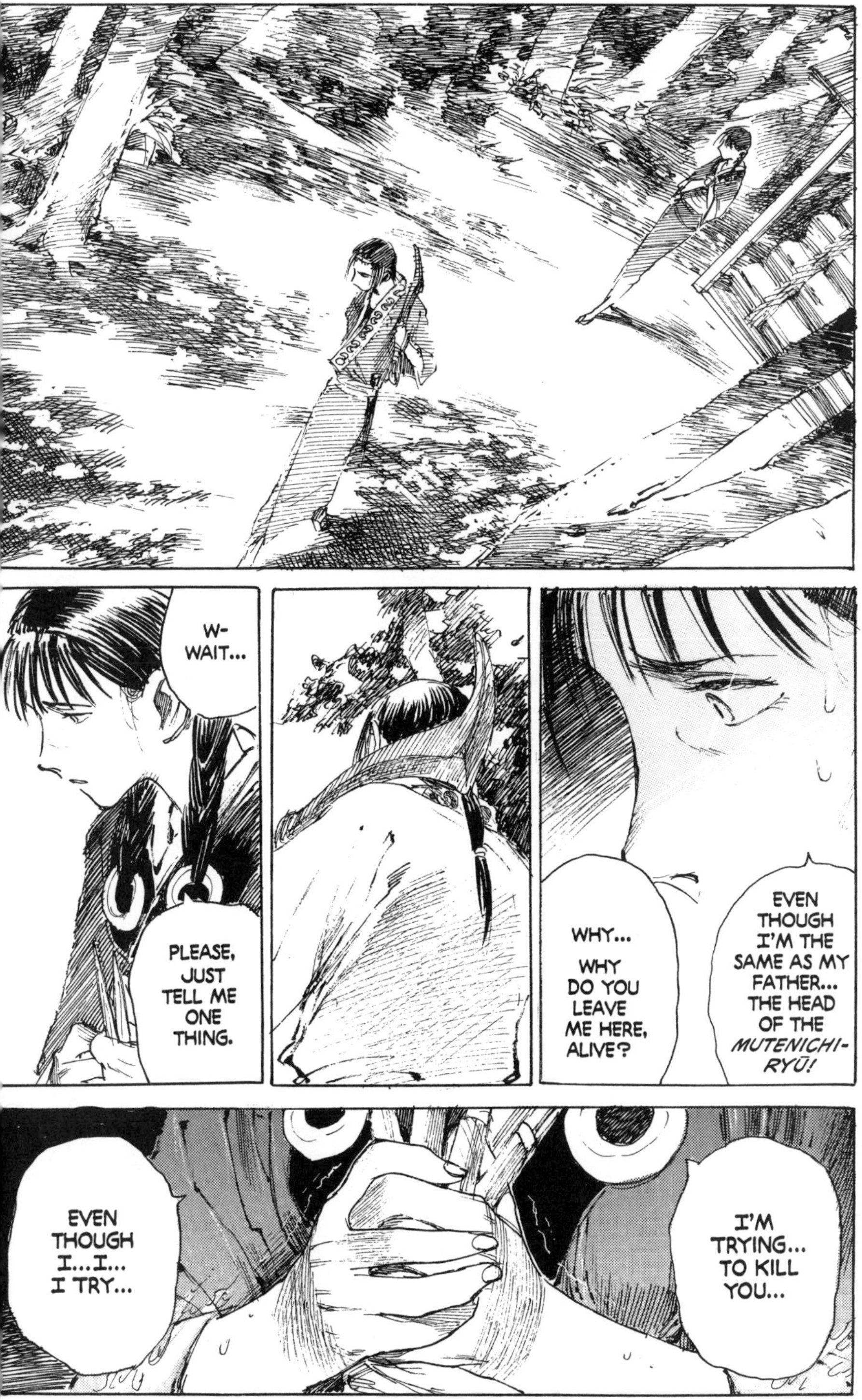
W-WAIT...
PLEASE, JUST TELL ME ONE THING.
WHY...
WHY DO YOU LEAVE ME HERE, ALIVE?
EVEN THOUGH I'M THE SAME AS MY FATHER... THE HEAD OF THE *MUTENICHI-RYŪ!*
EVEN THOUGH I...I... I TRY...
I'M TRYING... TO KILL YOU...

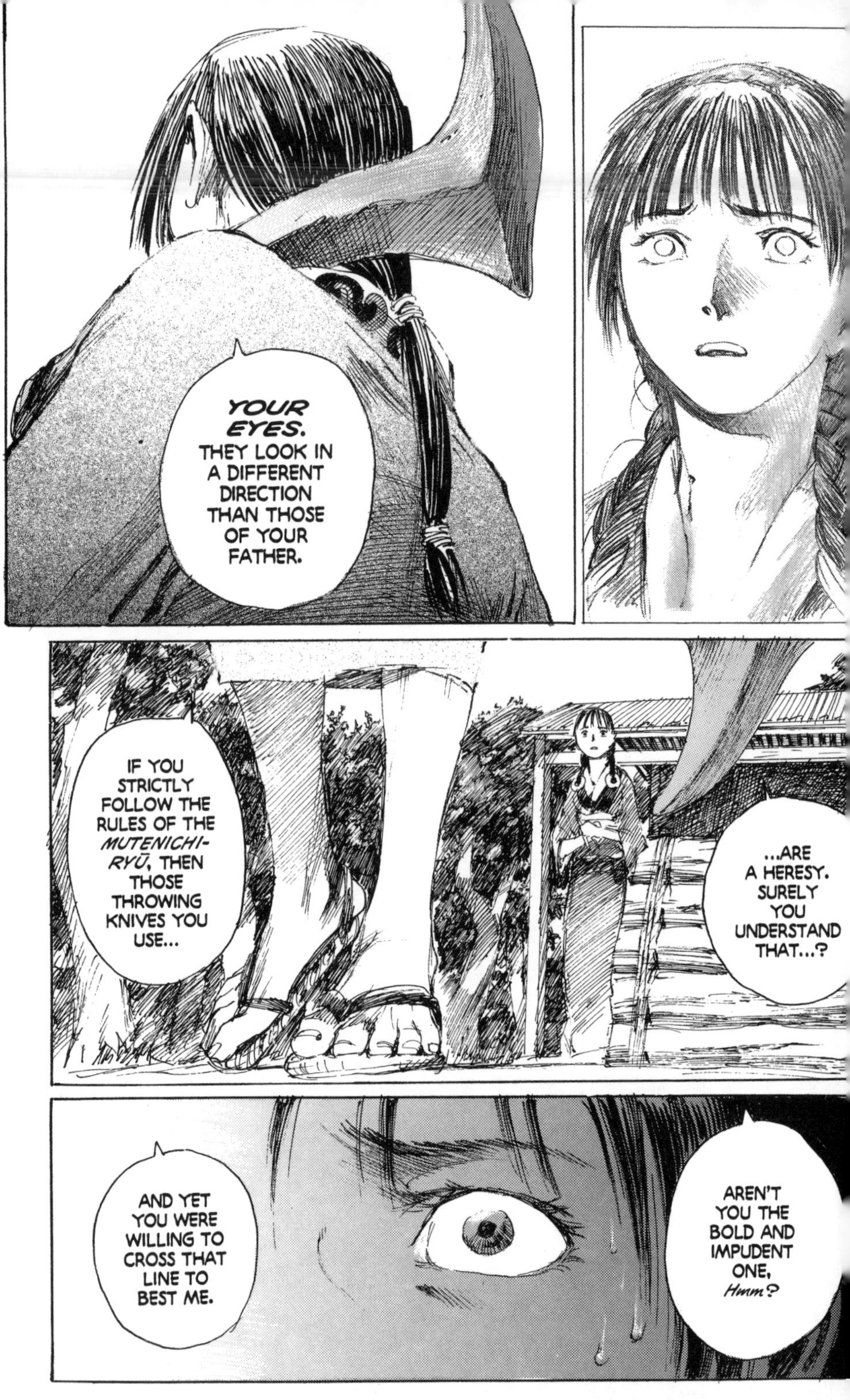
YOUR EYES. THEY LOOK IN A DIFFERENT DIRECTION THAN THOSE OF YOUR FATHER.
IF YOU STRICTLY FOLLOW THE RULES OF THE *MUTENICHI-RYŪ*, THEN THOSE THROWING KNIVES YOU USE...
...ARE A HERESY. SURELY YOU UNDERSTAND THAT...?
AND YET YOU WERE WILLING TO CROSS THAT LINE TO BEST ME.
AREN'T YOU THE BOLD AND IMPUDENT ONE, *Hmm?*

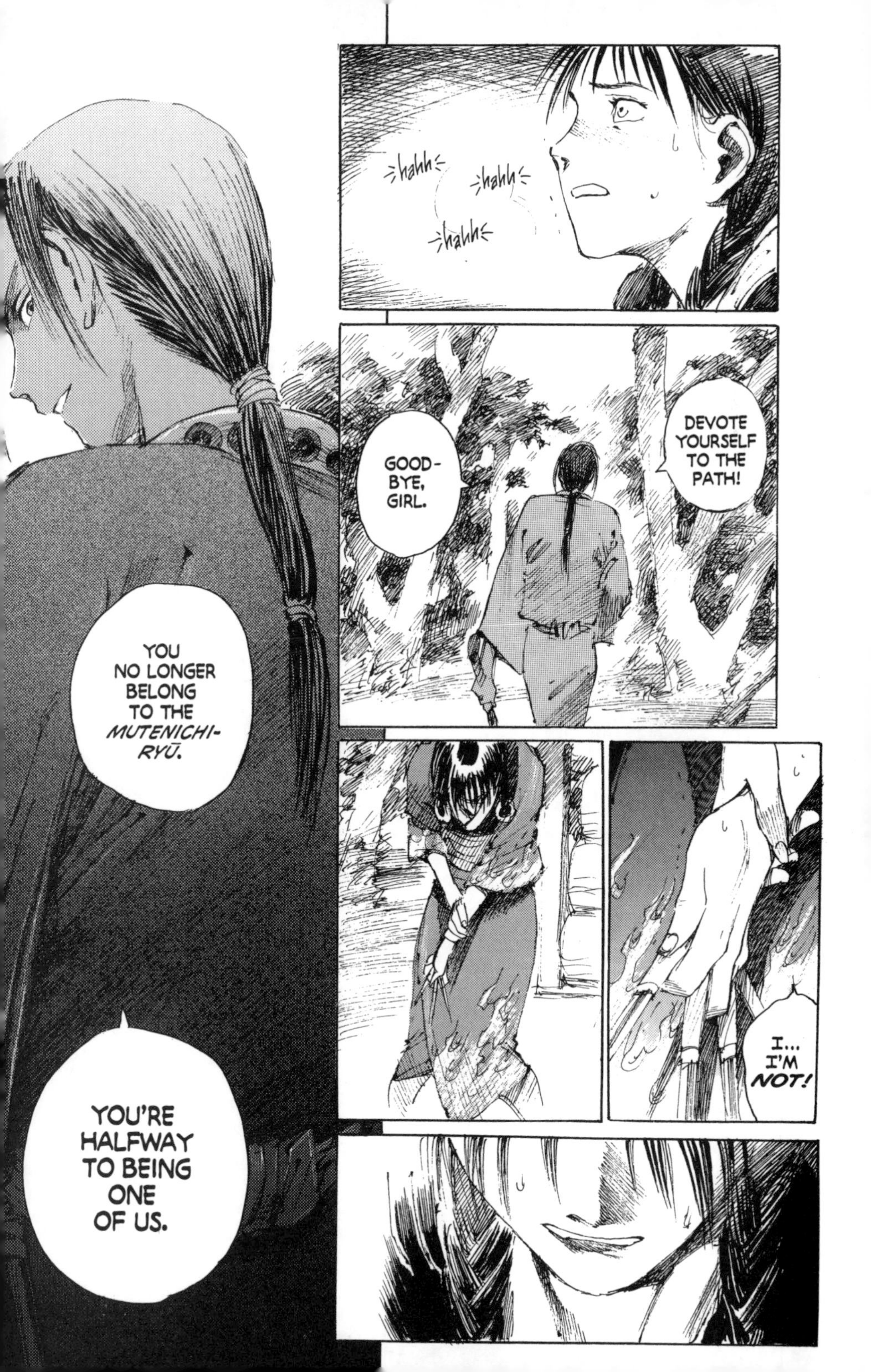
YOU NO LONGER BELONG TO THE *MUTENICHI-RYŪ*.
YOU'RE HALFWAY TO BEING ONE OF US.
hahh
hahh
hahh
GOOD-BYE, GIRL.
DEVOTE YOURSELF TO THE PATH!
I... I'M ***NOT!***

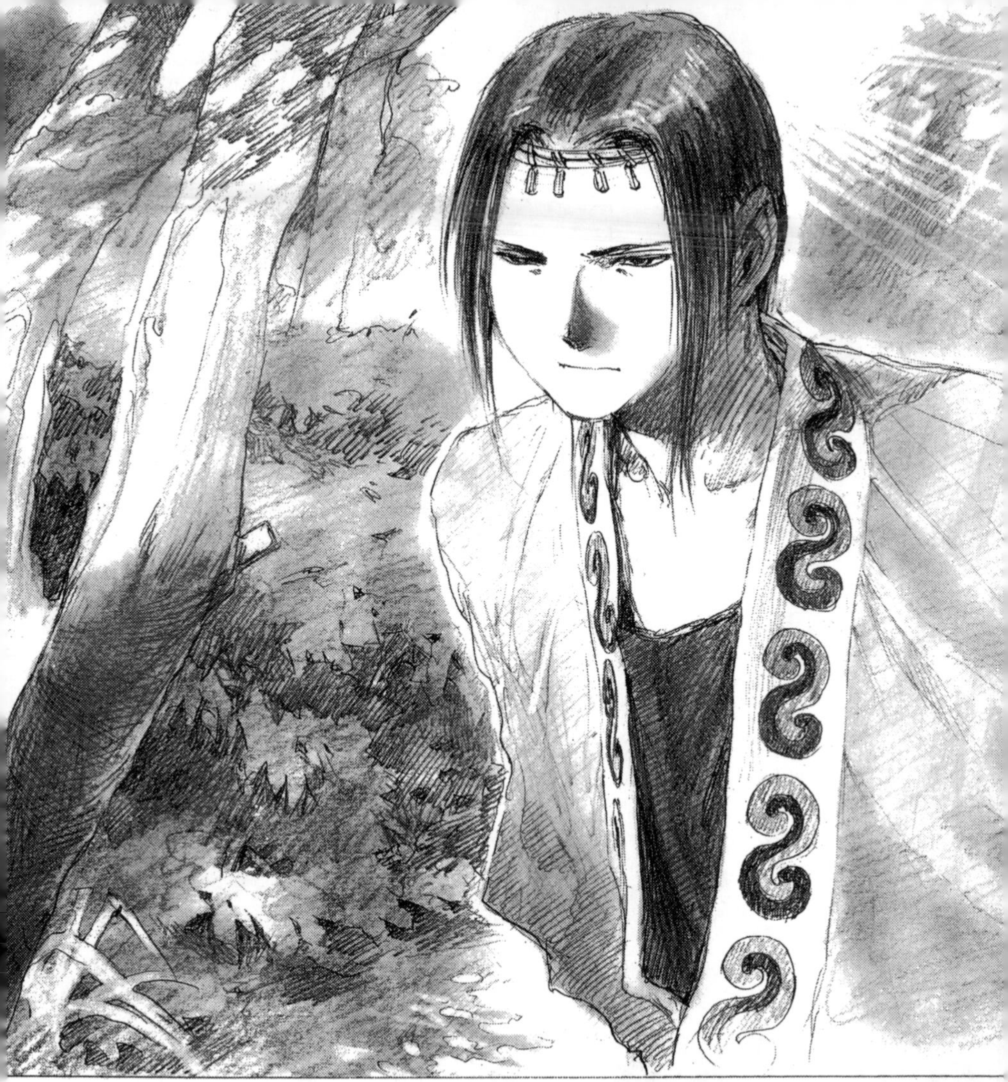
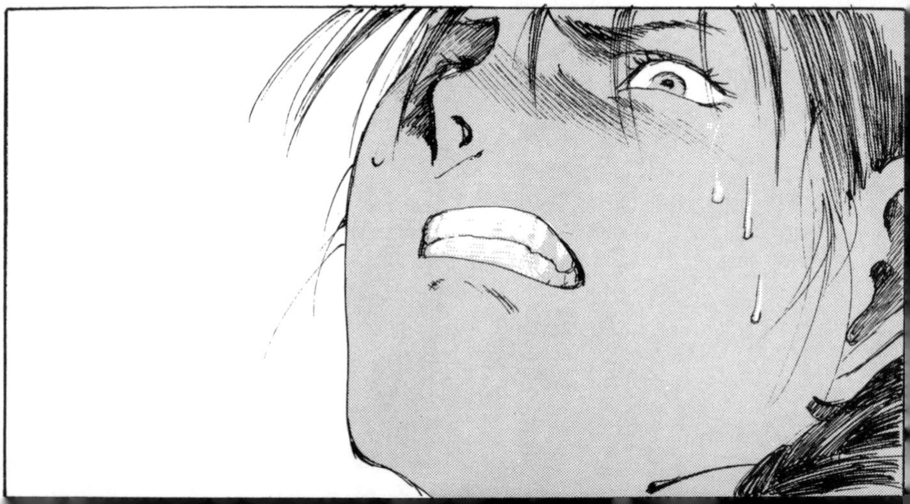

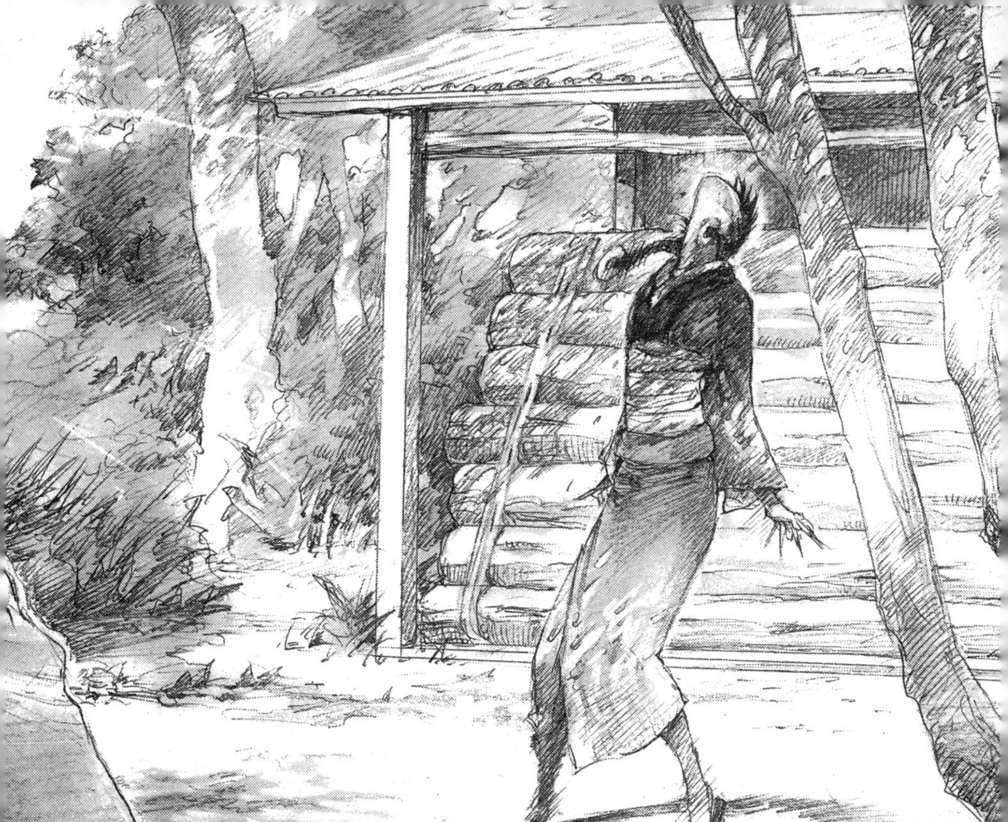
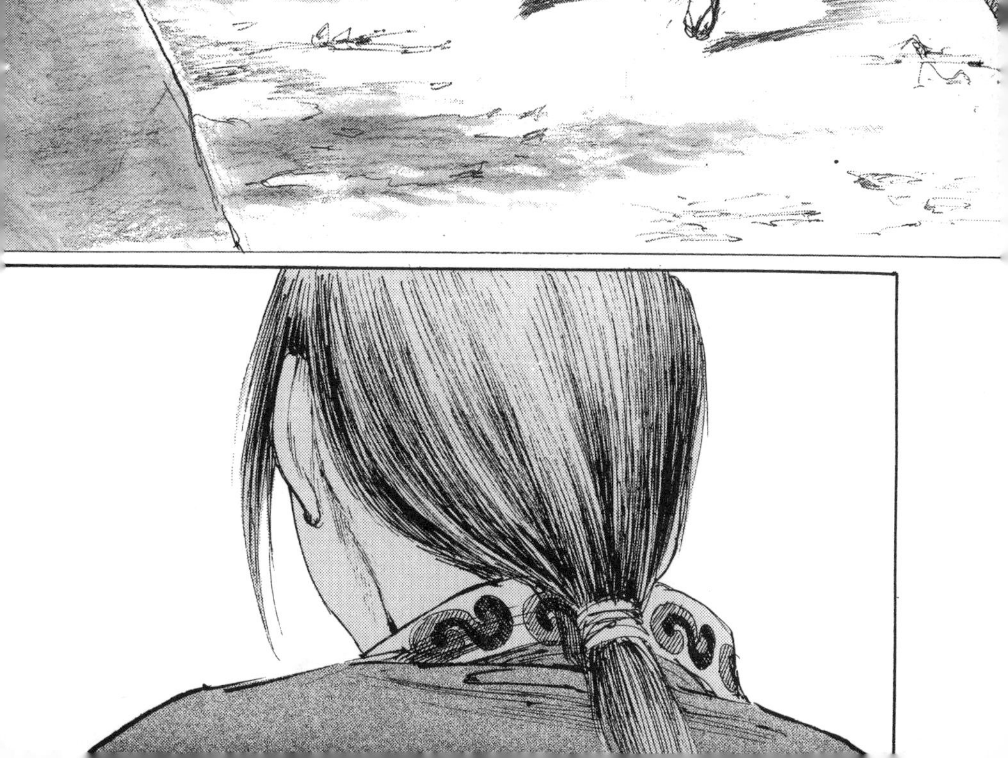

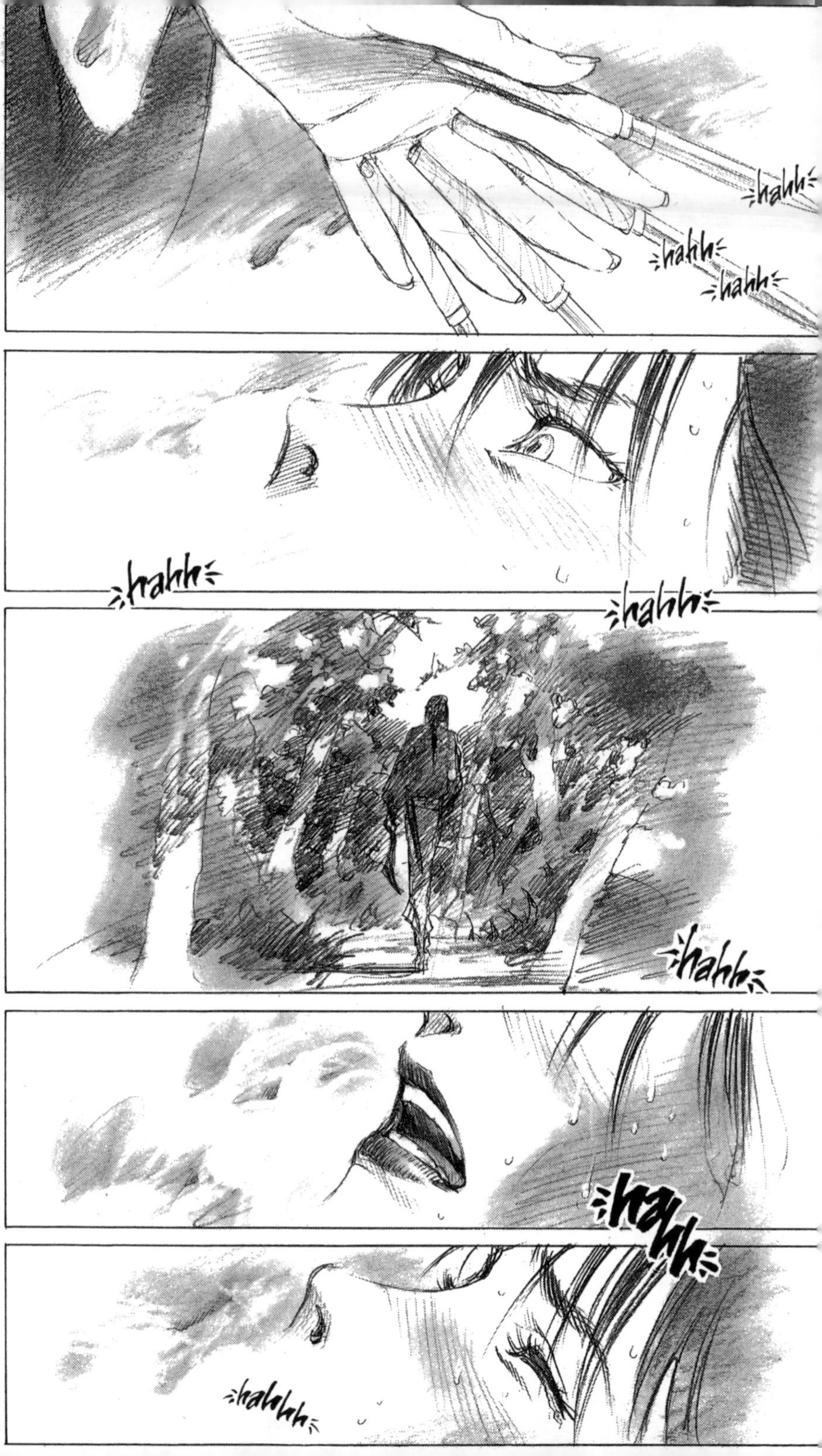
hahh
hahh
hahh
hahh
hahh
hahh
hahh
hahhh

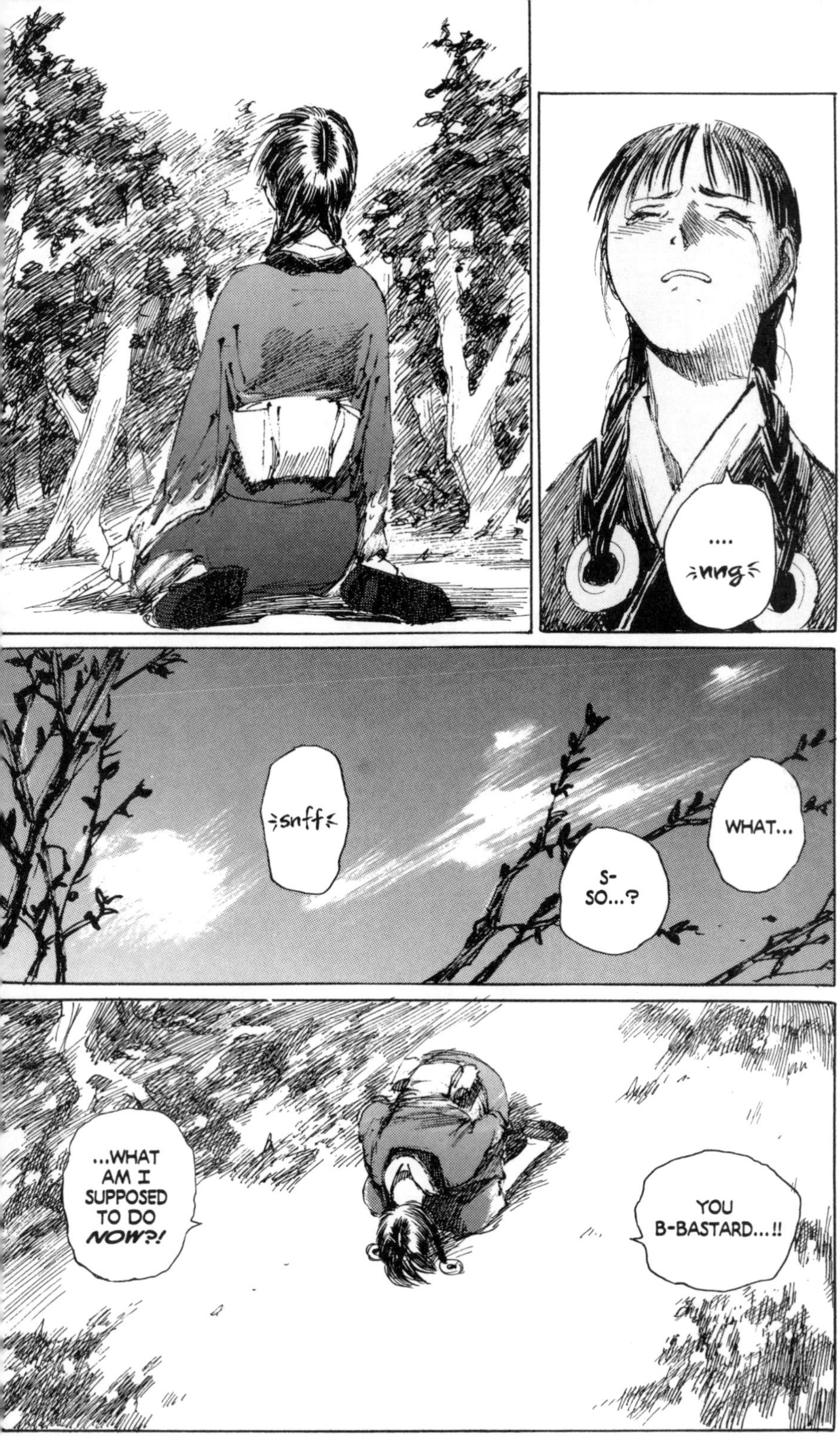
....
nng
snff
WHAT...
S-
SO...?
...WHAT AM I SUPPOSED TO DO *NOW?!*
YOU B-BASTARD...!!

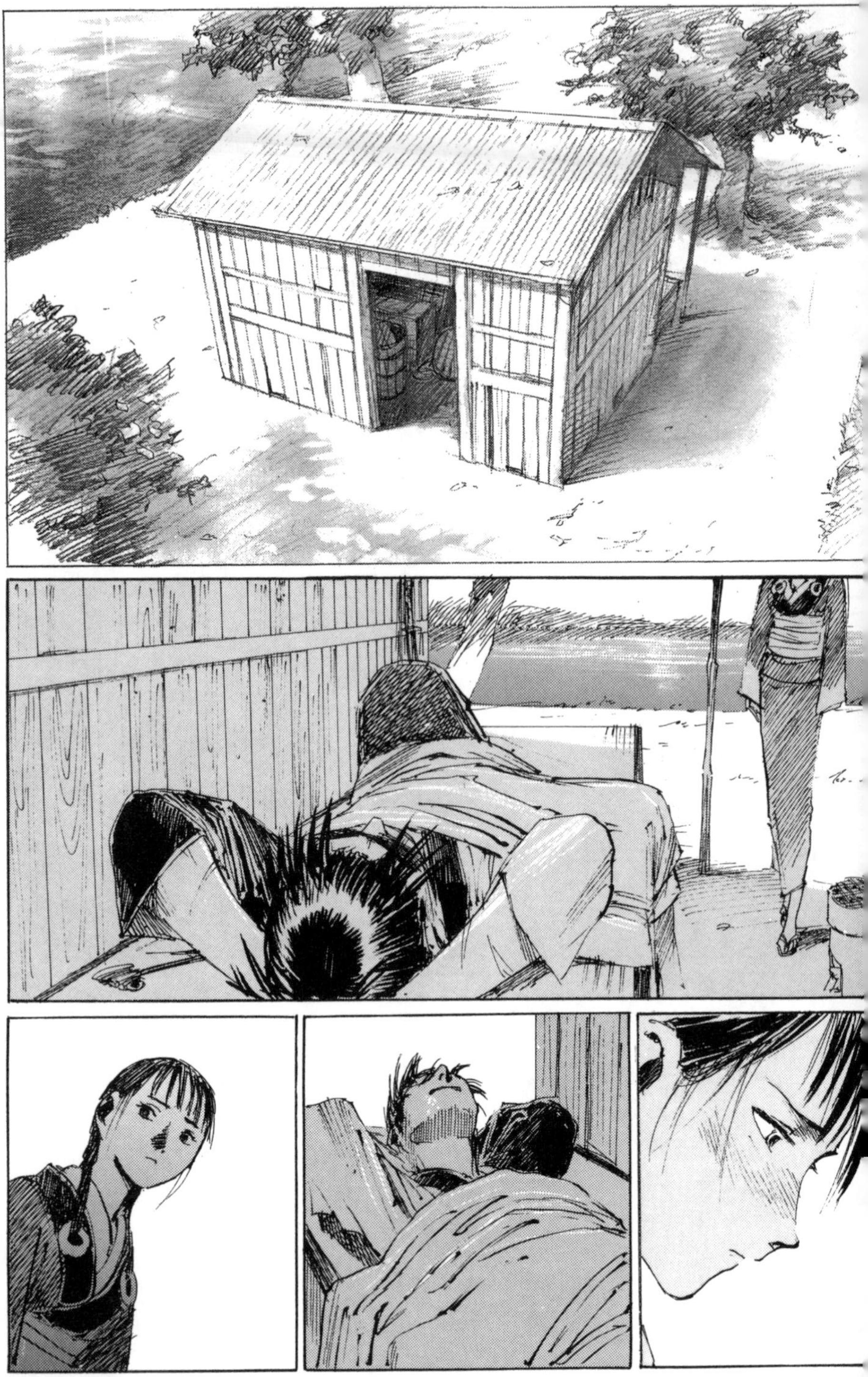

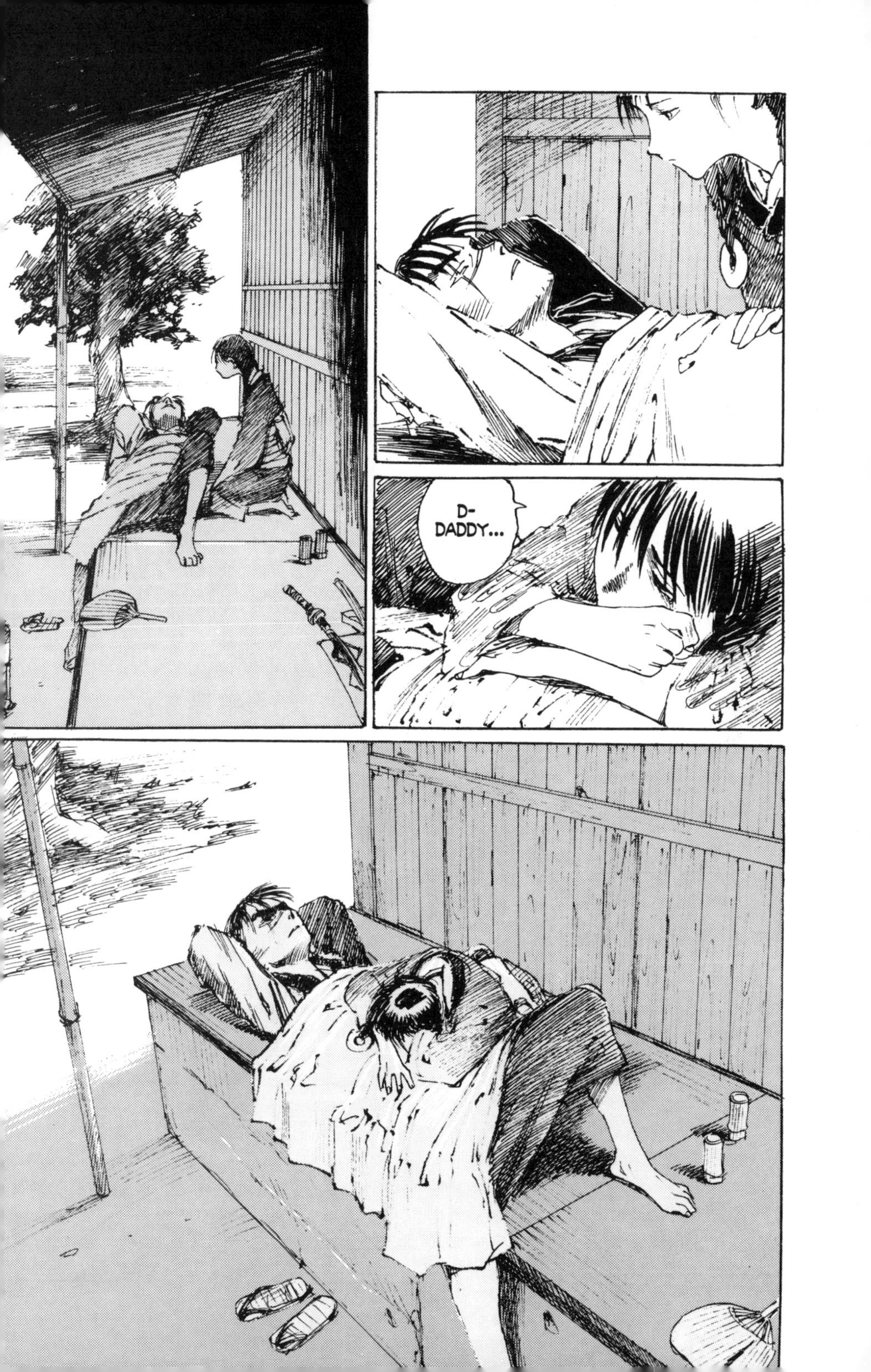
D-DADDY...

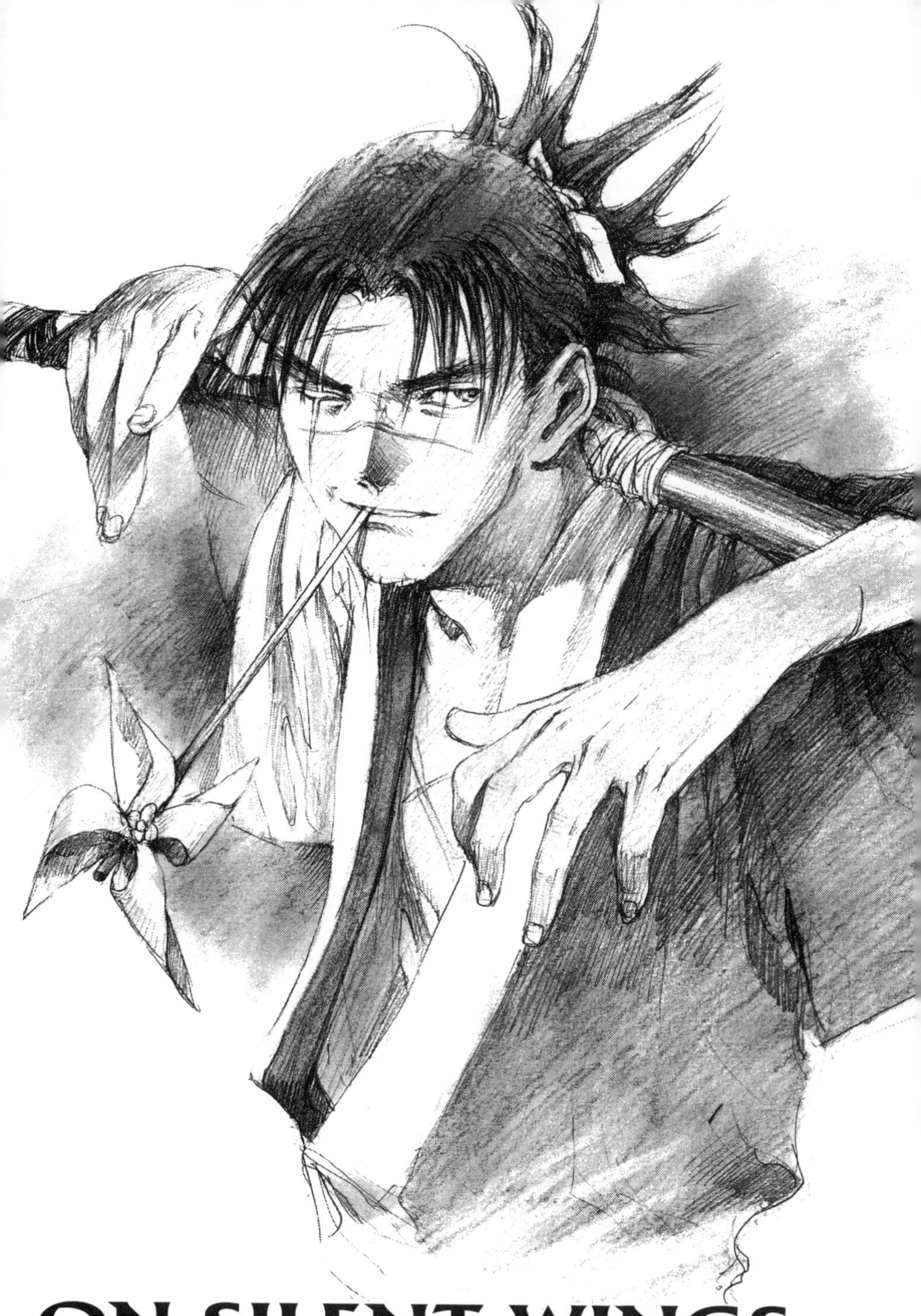

ON SILENT WINGS
Part 1

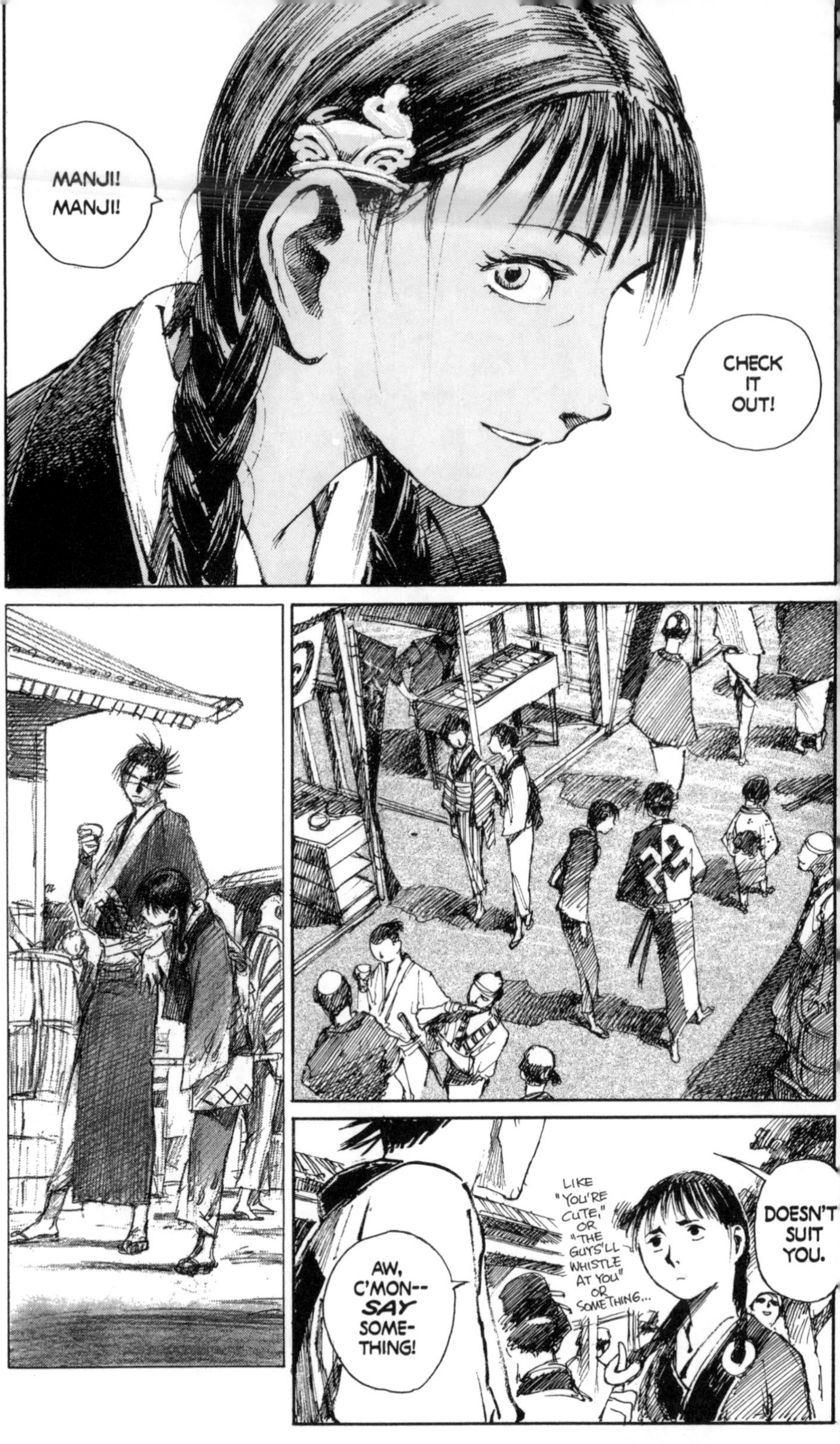
MANJI! MANJI!
CHECK IT OUT!
AW, C'MON-- SAY SOMETHING!
LIKE "YOU'RE CUTE," OR "THE GUYS'LL WHISTLE AT YOU" OR SOMETHING...
DOESN'T SUIT YOU.

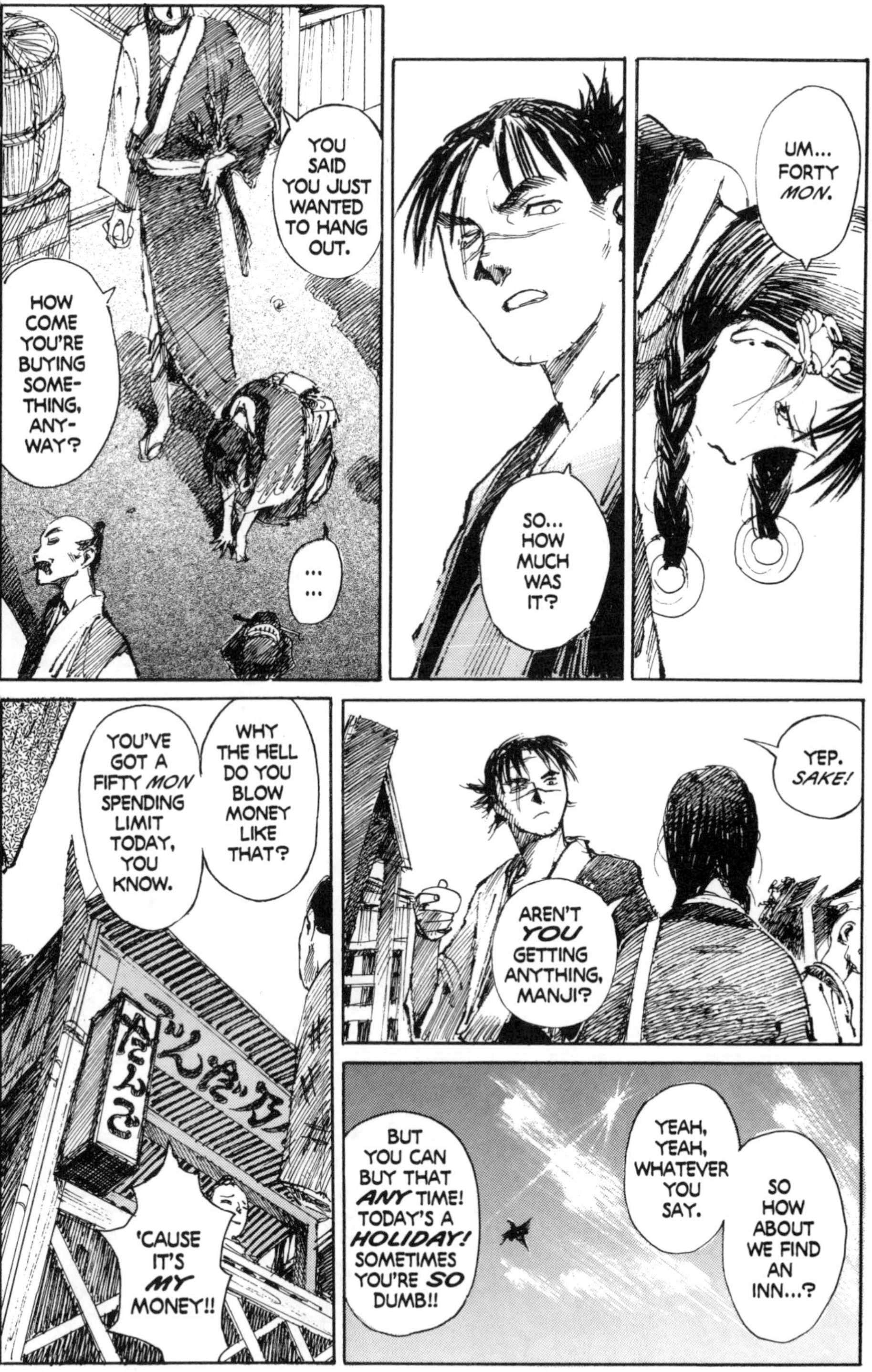
YOU SAID YOU JUST WANTED TO HANG OUT.
HOW COME YOU'RE BUYING SOME-THING, ANY-WAY?
......
SO... HOW MUCH WAS IT?
UM... FORTY *MON*.
YOU'VE GOT A FIFTY *MON* SPENDING LIMIT TODAY, YOU KNOW.
WHY THE HELL DO YOU BLOW MONEY LIKE THAT?
'CAUSE IT'S ***MY*** MONEY!!
YEP. *SAKE!*
AREN'T ***YOU*** GETTING ANYTHING, MANJI?
BUT YOU CAN BUY THAT ***ANY*** TIME! TODAY'S A ***HOLIDAY!*** SOMETIMES YOU'RE ***SO*** DUMB!!
YEAH, YEAH, WHATEVER YOU SAY.
SO HOW ABOUT WE FIND AN INN...?

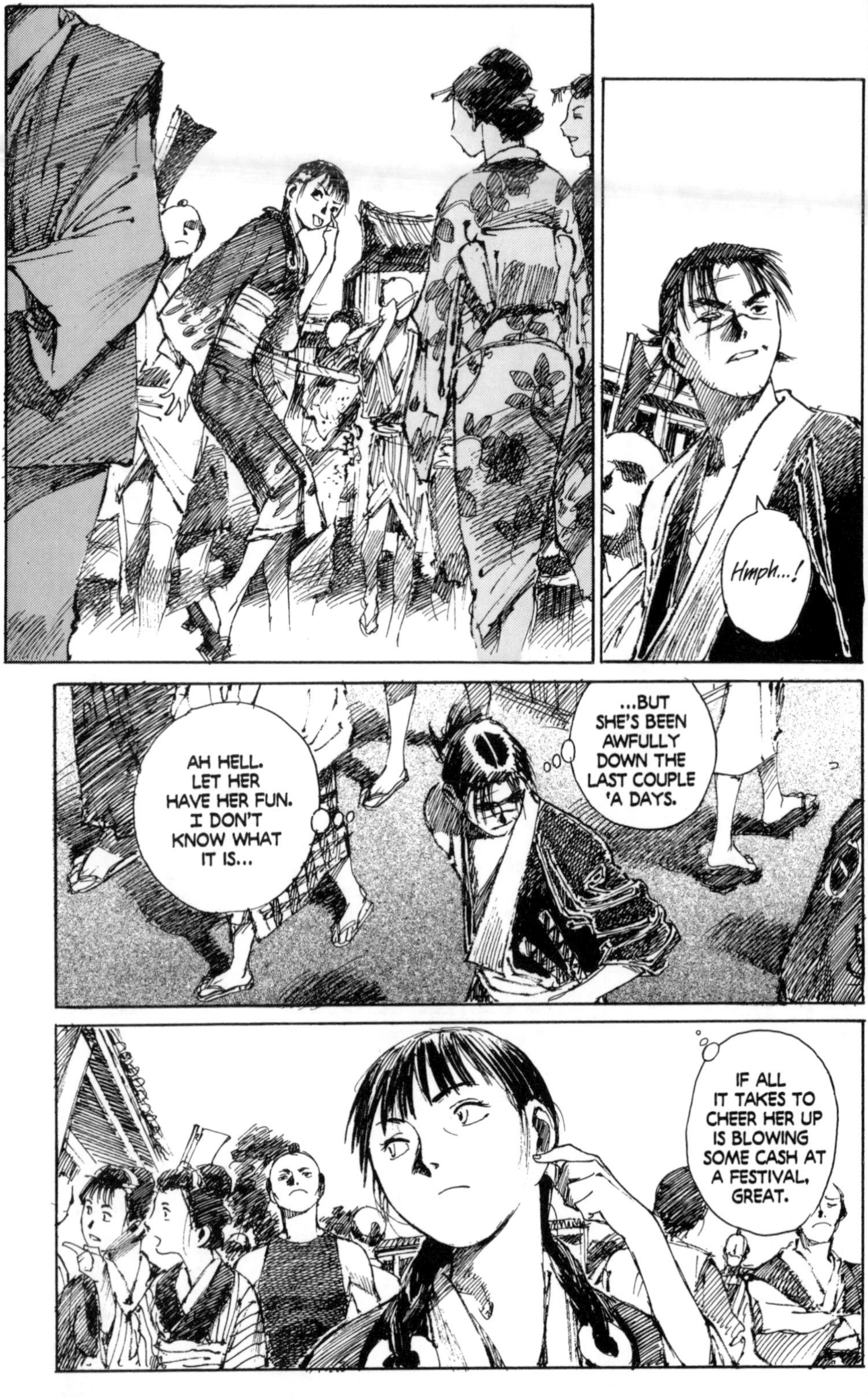
Hmph...!
AH HELL. LET HER HAVE HER FUN. I DON'T KNOW WHAT IT IS...
...BUT SHE'S BEEN AWFULLY DOWN THE LAST COUPLE 'A DAYS.
IF ALL IT TAKES TO CHEER HER UP IS BLOWING SOME CASH AT A FESTIVAL, GREAT.

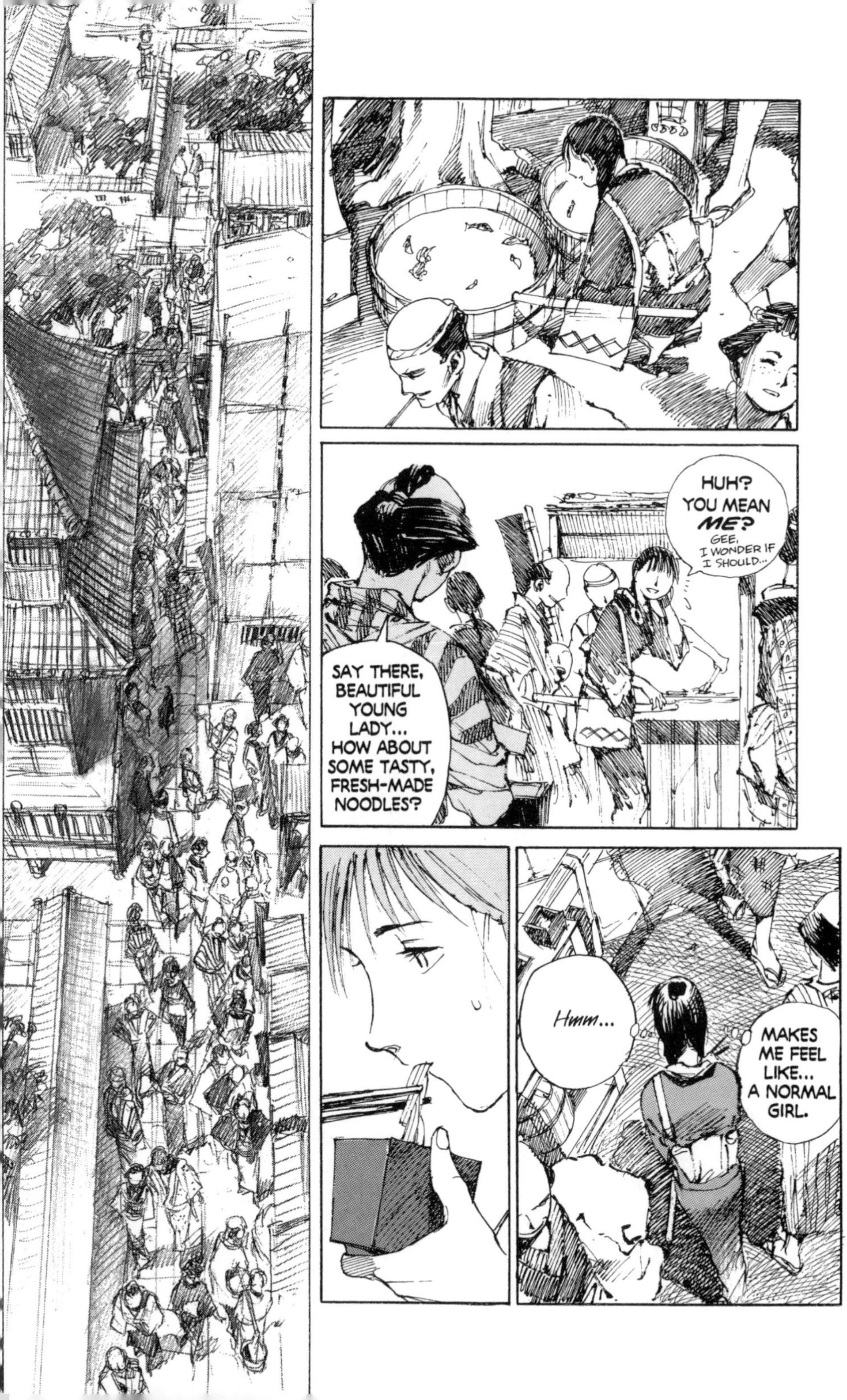
SAY THERE, BEAUTIFUL YOUNG LADY... HOW ABOUT SOME TASTY, FRESH-MADE NOODLES?
HUH? YOU MEAN *ME?*
GEE, I WONDER IF I SHOULD...
Hmm...
MAKES ME FEEL LIKE... A NORMAL GIRL.

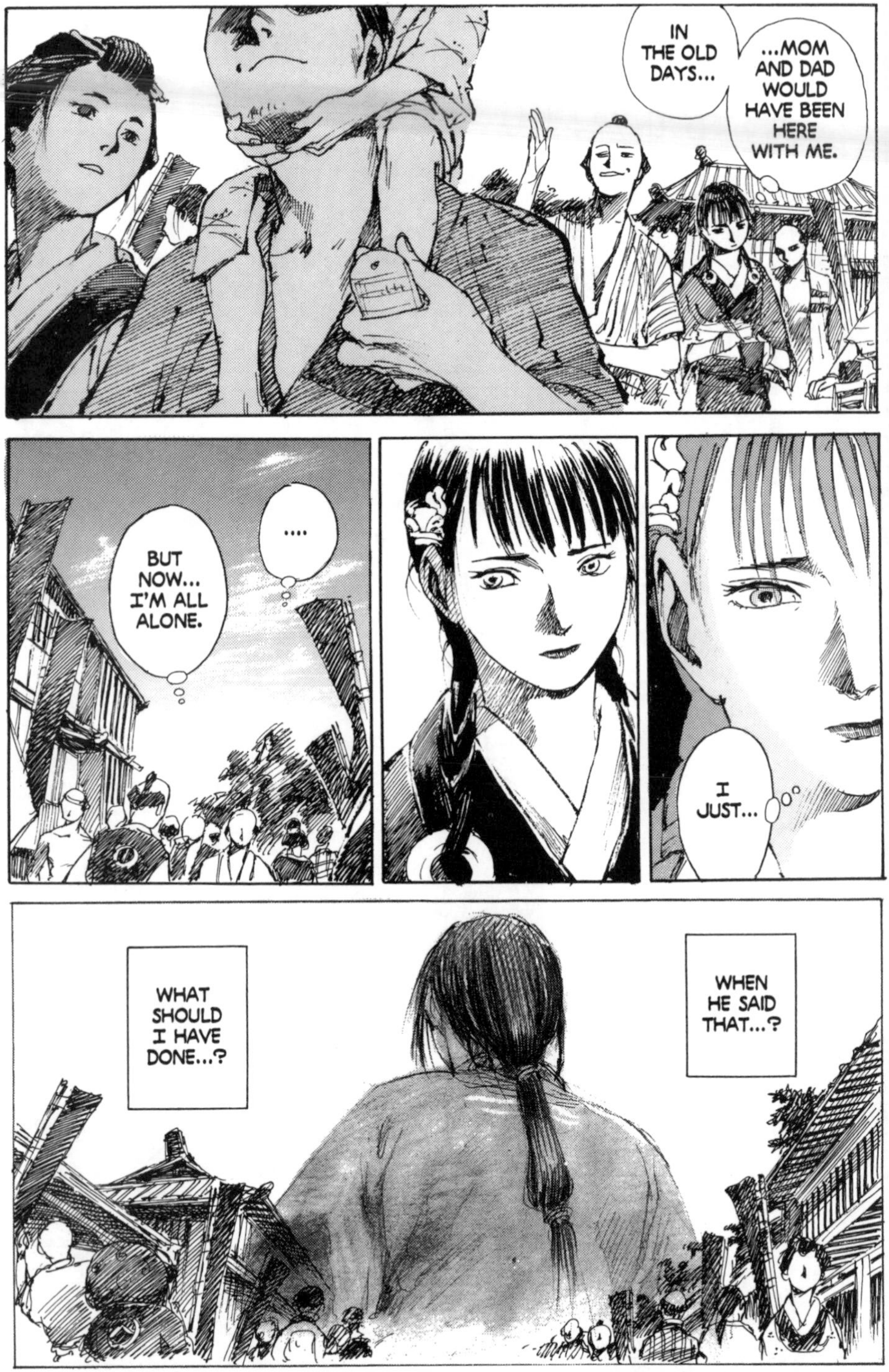
IN THE OLD DAYS...
...MOM AND DAD WOULD HAVE BEEN HERE WITH ME.
BUT NOW... I'M ALL ALONE.
....
I JUST...
WHAT SHOULD I HAVE DONE...?
WHEN HE SAID THAT...?

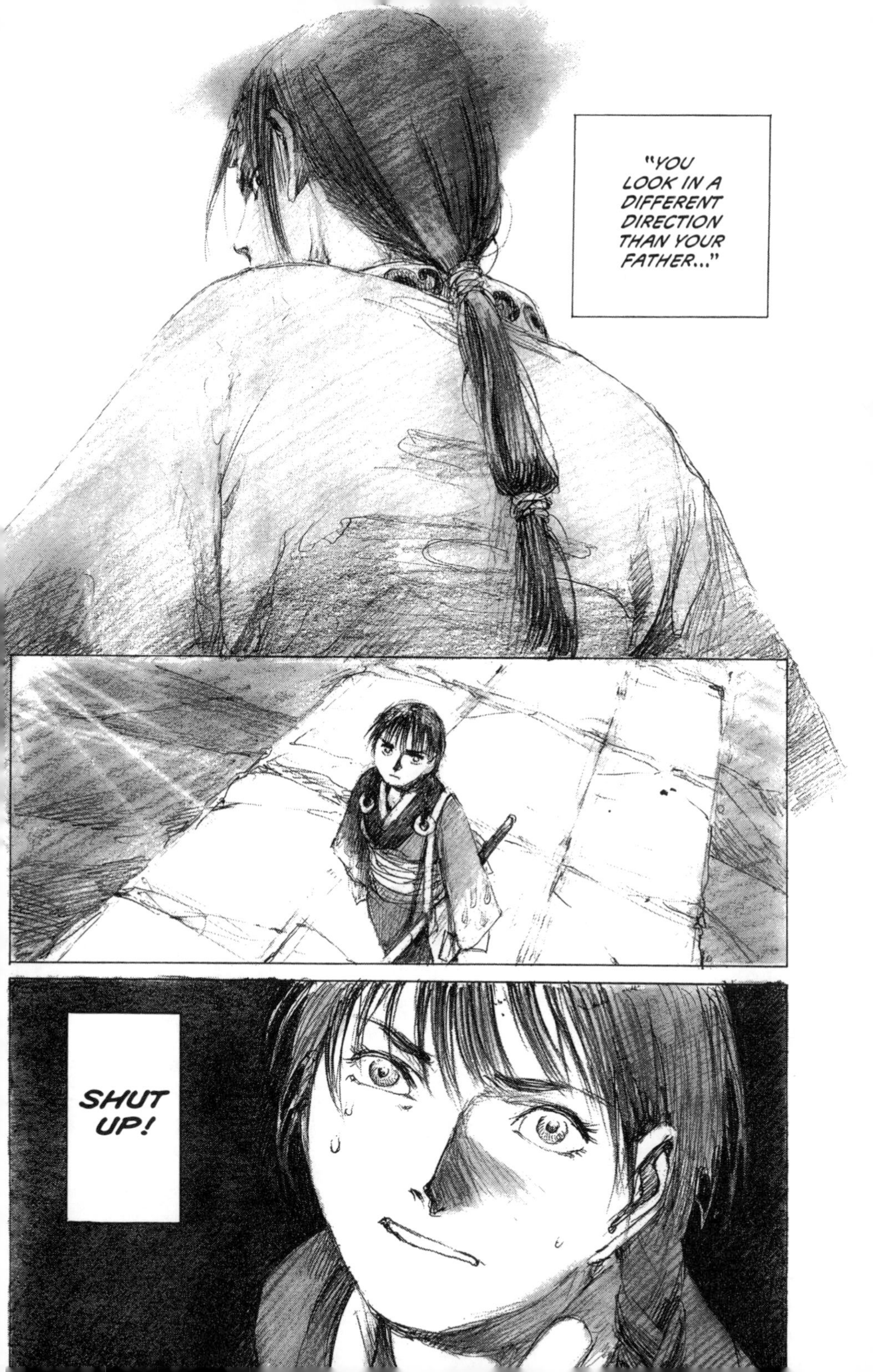
"YOU LOOK IN A DIFFERENT DIRECTION THAN YOUR FATHER..."
SHUT UP!

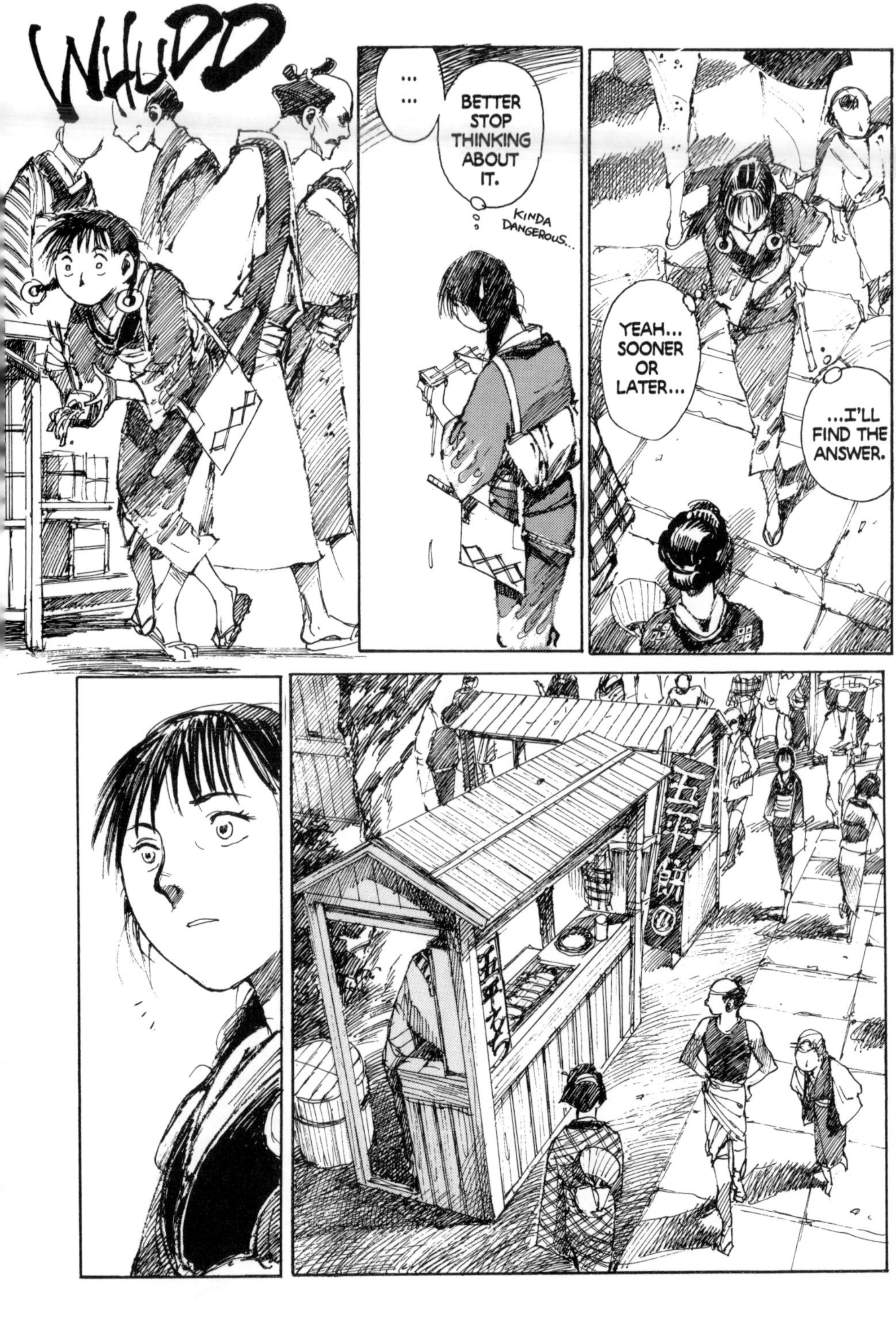
WHUDD
...
...
BETTER STOP THINKING ABOUT IT.
KINDA DANGEROUS...
YEAH... SOONER OR LATER...
...I'LL FIND THE ANSWER.

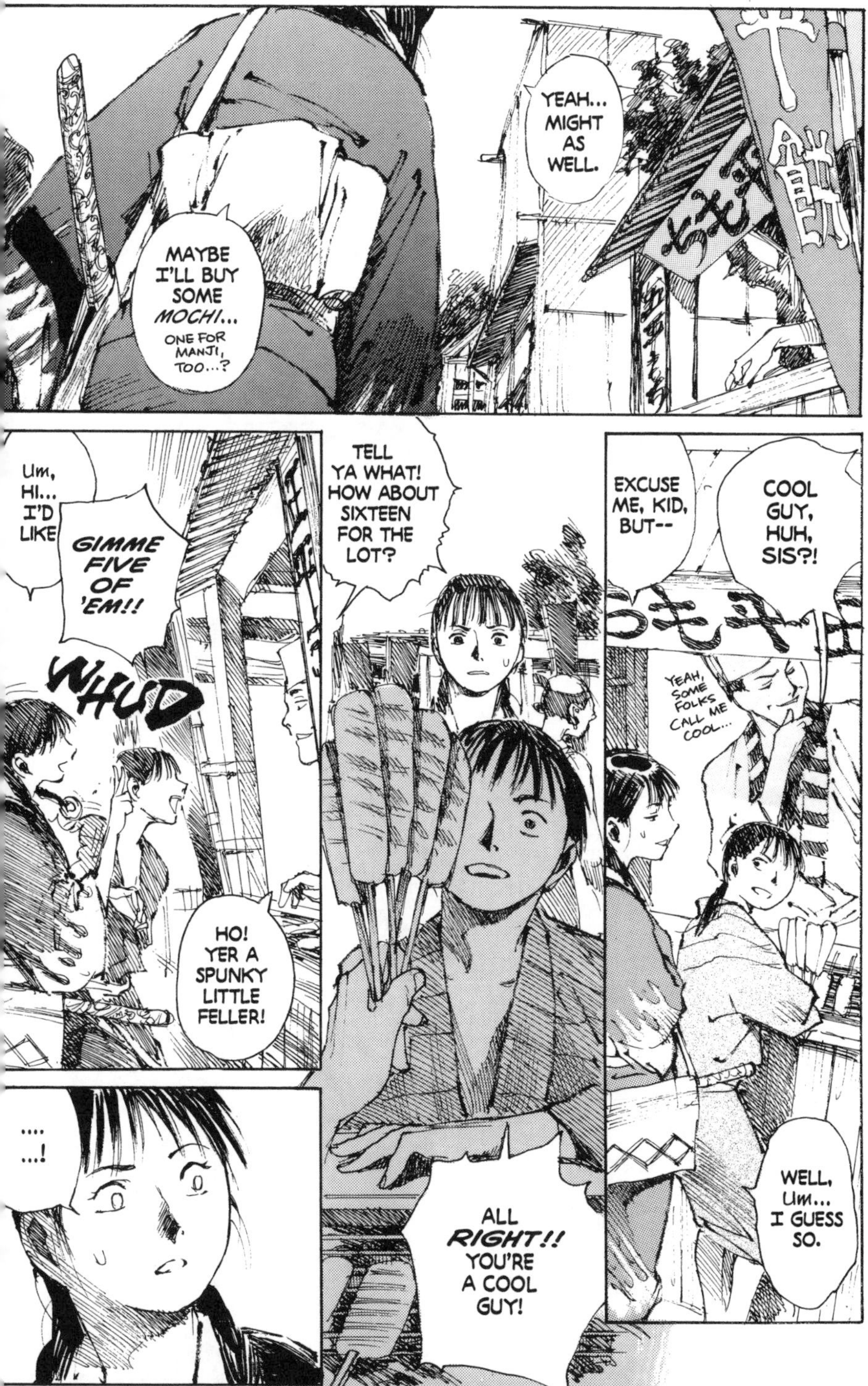
MAYBE I'LL BUY SOME *MOCHI*... ONE FOR MANJI, TOO...?
YEAH... MIGHT AS WELL.
UM, HI... I'D LIKE
GIMME FIVE OF 'EM!!
WHUD
HO! YER A SPUNKY LITTLE FELLER!
....
...!
TELL YA WHAT! HOW ABOUT SIXTEEN FOR THE LOT?
ALL *RIGHT!!* YOU'RE A COOL GUY!
EXCUSE ME, KID, BUT--
COOL GUY, HUH, SIS?!
YEAH, SOME FOLKS CALL ME COOL...
WELL, UM... I GUESS SO.

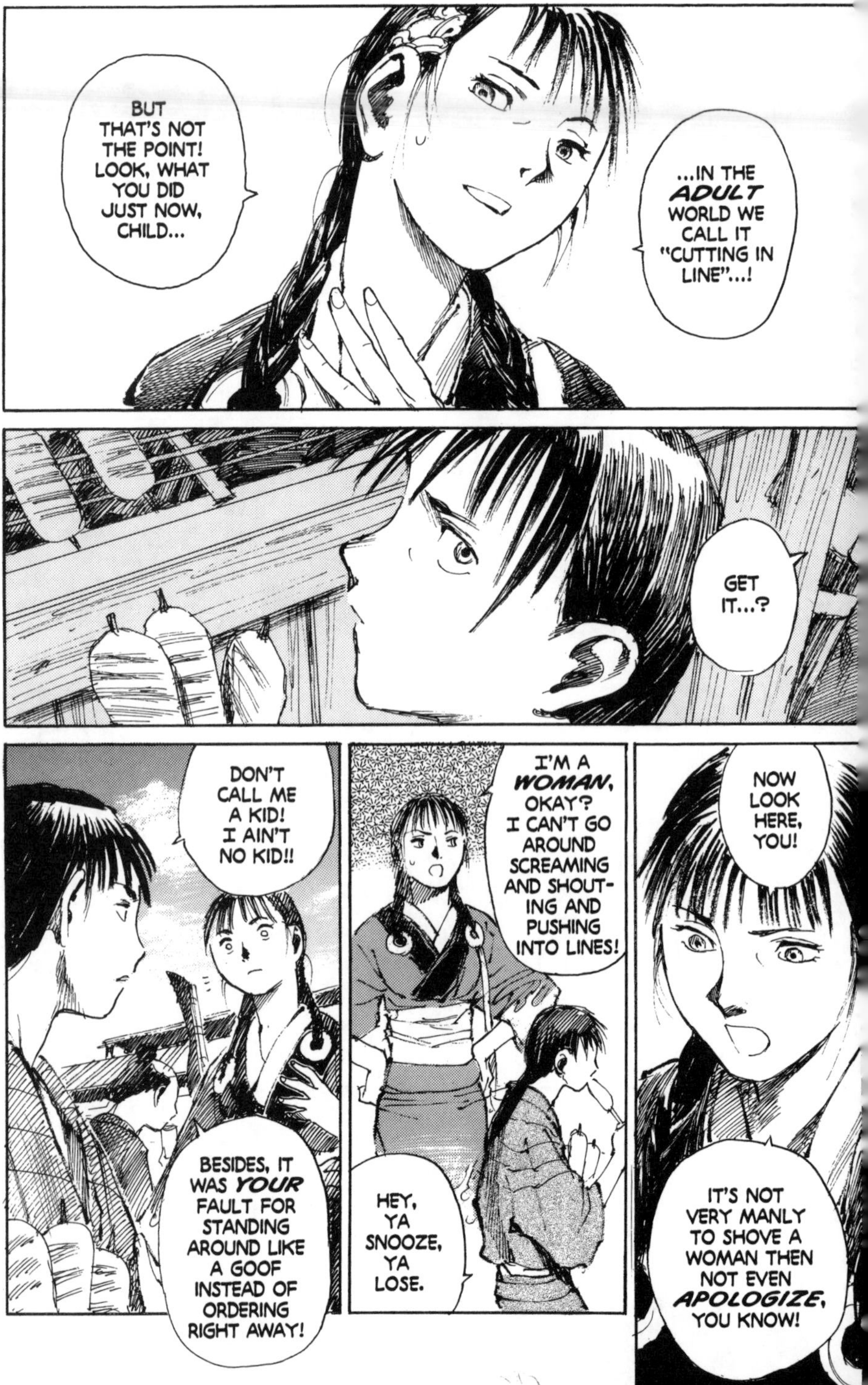
BUT THAT'S NOT THE POINT! LOOK, WHAT YOU DID JUST NOW, CHILD...
...IN THE *ADULT* WORLD WE CALL IT "CUTTING IN LINE"...!
GET IT...?
DON'T CALL ME A KID! I AIN'T NO KID!!
BESIDES, IT WAS *YOUR* FAULT FOR STANDING AROUND LIKE A GOOF INSTEAD OF ORDERING RIGHT AWAY!
I'M A *WOMAN*, OKAY? I CAN'T GO AROUND SCREAMING AND SHOUT-ING AND PUSHING INTO LINES!
HEY, YA SNOOZE, YA LOSE.
NOW LOOK HERE, YOU!
IT'S NOT VERY MANLY TO SHOVE A WOMAN THEN NOT EVEN *APOLOGIZE*, YOU KNOW!

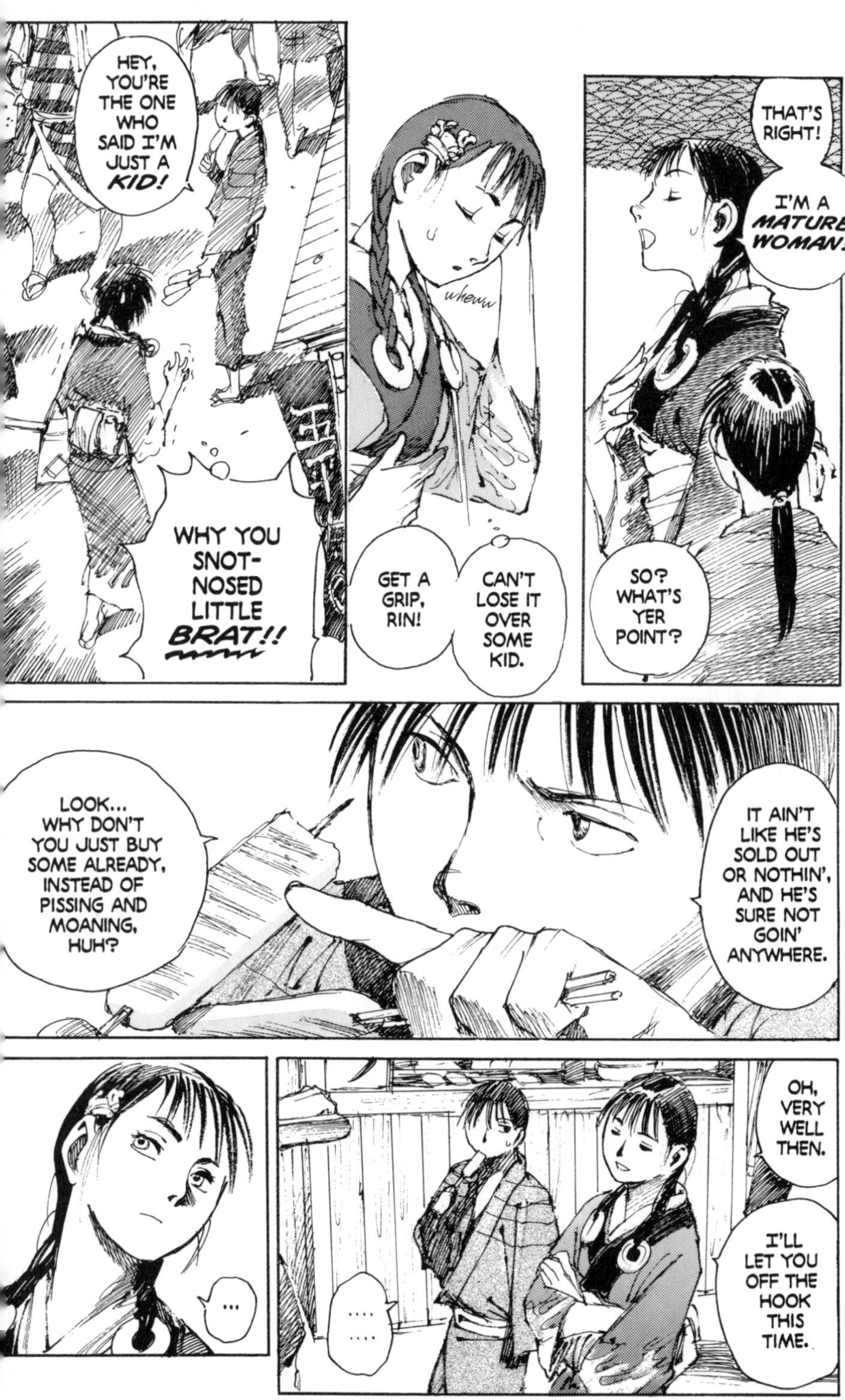
HEY, YOU'RE THE ONE WHO SAID I'M JUST A KID!
WHY YOU SNOT-NOSED LITTLE BRAT!!
GET A GRIP, RIN!
CAN'T LOSE IT OVER SOME KID.
THAT'S RIGHT!
I'M A MATURE WOMAN!
SO? WHAT'S YER POINT?
LOOK... WHY DON'T YOU JUST BUY SOME ALREADY, INSTEAD OF PISSING AND MOANING, HUH?
IT AIN'T LIKE HE'S SOLD OUT OR NOTHIN', AND HE'S SURE NOT GOIN' ANYWHERE.
...
OH, VERY WELL THEN.
I'LL LET YOU OFF THE HOOK THIS TIME.
....

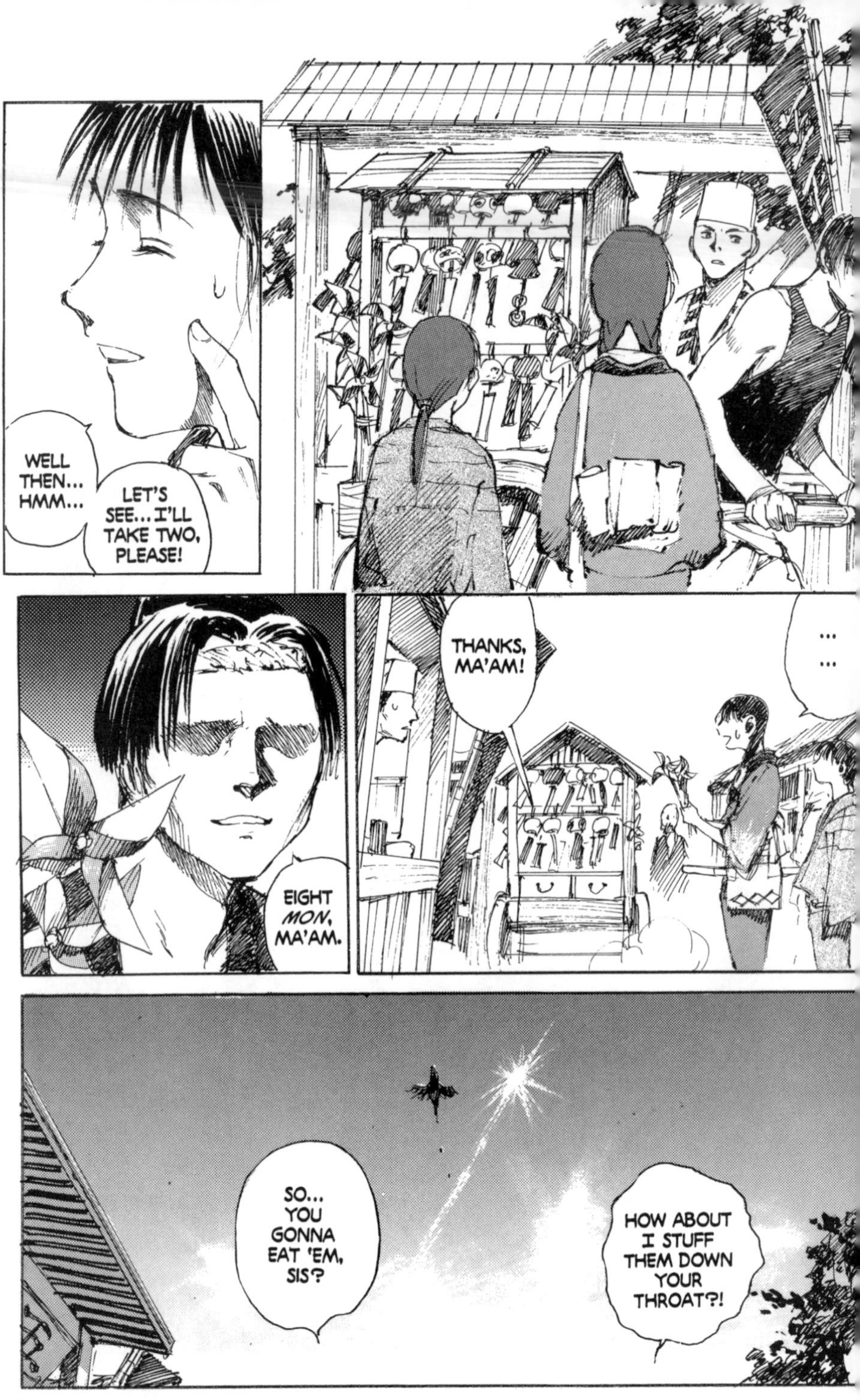
WELL THEN... HMM...
LET'S SEE... I'LL TAKE TWO, PLEASE!
EIGHT *MON*, MA'AM.
THANKS, MA'AM!
... ...
SO... YOU GONNA EAT 'EM, SIS?
HOW ABOUT I STUFF THEM DOWN YOUR THROAT?!

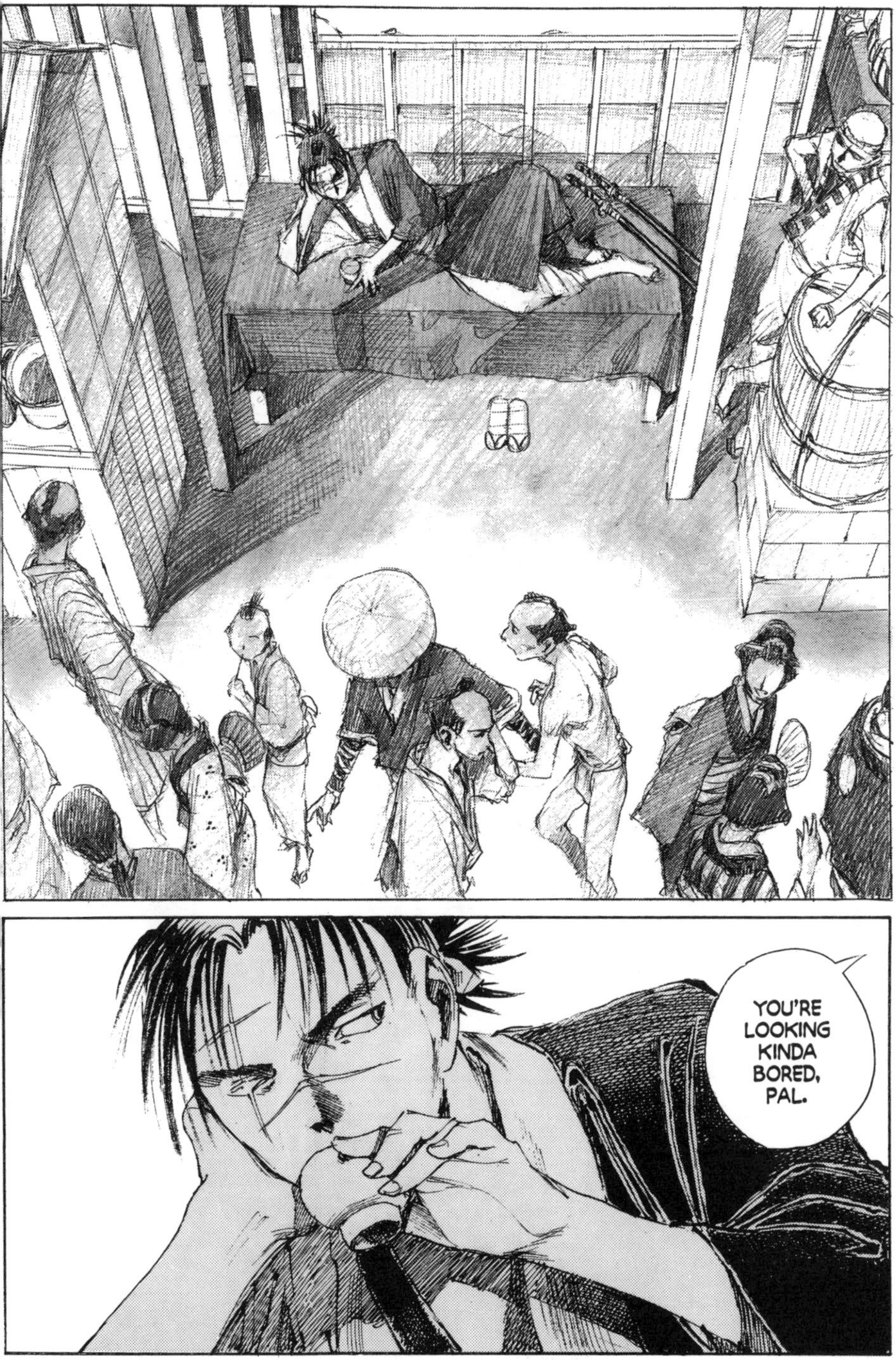
YOU'RE LOOKING KINDA BORED, PAL.

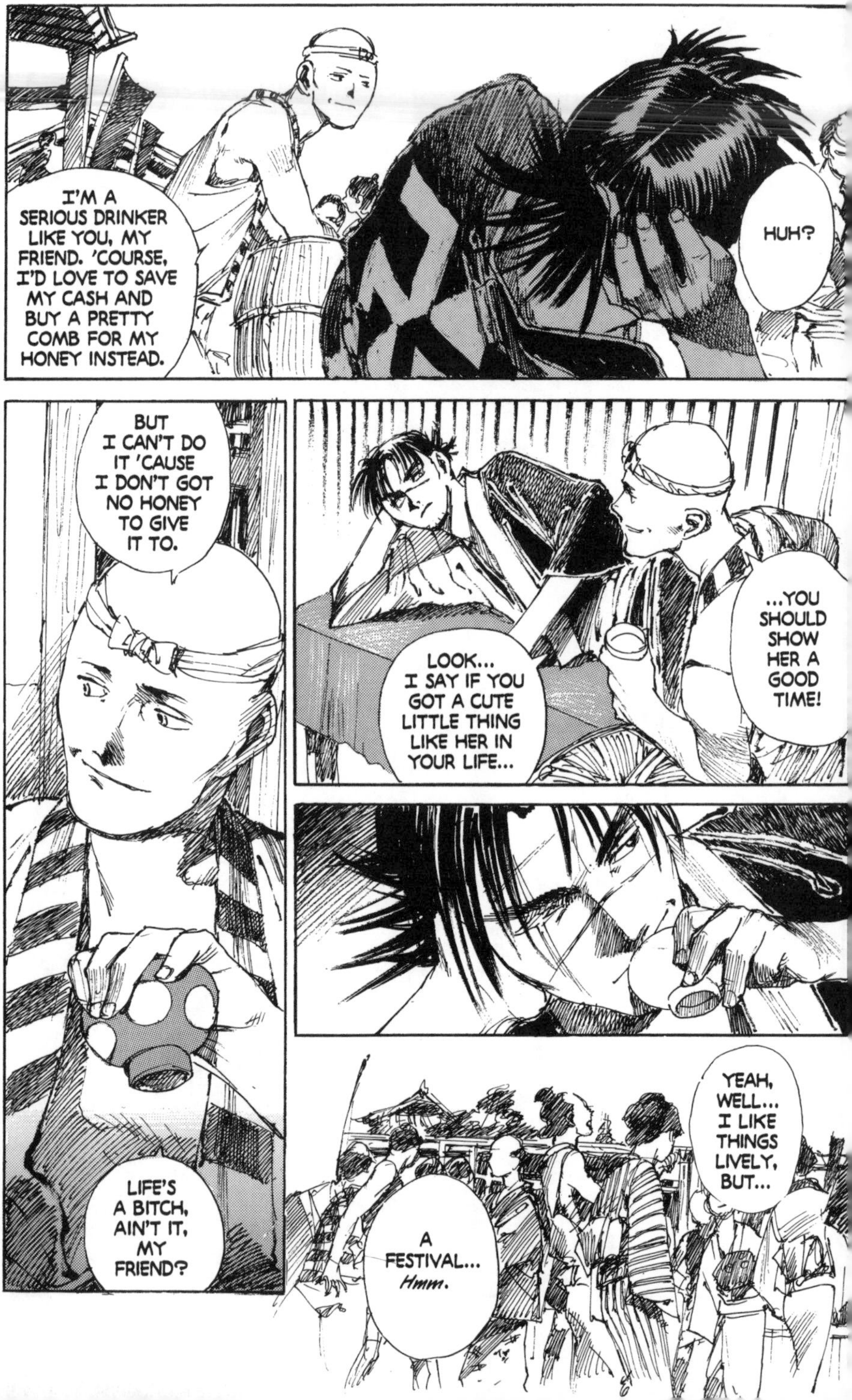
HUH?
I'M A SERIOUS DRINKER LIKE YOU, MY FRIEND. 'COURSE, I'D LOVE TO SAVE MY CASH AND BUY A PRETTY COMB FOR MY HONEY INSTEAD.
LOOK... I SAY IF YOU GOT A CUTE LITTLE THING LIKE HER IN YOUR LIFE...
...YOU SHOULD SHOW HER A GOOD TIME!
YEAH, WELL... I LIKE THINGS LIVELY, BUT...
A FESTIVAL... Hmm.
BUT I CAN'T DO IT 'CAUSE I DON'T GOT NO HONEY TO GIVE IT TO.
LIFE'S A BITCH, AIN'T IT, MY FRIEND?

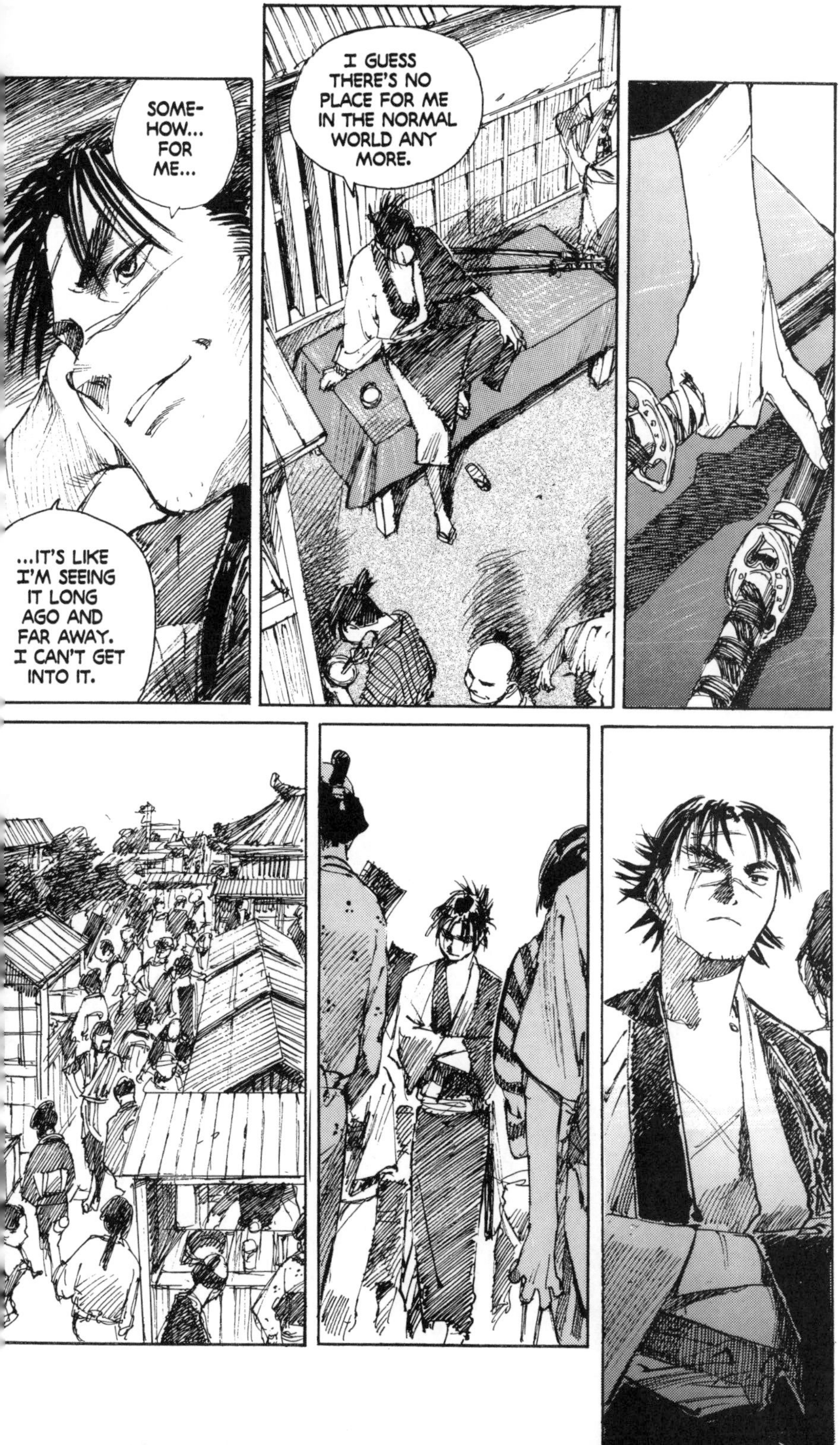
SOME-HOW... FOR ME...
...IT'S LIKE I'M SEEING IT LONG AGO AND FAR AWAY. I CAN'T GET INTO IT.
I GUESS THERE'S NO PLACE FOR ME IN THE NORMAL WORLD ANY MORE.

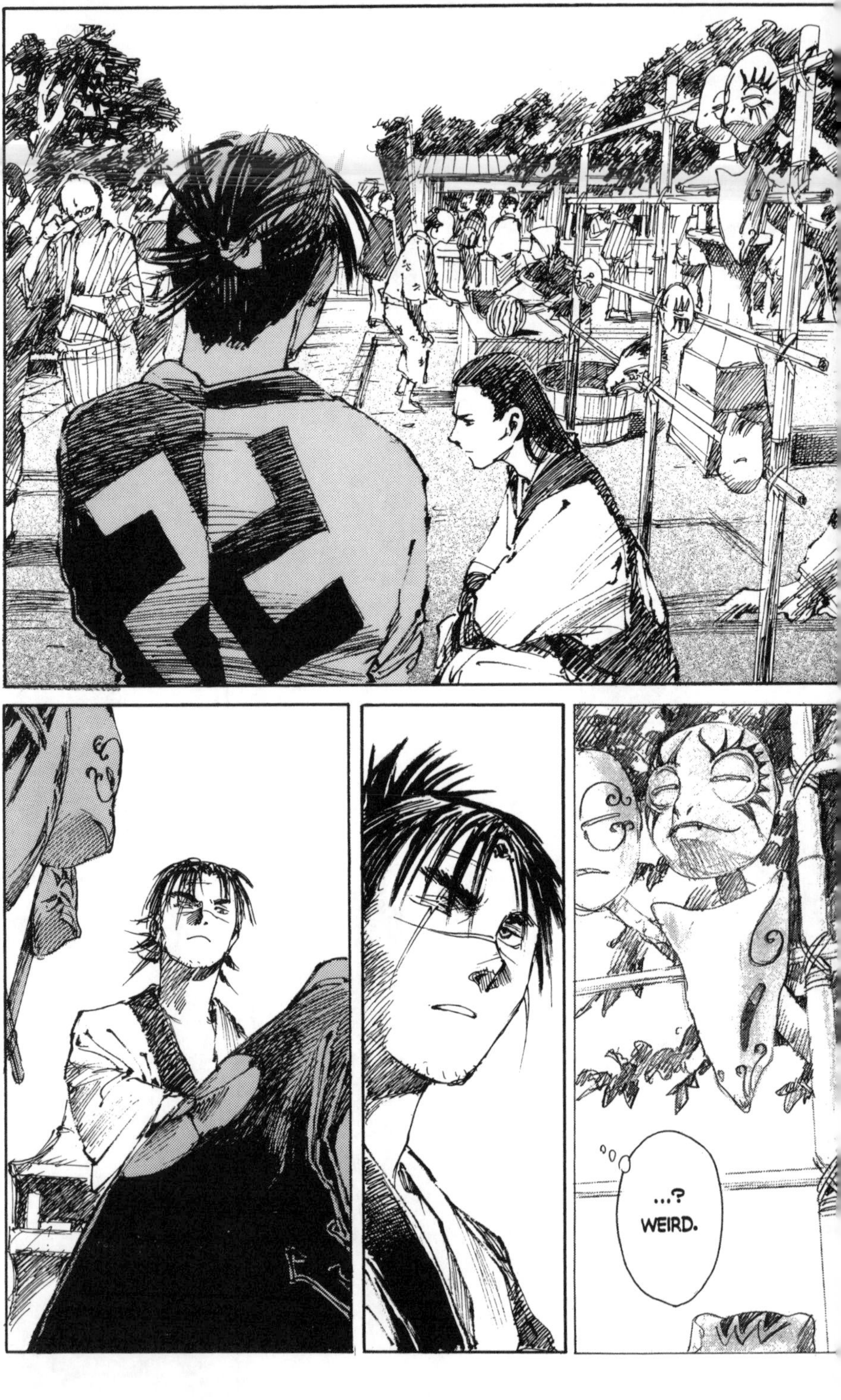
...?
WEIRD.

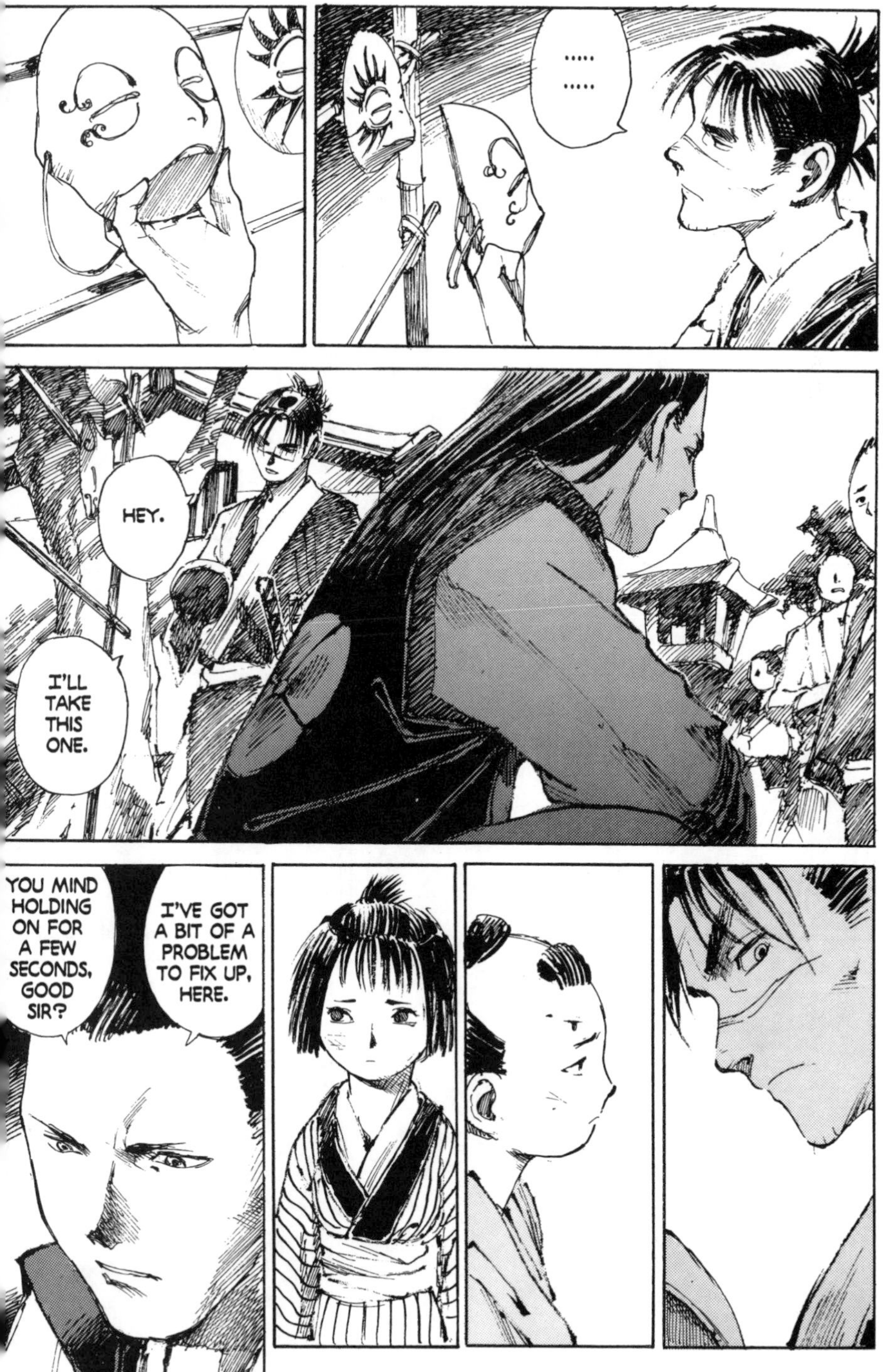
......
......
HEY.
I'LL TAKE THIS ONE.
YOU MIND HOLDING ON FOR A FEW SECONDS, GOOD SIR?
I'VE GOT A BIT OF A PROBLEM TO FIX UP, HERE.

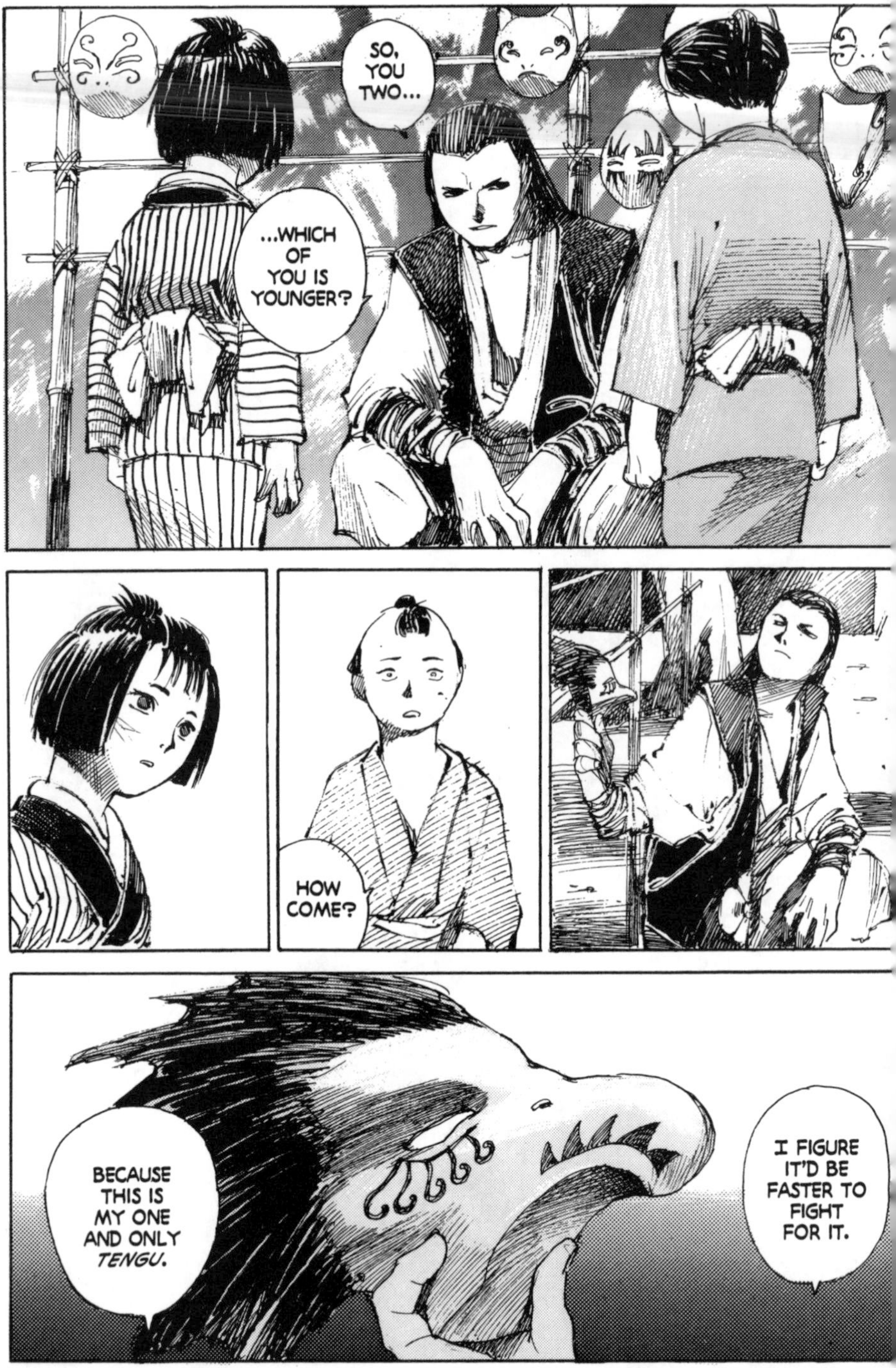
SO, YOU TWO...
...WHICH OF YOU IS YOUNGER?
HOW COME?
BECAUSE THIS IS MY ONE AND ONLY *TENGU*.
I FIGURE IT'D BE FASTER TO FIGHT FOR IT.

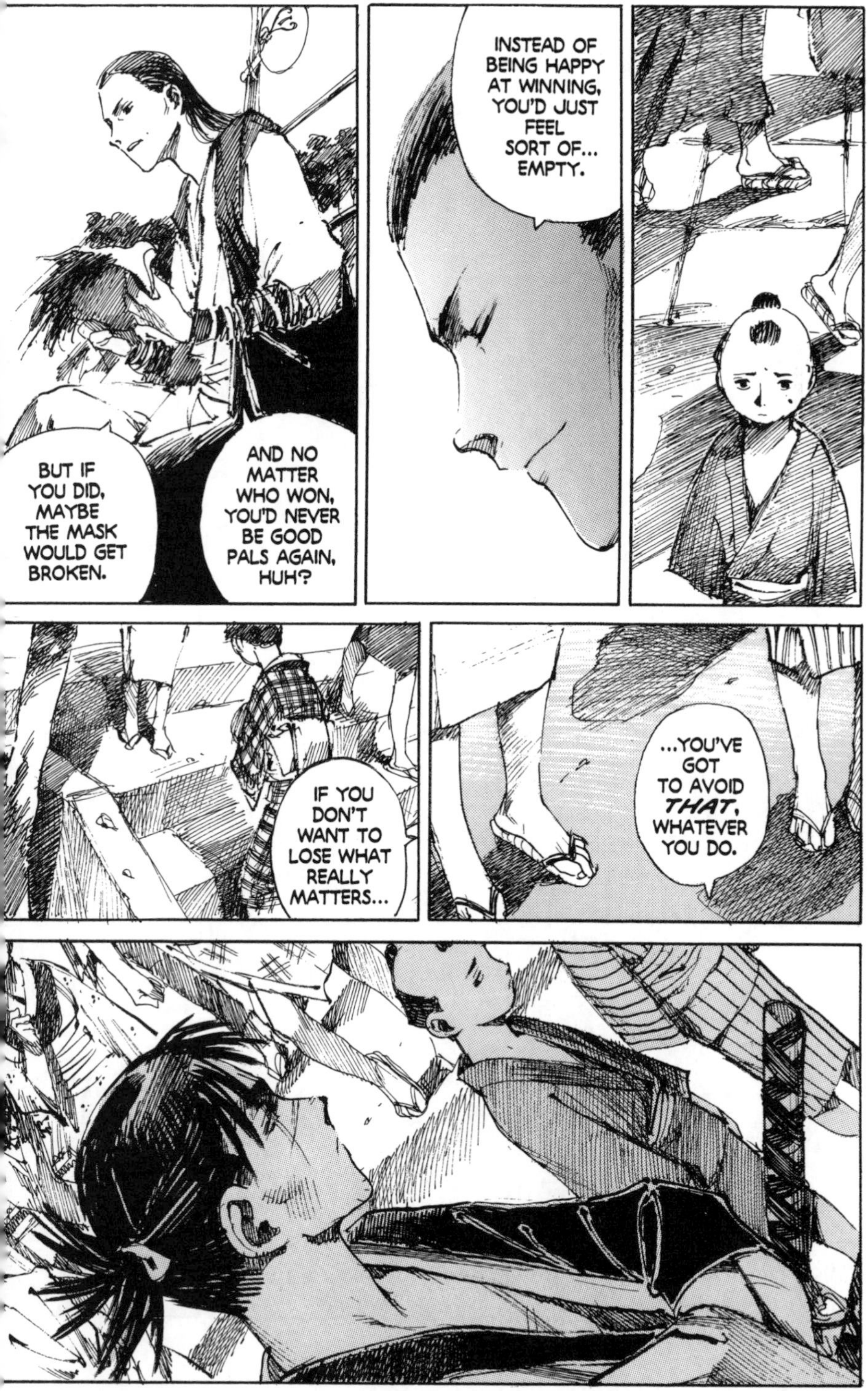
BUT IF YOU DID, MAYBE THE MASK WOULD GET BROKEN.
AND NO MATTER WHO WON, YOU'D NEVER BE GOOD PALS AGAIN, HUH?
INSTEAD OF BEING HAPPY AT WINNING, YOU'D JUST FEEL SORT OF... EMPTY.
IF YOU DON'T WANT TO LOSE WHAT REALLY MATTERS...
...YOU'VE GOT TO AVOID *THAT*, WHATEVER YOU DO.

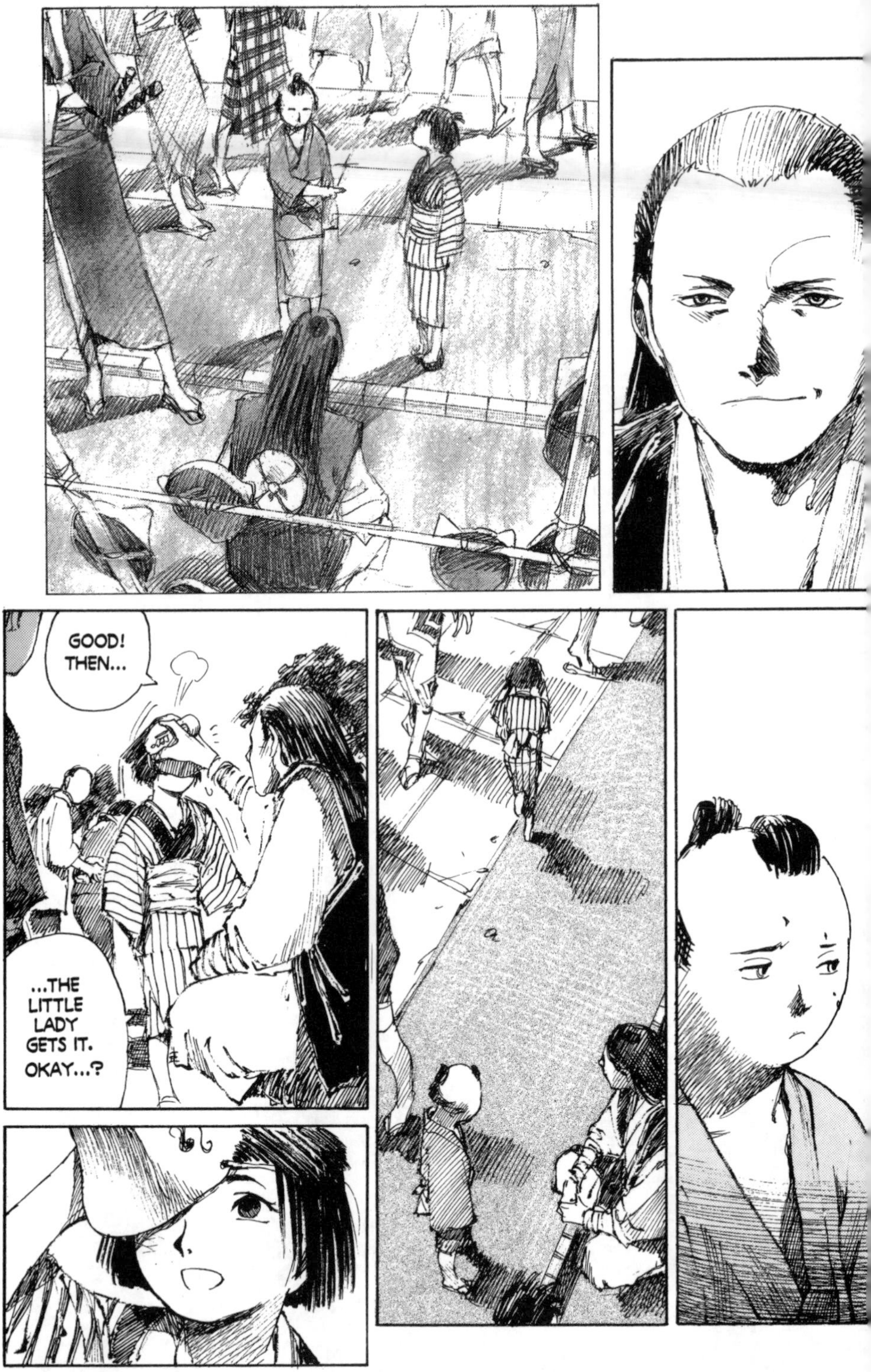
GOOD! THEN...
...THE LITTLE LADY GETS IT. OKAY...?

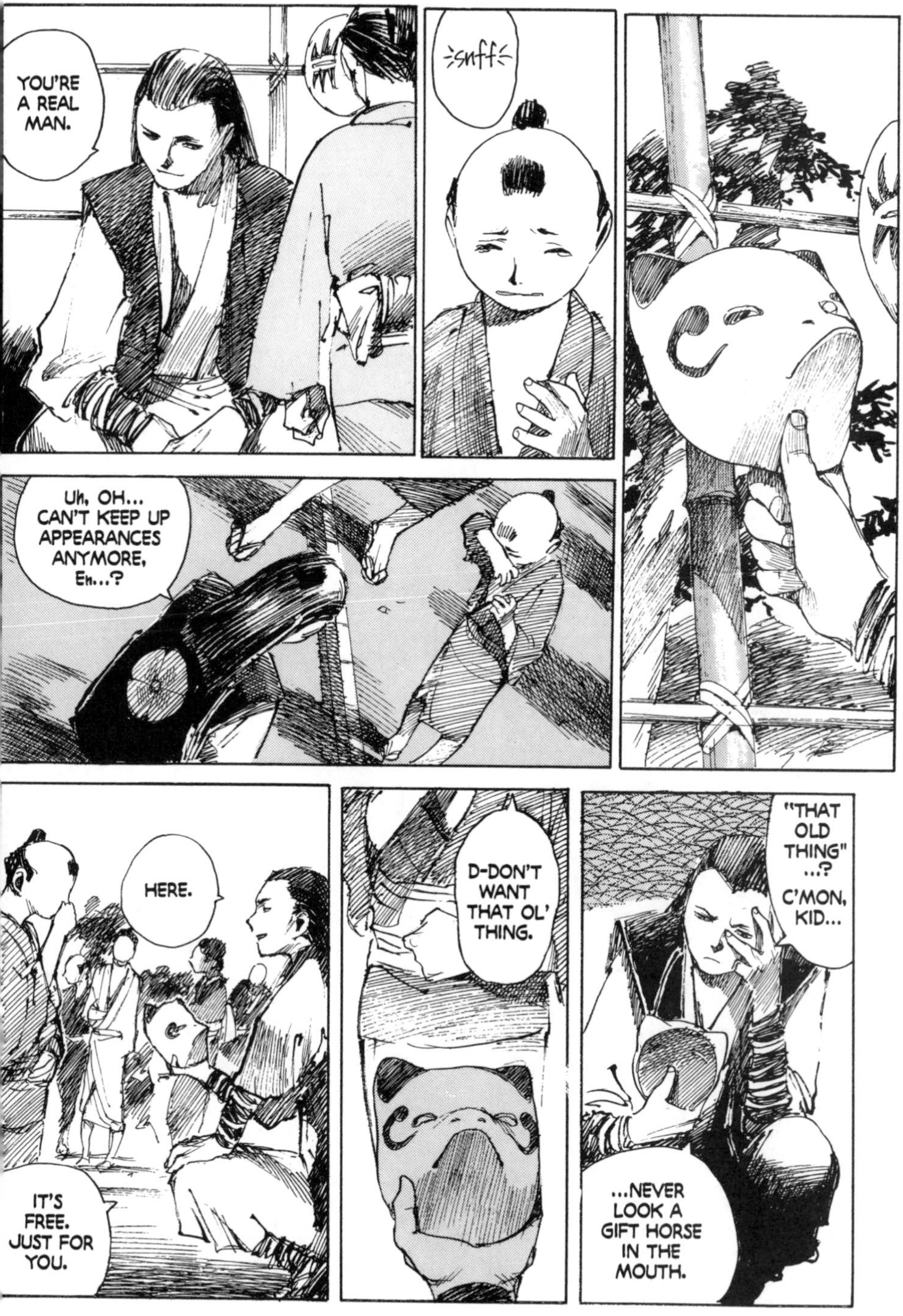
YOU'RE A REAL MAN.
snff
Uh, OH... CAN'T KEEP UP APPEARANCES ANYMORE, Eh...?
HERE.
IT'S FREE. JUST FOR YOU.
D-DON'T WANT THAT OL' THING.
"THAT OLD THING" ...? C'MON, KID...
...NEVER LOOK A GIFT HORSE IN THE MOUTH.

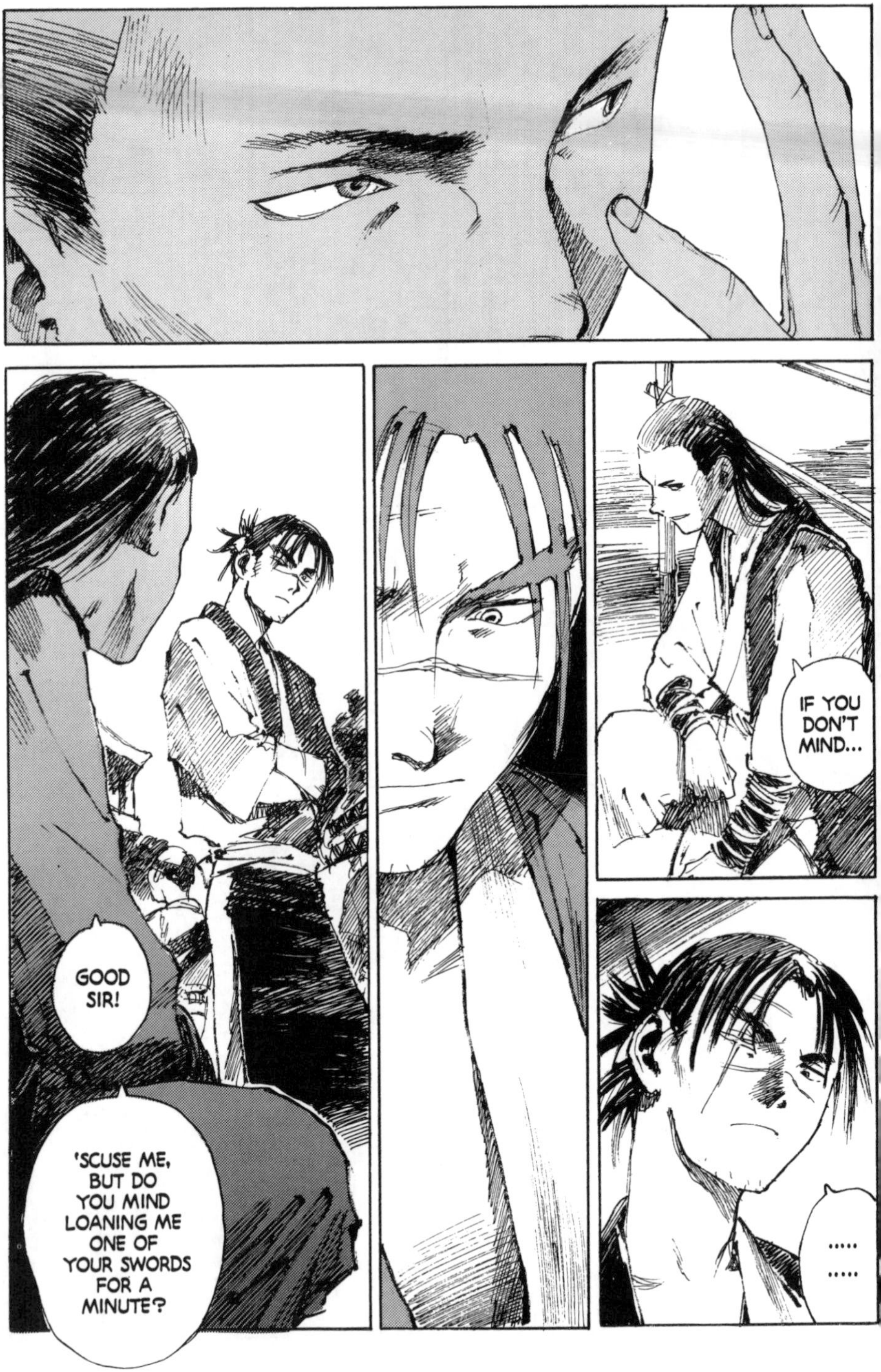
GOOD SIR!
'SCUSE ME, BUT DO YOU MIND LOANING ME ONE OF YOUR SWORDS FOR A MINUTE?
IF YOU DON'T MIND...
.....
.....

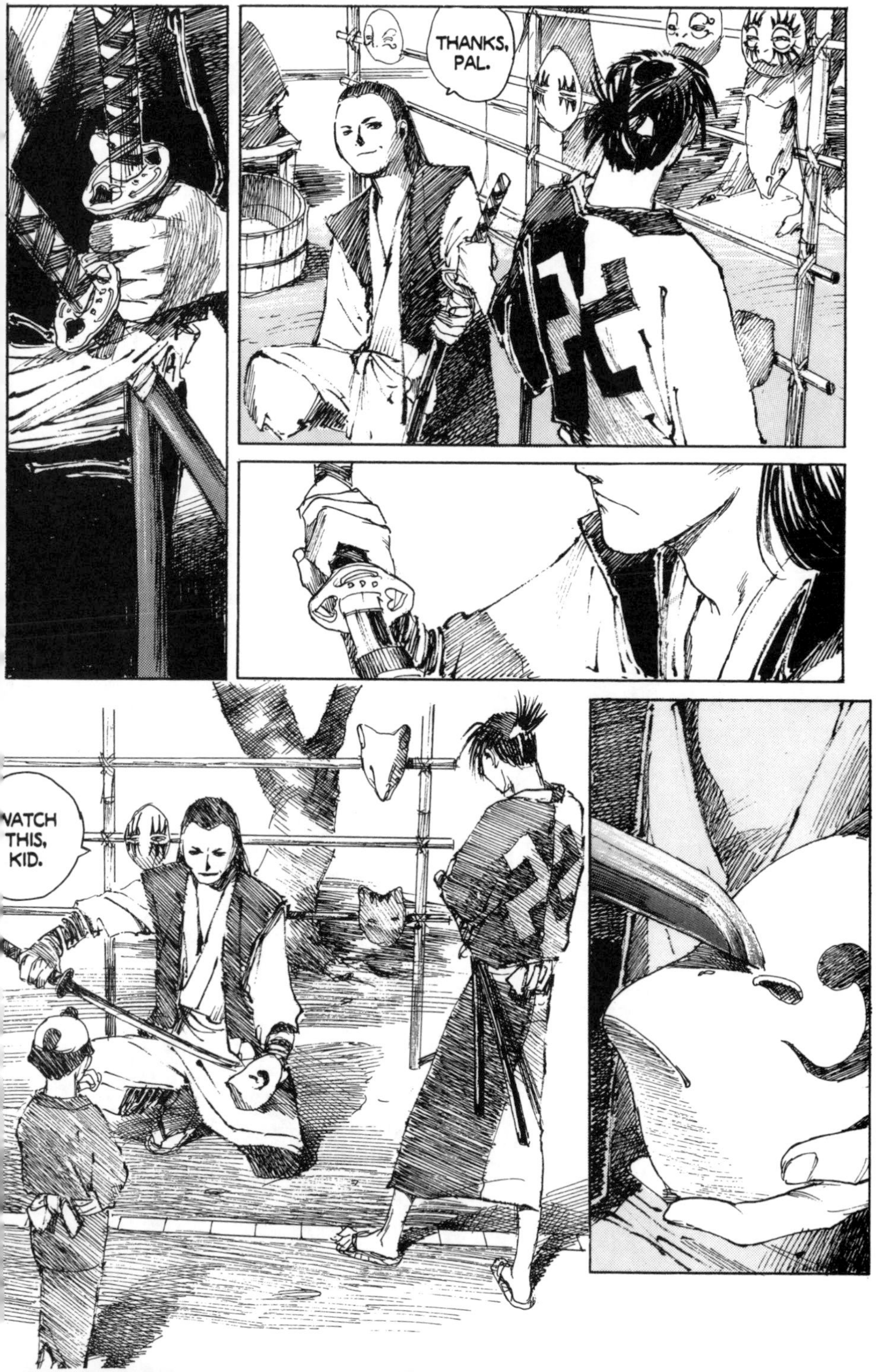
THANKS, PAL.
WATCH THIS, KID.

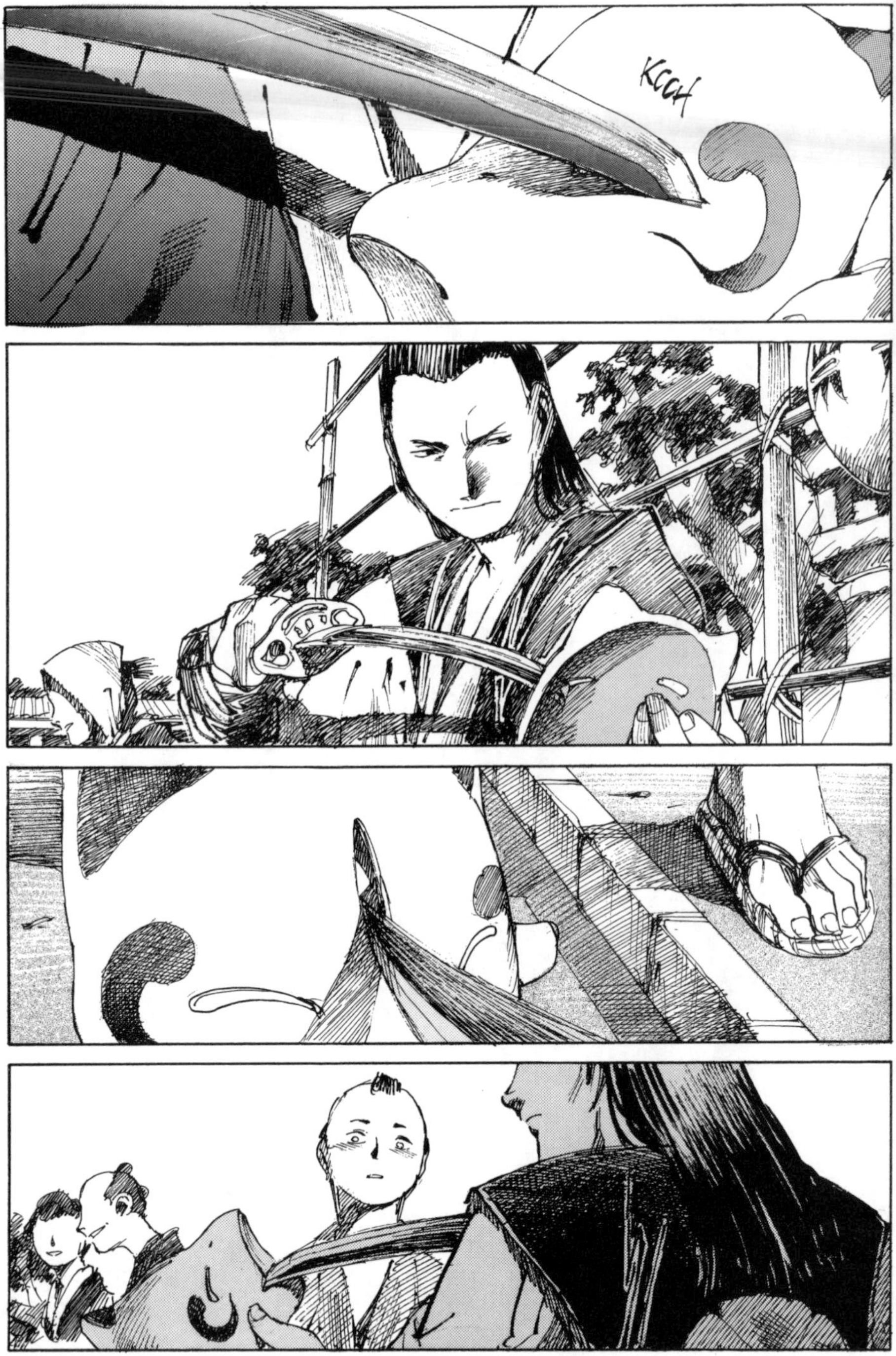
Kcch

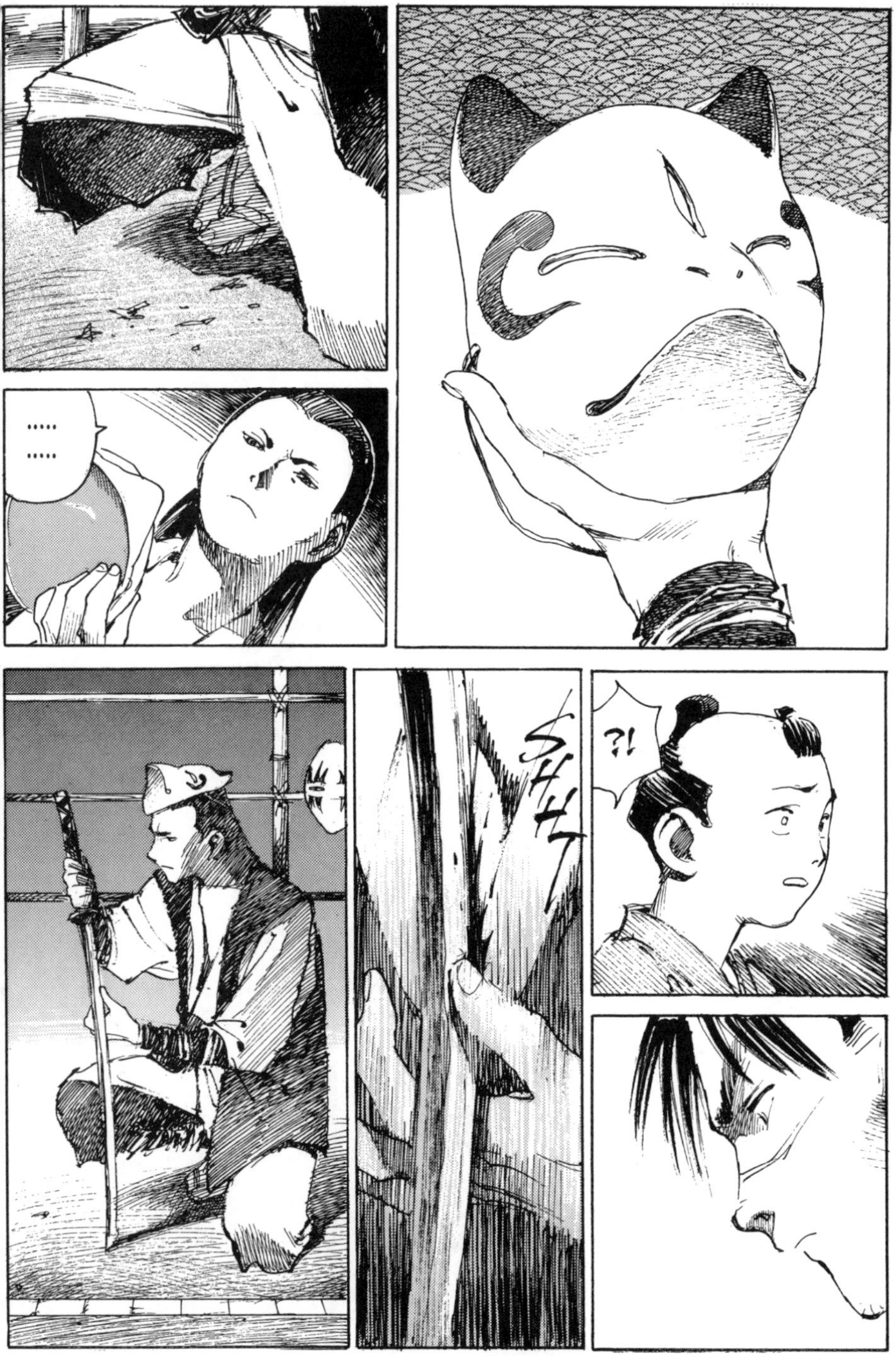
......
......
SHHT
?!

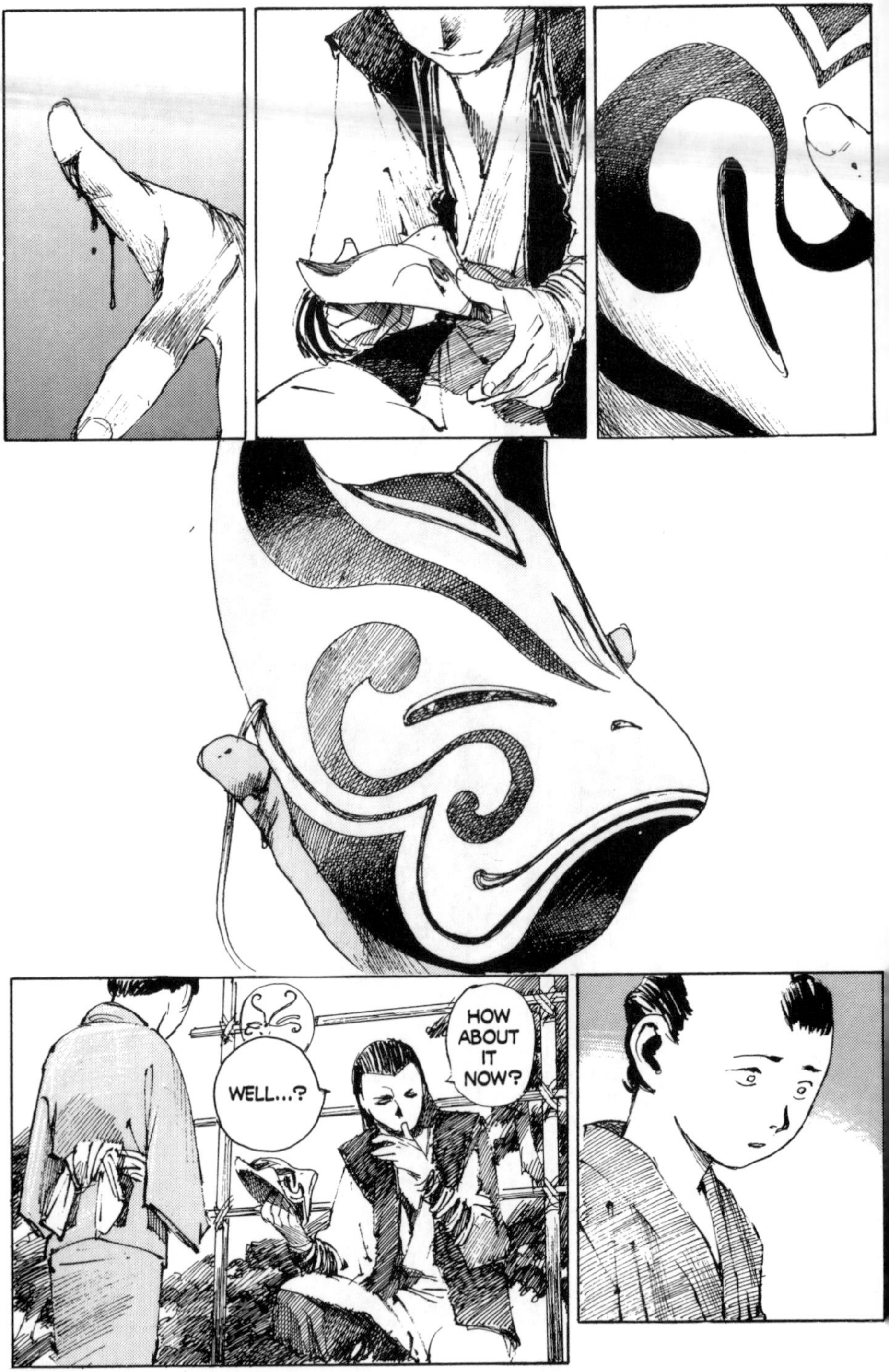
WELL...?
HOW ABOUT IT NOW?

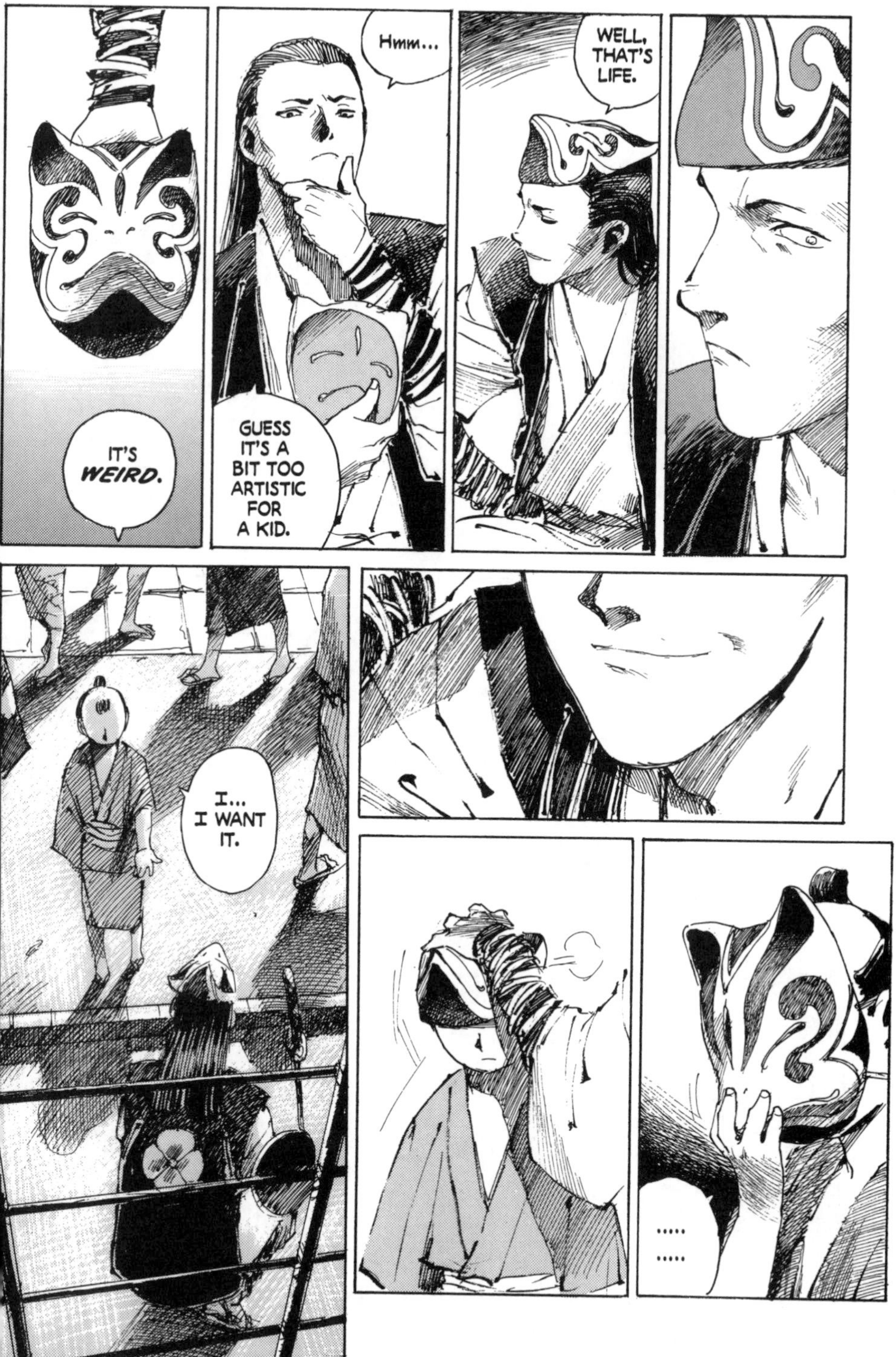
IT'S WEIRD.
Hmm...
GUESS IT'S A BIT TOO ARTISTIC FOR A KID.
WELL, THAT'S LIFE.
I... I WANT IT.
.....
.....

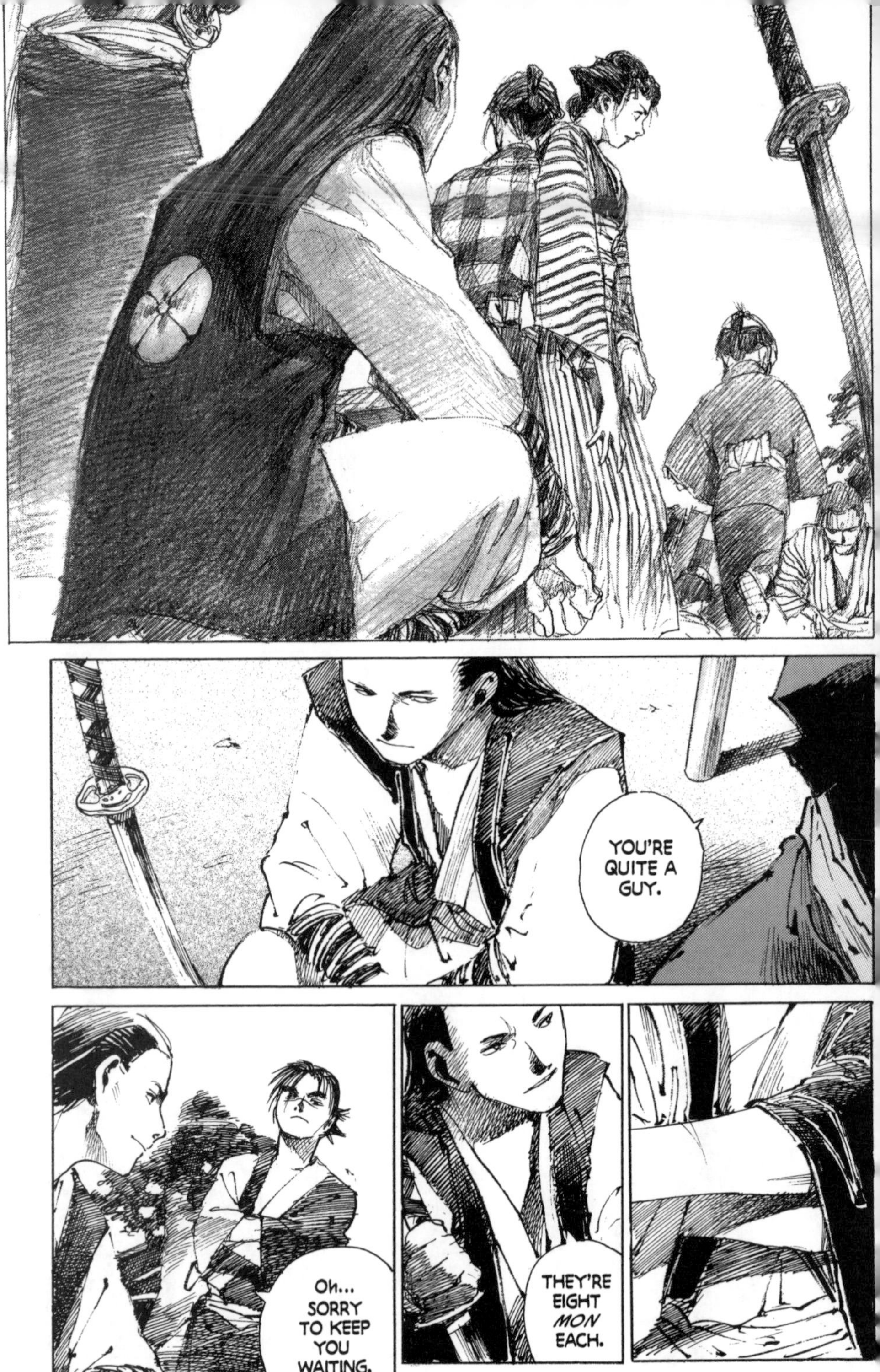
YOU'RE QUITE A GUY.
Oh... SORRY TO KEEP YOU WAITING.
THEY'RE EIGHT *MON* EACH.

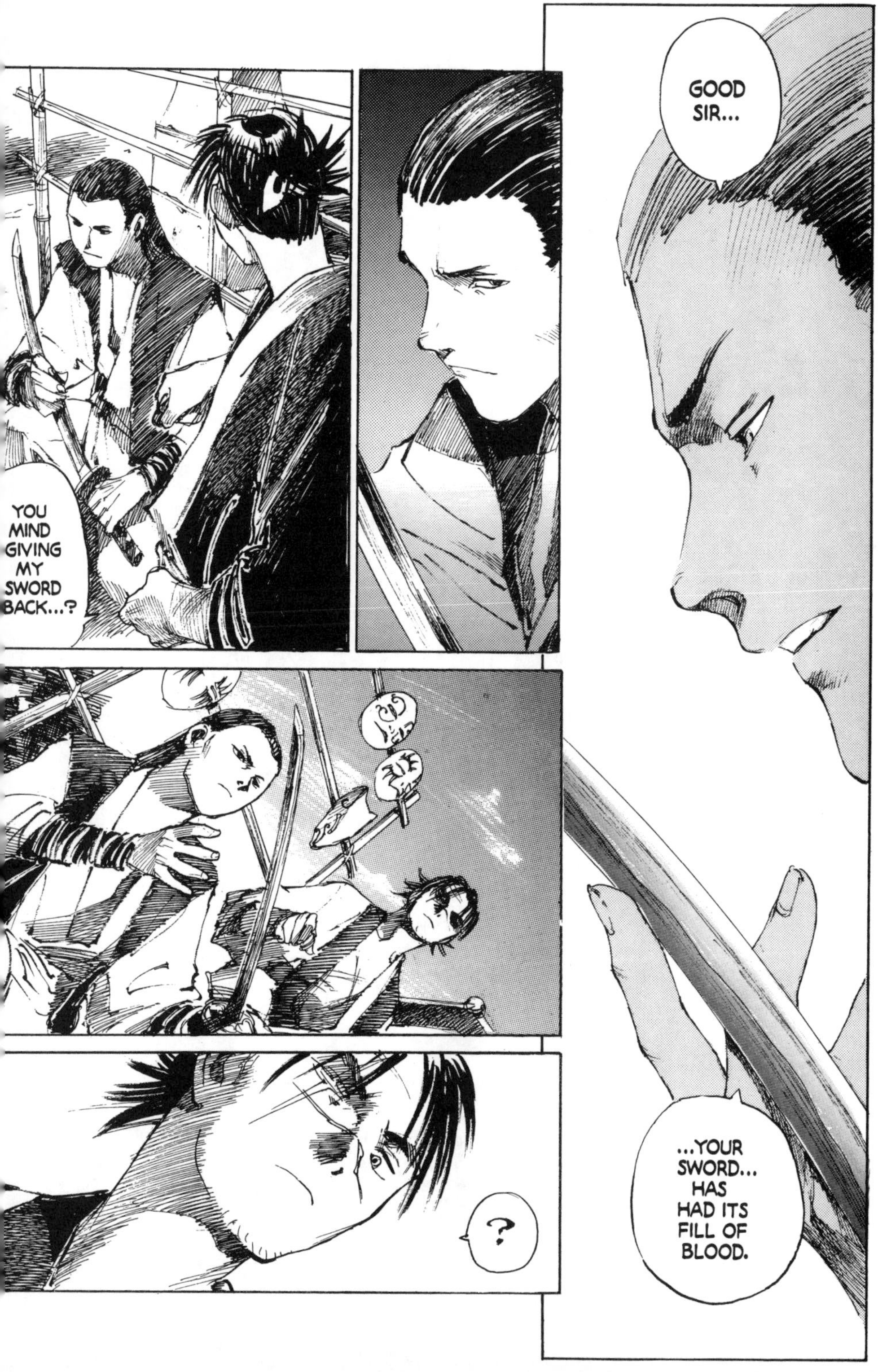
YOU MIND GIVING MY SWORD BACK...?
?
GOOD SIR...
...YOUR SWORD... HAS HAD ITS FILL OF BLOOD.

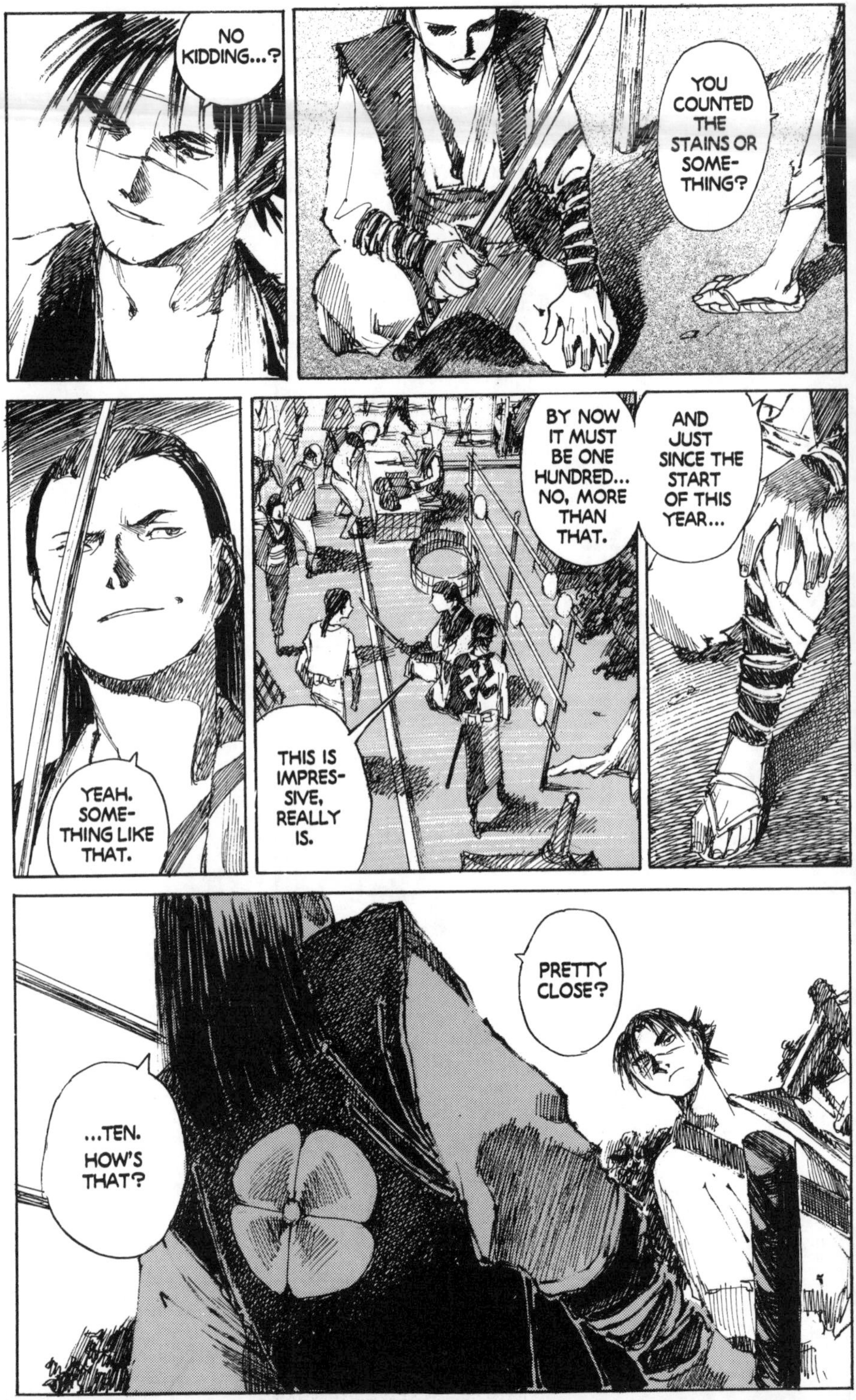
NO KIDDING...?
YOU COUNTED THE STAINS OR SOME-THING?
YEAH. SOME-THING LIKE THAT.
THIS IS IMPRES-SIVE, REALLY IS.
BY NOW IT MUST BE ONE HUNDRED... NO, MORE THAN THAT.
AND JUST SINCE THE START OF THIS YEAR...
...TEN. HOW'S THAT?
PRETTY CLOSE?

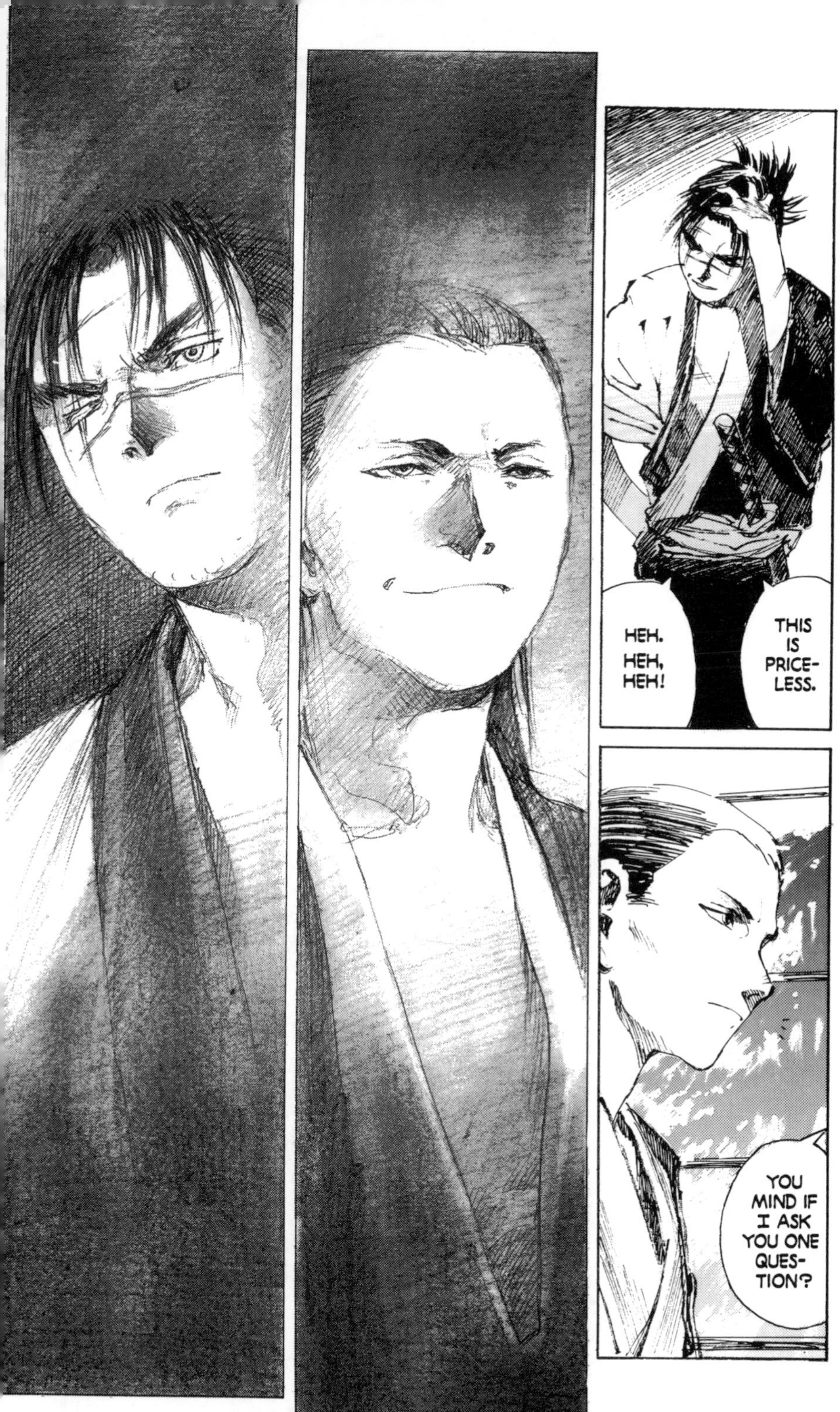
HEH. HEH, HEH!
THIS IS PRICE-LESS.
YOU MIND IF I ASK YOU ONE QUES-TION?

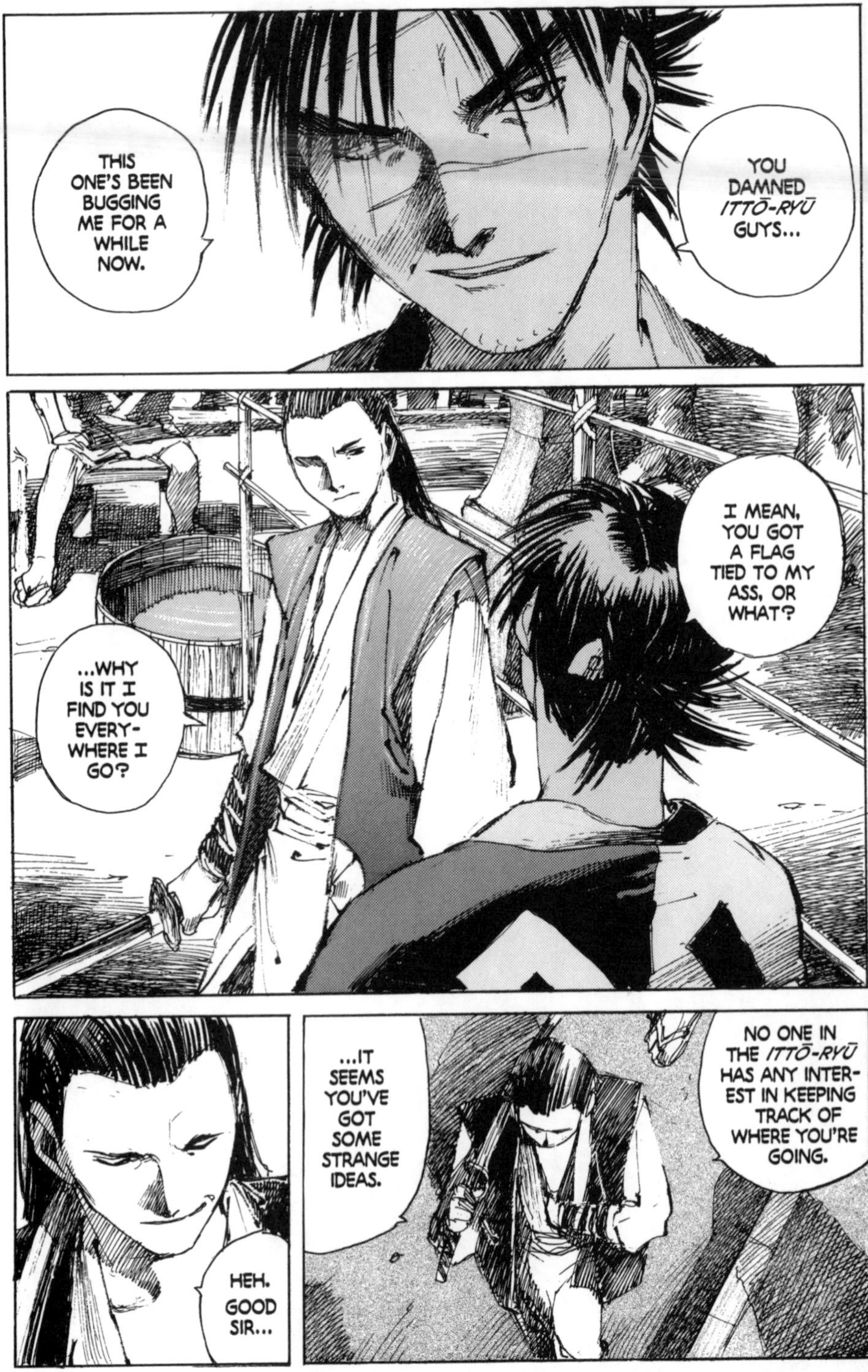
THIS ONE'S BEEN BUGGING ME FOR A WHILE NOW.
YOU DAMNED *ITTŌ-RYŪ* GUYS...
...WHY IS IT I FIND YOU EVERY-WHERE I GO?
I MEAN, YOU GOT A FLAG TIED TO MY ASS, OR WHAT?
HEH. GOOD SIR...
...IT SEEMS YOU'VE GOT SOME STRANGE IDEAS.
NO ONE IN THE *ITTŌ-RYŪ* HAS ANY INTER-EST IN KEEPING TRACK OF WHERE YOU'RE GOING.

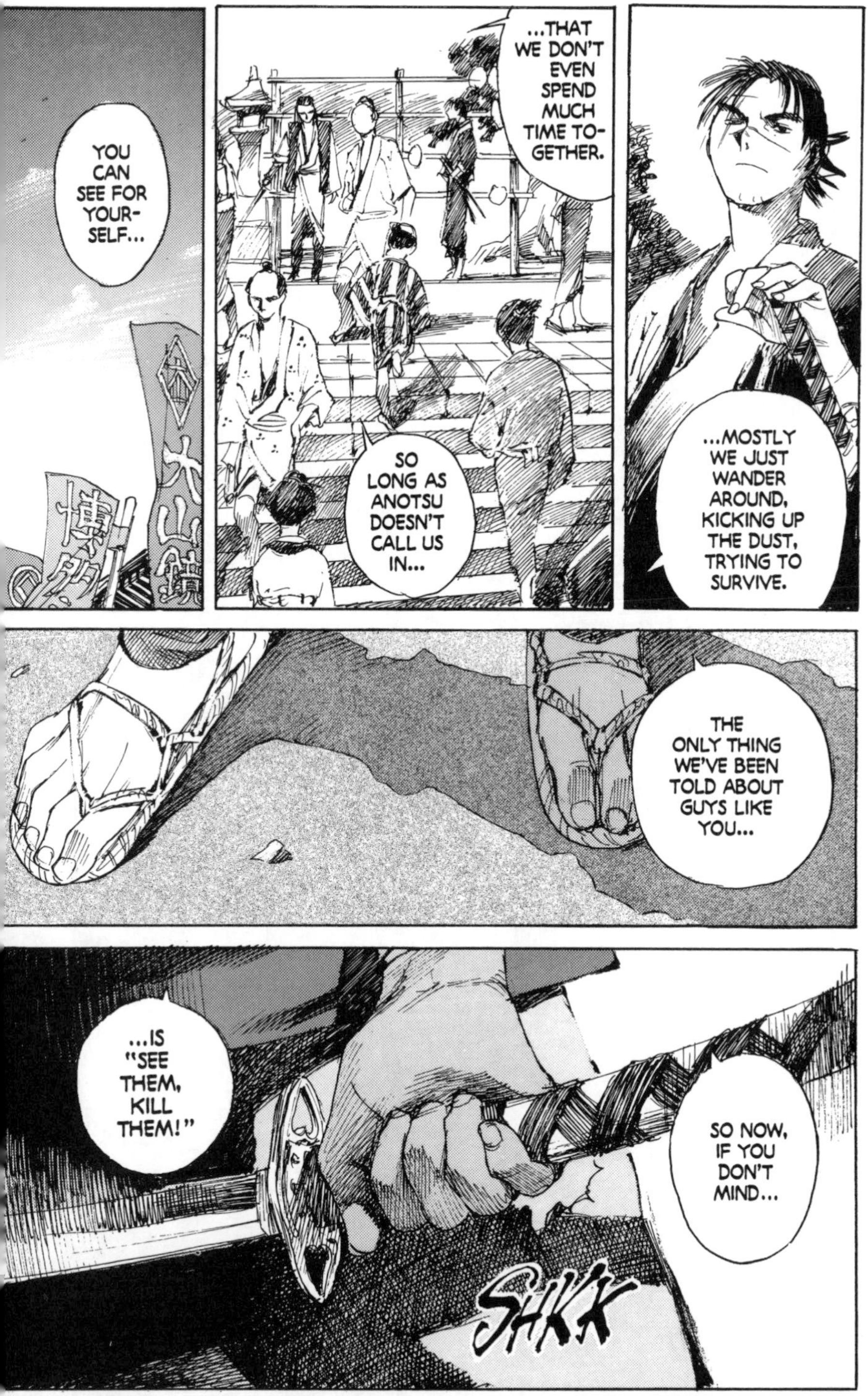
YOU CAN SEE FOR YOURSELF...
...THAT WE DON'T EVEN SPEND MUCH TIME TOGETHER.
SO LONG AS ANOTSU DOESN'T CALL US IN...
...MOSTLY WE JUST WANDER AROUND, KICKING UP THE DUST, TRYING TO SURVIVE.
THE ONLY THING WE'VE BEEN TOLD ABOUT GUYS LIKE YOU...
...IS "SEE THEM, KILL THEM!"
SO NOW, IF YOU DON'T MIND...
SHKK

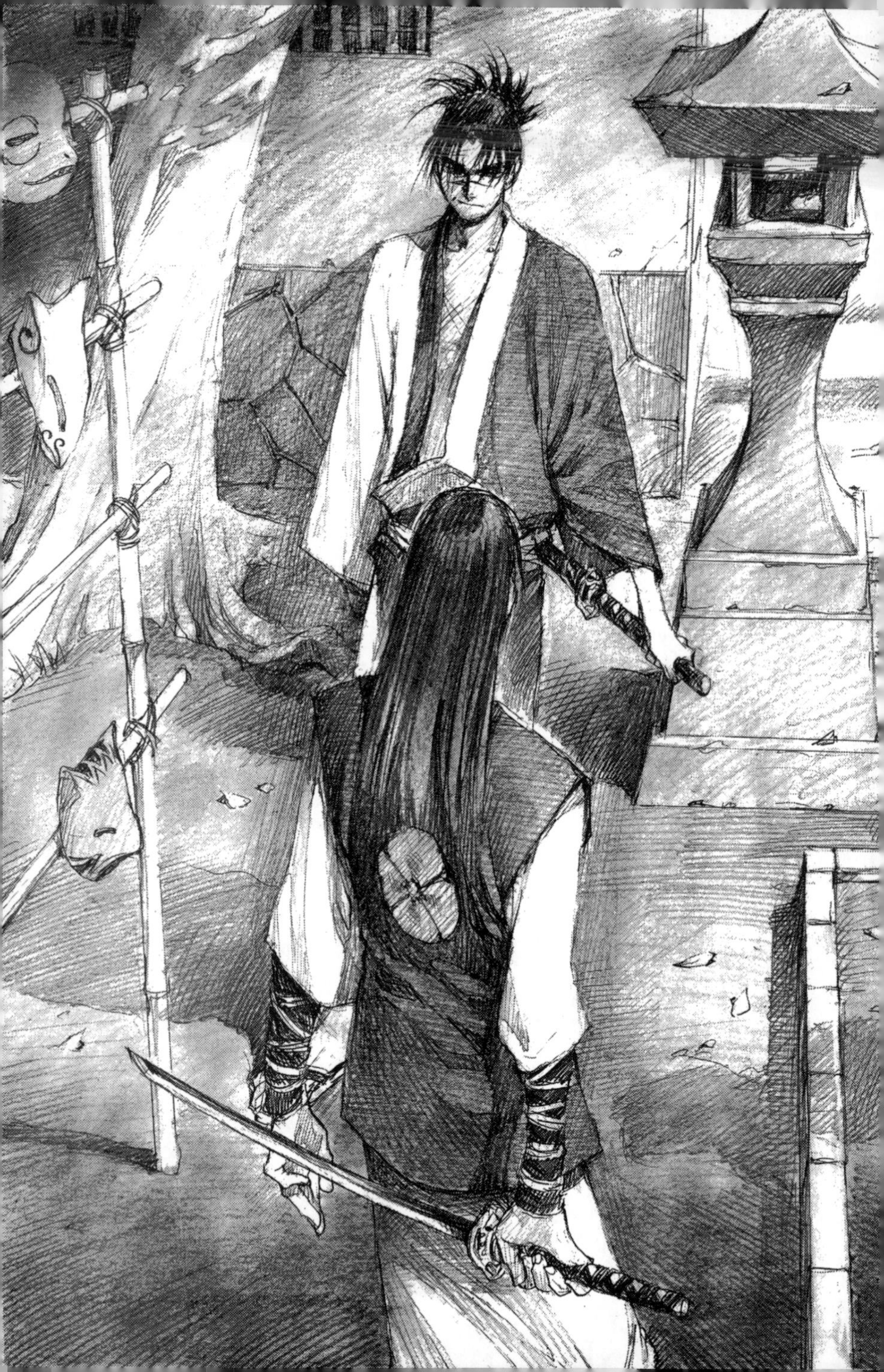

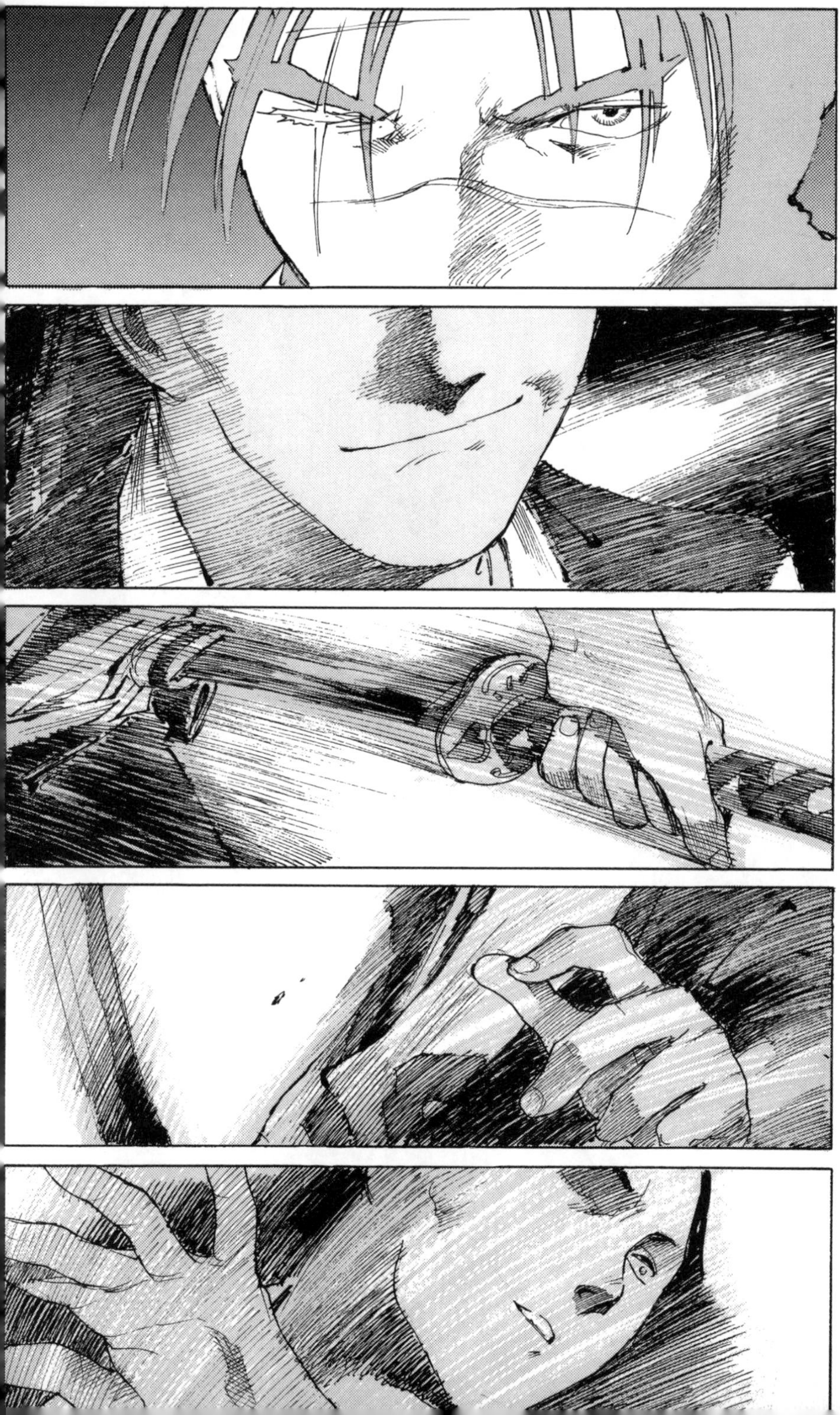

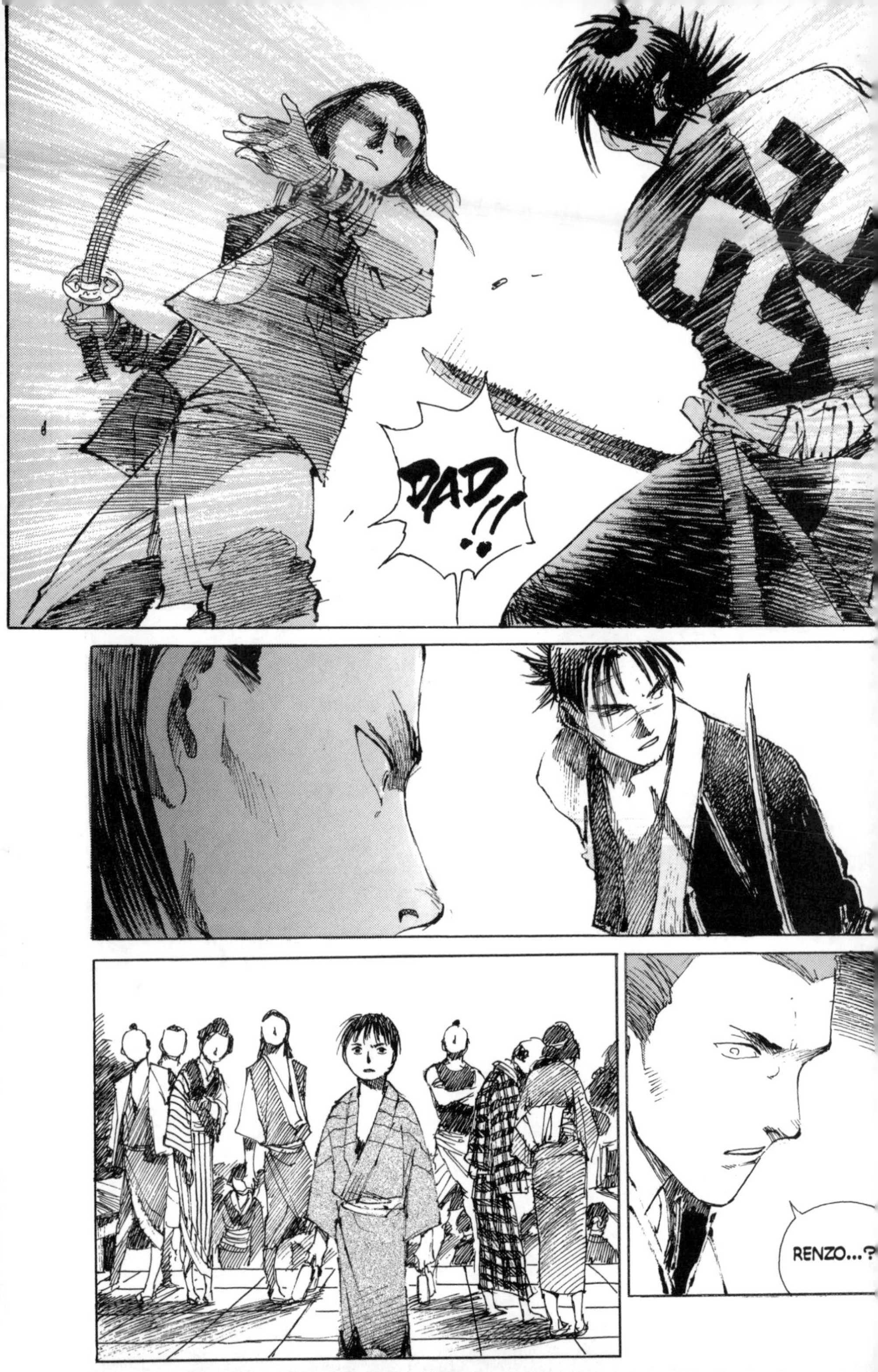
DAD!!
RENZO...?

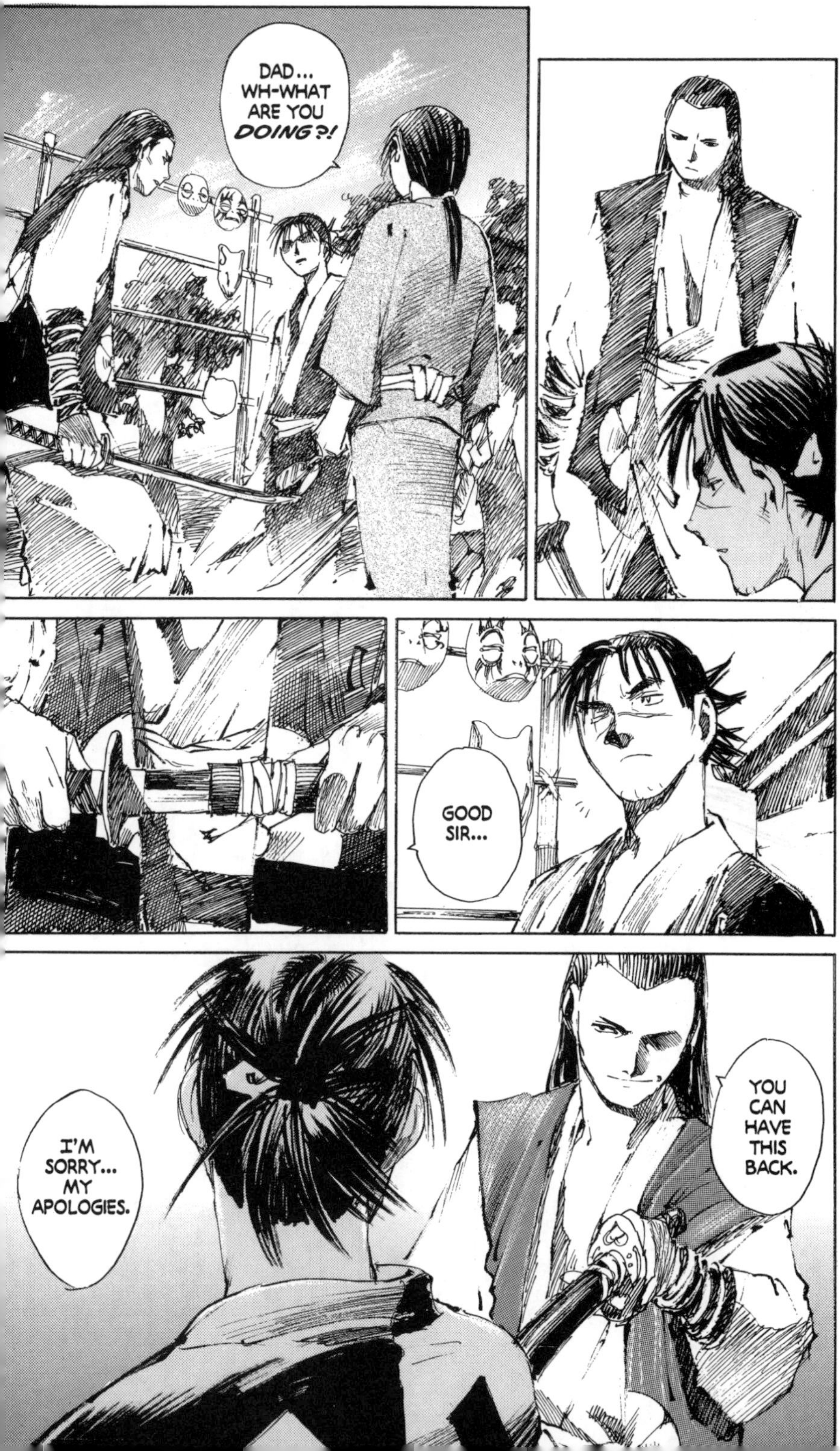
DAD... WH-WHAT ARE YOU *DOING?!*
GOOD SIR...
I'M SORRY... MY APOLOGIES.
YOU CAN HAVE THIS BACK.

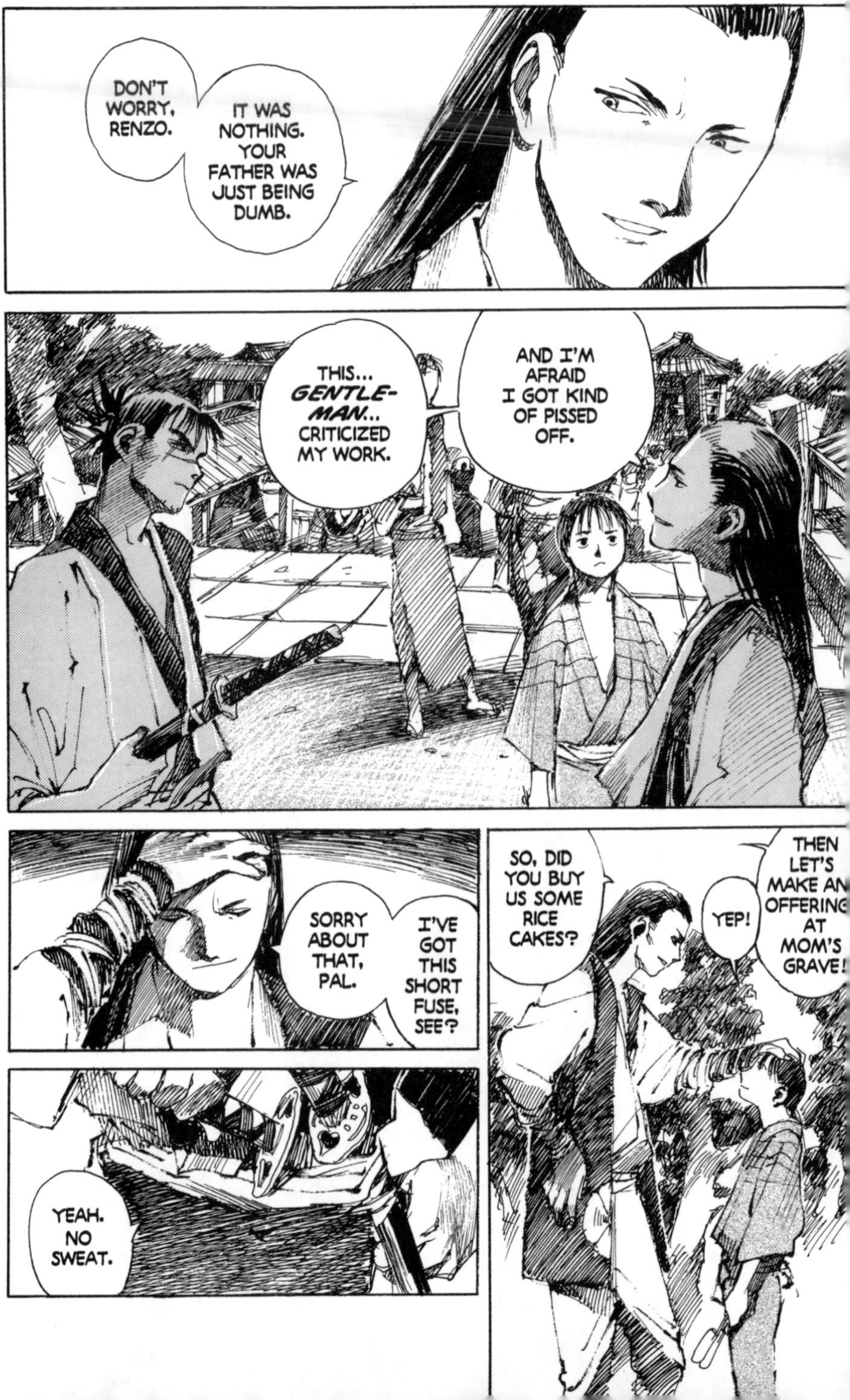
DON'T WORRY, RENZO.
IT WAS NOTHING. YOUR FATHER WAS JUST BEING DUMB.
THIS... GENTLE-MAN... CRITICIZED MY WORK.
AND I'M AFRAID I GOT KIND OF PISSED OFF.
SORRY ABOUT THAT, PAL.
I'VE GOT THIS SHORT FUSE, SEE?
YEAH. NO SWEAT.
SO, DID YOU BUY US SOME RICE CAKES?
YEP!
THEN LET'S MAKE AN OFFERING AT MOM'S GRAVE!

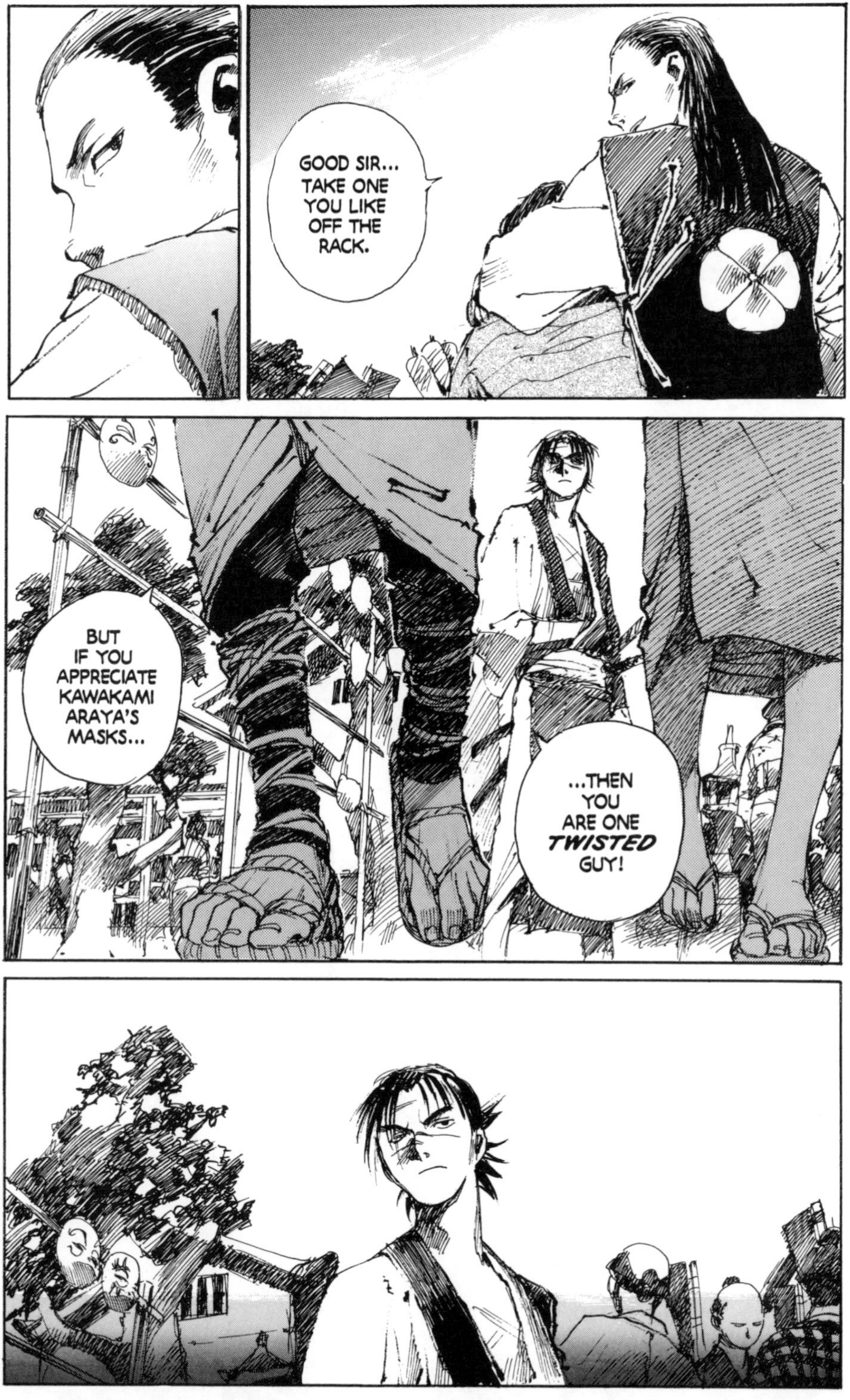
GOOD SIR... TAKE ONE YOU LIKE OFF THE RACK.
BUT IF YOU APPRECIATE KAWAKAMI ARAYA'S MASKS...
...THEN YOU ARE ONE *TWISTED* GUY!

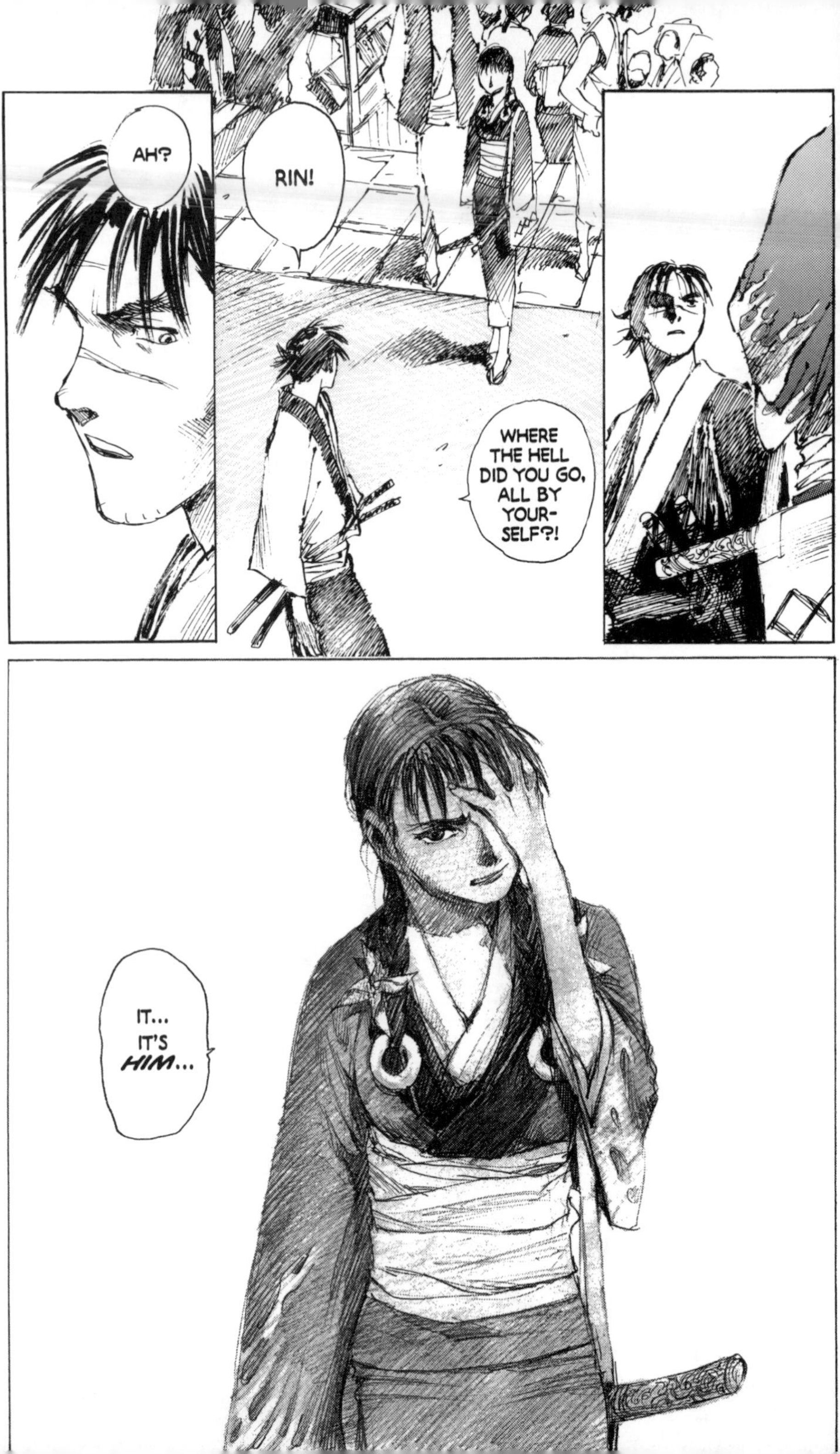
AH?
RIN!
WHERE THE HELL DID YOU GO, ALL BY YOUR-SELF?!
IT... IT'S *HIM*...

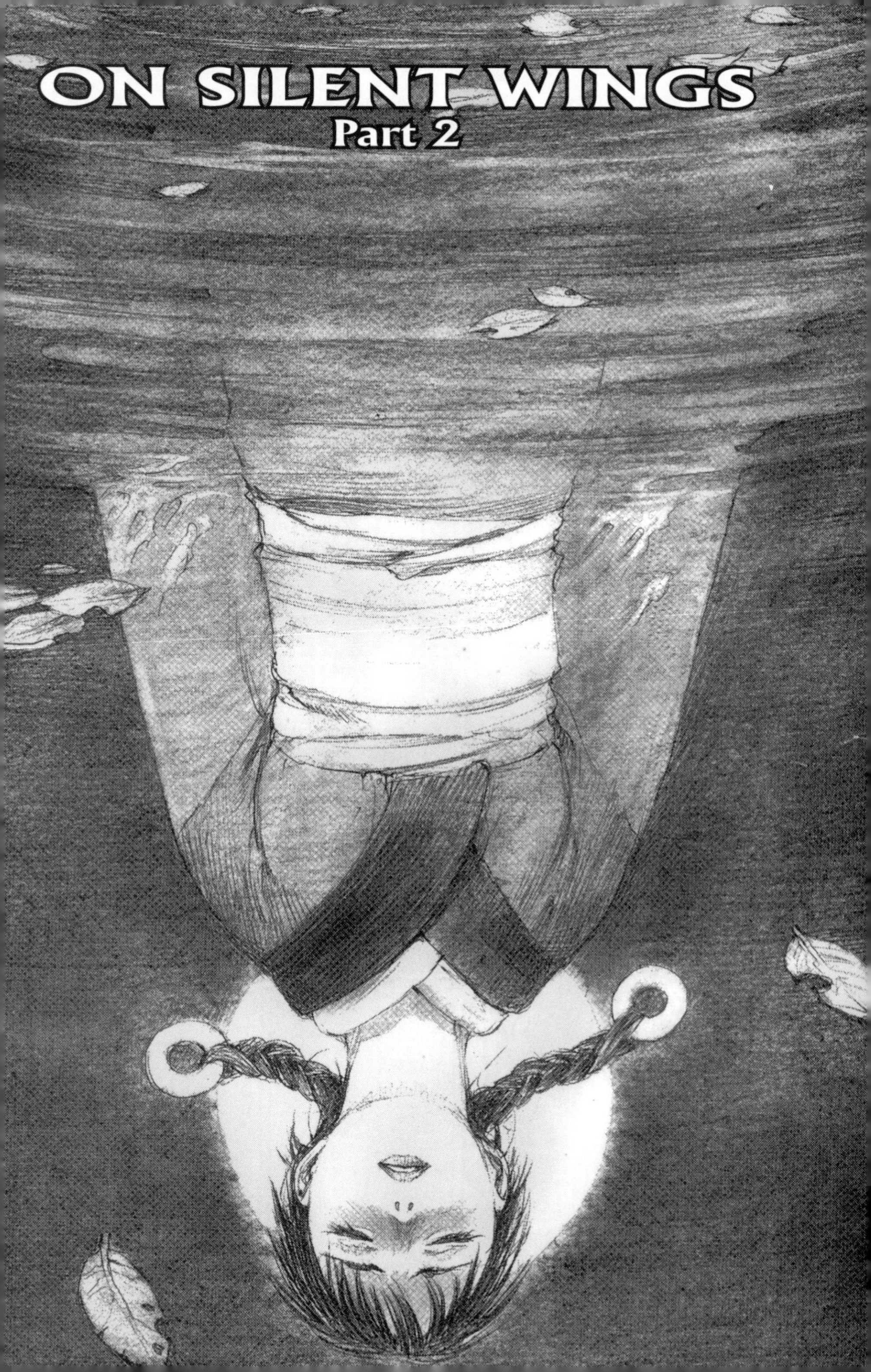
ON SILENT WINGS
Part 2

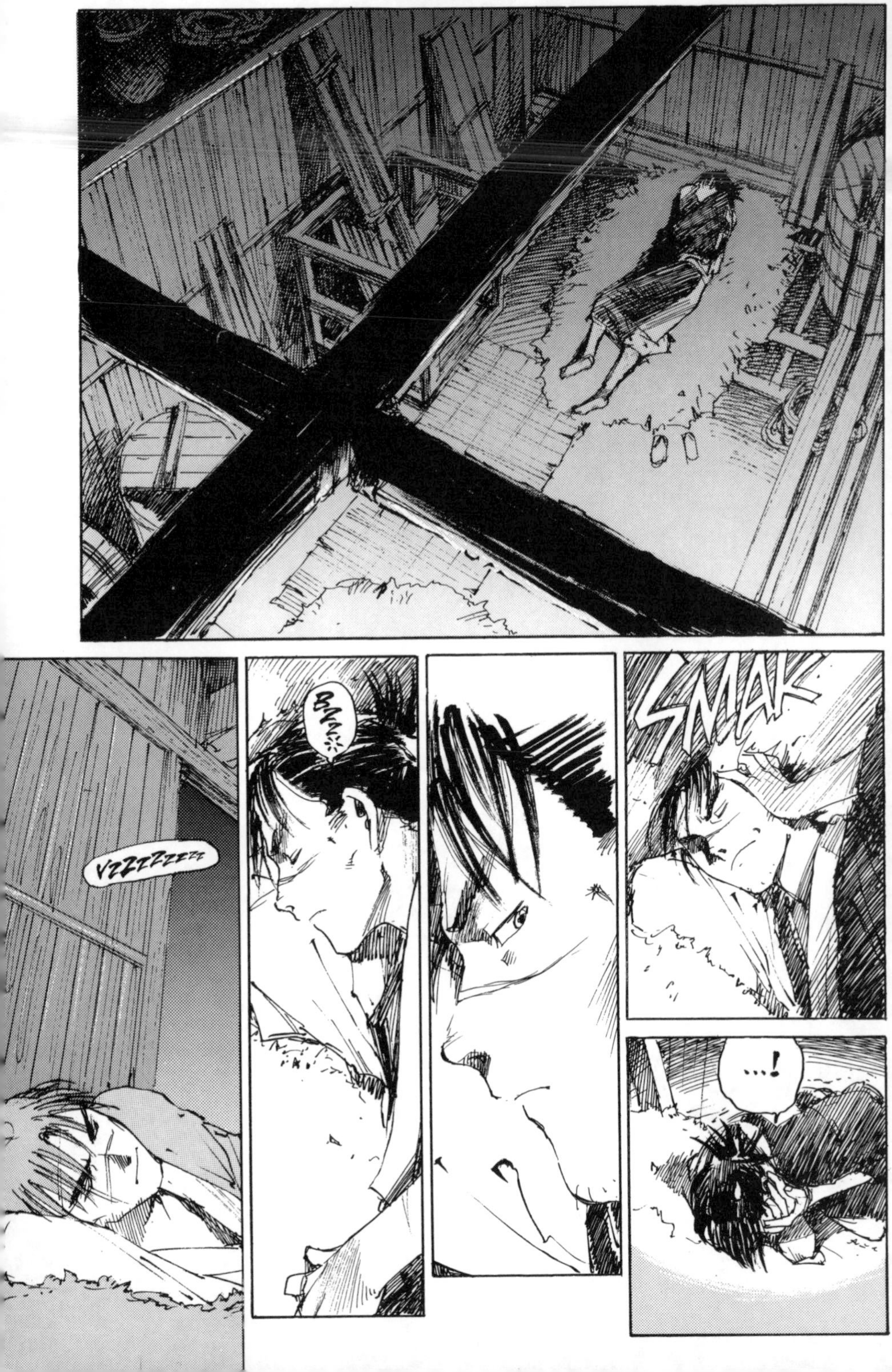
VZZZZZZZZ
BZZZ...
SMAK
...!

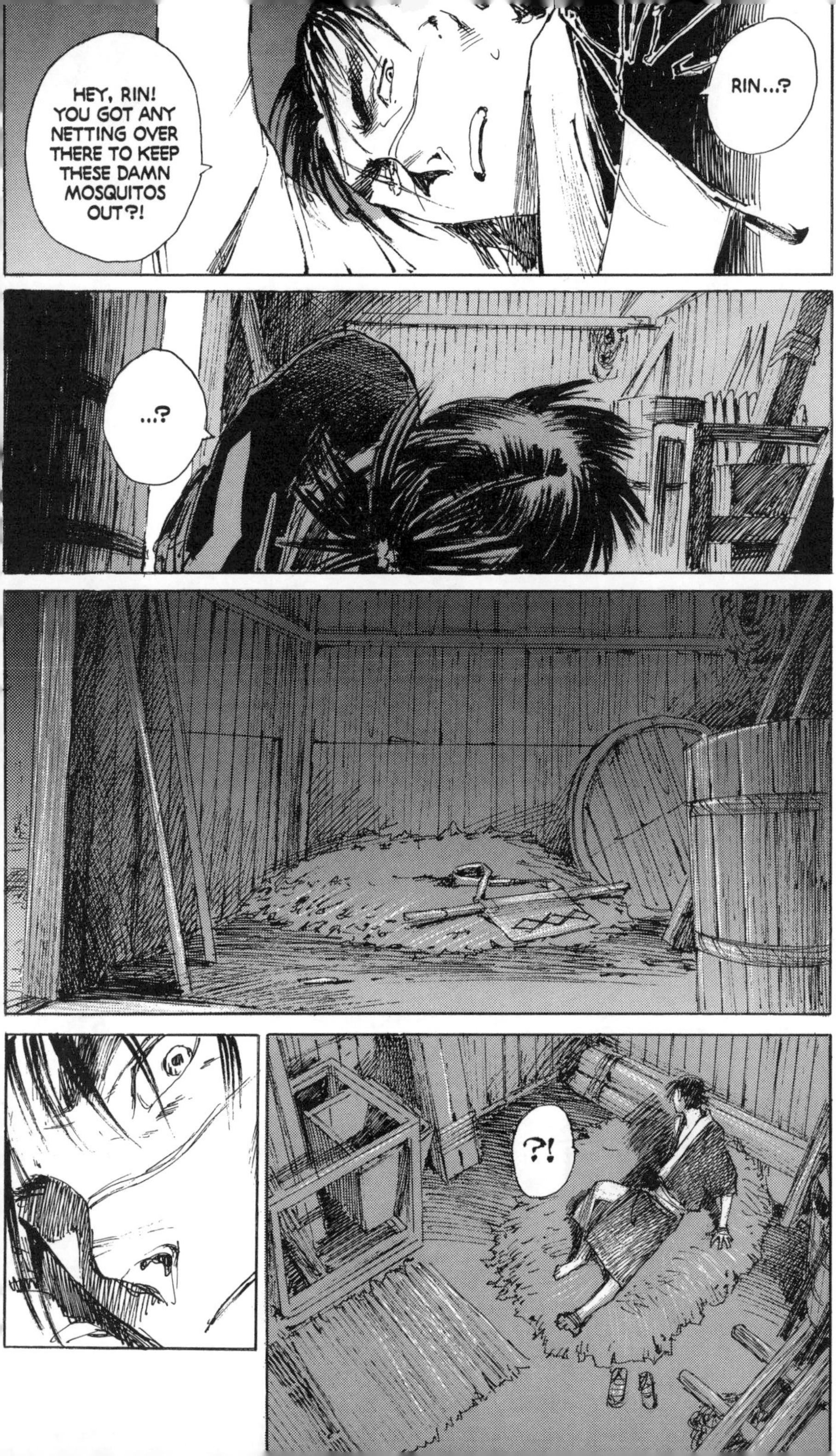
HEY, RIN! YOU GOT ANY NETTING OVER THERE TO KEEP THESE DAMN MOSQUITOS OUT?!
RIN...?
...?
?!

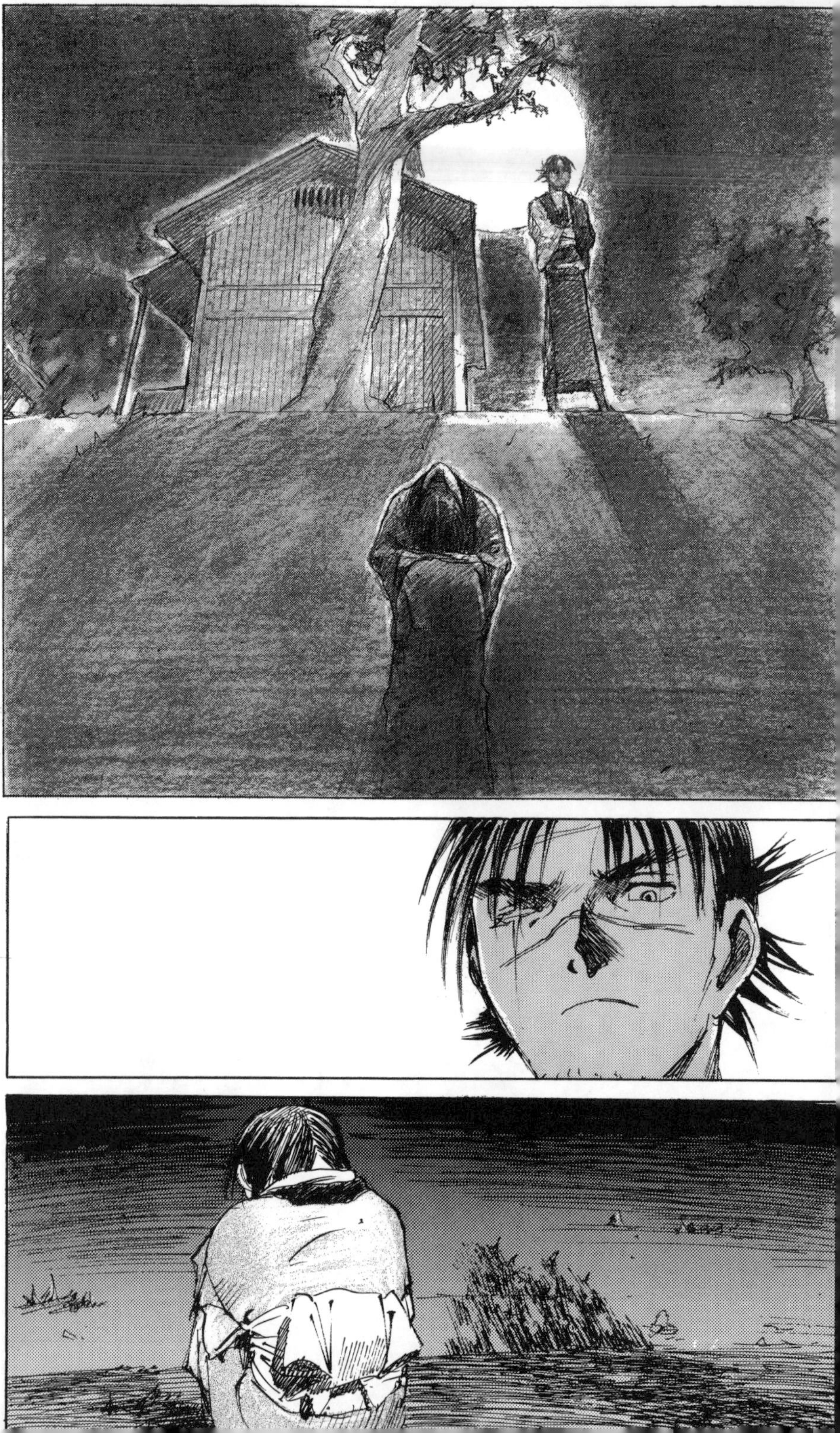

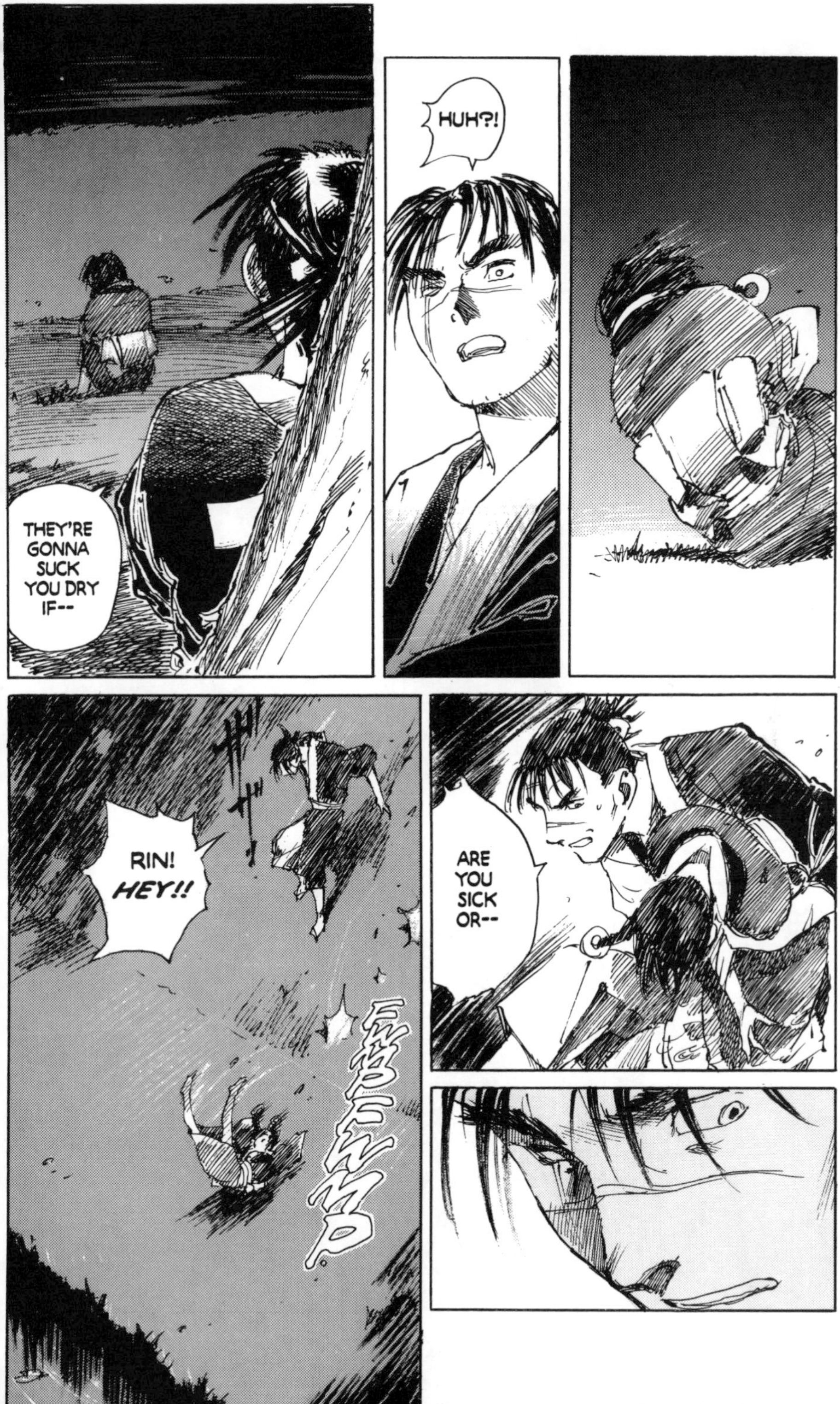
THEY'RE GONNA SUCK YOU DRY IF--
HUH?!
RIN! *HEY!!*
ARE YOU SICK OR--

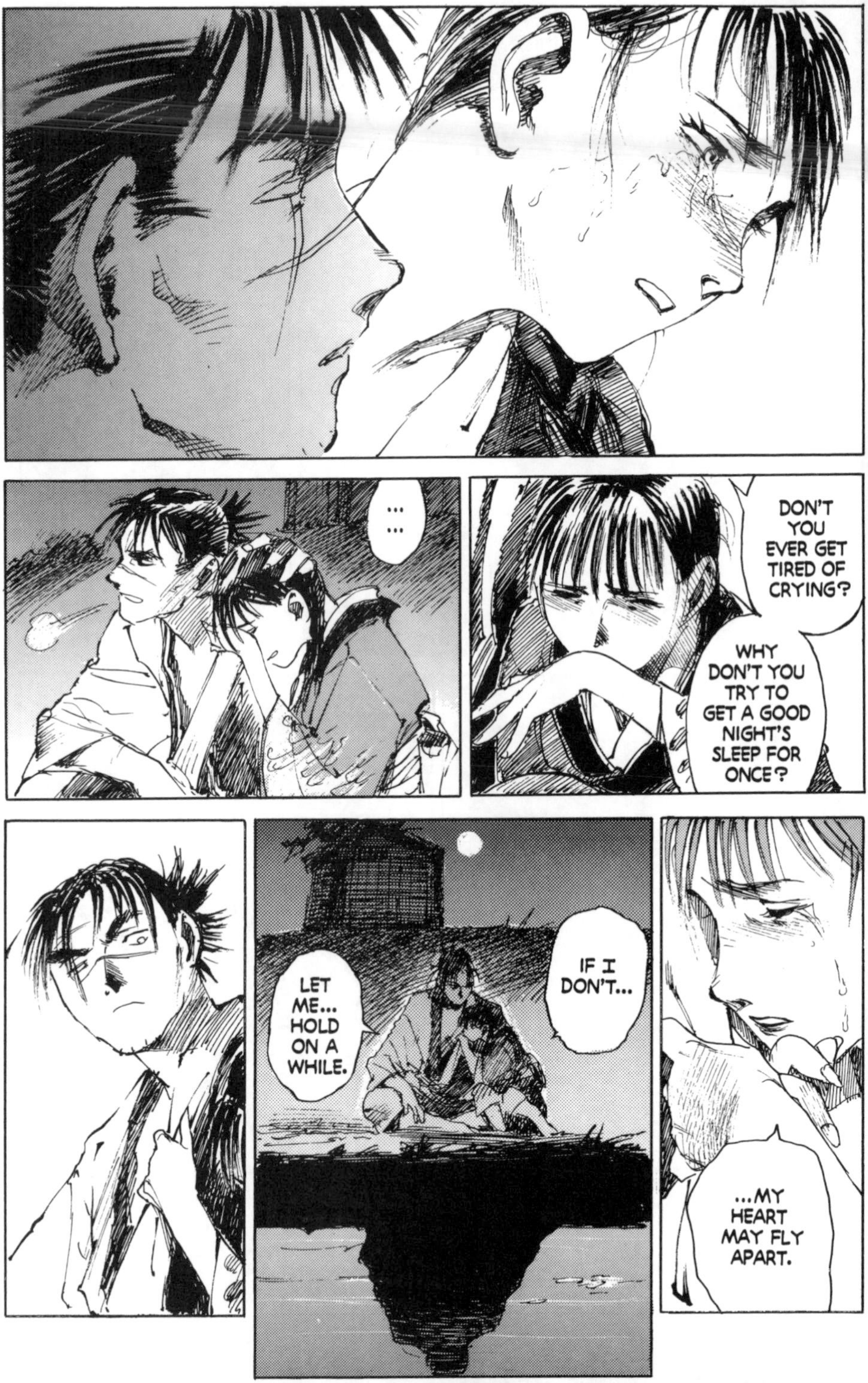
......
DON'T YOU EVER GET TIRED OF CRYING?
WHY DON'T YOU TRY TO GET A GOOD NIGHT'S SLEEP FOR ONCE?
LET ME... HOLD ON A WHILE.
IF I DON'T...
...MY HEART MAY FLY APART.

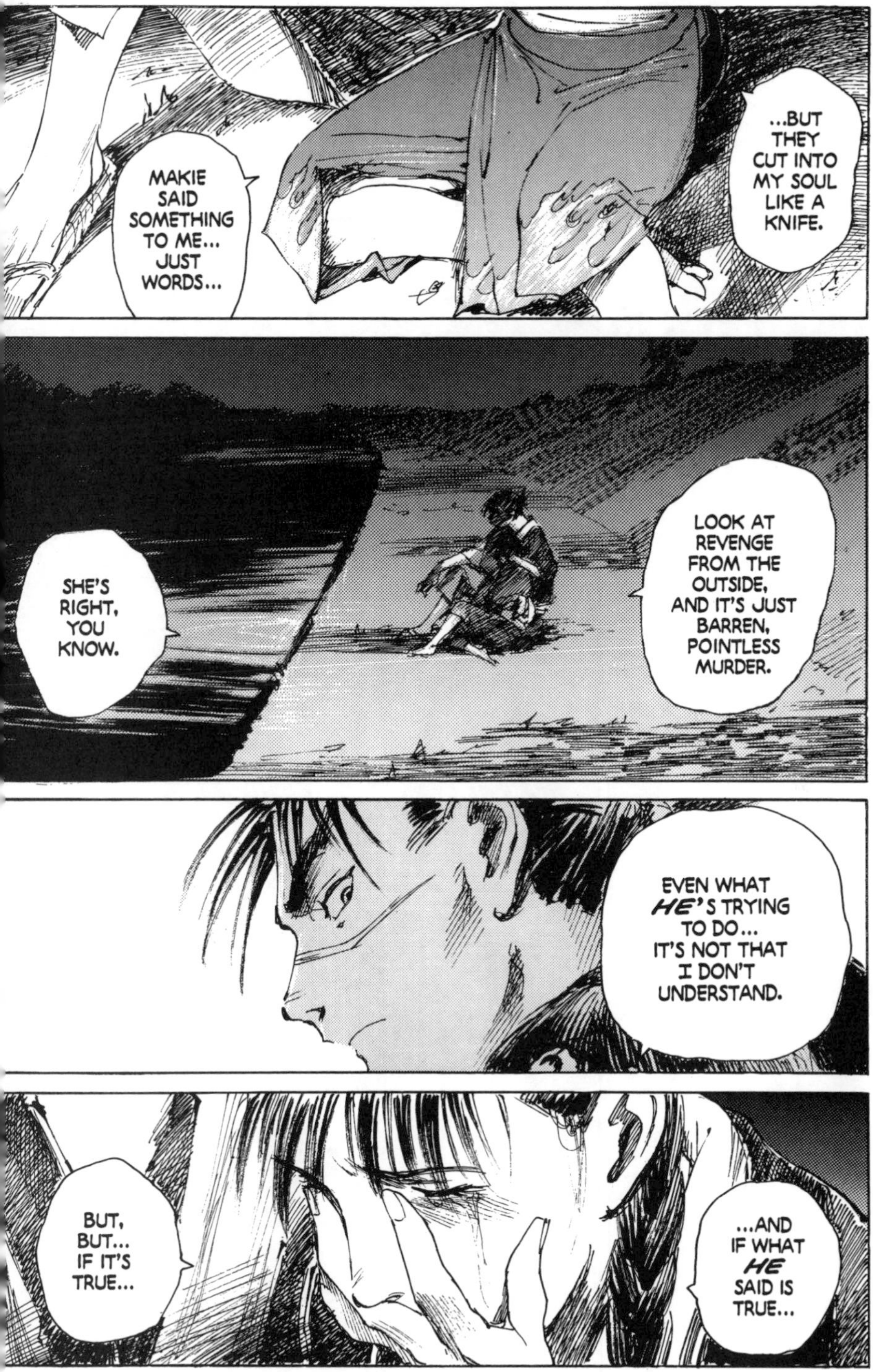
MAKIE SAID SOMETHING TO ME... JUST WORDS...
...BUT THEY CUT INTO MY SOUL LIKE A KNIFE.
SHE'S RIGHT, YOU KNOW.
LOOK AT REVENGE FROM THE OUTSIDE, AND IT'S JUST BARREN, POINTLESS MURDER.
EVEN WHAT *HE'S* TRYING TO DO... IT'S NOT THAT I DON'T UNDERSTAND.
BUT, BUT... IF IT'S TRUE...
...AND IF WHAT *HE* SAID IS TRUE...

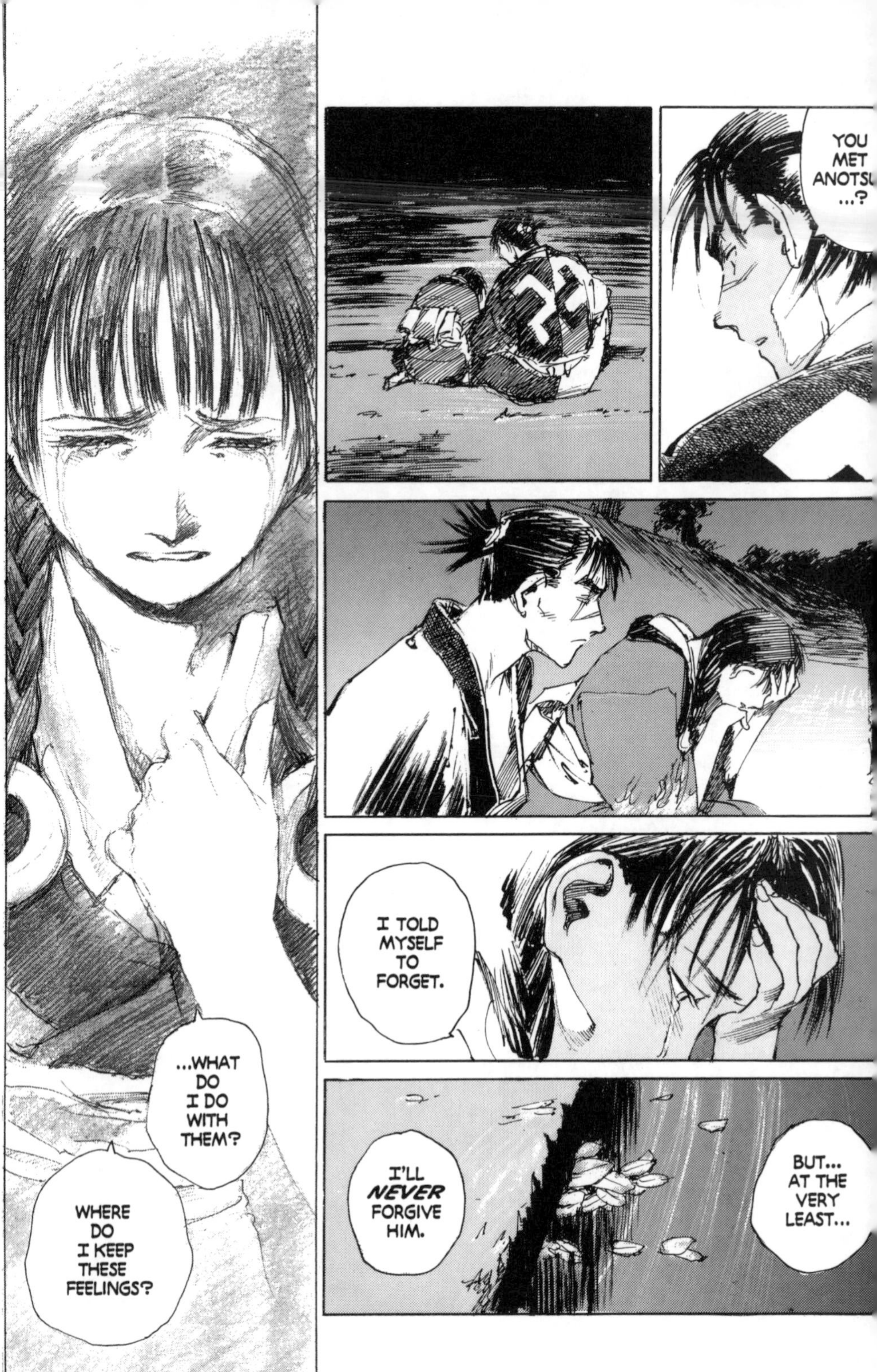
...WHAT DO I DO WITH THEM?
WHERE DO I KEEP THESE FEELINGS?
YOU MET ANOTSU ...?
I TOLD MYSELF TO FORGET.
I'LL *NEVER* FORGIVE HIM.
BUT... AT THE VERY LEAST...

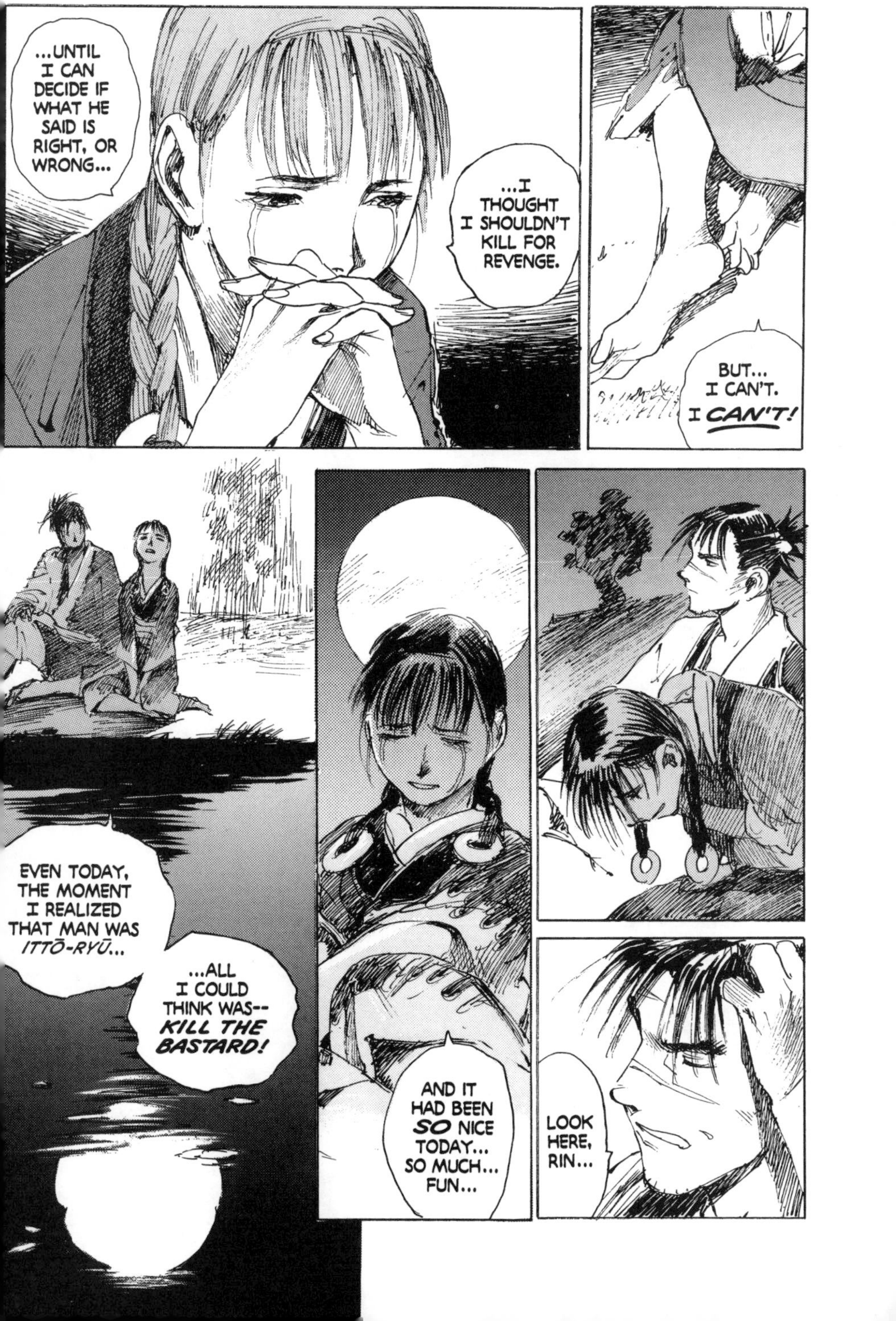
...UNTIL I CAN DECIDE IF WHAT HE SAID IS RIGHT, OR WRONG...
...I THOUGHT I SHOULDN'T KILL FOR REVENGE.
BUT... I CAN'T. I CAN'T!
EVEN TODAY, THE MOMENT I REALIZED THAT MAN WAS ITTŌ-RYŪ...
...ALL I COULD THINK WAS-- KILL THE BASTARD!
AND IT HAD BEEN SO NICE TODAY... SO MUCH... FUN...
LOOK HERE, RIN...

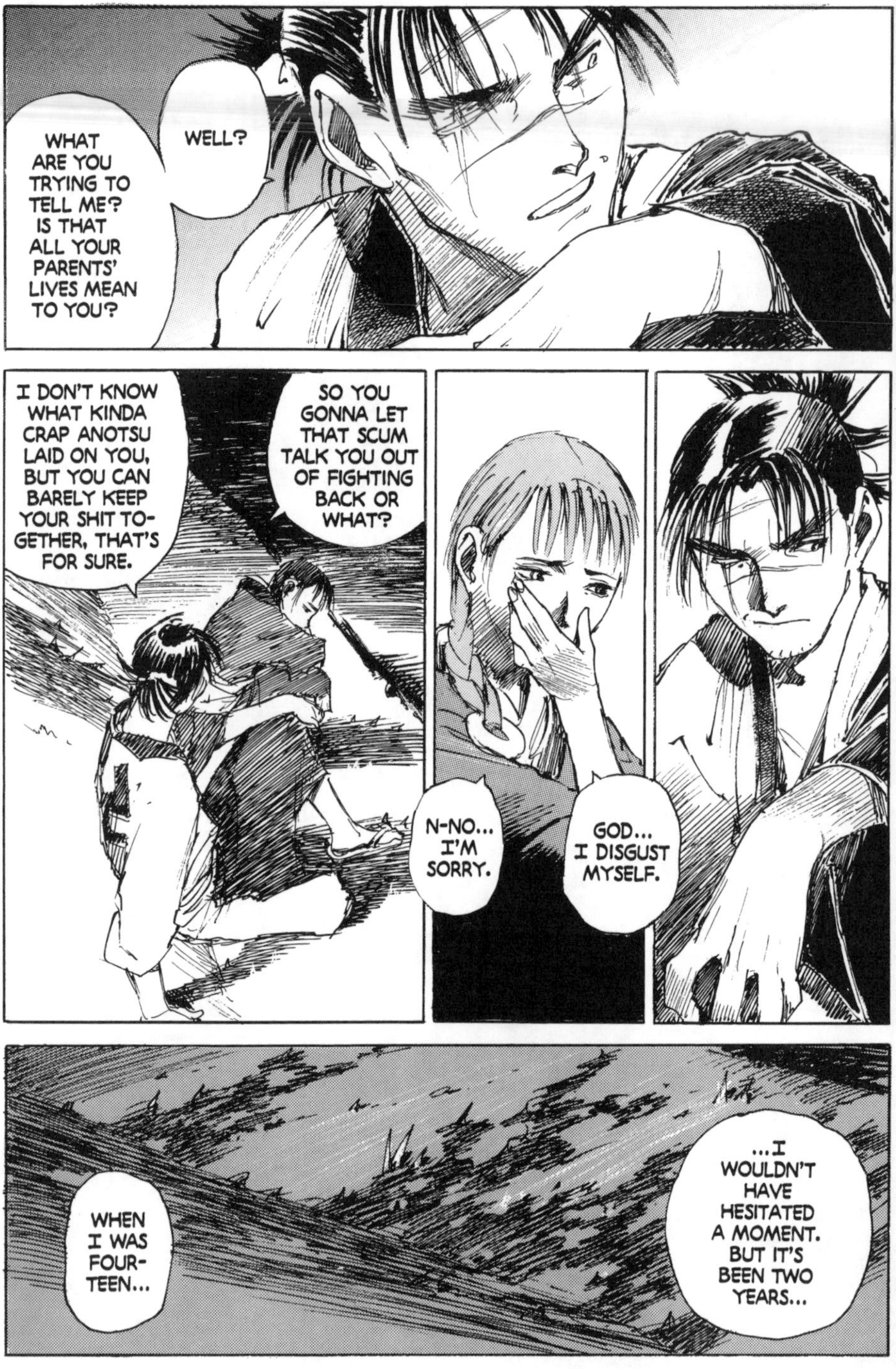
WHAT ARE YOU TRYING TO TELL ME? IS THAT ALL YOUR PARENTS' LIVES MEAN TO YOU?
WELL?
I DON'T KNOW WHAT KINDA CRAP ANOTSU LAID ON YOU, BUT YOU CAN BARELY KEEP YOUR SHIT TO-GETHER, THAT'S FOR SURE.
SO YOU GONNA LET THAT SCUM TALK YOU OUT OF FIGHTING BACK OR WHAT?
N-NO... I'M SORRY.
GOD... I DISGUST MYSELF.
WHEN I WAS FOUR-TEEN...
...I WOULDN'T HAVE HESITATED A MOMENT. BUT IT'S BEEN TWO YEARS...

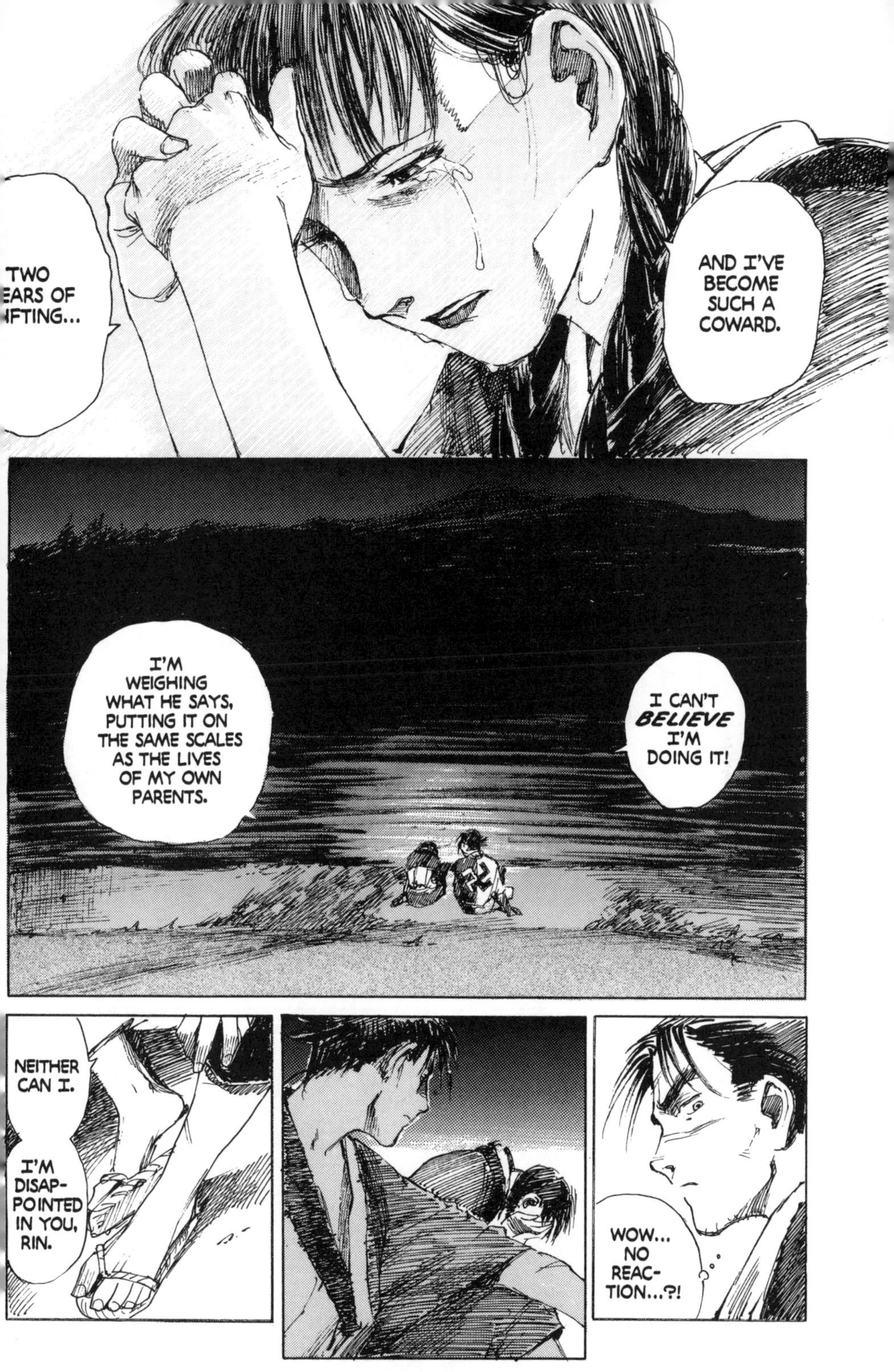
TWO EARS OF IFTING...
AND I'VE BECOME SUCH A COWARD.
I'M WEIGHING WHAT HE SAYS, PUTTING IT ON THE SAME SCALES AS THE LIVES OF MY OWN PARENTS.
I CAN'T *BELIEVE* I'M DOING IT!
NEITHER CAN I.
I'M DISAP-POINTED IN YOU, RIN.
WOW... NO REAC-TION...?!

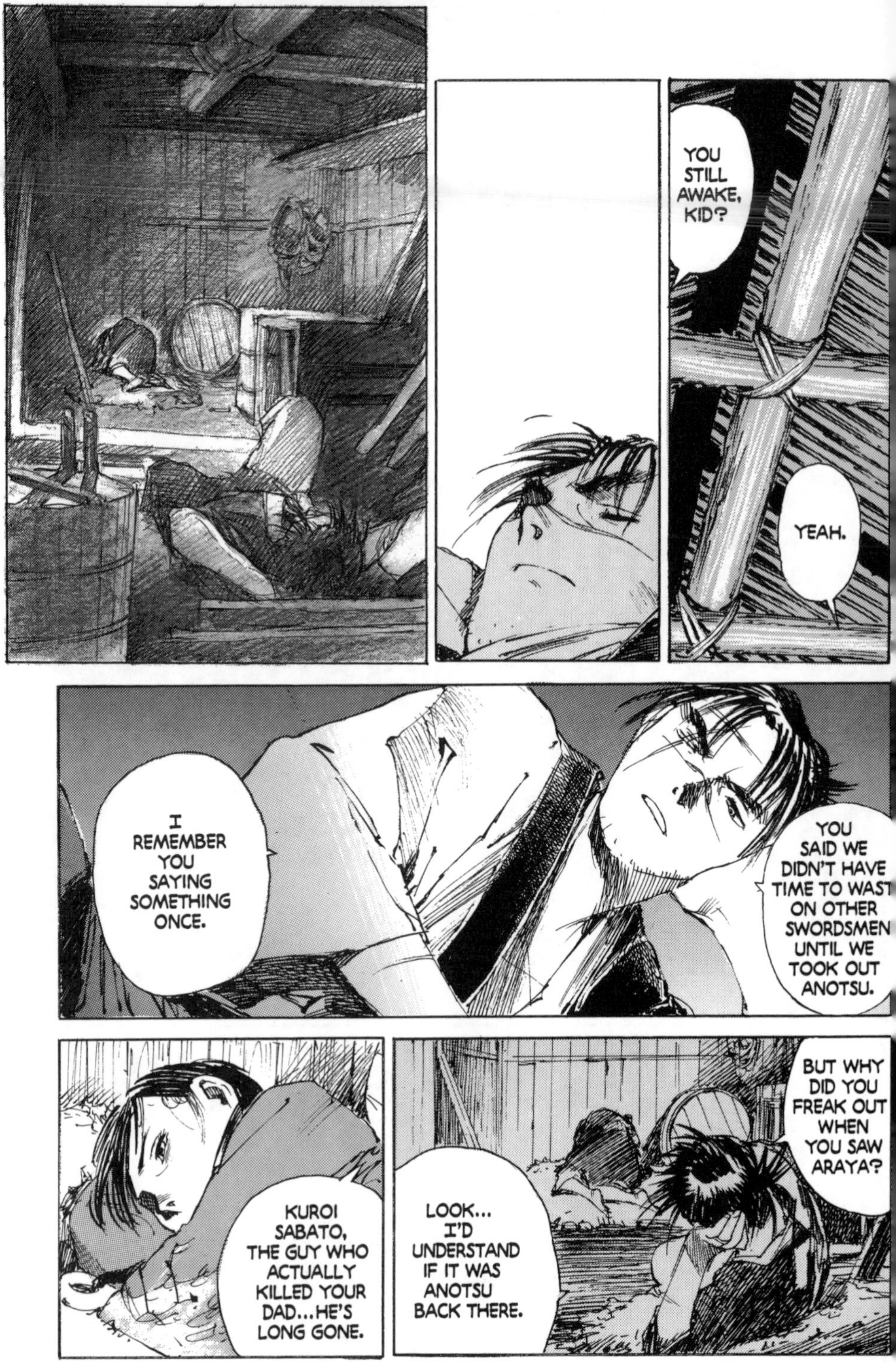
YOU STILL AWAKE, KID?
YEAH.
I REMEMBER YOU SAYING SOMETHING ONCE.
YOU SAID WE DIDN'T HAVE TIME TO WAST ON OTHER SWORDSMEN UNTIL WE TOOK OUT ANOTSU.
KUROI SABATO, THE GUY WHO ACTUALLY KILLED YOUR DAD...HE'S LONG GONE.
LOOK... I'D UNDERSTAND IF IT WAS ANOTSU BACK THERE.
BUT WHY DID YOU FREAK OUT WHEN YOU SAW ARAYA?

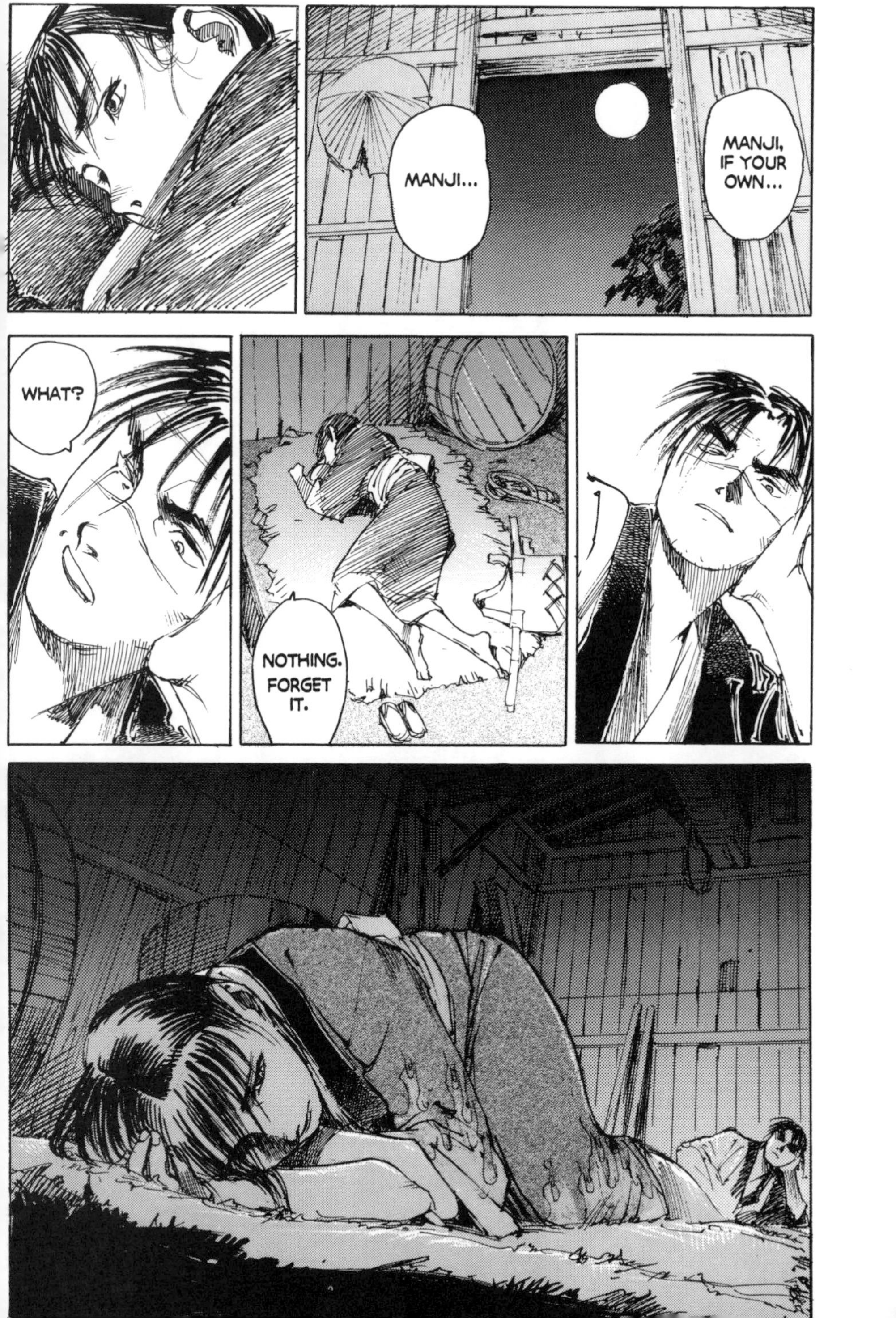
MANJI...
MANJI, IF YOUR OWN...
WHAT?
NOTHING. FORGET IT.

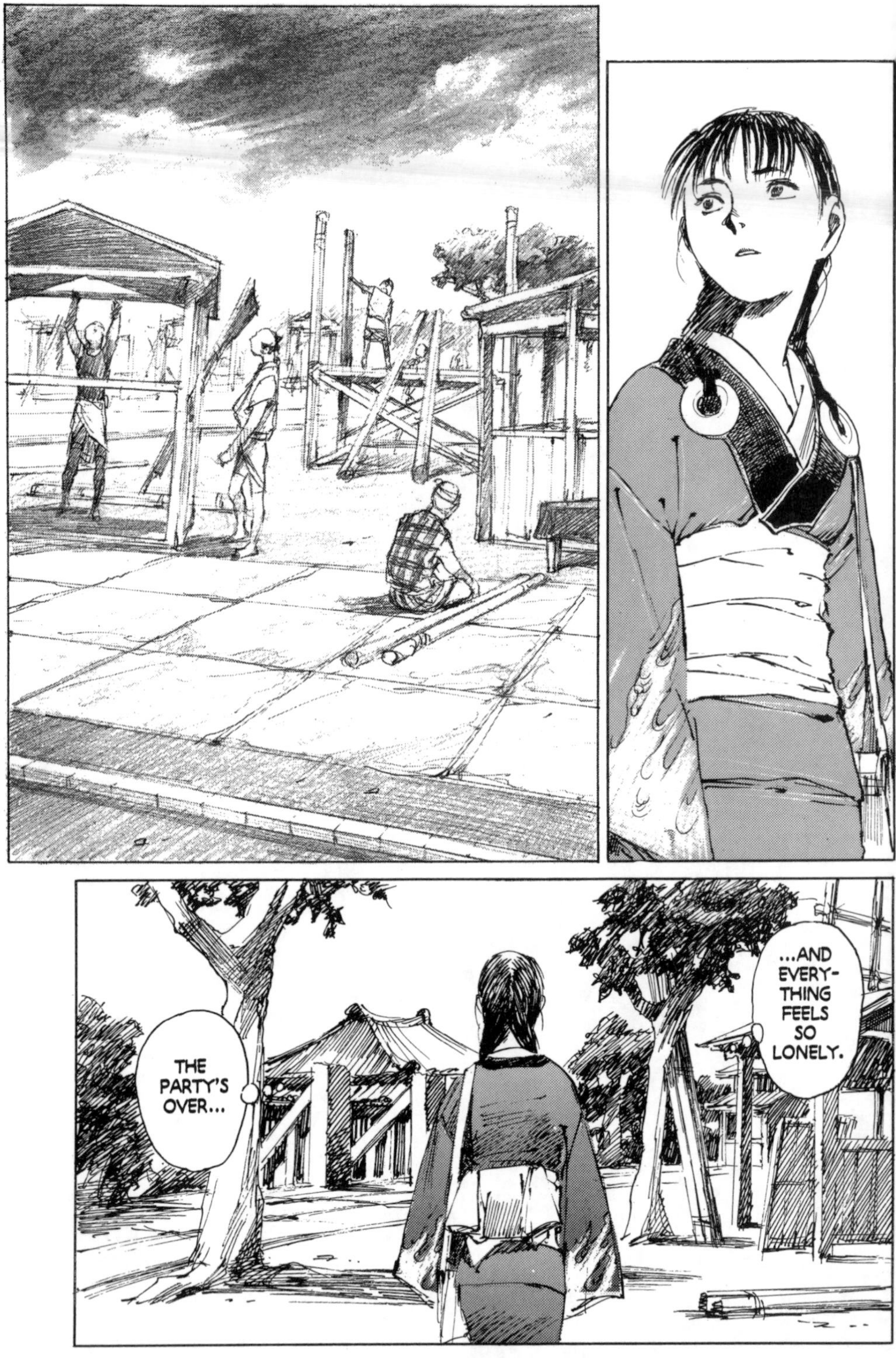
THE PARTY'S OVER...
...AND EVERYTHING FEELS SO LONELY.

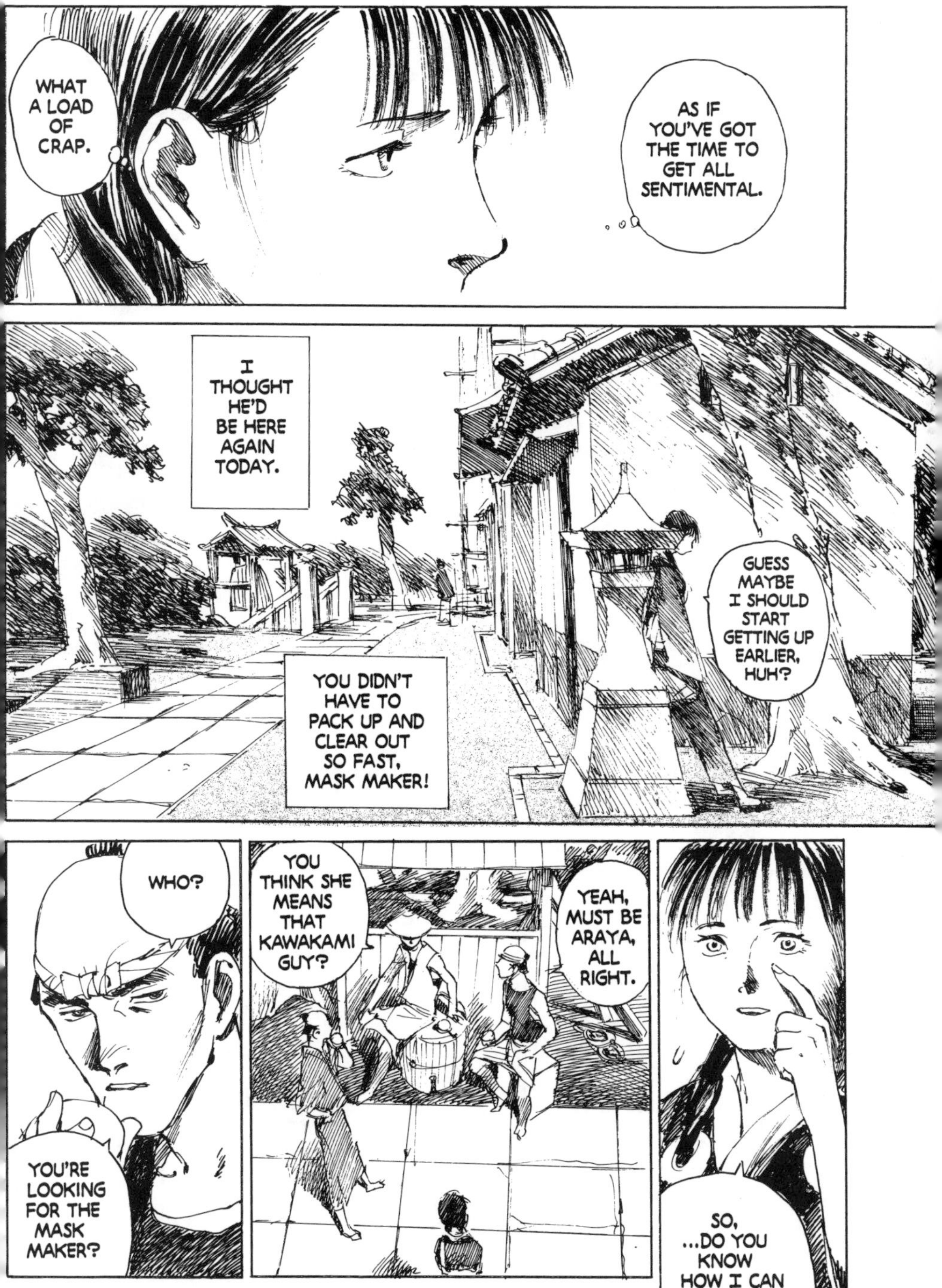
WHAT A LOAD OF CRAP.
AS IF YOU'VE GOT THE TIME TO GET ALL SENTIMENTAL.
I THOUGHT HE'D BE HERE AGAIN TODAY.
YOU DIDN'T HAVE TO PACK UP AND CLEAR OUT SO FAST, MASK MAKER!
GUESS MAYBE I SHOULD START GETTING UP EARLIER, HUH?
WHO?
YOU'RE LOOKING FOR THE MASK MAKER?
YOU THINK SHE MEANS THAT KAWAKAMI GUY?
YEAH, MUST BE ARAYA, ALL RIGHT.
SO, ...DO YOU KNOW HOW I CAN FIND HIM?

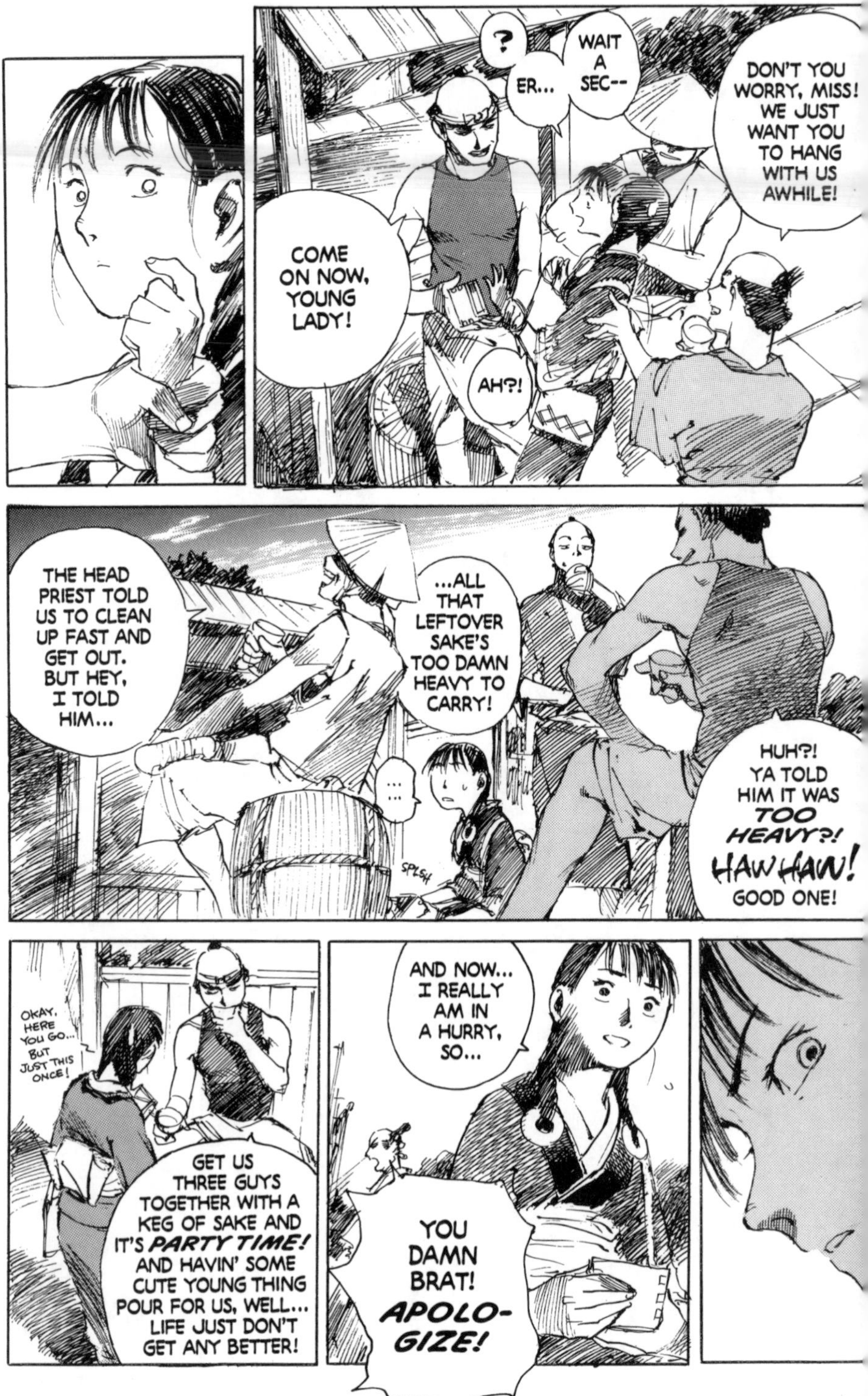
?
ER...
WAIT A SEC--
DON'T YOU WORRY, MISS! WE JUST WANT YOU TO HANG WITH US AWHILE!
COME ON NOW, YOUNG LADY!
AH?!
THE HEAD PRIEST TOLD US TO CLEAN UP FAST AND GET OUT. BUT HEY, I TOLD HIM...
...ALL THAT LEFTOVER SAKE'S TOO DAMN HEAVY TO CARRY!
......
SPLSH
HUH?! YA TOLD HIM IT WAS *TOO HEAVY?!* HAW HAW! GOOD ONE!
OKAY, HERE YOU GO... BUT JUST THIS ONCE!
GET US THREE GUYS TOGETHER WITH A KEG OF SAKE AND IT'S *PARTY TIME!* AND HAVIN' SOME CUTE YOUNG THING POUR FOR US, WELL... LIFE JUST DON'T GET ANY BETTER!
AND NOW... I REALLY AM IN A HURRY, SO...
YOU DAMN BRAT! *APOLO-GIZE!*

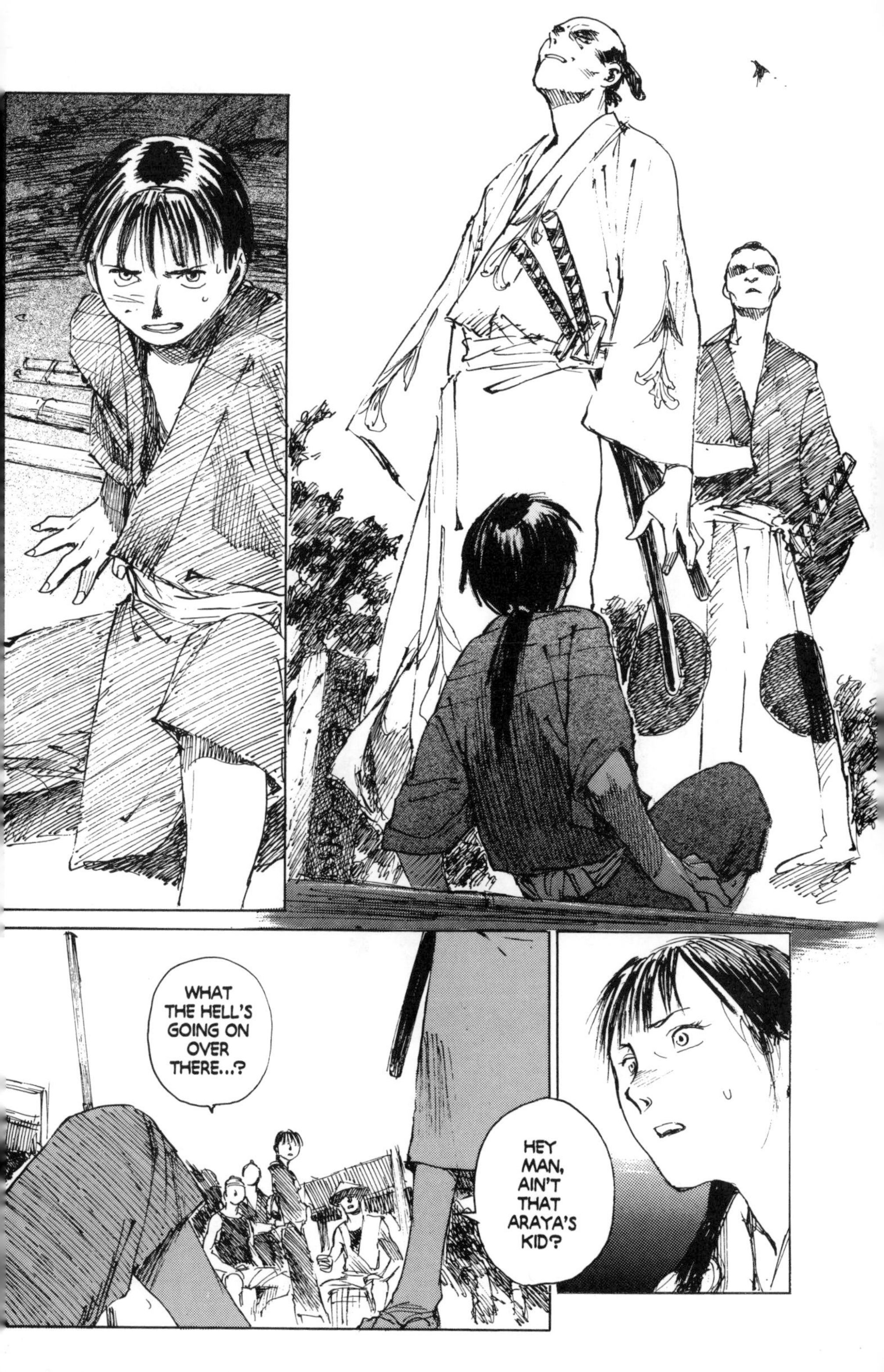
WHAT THE HELL'S GOING ON OVER THERE...?
HEY MAN, AIN'T THAT ARAYA'S KID?

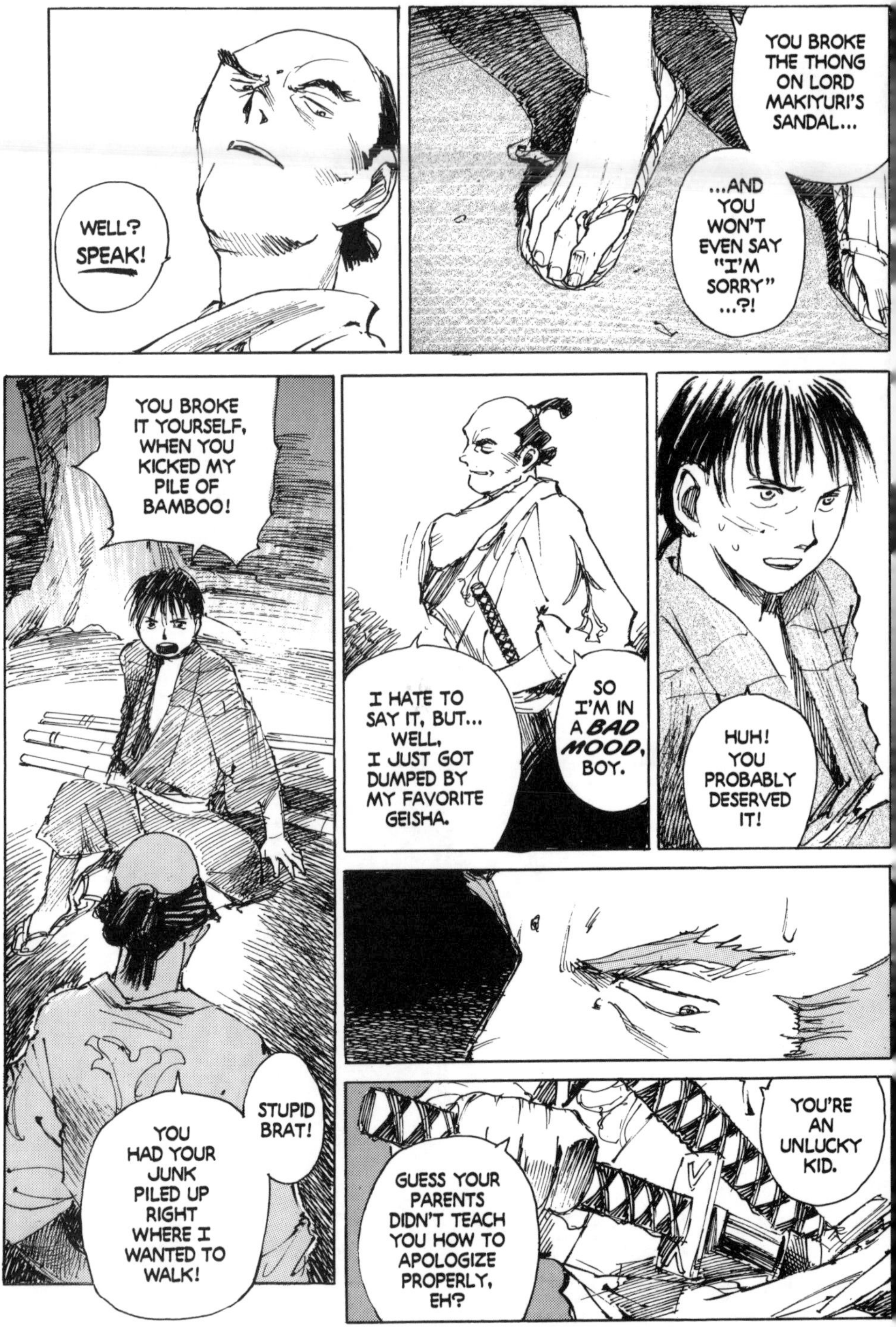

WELL? SPEAK!
YOU BROKE THE THONG ON LORD MAKIYURI'S SANDAL...
...AND YOU WON'T EVEN SAY "I'M SORRY" ...?!
YOU BROKE IT YOURSELF, WHEN YOU KICKED MY PILE OF BAMBOO!
STUPID BRAT!
YOU HAD YOUR JUNK PILED UP RIGHT WHERE I WANTED TO WALK!
I HATE TO SAY IT, BUT... WELL, I JUST GOT DUMPED BY MY FAVORITE GEISHA.
SO I'M IN A *BAD MOOD*, BOY.
HUH! YOU PROBABLY DESERVED IT!
GUESS YOUR PARENTS DIDN'T TEACH YOU HOW TO APOLOGIZE PROPERLY, EH?
YOU'RE AN UNLUCKY KID.

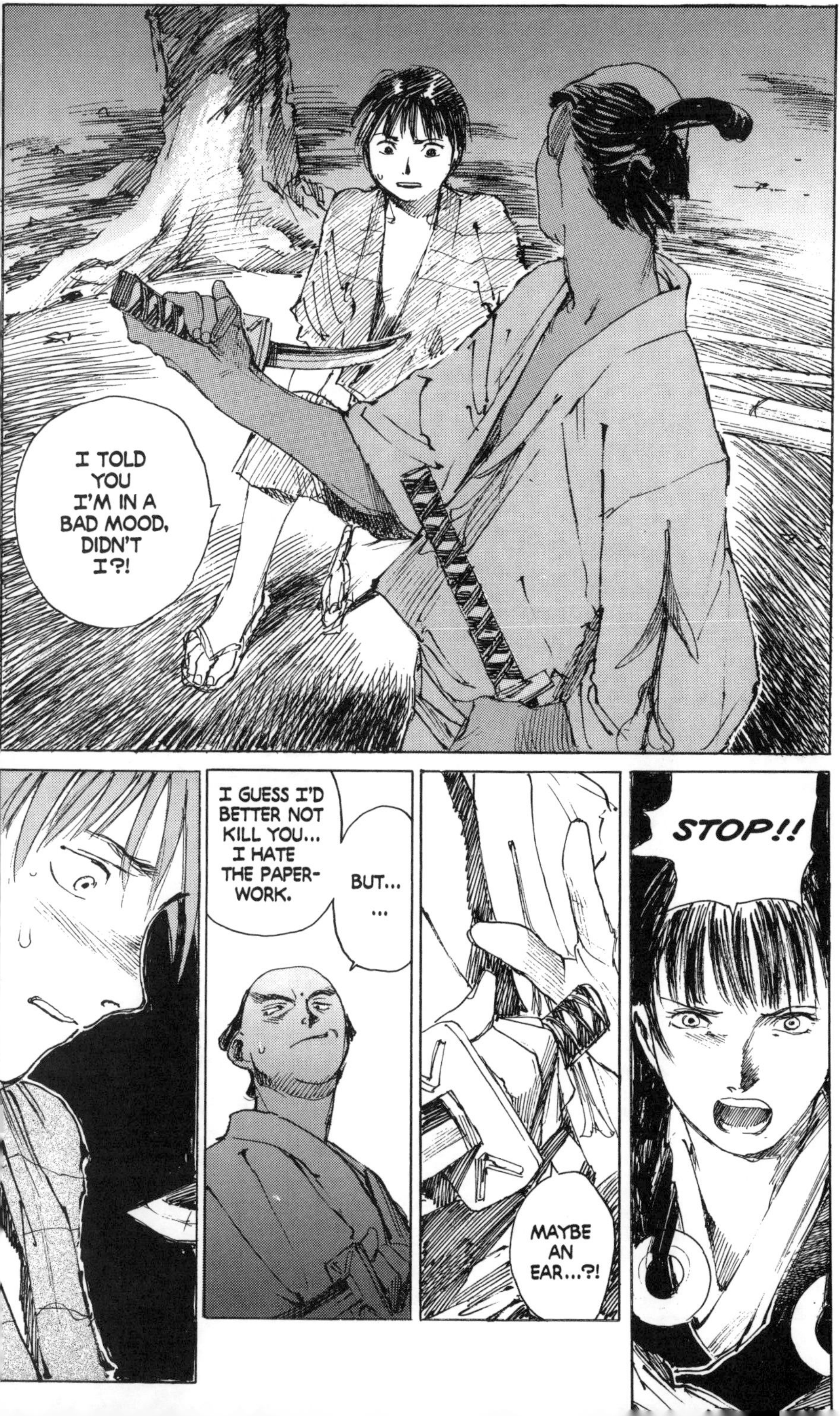
I TOLD YOU I'M IN A BAD MOOD, DIDN'T I?!
I GUESS I'D BETTER NOT KILL YOU... I HATE THE PAPER-WORK.
BUT... ...
MAYBE AN EAR...?!
STOP!!

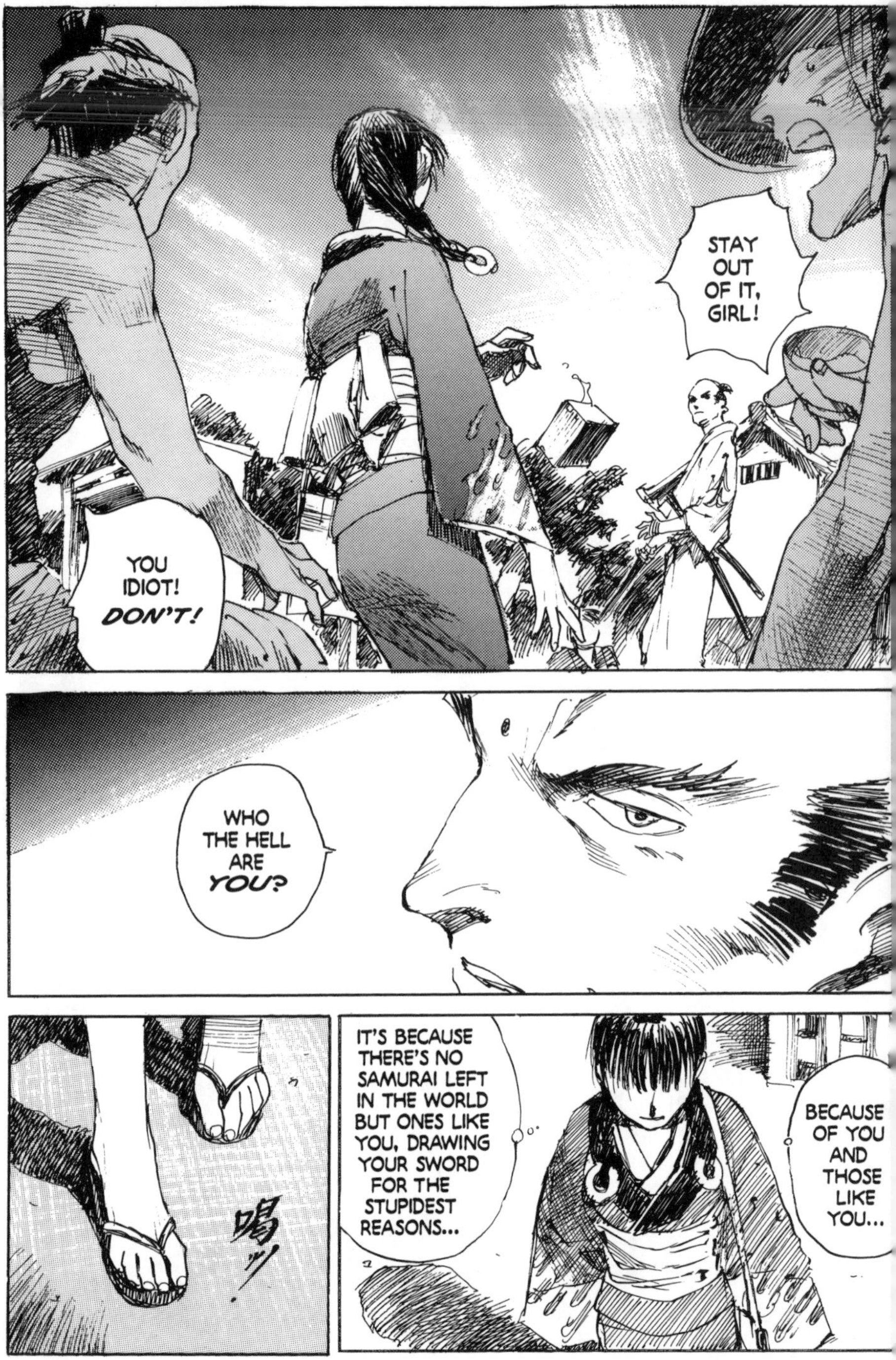
YOU IDIOT! DON'T!
STAY OUT OF IT, GIRL!
WHO THE HELL ARE YOU?
喝ッ
IT'S BECAUSE THERE'S NO SAMURAI LEFT IN THE WORLD BUT ONES LIKE YOU, DRAWING YOUR SWORD FOR THE STUPIDEST REASONS...
BECAUSE OF YOU AND THOSE LIKE YOU...

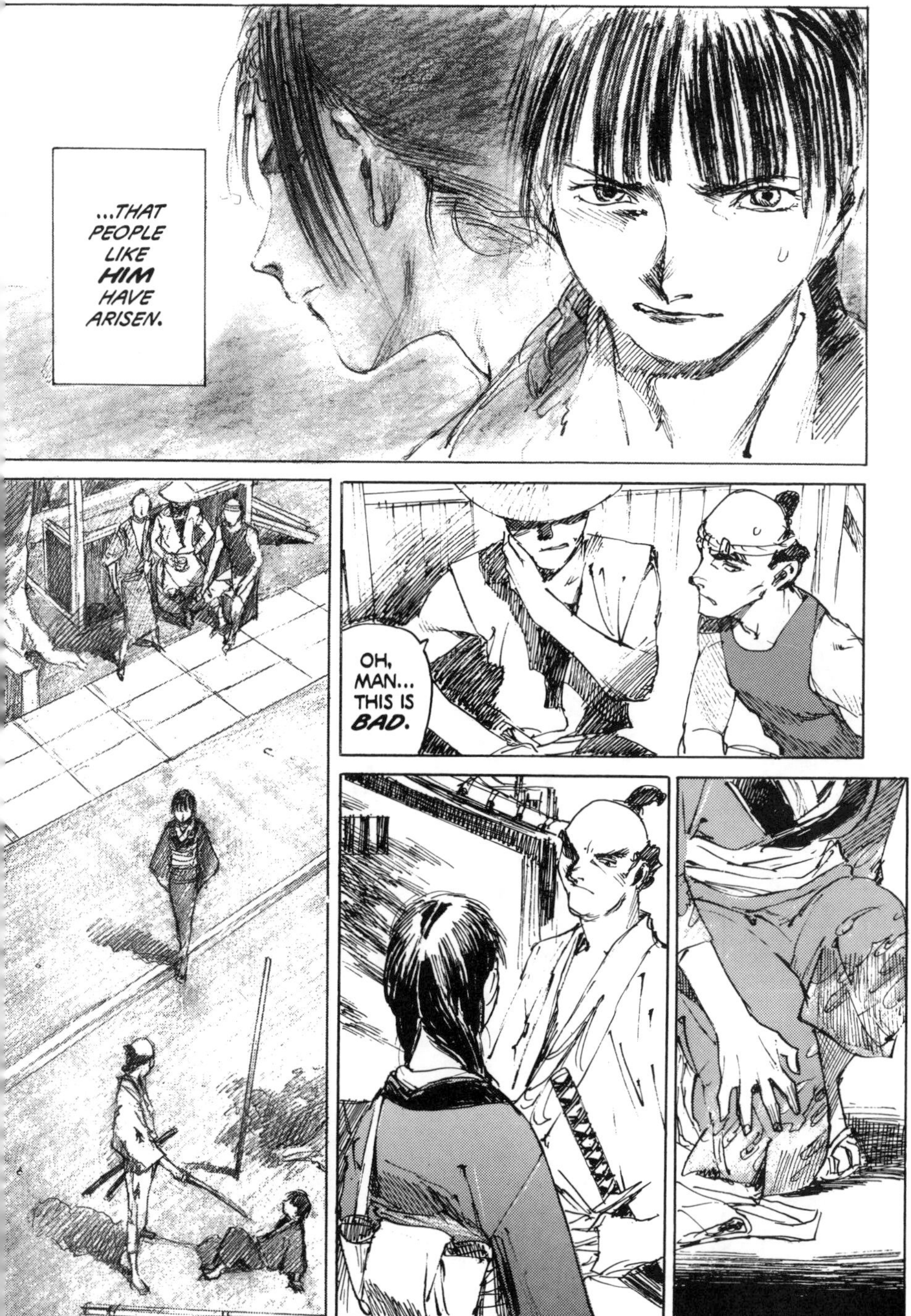
...THAT PEOPLE LIKE HIM HAVE ARISEN.
OH, MAN... THIS IS BAD.

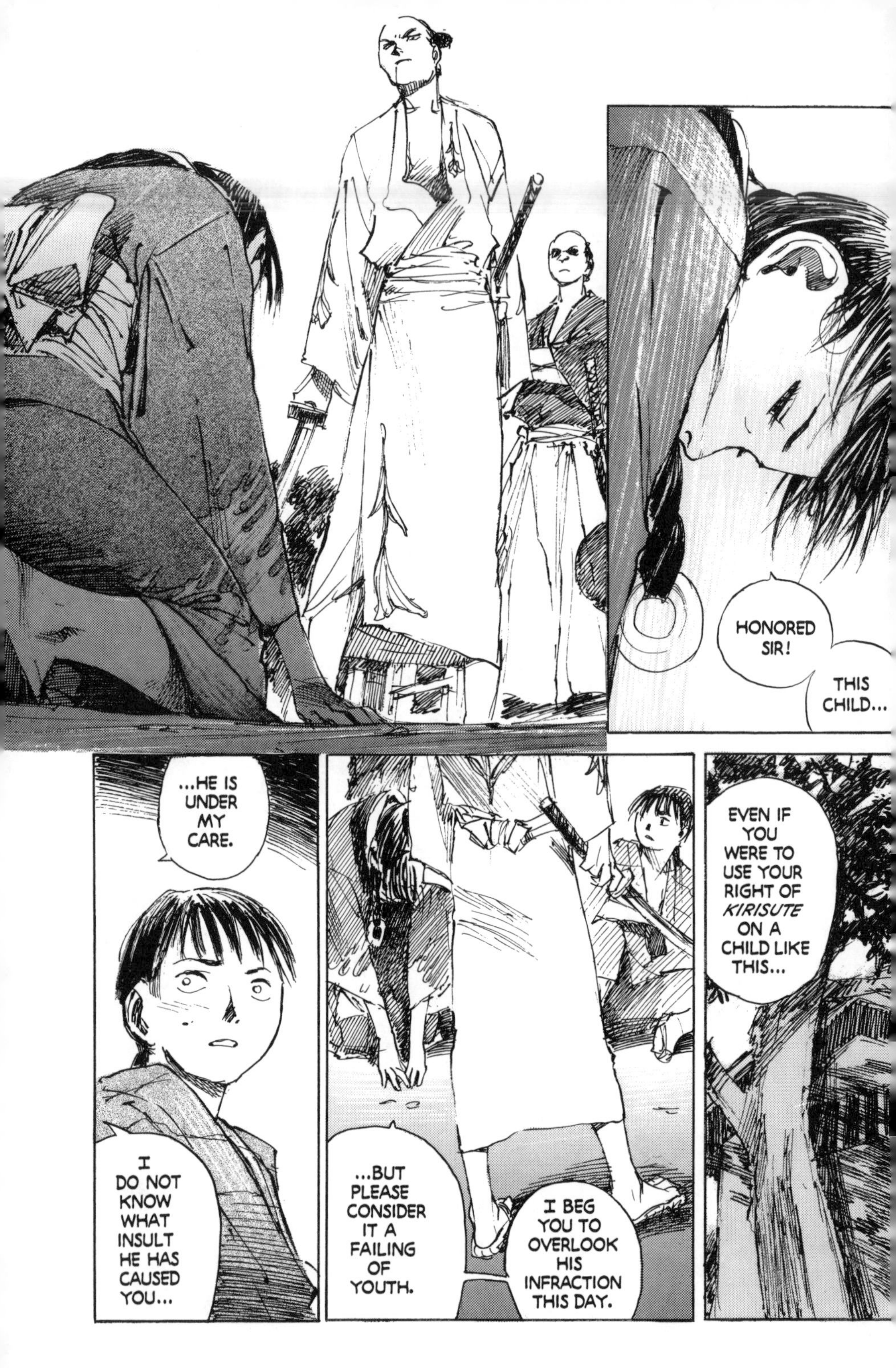
HONORED SIR!
THIS CHILD...
...HE IS UNDER MY CARE.
I DO NOT KNOW WHAT INSULT HE HAS CAUSED YOU...
...BUT PLEASE CONSIDER IT A FAILING OF YOUTH.
I BEG YOU TO OVERLOOK HIS INFRACTION THIS DAY.
EVEN IF YOU WERE TO USE YOUR RIGHT OF *KIRISUTE* ON A CHILD LIKE THIS...

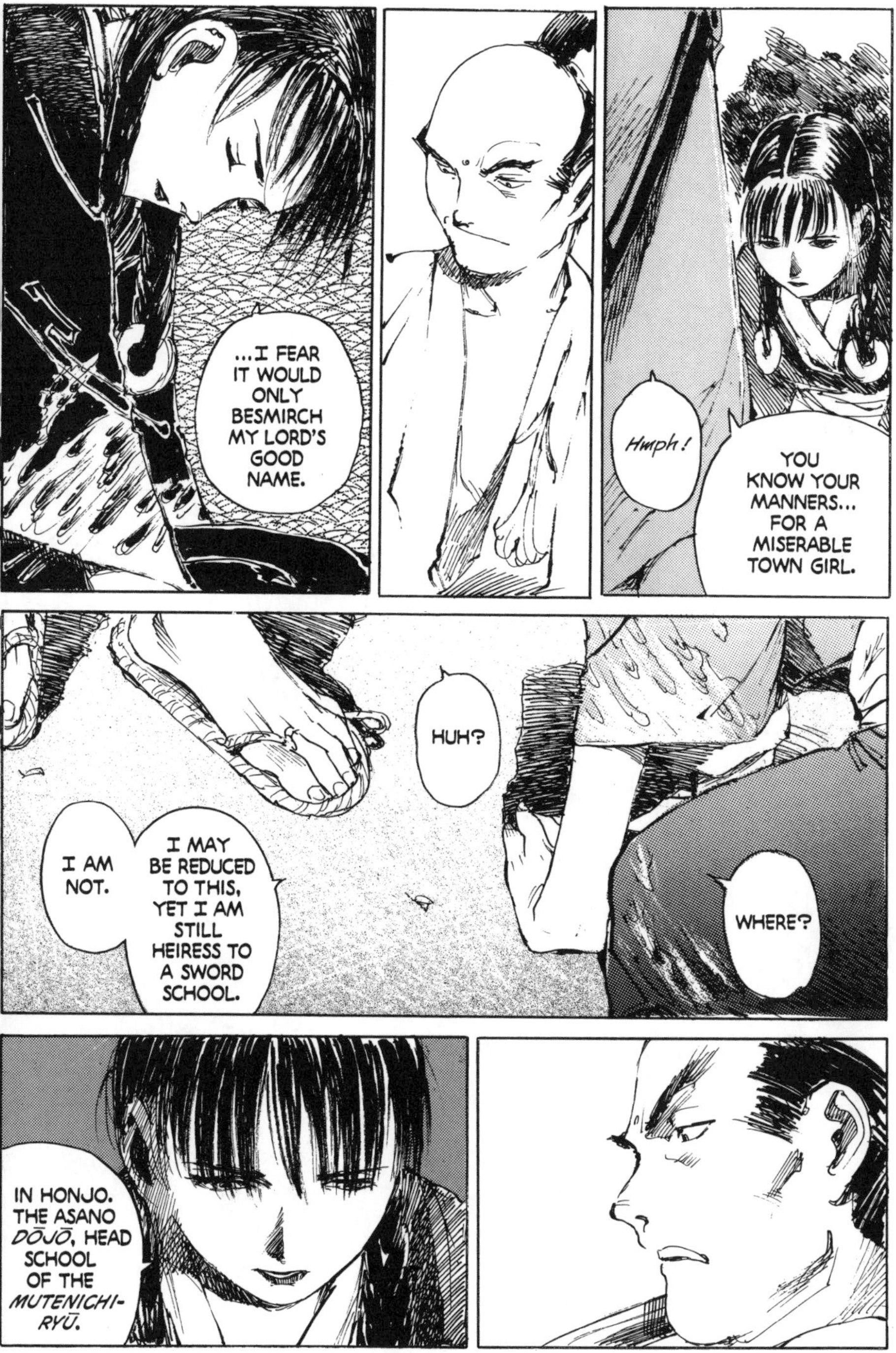
...I FEAR IT WOULD ONLY BESMIRCH MY LORD'S GOOD NAME.
Hmph!
YOU KNOW YOUR MANNERS... FOR A MISERABLE TOWN GIRL.
HUH?
I AM NOT.
I MAY BE REDUCED TO THIS, YET I AM STILL HEIRESS TO A SWORD SCHOOL.
WHERE?
IN HONJO. THE ASANO DŌJŌ, HEAD SCHOOL OF THE MUTENICHI-RYŪ.

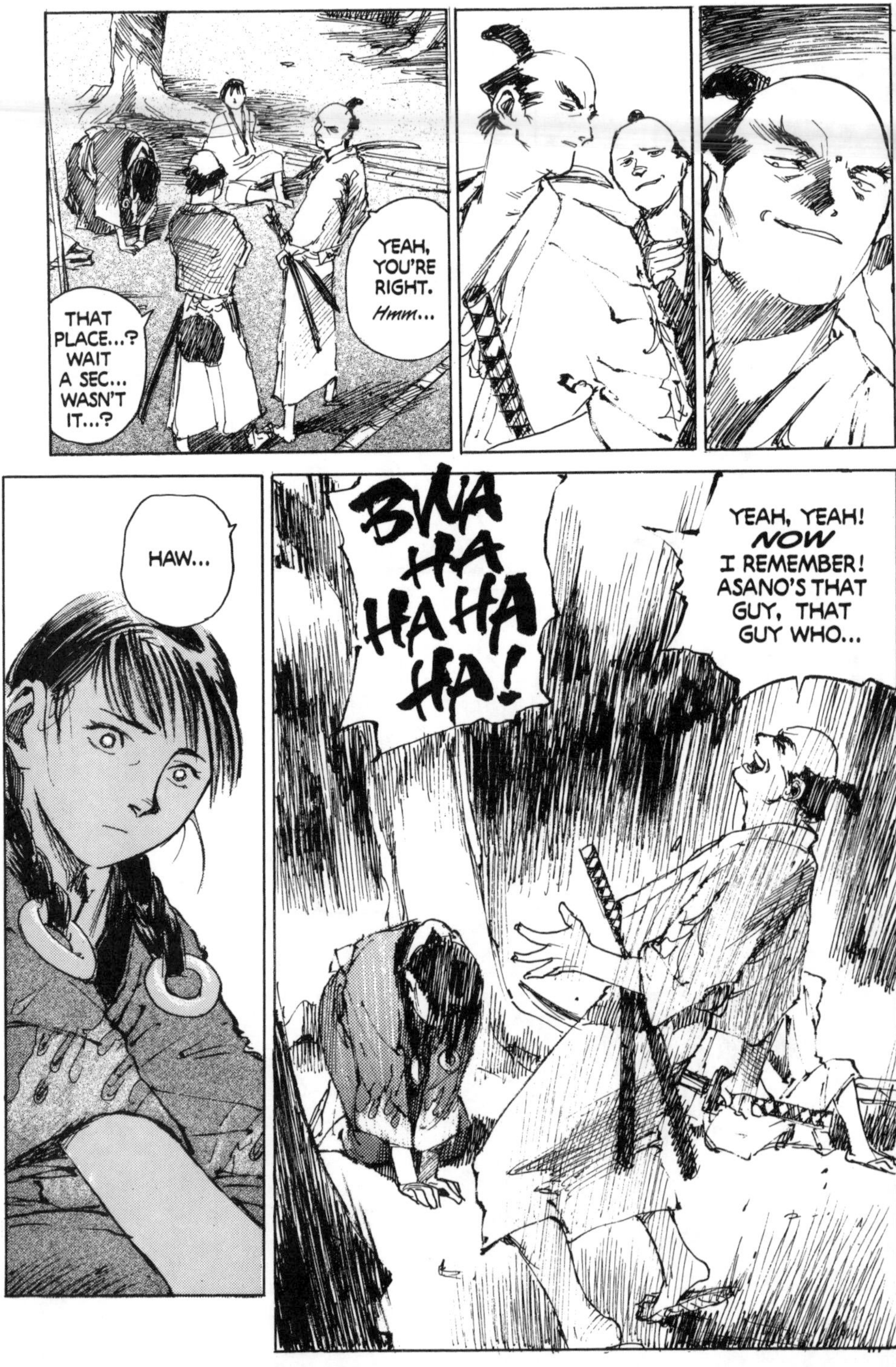
YEAH, YOU'RE RIGHT. *Hmm...*
THAT PLACE...? WAIT A SEC... WASN'T IT...?
HAW...
BWA HA HA HA HA HA!
YEAH, YEAH! ***NOW*** I REMEMBER! ASANO'S THAT GUY, THAT GUY WHO...

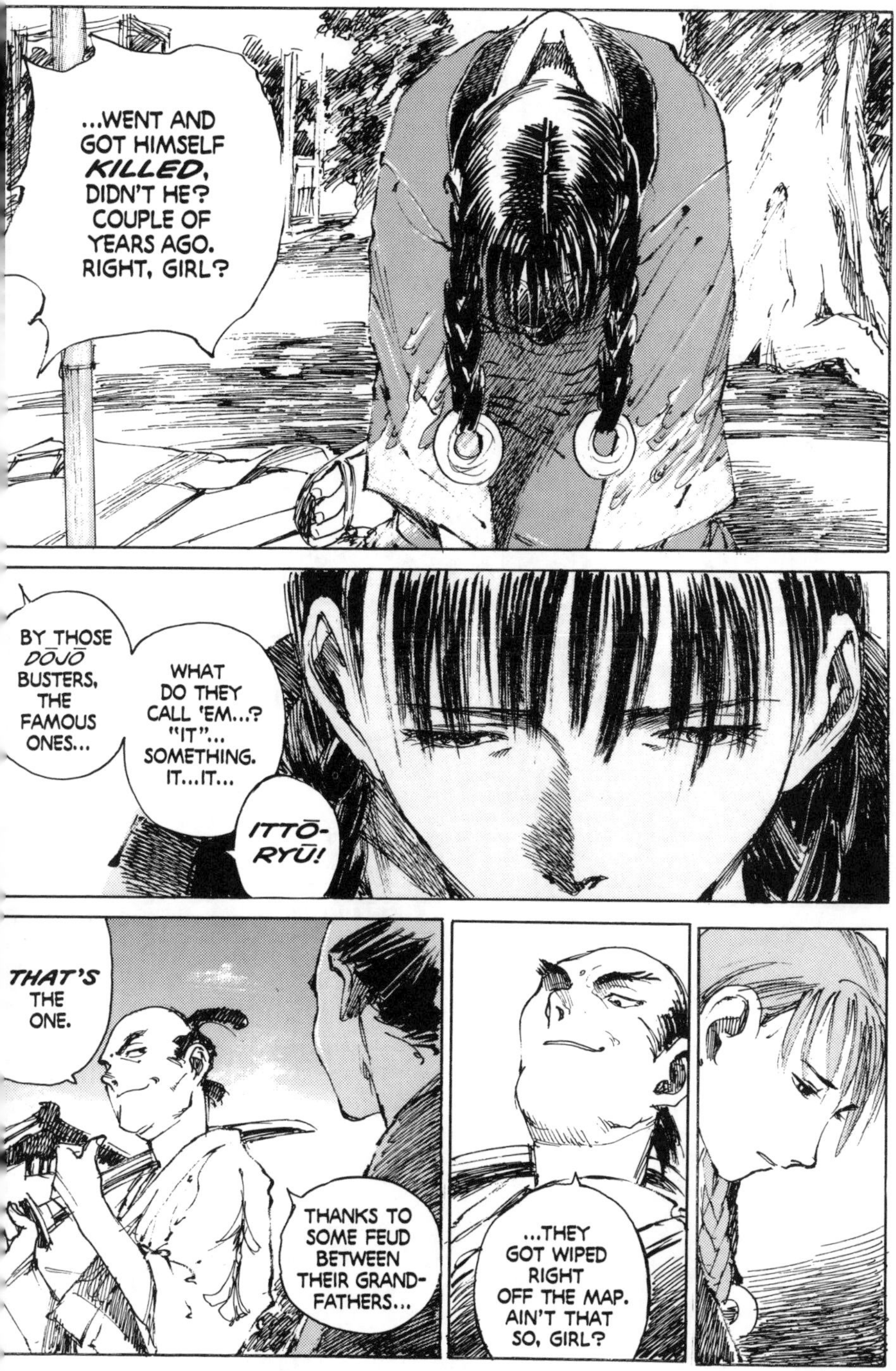
...WENT AND GOT HIMSELF *KILLED*, DIDN'T HE? COUPLE OF YEARS AGO. RIGHT, GIRL?
BY THOSE *DŌJŌ* BUSTERS, THE FAMOUS ONES...
WHAT DO THEY CALL 'EM...? "IT"... SOMETHING. IT...IT...
ITTŌ-RYŪ!
THAT'S THE ONE.
THANKS TO SOME FEUD BETWEEN THEIR GRAND-FATHERS...
...THEY GOT WIPED RIGHT OFF THE MAP. AIN'T THAT SO, GIRL?

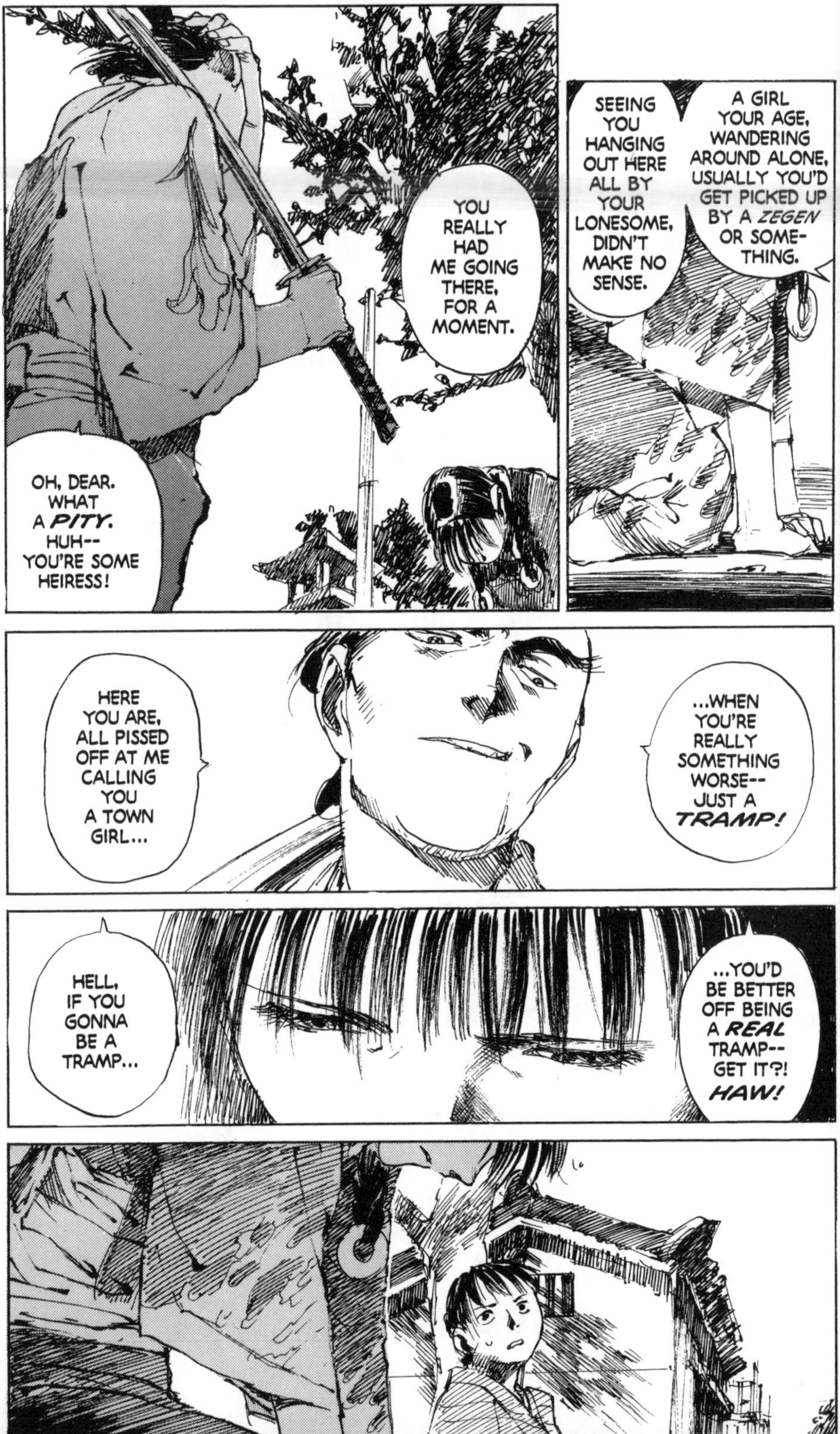
YOU REALLY HAD ME GOING THERE, FOR A MOMENT.
OH, DEAR. WHAT A *PITY.* HUH-- YOU'RE SOME HEIRESS!
SEEING YOU HANGING OUT HERE ALL BY YOUR LONESOME, DIDN'T MAKE NO SENSE.
A GIRL YOUR AGE, WANDERING AROUND ALONE, USUALLY YOU'D GET PICKED UP BY A *ZEGEN* OR SOME-THING.
HERE YOU ARE, ALL PISSED OFF AT ME CALLING YOU A TOWN GIRL...
...WHEN YOU'RE REALLY SOMETHING WORSE-- JUST A *TRAMP!*
HELL, IF YOU GONNA BE A TRAMP...
...YOU'D BE BETTER OFF BEING A *REAL* TRAMP-- GET IT?! *HAW!*

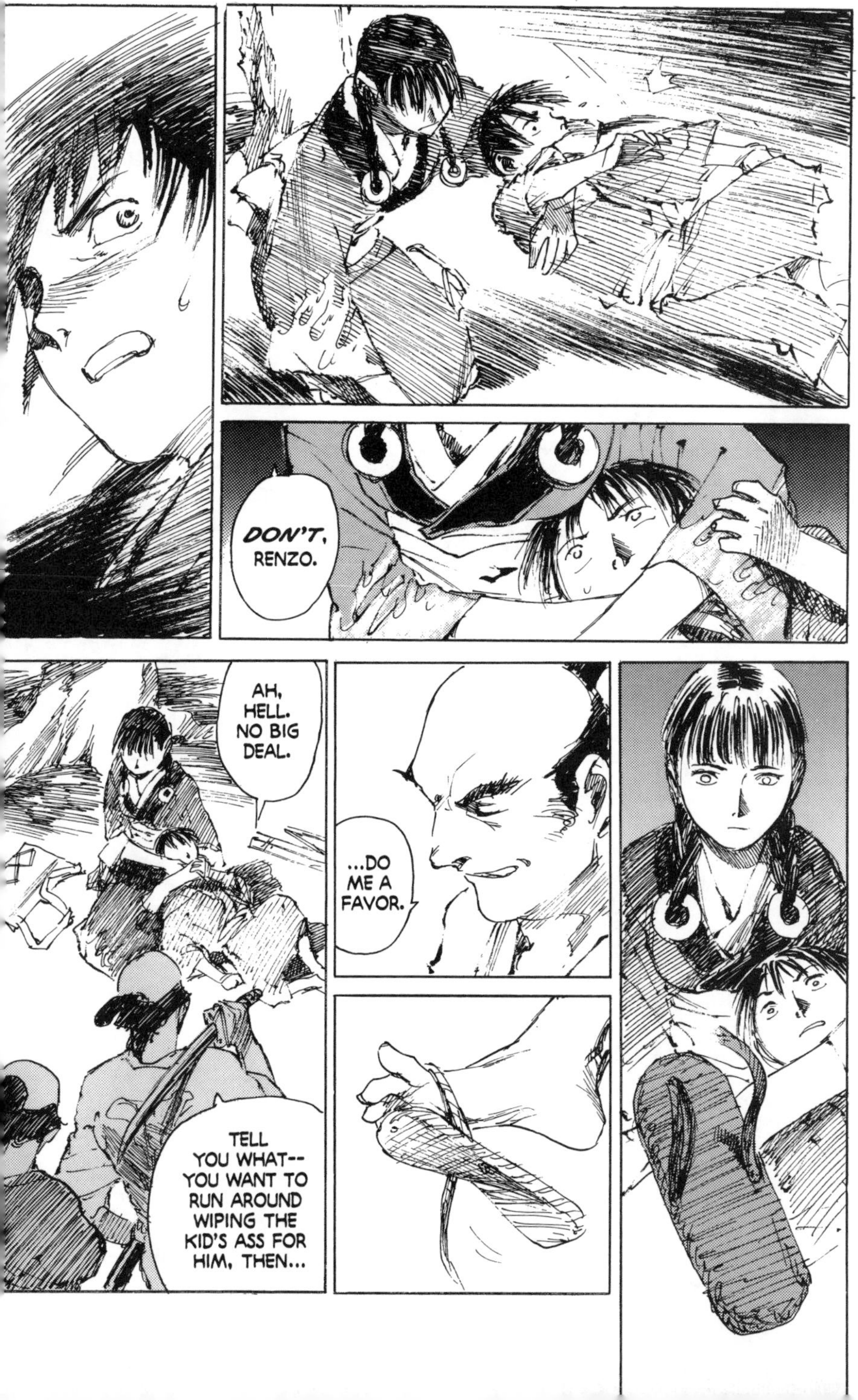
DON'T, RENZO.
AH, HELL. NO BIG DEAL.
...DO ME A FAVOR.
TELL YOU WHAT-- YOU WANT TO RUN AROUND WIPING THE KID'S ASS FOR HIM, THEN...

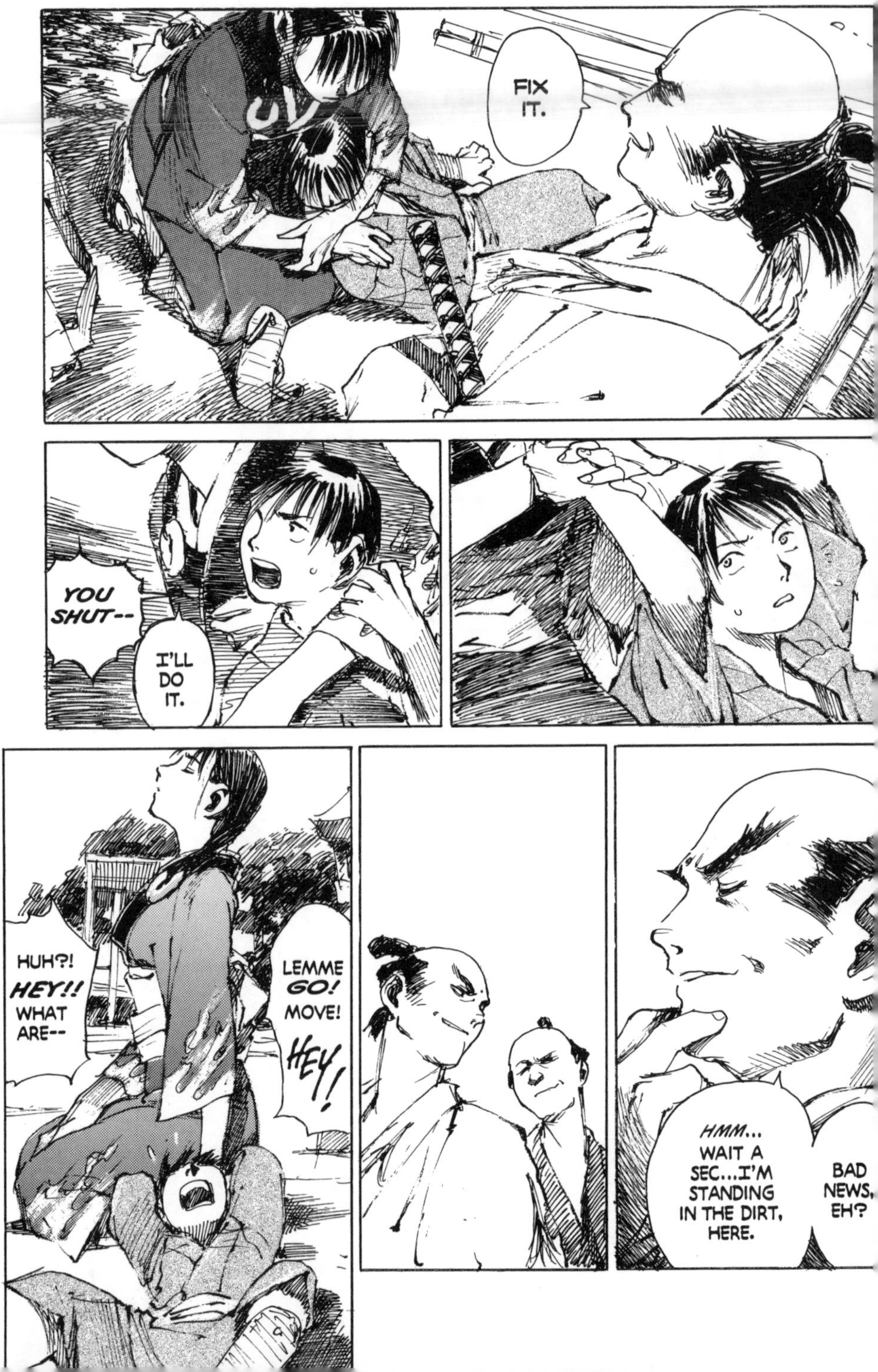
FIX IT.
YOU SHUT--
I'LL DO IT.
HUH?! *HEY!!* WHAT ARE--
LEMME *GO!* MOVE!
HEY!
HMM... WAIT A SEC...I'M STANDING IN THE DIRT, HERE.
BAD NEWS, EH?

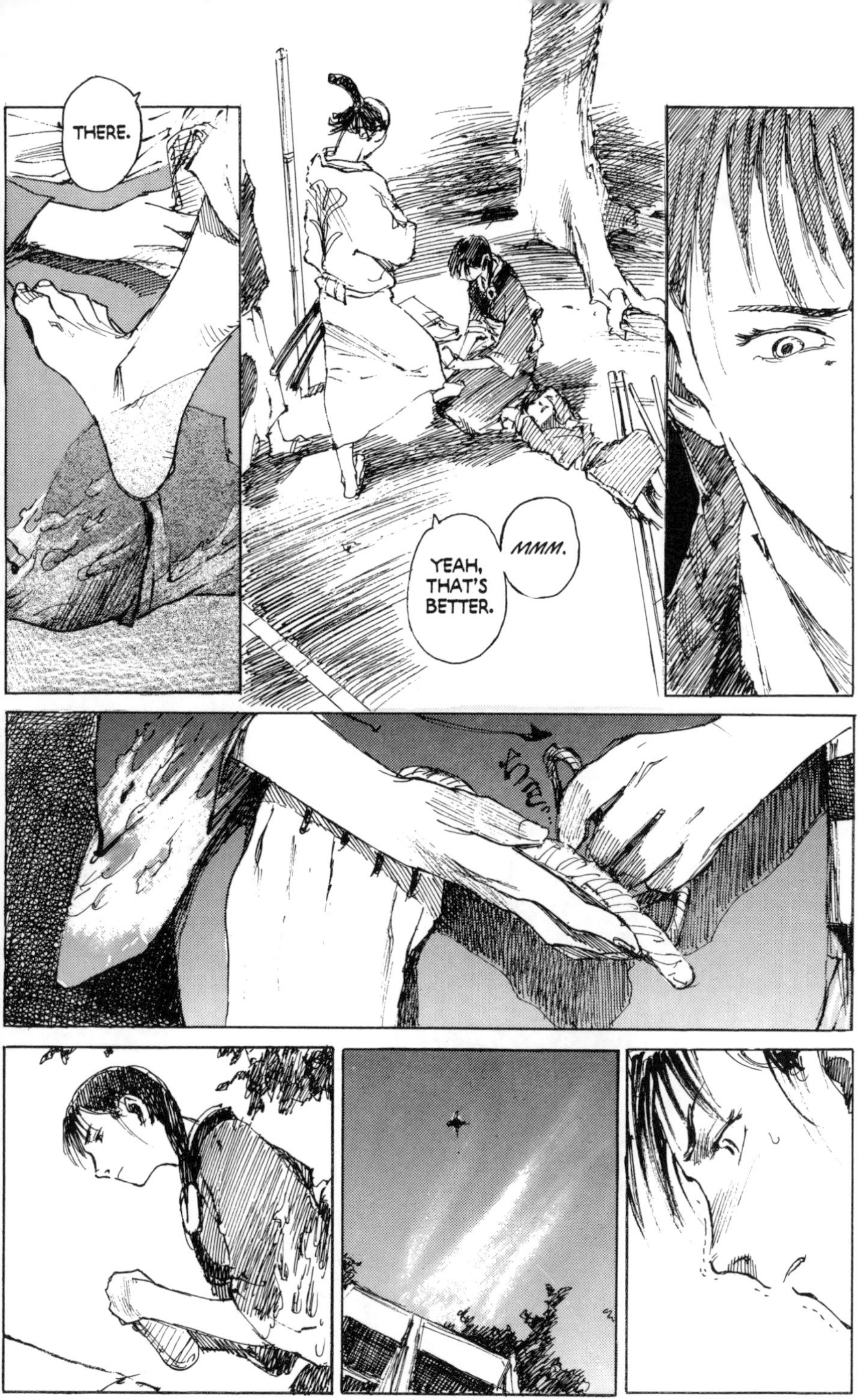
THERE.
MMM.
YEAH, THAT'S BETTER.

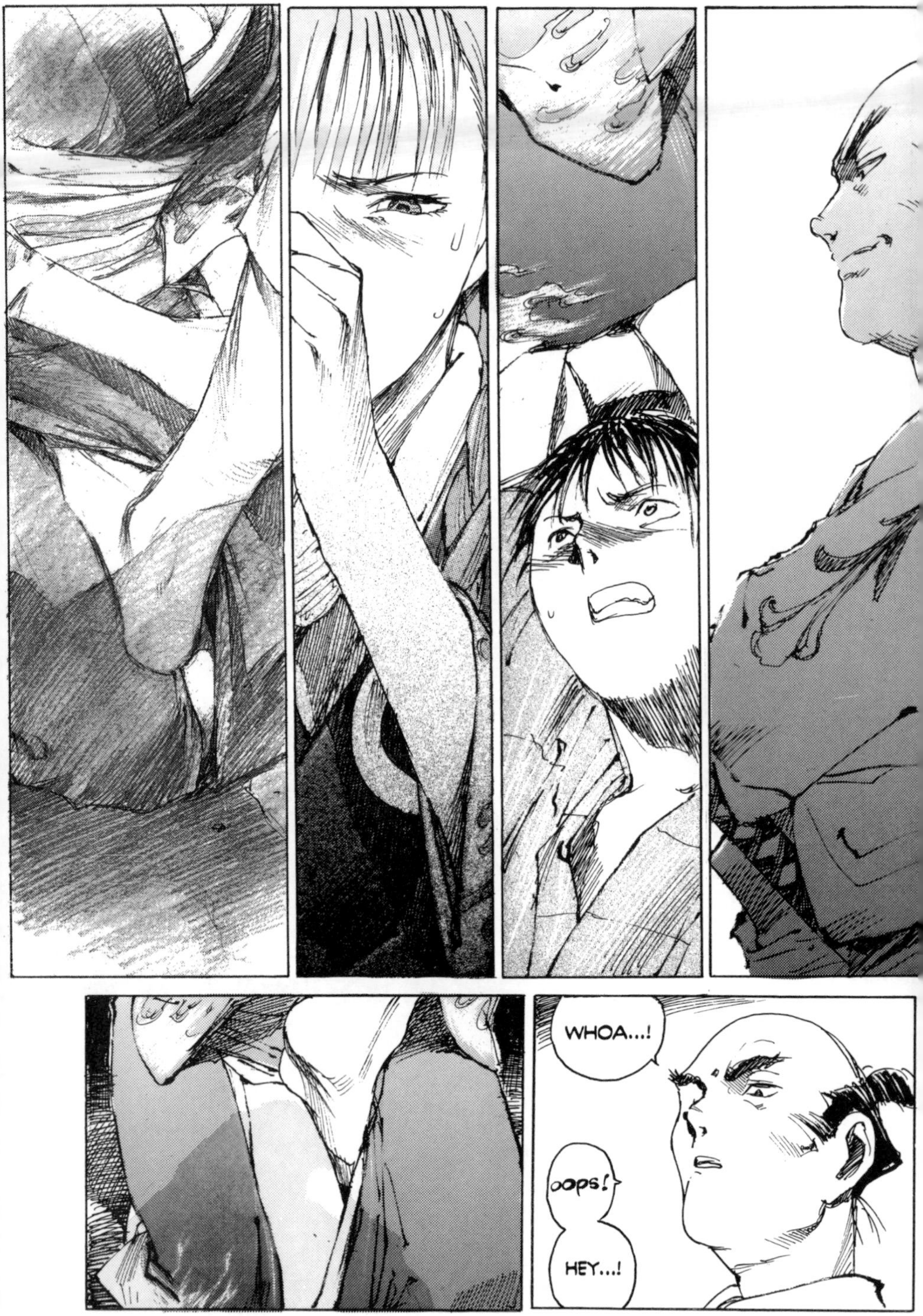
WHOA...!
oops!
HEY...!

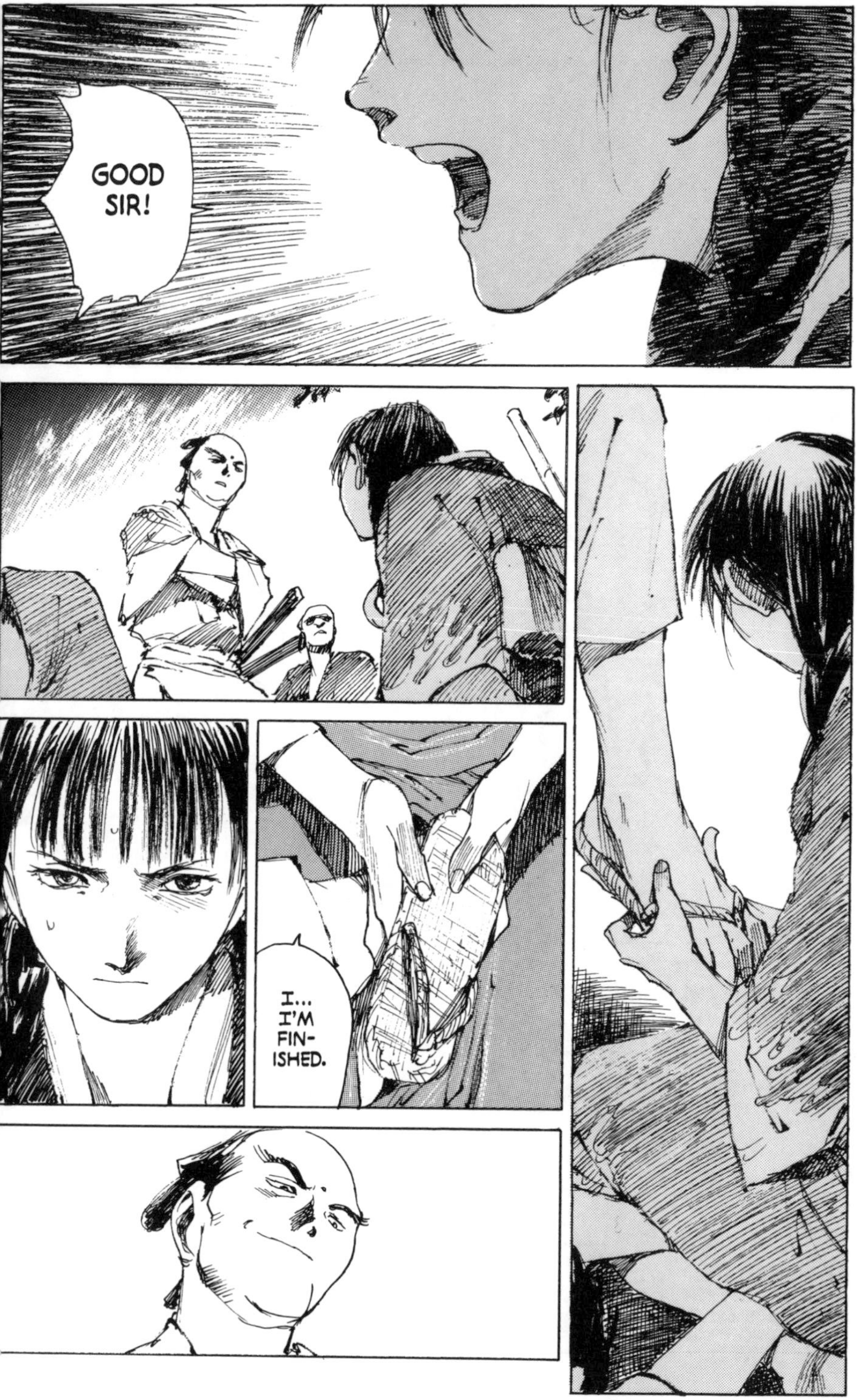
GOOD SIR!
I... I'M FIN-ISHED.

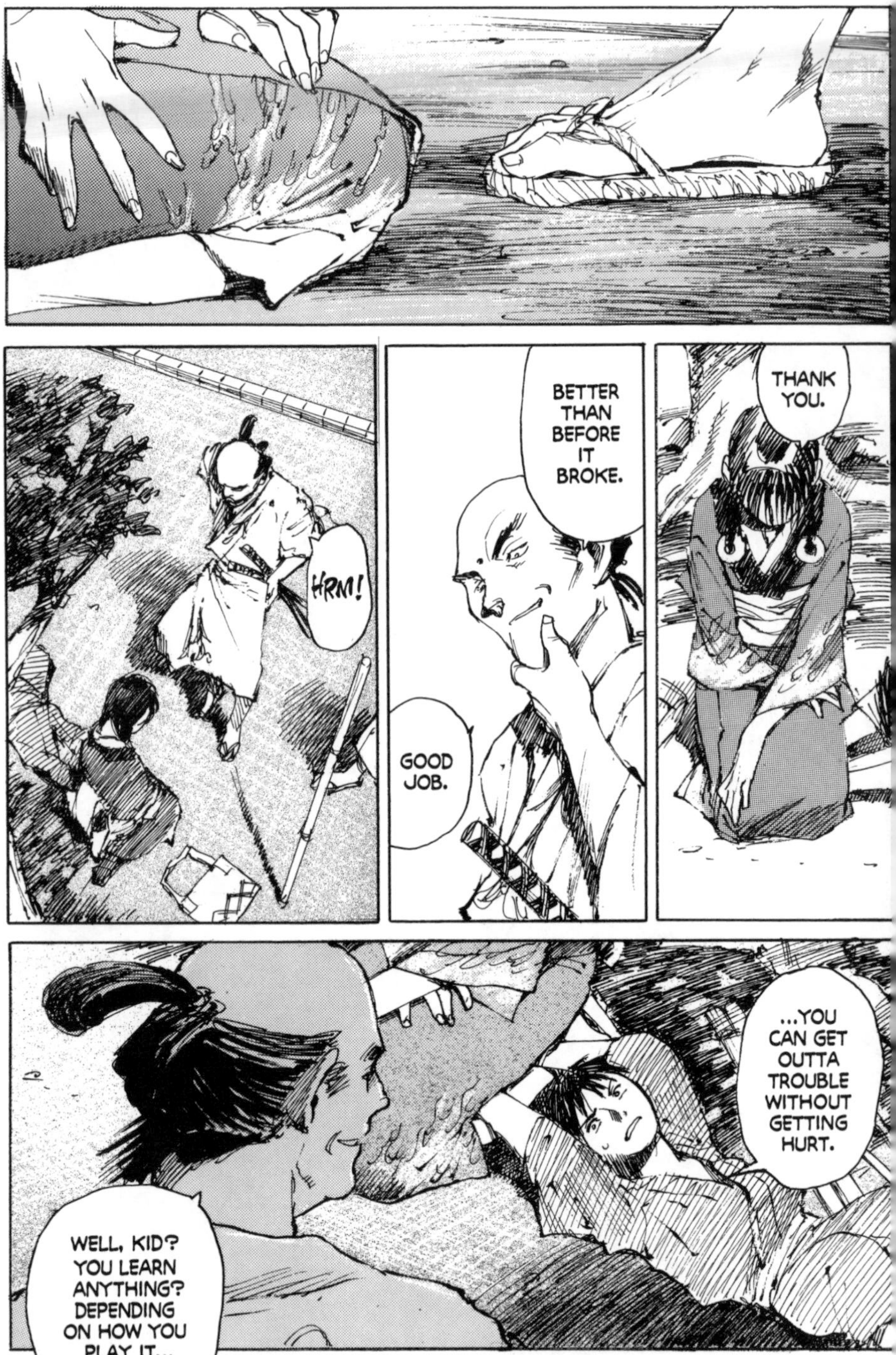
HRM!
BETTER THAN BEFORE IT BROKE.
GOOD JOB.
THANK YOU.
WELL, KID? YOU LEARN ANYTHING? DEPENDING ON HOW YOU PLAY IT...
...YOU CAN GET OUTTA TROUBLE WITHOUT GETTING HURT.

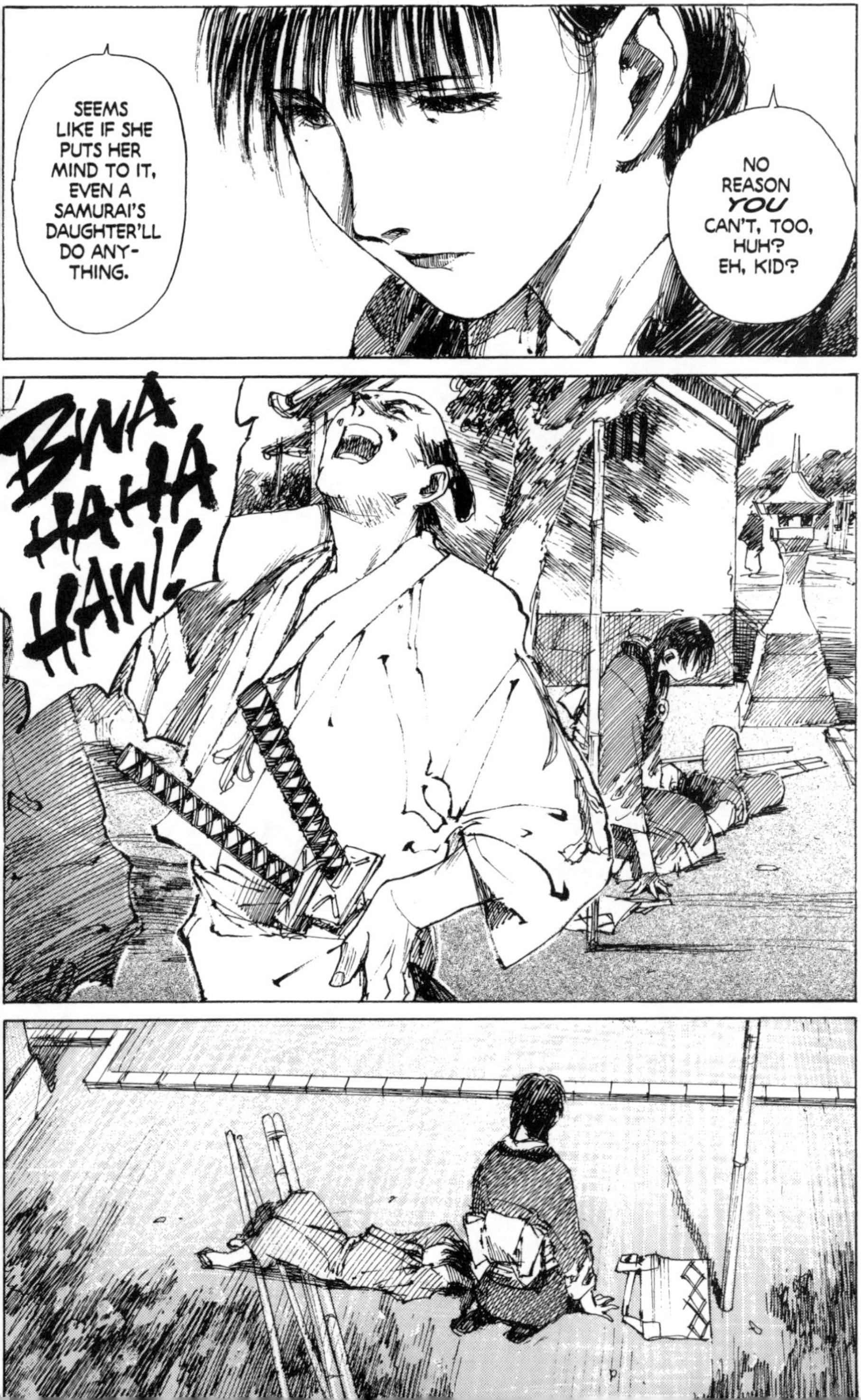
SEEMS LIKE IF SHE PUTS HER MIND TO IT, EVEN A SAMURAI'S DAUGHTER'LL DO ANY-THING.
NO REASON *YOU* CAN'T, TOO, HUH? EH, KID?
BWA HAHA HAW!

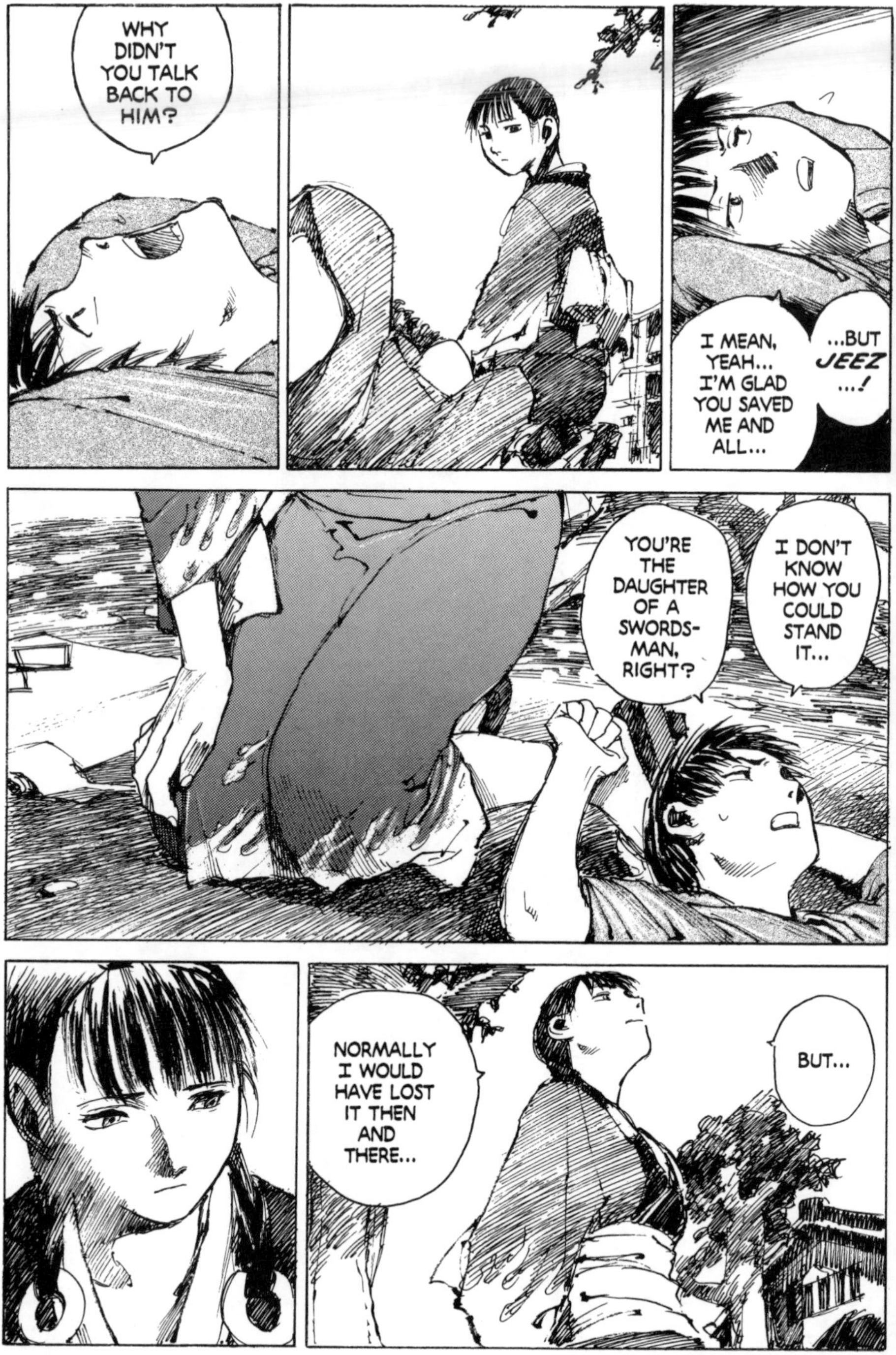
WHY DIDN'T YOU TALK BACK TO HIM?
I MEAN, YEAH... I'M GLAD YOU SAVED ME AND ALL...
...BUT JEEZ ...!
YOU'RE THE DAUGHTER OF A SWORDS-MAN, RIGHT?
I DON'T KNOW HOW YOU COULD STAND IT...
NORMALLY I WOULD HAVE LOST IT THEN AND THERE...
BUT...

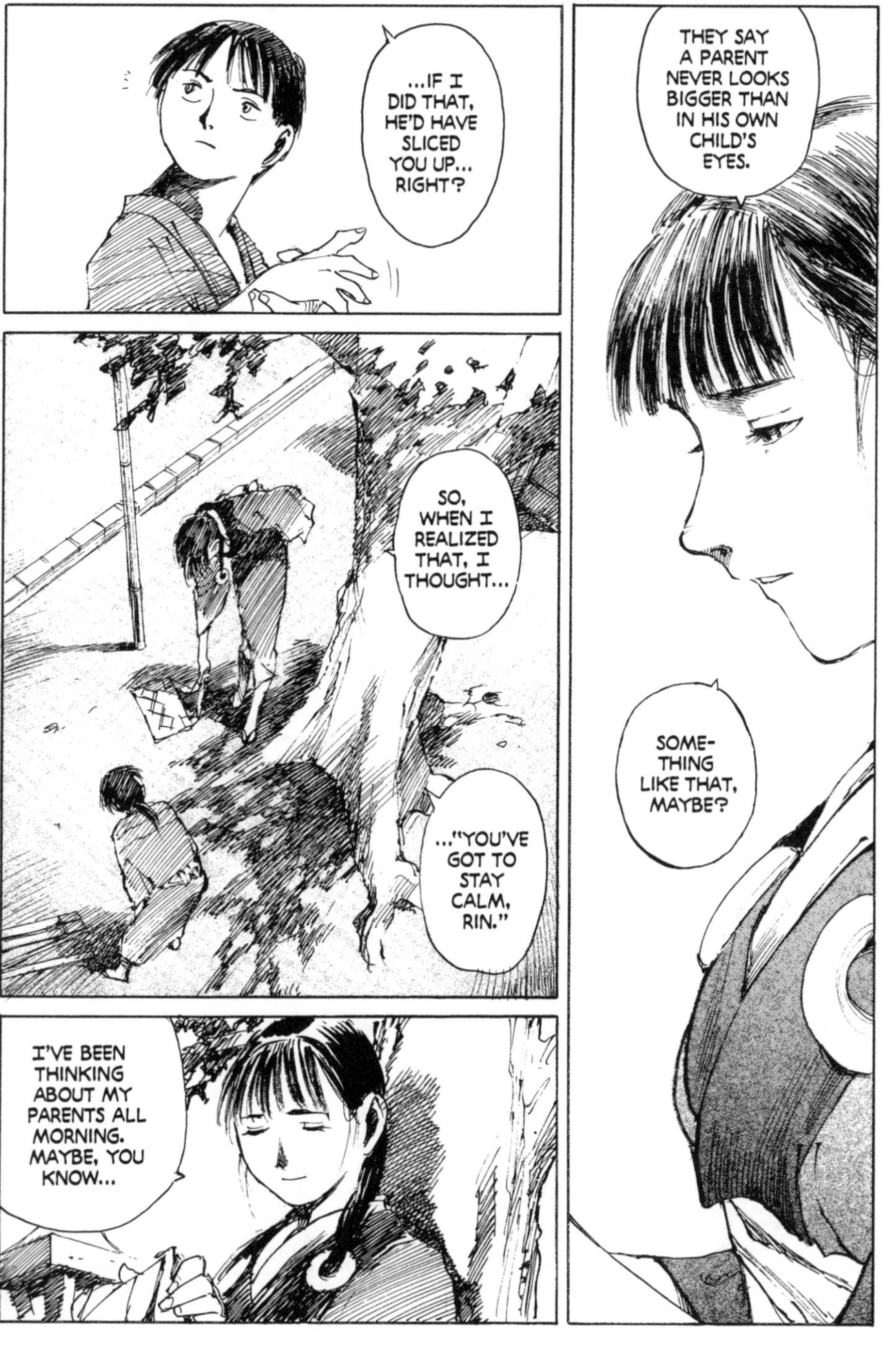
...IF I DID THAT, HE'D HAVE SLICED YOU UP... RIGHT?
SO, WHEN I REALIZED THAT, I THOUGHT...
..."YOU'VE GOT TO STAY CALM, RIN."
I'VE BEEN THINKING ABOUT MY PARENTS ALL MORNING. MAYBE, YOU KNOW...
THEY SAY A PARENT NEVER LOOKS BIGGER THAN IN HIS OWN CHILD'S EYES.
SOME-THING LIKE THAT, MAYBE?

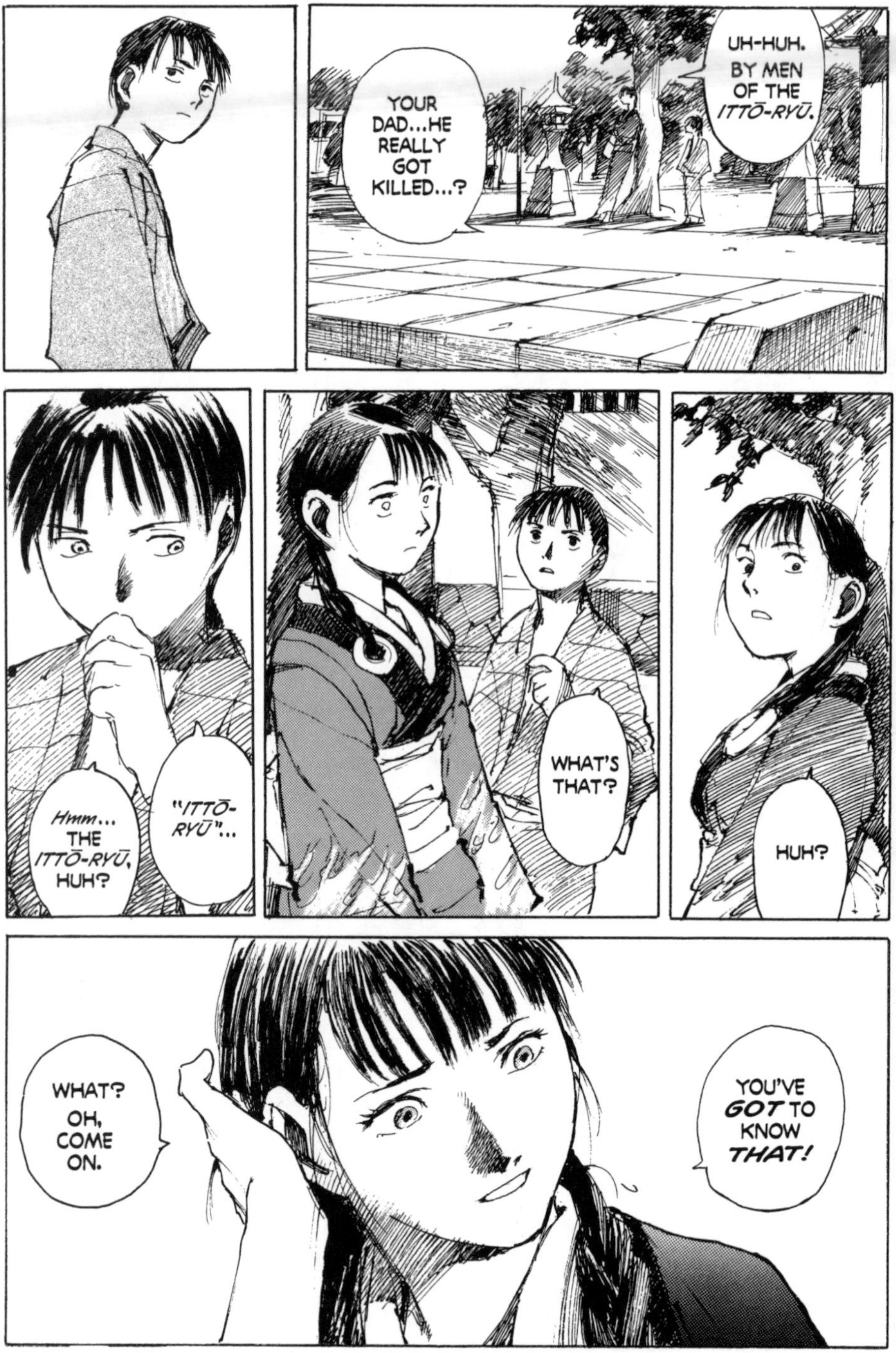
YOUR DAD...HE REALLY GOT KILLED...?
UH-HUH. BY MEN OF THE *ITTŌ-RYŪ*.
Hmm... THE *ITTŌ-RYŪ*, HUH?
"*ITTŌ-RYŪ*"...
WHAT'S THAT?
HUH?
WHAT? OH, COME ON.
YOU'VE ***GOT*** TO KNOW ***THAT!***

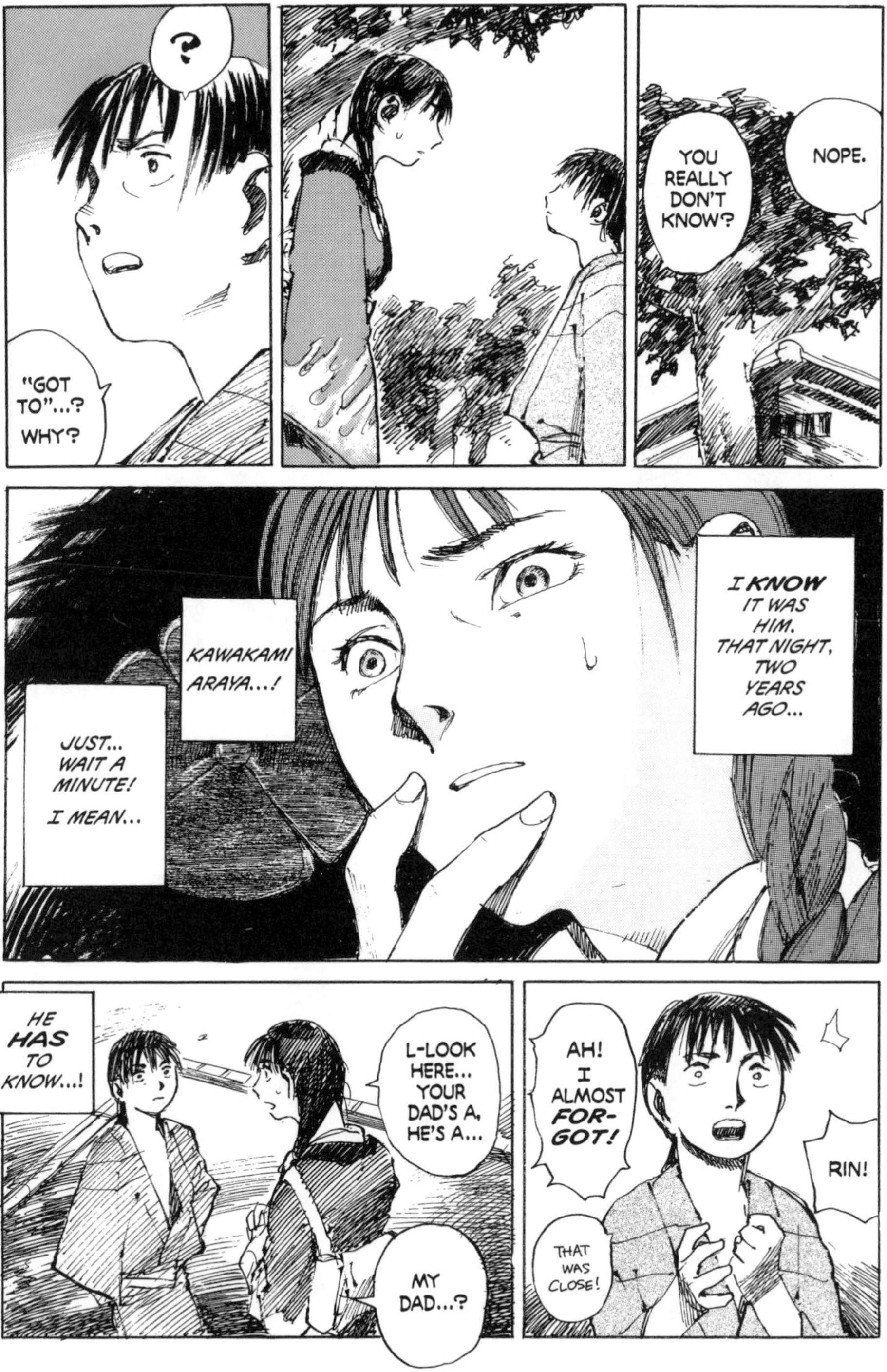
?
"GOT TO"...? WHY?
YOU REALLY DON'T KNOW?
NOPE.
JUST... WAIT A MINUTE! I MEAN...
KAWAKAMI ARAYA...!
I KNOW IT WAS HIM. THAT NIGHT, TWO YEARS AGO...
HE HAS TO KNOW...!
L-LOOK HERE... YOUR DAD'S A, HE'S A...
MY DAD...?
AH! I ALMOST FOR-GOT!
THAT WAS CLOSE!
RIN!

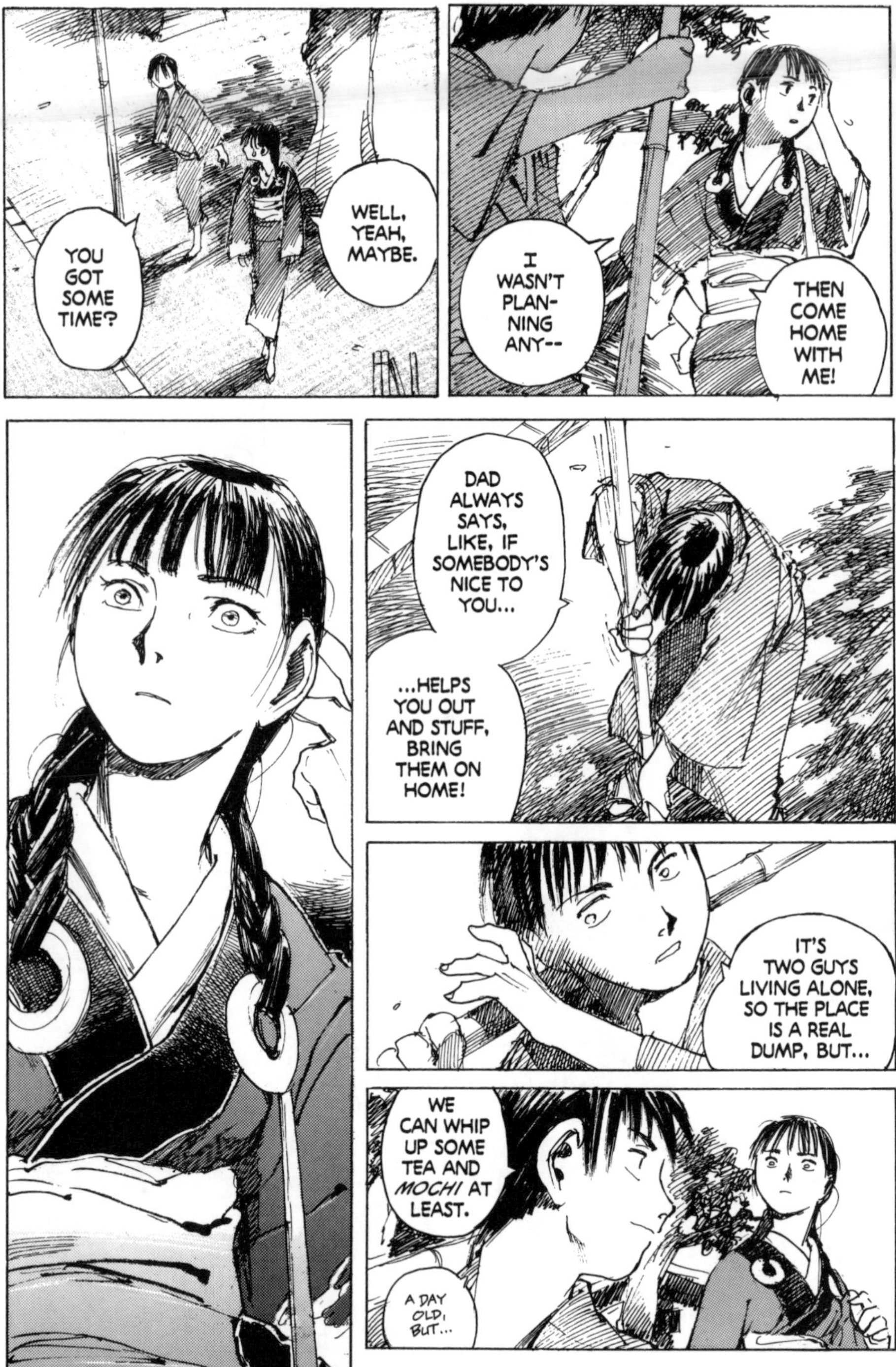
YOU GOT SOME TIME?
WELL, YEAH, MAYBE.
I WASN'T PLAN-NING ANY--
THEN COME HOME WITH ME!
DAD ALWAYS SAYS, LIKE, IF SOMEBODY'S NICE TO YOU...
...HELPS YOU OUT AND STUFF, BRING THEM ON HOME!
IT'S TWO GUYS LIVING ALONE, SO THE PLACE IS A REAL DUMP, BUT...
WE CAN WHIP UP SOME TEA AND *MOCHI* AT LEAST.
A DAY OLD, BUT...

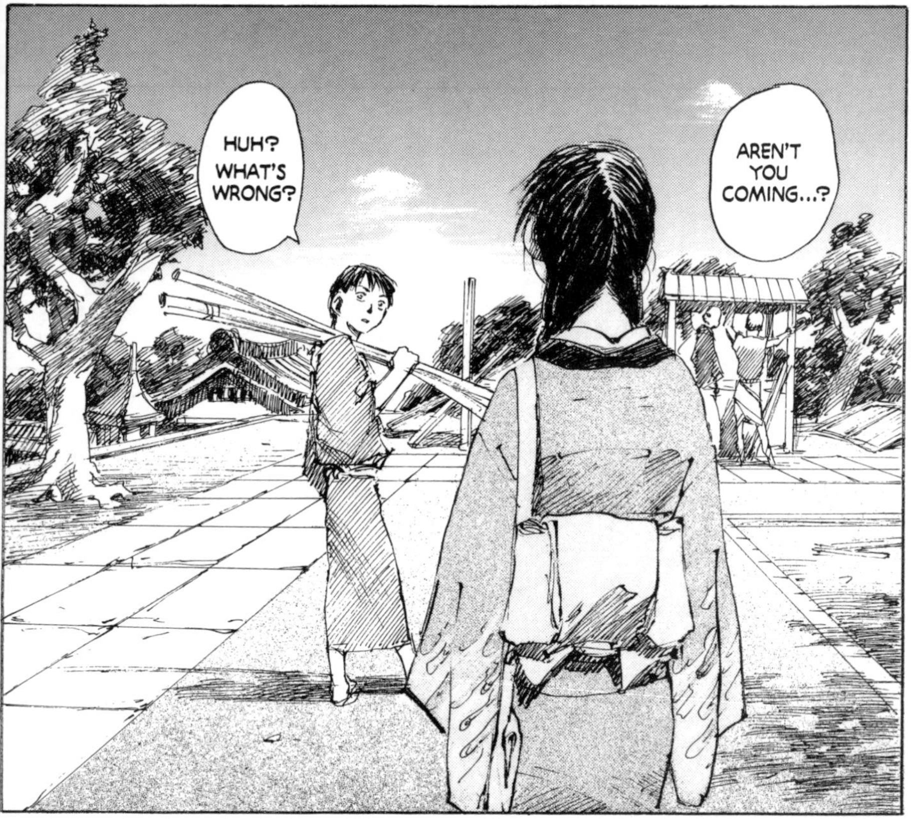
HUH? WHAT'S WRONG?
AREN'T YOU COMING...?

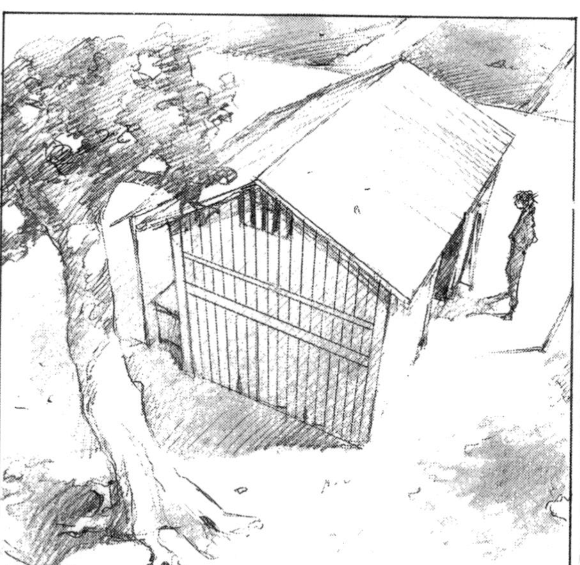

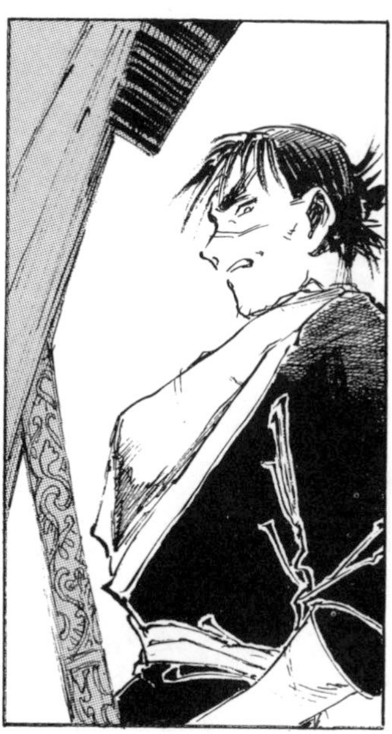

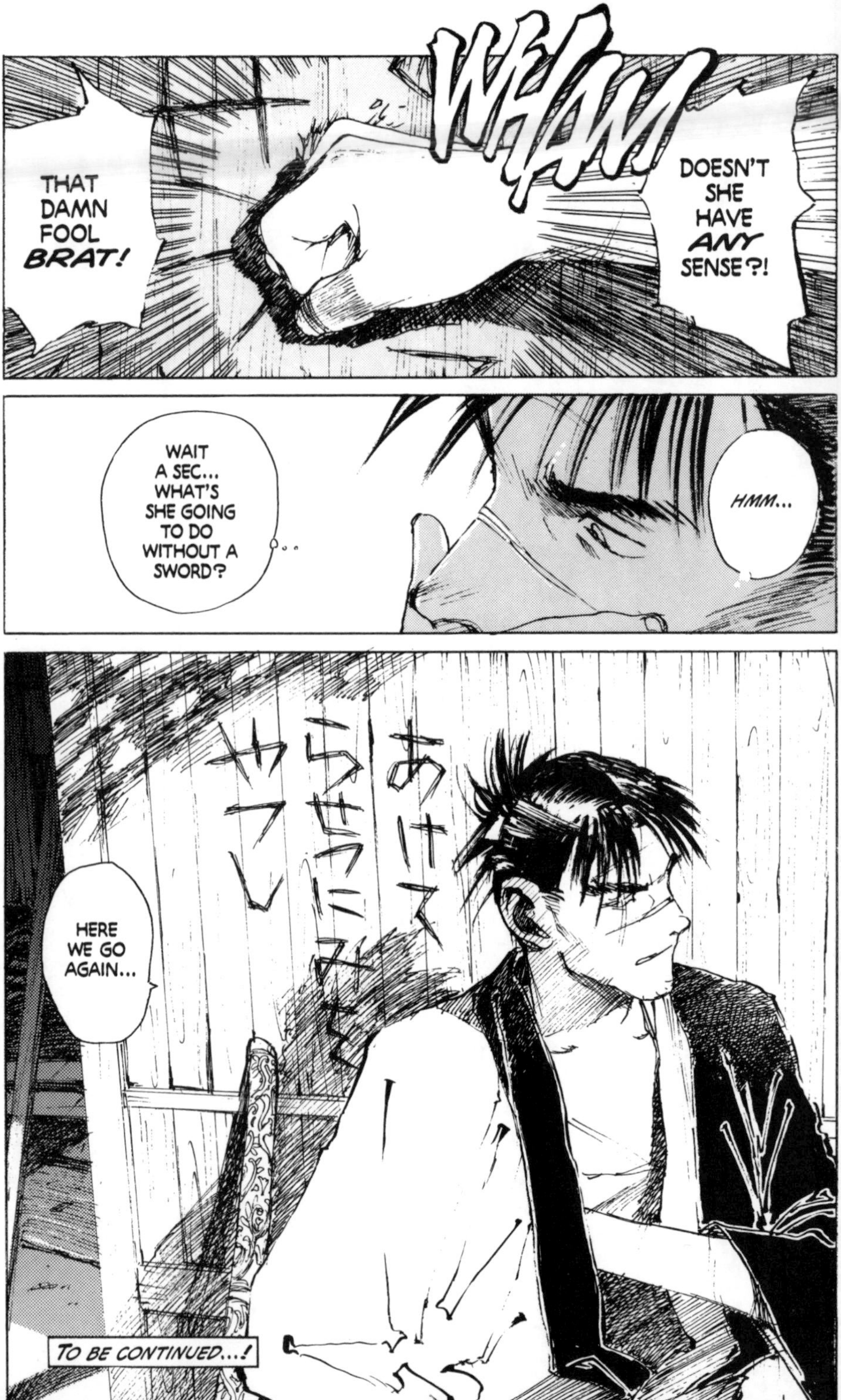
THAT DAMN FOOL BRAT!
WHAM
DOESN'T SHE HAVE ANY SENSE?!
WAIT A SEC... WHAT'S SHE GOING TO DO WITHOUT A SWORD?
HMM...
HERE WE GO AGAIN...
TO BE CONTINUED...!

GLOSSARY

Kenshi: swordfighter

Dōjō: training center for a sword school

Kata: basic movements of a martial art

Bokutō: wooden practice sword

Nihon-to: a Japanese sword: a *katana*

Mutenichi-ryū: swordfighting school led by Rin's father

Oda Nobunaga (1534 - 1582): a bold and innovative Japanese who nearly unified war-torn Japan before he was assassinated by an ambitious lieutenant

Mikawa: a region near today's Aichi Prefecture

Takeda Shingen (1521 - 1573): Nobunaga's most dangerous rival, widely considered to be the foremost general of his day. He died of illness during a campaign against Nobunaga's armies.

Kanei: historical period (1584 - 1645): during the reign of Emperor Gomizuno-o

Miyamoto Musashi (1584 - 1645): the most famous samurai in Japanese history, who dedicated his life to mastering the sword: author of the famous *Gorishino* (*The Book of Five Rings*) on the way of the warrior

Itoichi-ryū: the sword school founded by Miyamoto Musashi, distinguished by its revolutionary two-sword technique: also known as *Niten-ryū*

Daimyō: a feudal lord, ruler of a *Han* (feudal fief)

Hanshi: retainer to a *Daimyō*: literally, "warrior of the *Han*"

Ittō-ryū: the sword school of Kagehisa Anotsu

Bushido: the way of the warrior: the Japanese ethic of the warrior life

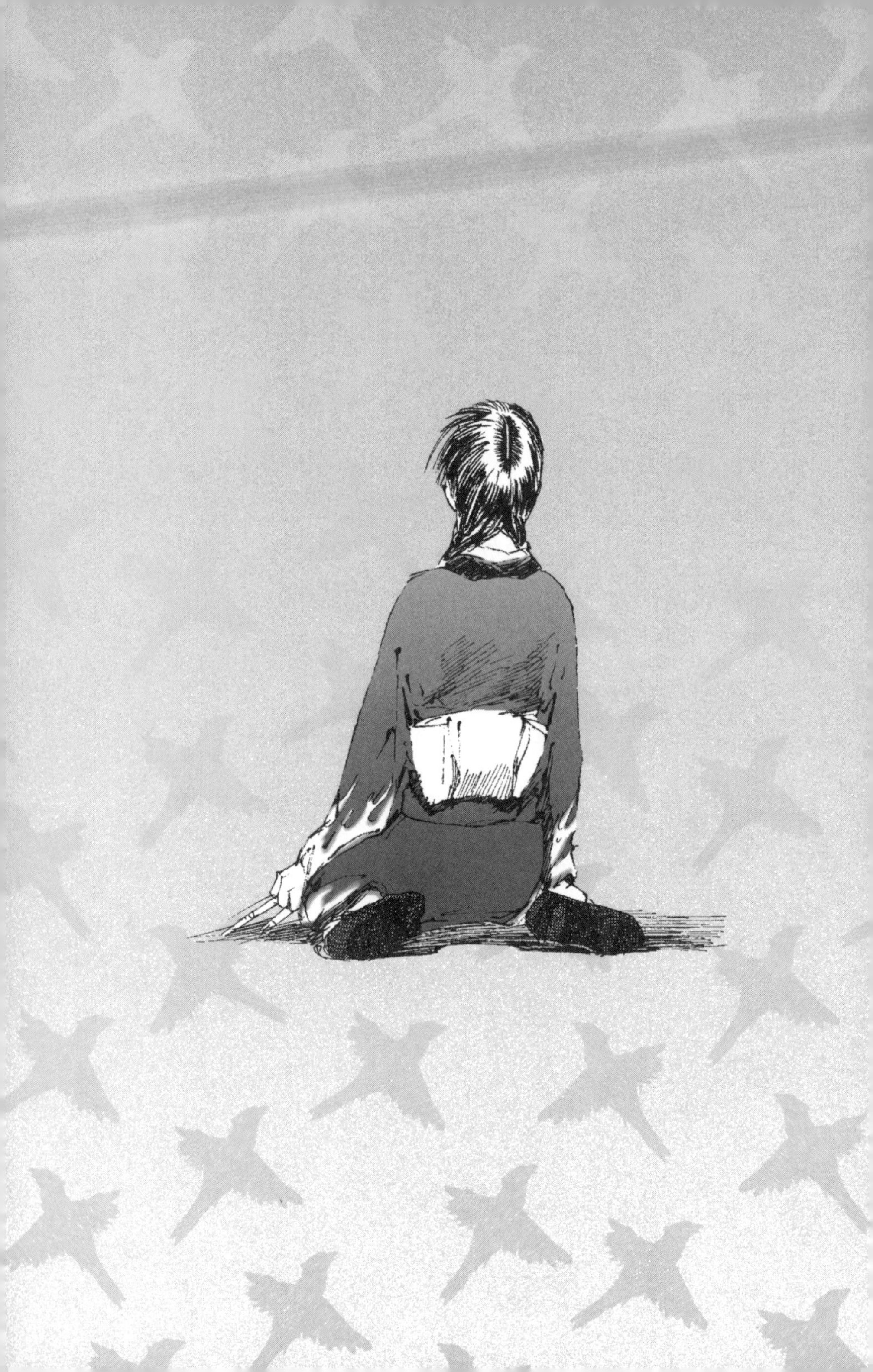

ALSO AVAILABLE:

BLOOD OF A THOUSAND
ISBN: 1-56971-239-5 $14.95

CRY OF THE WORM
ISBN: 1-56971-300-6 $14.95

DREAMSONG
ISBN: 1-56971-357-X $12.95

ON SILENT WINGS
ISBN: 1-56971-412-6 $14.95

ZIPPO LIGHTER #1
19-063 $29.95

ZIPPO LIGHTER #2
19-169 $29.95

To find a comics shop in your area, call 1-888-266-4226

For more information or to order direct:
•On the web: www.darkhorse.com •E-mail: mailorder@darkhorse.com
•Phone: 1-800-862-0052 or (503) 652-9701 Mon.-Sat. 9 A.M. to 5 P.M. Pacific Time

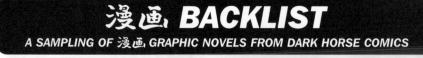

漫画 BACKLIST

A SAMPLING OF 漫画 GRAPHIC NOVELS FROM DARK HORSE COMICS

MASAMUNE SHIROW
APPLESEED
BOOK ONE

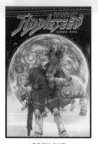

BOOK ONE
ISBN: 1-56971-070-8 $14.95

PROMETHEUS UNBOUND
MASAMUNE SHIROW
APPLESEED

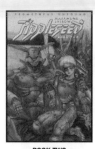

BOOK TWO
ISBN: 1-56971-071-6 $14.95

APPLESEED
BOOK THREE

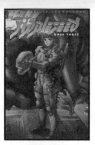

BOOK THREE
ISBN: 1-56971-072-4 $14.95

APPLESEED
BOOK FOUR

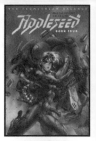

BOOK FOUR
ISBN: 1-56971-074-0 $14.95

MASAMUNE SHIROW
APPLESEED
DATABOOK

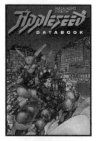

DATABOOK
ISBN: 1-56971-103-8 $12.95

BUBBLEGUM CRISIS
GRAND MAL
ADAM WARREN

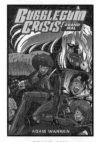

GRAND MAL
ISBN: 1-56971-120-8 $14.95

CARAVAN KIDD
JOHJI MANABE
1

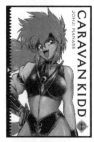

VOLUME ONE
ISBN: 1-56971-260-3 $19.95

CARAVAN KIDD
JOHJI MANABE
2

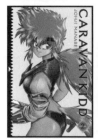

VOLUME TWO
ISBN: 1-56971-324-3 $19.95

CARAVAN KIDD
JOHJI MANABE
3

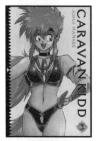

VOLUME THREE
ISBN: 1-5-6971-338-3 $19.95

The DIRTY PAIR

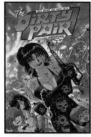

DANGEROUS ACQUAINTANCES
ISBN: 1-56971-227-1 $12.95

The DIRTY PAIR

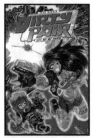

FATAL BUT NOT SERIOUS
ISBN: 1-56971-172-0 $14.95

DIRTY PAIR
A PLAGUE OF ANGELS

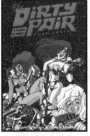

A PLAGUE OF ANGELS
ISBN: 1-56971-029-5 $12.95

Adam Warren
The DIRTY PAIR
SIM HELL

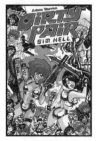

SIM HELL
ISBN: 1-56971-159-3 $13.95

The DIRTY PAIR

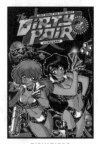

BIOHAZARDS
ISBN:1-56917-339-1 $12.95

MASAMUNE SHIROW'S
DOMINION
CONFLICT 1

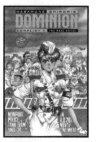

CONFLICT 1: NO MORE NOISE
ISBN: 1-56971-233-6 $14.95

KATSUHIRO OTOMO'S
DOMU
A CHILD'S DREAM
FROM THE CREATOR OF AKIRA

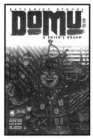

A CHILD'S DREAM
ISBN: 1-56971-140-2 $17.95

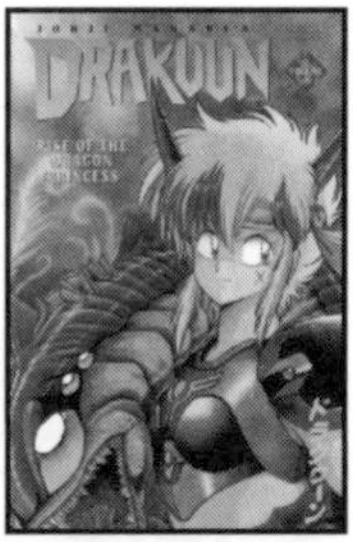
DRAKUUN
RISE OF THE DRAGON PRINCESS

RISE OF THE DRAGON PRINCESS
ISBN: 1-56971-302-2 $12.95

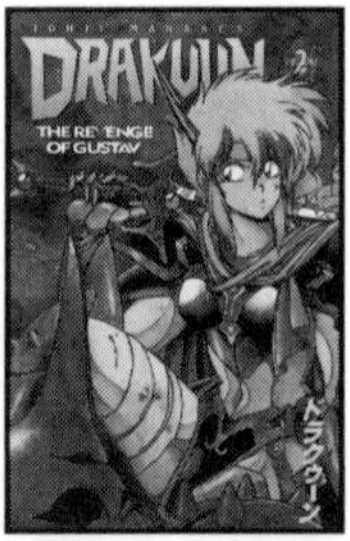
DRAKUUN
2
THE REVENGE OF GUSTAV

THE REVENGE OF GUSTAV
ISBN: 1-56971-368-5 $14.95

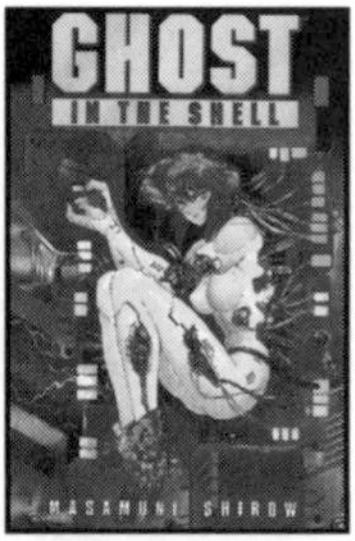
GHOST
IN THE SHELL
MASAMUNE SHIROW

GHOST IN THE SHELL
ISBN: 1-56971-081-3 $24.95

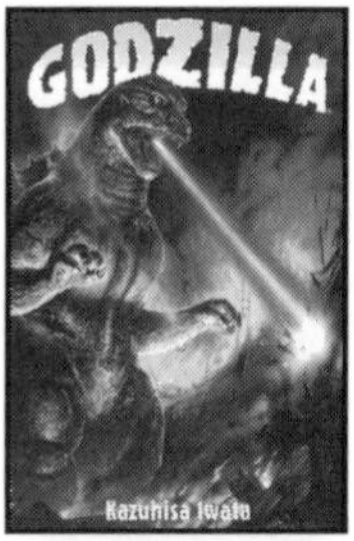
GODZILLA
Kazuhisa Iwata

GODZILLA
ISBN: 1-56971-063-5 $17.95

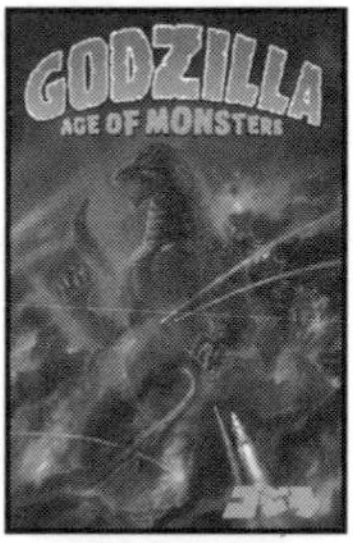
GODZILLA
AGE OF MONSTERS

AGE OF MONSTERS
ISBN: 1-56971-277-8 $17.95

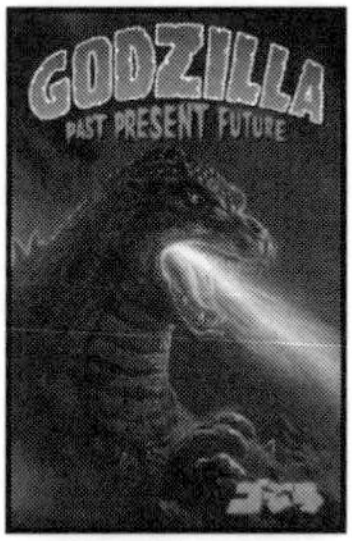
GODZILLA
PAST PRESENT FUTURE

PAST, PRESENT, & FUTURE
ISBN: 1-56971-278-6 $17.95

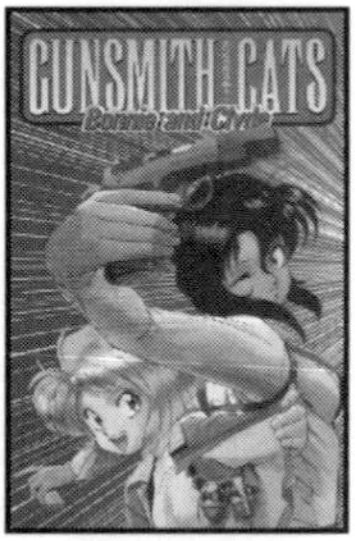
GUNSMITH CATS
Bonnie and Clyde

BONNIE AND CLYDE
ISBN: 1-56971-215-8 $13.95

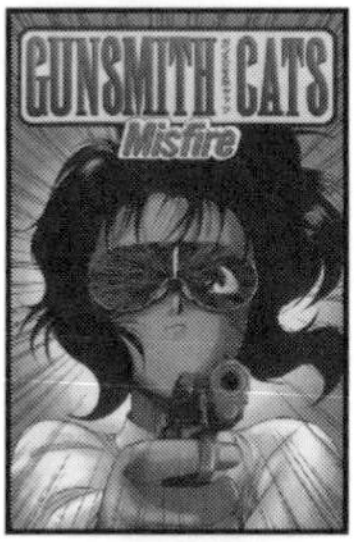
GUNSMITH CATS
Misfire

MISFIRE
ISBN: 1-56971-253-0 $12.95

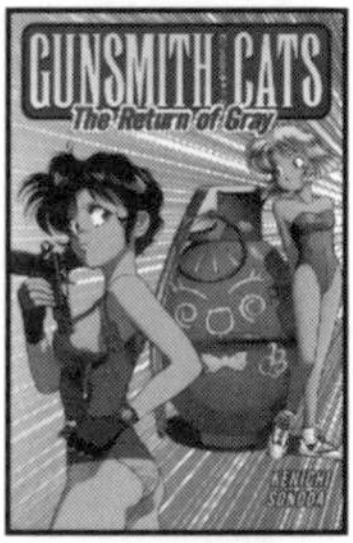
GUNSMITH CATS
The Return of Gray
KENICHI SONODA

THE RETURN OF GRAY
ISBN: 1-56971-299-9 $17.95

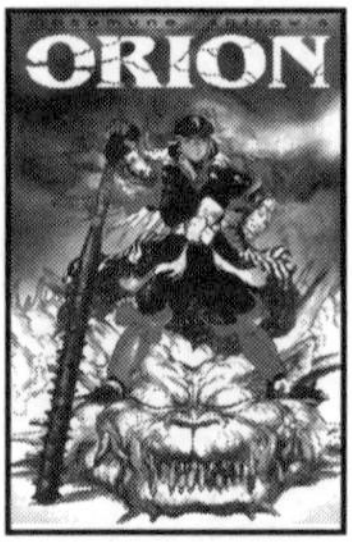
ORION

ORION
ISBN: 1-56971-148-8 $17.95

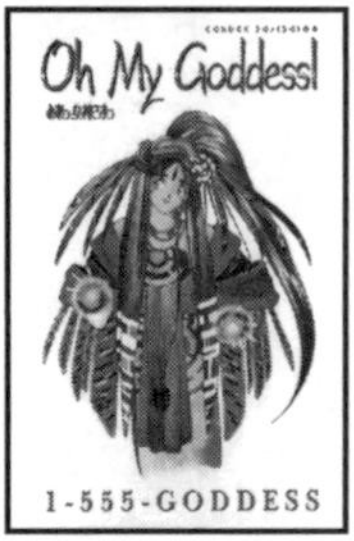
Oh My Goddess!
1-555-GODDESS

1-555-GODDESS
ISBN: 1-56971-207-7 $13.95

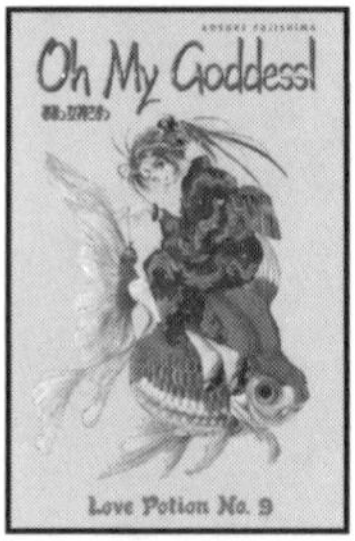
Oh My Goddess!
Love Potion No. 9

LOVE POTION NO. 9
ISBN: 1-56971-252-2 $14.95

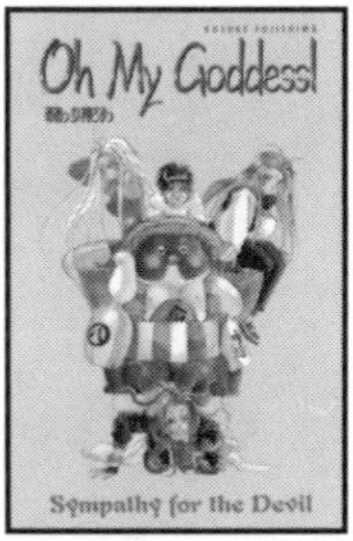
Oh My Goddess!
Sympathy for the Devil

SYMPATHY FOR THE DEVIL
ISBN: 1-56971-329-4 $13.95

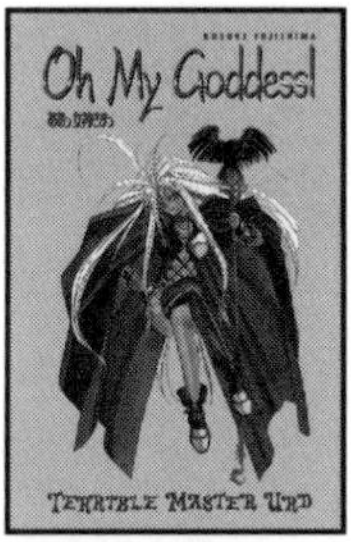
Oh My Goddess!
TERRIBLE MASTER URD

TERRIBLE MASTER URD
ISBN: 1-56971-369-3 $13.95

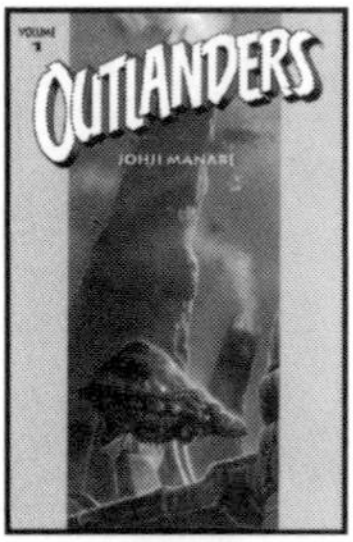
OUTLANDERS
JOHJI MANABE

VOLUME 1
ISBN: 1-56971-161-5 $13.95

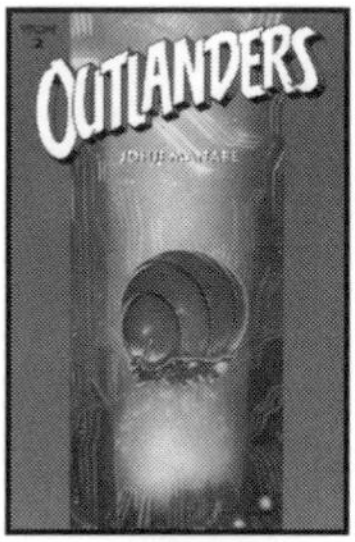
OUTLANDERS
JOHJI MANABE

VOLUME 2
ISBN: 1-56971-162-3 $13.95

AVAILABLE AT YOUR LOCAL COMICS SHOP OR BOOKSTORE
To find a comics shop in your area, call 1-888-266-4226 • For more information or to order direct:
• On the web: www.darkhorse.com • E-mail: mailorder@darkhorse.com
• Phone: 1-800-862-0052 or (503) 652-9701 Mon.-Sat. 9 A.M. to 5 P.M. Pacific Time

VOLUME 3
ISBN: 1-56971-163-1 $13.95

VOLUME 4
ISBN: 1-56971-069-4 $12.95

VOLUME 5
ISBN: 1-56971-275-1 $14.95

VOLUME 6
ISBN: 1-56971-423-1 $14.95

HOUSE OF DEMONS
ISBN: 1-56971-059-7 $12.95

CURSE OF THE GESU
ISBN: 1-56971-175-5 $12.95

BLACK MAGIC
ISBN: 1-56971-360-X $16.95

SPIRIT OF WONDER
ISBN: 1-56971-288-3 $12.95

A NEW HOPE—MANGA #1
ISBN: 1-56971-362-6 $9.95

A NEW HOPE—MANGA #2
ISBN: 1-56971-363-4 $9.95

A NEW HOPE—MANGA #3
ISBN: 1-56971-364-2 $9.95

A NEW HOPE—MANGA #4
ISBN: 1-56971-365-0 $9.95

THE EMPIRE STRIKES BACK—MANGA #1
ISBN: 1-56971-390-1 $9.95

THE EMPIRE STRIKES BACK—MANGA #2
ISBN: 1-56971-391-X $9.95

THE EMPIRE STRIKES BACK—MANGA #3
ISBN: 1-56971-392-8 $9.95

THE EMPIRE STRIKES BACK—MANGA #4
ISBN: 1-56971-393-6 $9.95